flying with my Angel

SURVIVING RELIGION, SEX AND HELICOPTERS

PHIL LATZ

*Hope you enjoy a good
read*

Regards

Phil

**ZYTAL
PRESS**

National Library of Australia Cataloguing-in Publication Data:

Latz, Phil (Philip John), 1937-

Flying with my angel : surviving religion, sex and helicopters

1st edition

ISBN: 9780980445107 (pbk.) :

1. Latz, Phil (Philip John), 1937. 2. Bush pilots–Australia–Biography. 3.
Helicopter pilots–Australia–Biography. 4. Air pilots–Australia–Biography. 5.
Bush pilots–Biography. 6. Helicopter pilots–Biography. 7. Air pilots–Biography.

629.1309

Published by Zytal Press, 2007
C/o Post Office, Stokers Siding, NSW, 2484.

Printed and bound in Australia by McPherson's Printing Group,
Maryborough, Victoria

Cover photography:
Shows author at 20 months on a camel named Darkie at Hermannsberg, by
Mr Rex Batterbee.
Author next to the Mil Mi 26 Helicopter, NATO codenamed 'HALO',
courtesy of *Flight International*

Cover layout and design by Heather McDonald

Acknowledgements

To my friend and mentor James, whose encouragement, coaching, wise help and advice has enlivened and brought this project to fruition. Without his editorial input, a much lesser version may have languished on the vine.

Likewise, my thanks to Cathy who suffered my early amateurish attempts and guided my 'growing up' period in the world of words and provided invaluable copyediting. Also to my loving partner Dinah, for her patience and support during this book's long road to completion.

Much gratitude and thanks go to all the many helpers and crew with whom I had the privilege to work, they helped me survive. The real heroes are slaving behind the scene; pilots push buttons and try to stay out of harms way.

Authors Notes

The christian names assigned to people may or may not be correct. Surnames are correct. The timing of some events may be distorted due to flawed recollection or lack of records.

Some people may find what are now considered sexist or racist terms, but these words were in common usage during that time and locality. Some descriptive nouns may now be regarded as offensive - kanaka, gin, house Mary for example. I do not wish to distort history for the sake of political correctness so please read them in that context.

I have endeavoured to use the spelling of the era.

To my Aboriginal friends, I regret the injustices that occurred to them but I was only a child at the time and accepted the actions and views of my peers. Also please accept my apologies for any inaccuracies or omissions, memory being imperfect.

I have used feet to show height above sea level in aviation stories, these being standard in the West. To convert to metres, multiply by 0.305.

Life is like playing a violin solo in public ~
learning the instrument as you go.
~ Anonymous

I would rather that my spark should burn out in a
brilliant blaze than it should be stifled by dry rot.
I would rather be a superb meteor, every atom of me in
magnificent glow, than a sleepy and permanent planet.
The proper function of man is to live, not to exist.
~ Jack London

ABOUT THE AUTHOR

Phil Latz grew up in the desert among the indigenous people of Central Australia where supplies and mail arrived by pack camel. His secondary schooling and employment were 1600 km away from home. Notwithstanding, he graduated in many differing fields of endeavour while working around Australia and learning to fly and maintain aeroplanes and helicopters. Over 20 years flying, training and management tasks worldwide followed, plus many house and country moves overseas. He has now retired and lives in the Tweed Valley, northern NSW.

Phil is published in various magazines with worldwide distribution and was also responsible for producing certified English language manuals for several large Russian helicopters. He has commissioned a CD containing 'translations' of operating aspects, limits and photographs of the Mil Mi 26, the worlds largest helicopter.

CONTENTS

*Indigenous people of Australia
are advised that this book contains
images of, and references to,
deceased Aboriginal people.*

PROLOGUE, 5th March, 1968

After regaining consciousness, I remembered the silence. It had chilled my soul. The bubble of the helicopter I was piloting lay smashed on the rocks and the instrument panel now lay at a drunken angle. I automatically switched off the battery and ignition even though the engine had stopped, either with the force of the impact or while destroying the rotor blades against the rockface to my right. I unfastened my seatbelt and stepped out of the wreckage to check the photographer, Boris, who was slumped in his seat.

Hearing a hissing sound, I saw its source to be petrol dripping onto a hot exhaust pipe.

"Boris, wake up - can you hear me?"

His eyes flickered open.

"Are you hurt, can you get out?" He nodded, I unfastened his belt and helped him over the ridge we had struck so he'd be safe if the helicopter caught fire. Blood was running down his right leg from a nasty cut on the shin. I ran back to get the first aid kit from the cockpit.

There was no sign of Beverly, the model we had been filming, or Bob, the producer – just the continuous array of sandstone ridges stretching away in the silence across the top of Uluru.

I remember thinking, what a way for a local boy to make a hit!

My mind quickly returned to the present and wondered why this disaster had occurred to me. My guardian angel had saved me from injury or death, even though I had outgrown my religious upbringing, but why did I have to suffer this calamity? What had I done right or wrong in my past life on planet earth, a speck among billions in the cosmos? Did I deserve this catastrophe?

If nothing else, mine had been an interesting and often exciting quest. It began with my birth near the banks of the Todd River in the Australian Inland Mission Hostel in Alice Springs, Central Australia.

CHAPTER 1

Every takeoff is optional. Every landing is mandatory.
~ The Aviators Guide Book

I've often imagined the setting for my first breath on this earth at 5am, on 21st of February 1937.

Not a leaf moved. The gums on the Todd River stood mute in the pale dawn light, magpies yet to sing their morning chorus.

The air refreshing, inviting breath, soon to be changed as the searing February sun fried all below.

My mother, Dora Latz, was one of the few white female settlers in outback Central Australia. She and my father were lay workers at Hermannsburg Lutheran Mission, 120 km south-west of the Alice, and I was their first born. Fortunately, my birth was uncomplicated. The only doctor within a thousand kilometres was away, the two resident nurses catering for us.

After two weeks Mother left the hostel and stayed with the Johannsen family in town while awaiting transport. We waited in the Alice for several weeks before being lucky enough to obtain a lift home in a vehicle driven by tourists.

My parents first met in 1934 when father was en-route to the mission to begin construction of a water pipeline. He stayed with the Lange family for several days. They lived close to my mother's home, some 220 kilometres north of Adelaide in South Australia. By chance, my mother happened to be working at Lange's. Her diary entry reads:

'He got out of the car in his great long navy overcoat and wearing glasses and a rather bewildered air on his face and my maternal feelings went to him immediately (up in the cow-yard milking I was too when that happened) and I think I must have fallen in love with him immediately. There seemed to be something about him that seemed as if he needed a bit of mothering (the coat was too big and the sleeves too long) and there was a sort of a finished – with – love affairs look about him that I sort of felt then, but could not analyse.

And then, because he did not suggest letter writing to me when he left three days later for Hermannsburg I was absolutely disappointed and to hide my hurt pride went and imagined myself in love with a boy 6 years younger than I and whom I really did like but oh how I hurt him when I broke off with him 13 months later.'

Mother suffered a period of ill health and was invited to visit Hermannsburg for a month's holiday by the Mission Superintendent, Rev. F. W. Albrecht as the dry desert air was believed to promote healing. Also, mother's sister Ruth Pech was governess of the Albrecht household. During this holiday my parent's romance blossomed, culminating in a marriage proposal. Mother's parents' approval of the engagement arrived via telegram, in Morse Code, on the pedal radio on 4th November 1935. The engagement was celebrated at Rev. Albrecht's house where father presented a token engagement ring he made from a sixpenny piece. My parents married in April 1936 at Appila, 220 km north of Adelaide in South Australia, returning to the Mission soon after.

Our house, one of the original buildings, was erected in the 1880s by Mr C.H. Eggars, an early Mission worker, with help from the local Aranda people. It is reputedly the second oldest house in the Northern Territory still standing. The metre thick outside walls were heaped sandstone, glued together with a slurry of red ant's nest sand, spinifex spines and lime, with a coat of whitewash completing the job.

The floors were smooth river stones, arrayed like crazy tiles and held together by pouring a mixture of hot fat and ashes between the gaps. As children we sometimes bored holes in the floor with a hot poker from mother's wood burning kitchen stove. Many a stubbed toe resulted from the unevenness of the floor, while getting furniture positioned steady and level was like asking a small child to sit still.

Initially, the ceilings of our house were whitewashed hessian secured to she-oak beams. In time, plasterboard replaced the hessian as small animals tended to fall through the latter.

The outhouse, a bucket under the seat, stood a few metres behind the house. Dozens of poisonous Redback Spiders lived beneath the throne. To my knowledge, no one was ever bitten. It was pointless trying to remove them, they were just part of the furniture in most Australian backyard toilets.

A cellar was built under the front bedroom. I can remember the darkness being suggestive of mystery and danger. It was also closer to hell as we were told at Sunday School. A carpet snake lived in the cellar from

3

time to time. We had little fear of it as it was favourably regarded as an excellent vermin exterminator.

During the day Snake often slept coiled around the bars of the cellar vent, set in the wall just above the front veranda floor. We were not allowed to poke Snake to awaken it during our playtime, for fear of it finding another, less troublesome household.

Snakes of all kinds, most highly venomous, were regular visitors during the summer months and were quickly dispatched by parents or our aboriginal housemaids. A metre length of thick fencing wire, one end bent over several times to form a handle, was the usual weapon. It was cheap, effective and could be parked in various parts of the house. When a venomous snake appeared, an adult grabbed the nearest wire and broke its back with a swift blow, rendering it immobile. It could then be carried outside and killed.

One hot summer evening at dinner when the geckos were busy on the flyscreen and the Tilly lamp was hissing away as usual, someone said 'What's that under the table?' Silence as several heads went down and then Mother said - 'It's a snake heading for the kitchen.' Father grabbed the wire parked next to the sofa and after one quick step the 1.5 metre long snake was immobilised. It had been slithering around our bare feet! The snake was identified as a deadly King Brown and had no doubt spent the day coiled around a sofa leg.

We had minimal furniture. Most was made by my father from local timber, redundant four gallon (18 litre) kerosene tin shipping boxes and old tea chests. Some of Dad's creations have been displayed locally and Interstate, at exhibitions of Early Settlers' work, which showed the ingenuity required in adapting very limited materials to make furniture. For example, rawhide, untanned cow skin, was stretched over appropriately shaped and dovetailed hardwood tree branches, formed to make the base of our parents double bed. The frame of our sofa was of similar construction; the cushions fashioned by stuffing washed goats hair inside locally tanned kangaroo skin covers. This resulted in a comfortable sofa that was still in use 60 years later.

All the resident families on the Mission were assigned several female helpers. Our senior housegirl had the use of a detached room at the rear of our house. A young servant girl assisted during the day. That poor lass would be locked up in a dormitory with other single females and schoolgirls every night to ensure males didn't get at them. The idea was to expose the Aboriginals to our standards of behaviour, hygiene, to teach

4

them English and practical skills in cooking, cleaning and sewing. While the housegirls washed clothes, swept and ironed, wives attended to important communal tasks, providing welfare for the floating population of up to four hundred aborigines.

Consequently, during childhood, I did not perform mundane chores such as bed-making or washing dishes. The male kids ran wild in our 3,000 square km backyard, which contained the Finke River and James Ranges.

In common with other children at Hermannsburg, I grew up with three languages, in three different cultures, in three totally different societies. This was certainly not the norm in Australia in the 30s but we did not know that. I spoke German to my parents, English to visitors, and Aranda (the local aboriginal language) to the natives. Mother mentioned that one Christmas; carol singing around the tree utilised all three, sometimes simultaneously by different singers.

All of the original Mission houses were built on the north bank of the Finke. The main watercourse was a half kilometre away and only once in my memory did it flood to our vegetable garden, on the lower bank of the river. Several mature date palms and grapevines produced perennial crops. The dates, planted around 1878, were over 10 metres high and we began eating the fruit when the dates turned yellow, and when fully ripe, were obliged to pick them to share with others. Access was gained by a rope attached to the crown, which enabled us to 'walk' up the trunk by pulling hand over hand on the rope

This garden provided virtually the only vegetables available for our table, apart from onions and potatoes. In the early days foods not produced on the Mission were ordered from Adelaide, and could take up to three months to arrive. Refrigeration was not available, but this was of no concern as we pulled carrots, kohlrabi, corn or other ripe vegetables from the garden and ate them raw while barely missing a stride on our way to some new adventure.

Coffee was far too expensive so Mother browned wheat and barley grains in the oven and when ground, used them as a substitute.

To beat the summer heat we spent much time swimming. Underwear or bathing costumes were unheard of so being naked was a natural thing. This made it difficult for parents to have children decently attired for church on Sundays. I remember a photo session when Mission staff and their offspring were to have a group shot taken. Martin Albrecht, the youngest son of the Reverend, refused to be properly dressed and kept escaping. The orderly rows of adults and children slowly disintegrated amid parents' cajoling, threats, and children's tears. After much turmoil, Martin escaped to the high country, shedding his Sunday clothes as he fled. Ultimately, the photo session was abandoned. I suspect Martin got more than soup that night as a leather strap across the backside was the usual discipline for me, and the Albrechts used similar methods.

The Mission, having been founded by German Lutherans, employed dedicated Christians from South Australia and Victoria. Most Lutheran Church services were still conducted in German, although many of the congregation were second, and in my case, third generation Australian born. I suspect that few of us Mission kids understood much of the ecclesiastical nuances of German services. The Aranda language versions frequently preached on the Mission also did little - except try our patience. The mental torture was also matched by physical, after being forced to wear shoes too narrow for our wide, normally unrestrained feet.

The reward of a Sunday roast still seemed light years away at the beginning of the sermon. Much imagination and restraint was necessary to avoid being carried outside in disgrace amid the disparaging eyes of mothers who had taught **their** children to behave!

Naturally, grace was always said before and after meals. The evening meal was followed by reading from an approved devotion book. This was in German until the war years when it was considered politic to switch to English. I believe those whose education had been conducted in German found it hard to make the change.

During my childhood days the Mission contained four large houses for married staff and boarders, separate bachelor and visitor rooms, the church and a morgue. Also, an aboriginal school, workshops, tannery, meat house, dispensary and kitchen cum mess for aboriginal children. In time, permanent houses were built for responsible aboriginal leaders.

White staff oversaw the growing of vegetables for the aboriginals in a large dedicated garden. In my day I believe five or six cattle were killed and butchered every week. Free meat was distributed to the sick and aged, women, children and workers early on Monday, Wednesday and Friday mornings. White families had a choice of free beef and so tongue, brains, heart, liver, kidney, as well as the normal fillets, were staple fare at our table. The disadvantage – there was beef or more beef unless an expensive tin was opened or one of Mother's chickens lost its head. Sometimes a goat from the Mission herd was butchered. I remember one occasion when several visiting church leaders dined at our table.

'Delicious meal Mrs Latz, lovely lamb,' commented one and the others agreed.

'Sorry, but there are no sheep in the Territory,' my mother said innocently. 'That was goat you ate tonight. It's a treat for us, after months of beef.'

On hearing this, the guests rushed outside and vomited. We could not begin to understand such people.

When the men branded and castrated calves in the nearby stockyard we joined them unless constrained by schoolwork. The 'rocky mountain oysters', bulls balls were thrown over the rails, caught and cooked in the fire used to heat branding irons. They were a delicacy that my aboriginal friends and I greatly enjoyed.

Milk could only be obtained from cows in calf, or goats. I was fortunate to be weaned on goats' milk, which is supposedly superior to cows. With no electricity or fridge's, Mother's homemade butter and cheese could be kept at a reasonable temperature in our cool safe. This cooler, also known as a Coolgardie or drip safe, comprised four walls about 10 cm thick containing lumps of charcoal, held in place by chicken wire inside and out. The top held a water tray with hessian bags draped over the outside edge of the safe. These acted as wicks, keeping the charcoal sides damp while evaporation kept the inside cool. One side of the safe was hinged to form a door. During humid weather, the cooling process slowed and food could go mouldy. Fortunately, this occurred infrequently. Meat was salted to preserve it. Originally, salt was gathered from dry lakes 320 kilometres to the south and transported to the Mission by camel.

Pioneer women had to be tough and enterprising. My mother suffered health problems all her life and writes of being very distressed when the mercury stayed above the century (38°C) for weeks on end. Having only a wood stove on which to cook did not help either. Often, in the warmer months we slept on the front lawn; it was just too hot to sleep inside.

When mother received an inheritance from her father, it was used to purchase a kerosene refrigerator, which cost £65 ($130) in 1939. As Father's salary was only just over £100 per annum ($200), it could not have been afforded otherwise. This was the first refrigeration unit on the Mission, and the Albrecht's 'rented' one daily tray of iceblocks for which they paid sixpence (50 cents) a week.

My parents' long working hours and other privations went unnoticed by us children as we were well fed, watered, much loved and enjoyed great freedom. Whether their Missionary efforts were misguided or not is for others to judge, we were just busy having fun as kids.

Mother recorded that at age four I began asking difficult questions about religion and the beginning of life. At this age I was also caught smoking, having 'borrowed' some of father's cigarettes. A lecture on stunting one's growth had no effect for the following morning I was dobbed in by the housegirls who saw me puffing away again. It seems I had four Red Capstans before breakfast, which did not blunt my appetite, at least according to her diary entry. Her next sentence deals with my punishment – the strap. I don't remember getting the strap across my backside for stealing cigarettes but I do remember that a very careful climb was required to reach the cigarette tin, stored inside a cupboard on a shelf one and a half metres above the floor.

At about this time in my life, the Japanese bombed Darwin. The adults were very concerned. When WW II was declared in 1939, Hermannsburg did not hear of the news for weeks. Ration cards appeared and mother kept serial No. S 679585 for tea and butter, with my name typed on it. On one of our rare visits (the Mission now had a vehicle) to the Alice in 1942, air raid sirens sounded. I was five and can remember the town being evacuated. We drove some kilometres out and parked under a tree. I was disappointed when nothing happened – no Japanese aircraft, no bombs falling, no explosions in town, so I resorted to chasing lizards.

I now know that Alice Springs was beyond the range of Japanese carrier borne aircraft but the civilian population was probably unaware of this. Perhaps the Australian Military were rehearsing for a worst case scenario.

The bombing also resulted in Military Intelligence sharpening their pencils and visiting Hermannsburg to check on the German speaking staff. The local Head of Intelligence thumbed through the same diary I have quoted, but until May 1940 Mum wrote in German - with odd bits of English thrown in. She was asked to verbally translate parts of her own diary and letters from family. Honour was satisfied and Intelligence could report that the Mission had been searched, the staff interviewed and checked for evidence of subversive activity.

Hysterical speculation was mollified by the appointment of an Independent Protector of Aboriginals –a spy to spy on supposed spies. Mr Rex Battarbee, our Protector, was wounded in the First World War, took up art and became a respected watercolour artist. Prior to the bombing in Darwin, he had been our boarder for several years, between painting trips out bush.

As a child I remember Rex having a bent left wrist and a deformed hand. He was a gentle soul, sometimes giving us sweets. As chronicled in books on the aboriginal art movement, Rex taught Albert Namatjira to paint in watercolours. This occured during a trip when Albert was Rex's camel boy.

The Rev. Albrecht, arranged this opportunity to help Albert begin painting. The Reverend felt this could lead to a greater acceptance of aboriginals, even to providing them a source of income. During the early days of the aboriginal art movement my mother served on the Mission Arts Advisory Council. I remember our house being littered with paintings. Mission staff evaluated and priced them, before being sent to exhibitions in capital cities. This inevitably led to accusations that the Mission was profiteering from these works which was not the case. To avoid criticism, the Mission completely disengaged from aboriginal artwork sales and monetary affairs. Prior to his watercolour painting, I believe my father taught Albert Namatjira to blacksmith.

Christmas in 1938, saw Mother and I travelling south to Port Augusta on the weekly Ghan passenger service. This train had replaced the Afghan camel teams previously plying the route although there appears to be some contention as to why it was called The Ghan. Conditions in the third Class carriages were primitive. The only sustenance available was water – and even that managed to dry up on occasion. We carried food and bedding for the scheduled three-day journey. Only hard wooden seats were provided, so children slept under them, being safer. Others slept whenever and wherever they could, often treated to drunken behaviour and foul language by male travellers who indulged at the frequent hotels along the line. As the couplings between carriages had a lot of slack, severe jolting occurred with passengers thrown on top of each other. A hot drink could be hazardous, except when the train was stationary. Making tea entailed a two hundred metre walk through the dust to the front of the train, where hot water was passed down by the engine driver. Luckily, stops were frequent and often lasted for several hours.

With small children, 40°C heat and dusty soot blowing in the windows, it was stressful travelling for mothers. Sleepers and a dining car were available but we could not afford such luxuries.

It was an arduous journey for my pregnant mother, with me just 22 months old. Her sister, on leave from mission work in New Guinea, was already at the family home. Their happy reunion was marred by complications at my brother's birth. An obstruction caused my first brother to be stillborn.

In January 1940 Mother had a curette performed in the Alice and became pregnant again later that year. One benefit of the war was that a fully equipped hospital was built in the Alice, supplemented with Army Doctors to cater for troops. X-rays taken at 7 months into the pregnancy indicated possible complications at birth. When Mother began having pains a few weeks later a radio call brought the Flying Doctor and she was flown to the Alice as a precaution. This occurred just before the Mission's radios were confiscated for being a potential source of 'spying'. It was her first flight; the aircraft being a specially outfitted Tiger Moth bi-plane. These aircraft normally had two open cockpits, one behind the other, which required occupants to wear a helmet and goggles in flight, as I did when learning to fly Tigers 18 years later. Connellan's aircraft was modified to allow carriage of a stretcher behind the pilot and a perspex canopy enclosed both areas. Mother later wrote that she enjoyed the flight, even though the aircraft behaved like a bucking horse in the turbulence from thunderstorms.

I had been asking for a brother for some time and happily Peter arrived safely on April 5th, 1941, the same date as our father's birthday. It was an induced birth and neither the Sister nor Doctor were present when Peter decided to appear. Mother wrote that she was very proud to have done it all on her own. She was now 32 years old and father 45.

After wanting a brother to play with, it seems I was not happy with the attention he received, becoming a difficult child. This is when I took up smoking and copped the strap after repeat offences. I must have sensed that father favoured my young brother who was gentler, more affectionate and less trouble. So I bullied and picked on him and got belted for it. Mother's diary entry reads,

'With Peter, generally words are quite enough.' 'Talk about the many and severe thrashings Philip had to have.'

She also records that I was afraid of rain. It was such an unusual event that I rushed inside screaming after a few drops fell on me. I still recall that it, extraordinarily, once rained for 2 days and nights without stopping. Another unusual occasion was once having great difficulty finding my way home during a severe dust storm. I made it into the Mission compound before the swirling dust reduced visibility to several metres. The last hundred metres to our house took a long, long time – being largely a matter of feel. If I opened my eyes they filled with sand. It sounds rather silly to be lost fifty metres from home, but this incident taught me a valuable lesson.

Early in May 1942 Mother became pregnant but miscarried at eleven weeks. This happened at home with Reverend Gross's wife attending. Mother wrote that thanks to a bedpan at least the bed was not messed up. Mother's sister in South Australia also miscarried at about the same time and Mother mentions that sharing the knowledge of this misfortune made them both feel better.

After another pregnancy in 1943, Mother went to Alice Springs for the confinement early in January 1944. Again, her penchant for a quick performance resulted in neither nurse or doctor being present at the 9 p.m. birth. While other patients in the ward tried to contact Sister Kerr, Mother sat up to look at her newborn. She noticed a purplish-blue raised blister on his spine. Sister arrived a minute or two after Norman's first and only cry and immediately called for the Doctor. He arrived quickly and while examining the baby mother asked him what the blister was. He evaded her question. Then, after Sister asked for Mother's religion, she queried the doctor again and he admitted that Norman was a spinabifida child.

Because it was thought that Norman might only live for a day, Kurt Johannsen drove out to Hermannsburg that night, collected my Father and Rev. Albrecht and was back in the Alice by 7 a.m. It was a valiant effort on his part. My twelve hour old brother was christened and Mother wrote:

'It was a great comfort to us to have our poor little darling received into the kingdom of God in preparation for the return to the heavenly home.'

A distressing conclusion to what should have been a happy event. My sad parents drove back to the Mission, waiting for the inevitable. Mother visited Norman in hospital several times over the next few months, only to see his condition worsening. She did not feed or nurse him, it was felt this would have made matters worse for her. Luckily mother's brother, Adolf Pech, had been drafted into the Army and happened to be serving in the Alice at the time. He visited the hospital, checked Norman's condition and reported to my parents.

Norman died ten weeks after birth and was buried in the Hermannsburg cemetery. I helped carry the cross and led the funeral procession through the parched sand to his grave. This event remains one of my early memories but I was not badly affected as I had never seen Norman.

Mother became pregnant again in mid year. It seems that was never a problem even with father frequently away from home. Being responsible for around three thousand head of cattle, father spent a lot of time mustering, branding and droving them to the Alice. He also often accompanied them south on the cattle train. General supervision of the welfare of the stock, stockmen and their horses left little time for us. He was also the general handyman at the Mission and was respected by the aboriginals. They worked well for him, which was not always the case with other supervisors.

Mother, as a good Mission-wife, spent much of her time working for the welfare of the community. Church dignitaries, V.I.P.s and ordinary visitors had to be 'put up.' We invariably had boarders living in the house and accommodated numerous visitors at our table. She also managed to maintain our vegetable garden.

Mother was also responsible for the school clothing of about 80 aboriginal children (they obviously could not attend a Mission school naked) and making soap for washing. At one stage, as a public service, she even catered for weekly tourist buses.

Then of course, there was the family. Bread and cakes had to baked, fruit and vegetables preserved, butter and cheese made, and the vinegar producing plant in the cellar fed. Tucker boxes had to be packed for Father's constant trips away and it was left to Mother to organise aboriginal staff during his absence. She also had to care for, and keep us from running totally wild. Stocks of home remedies were kept to cater for gastric problems, sore throats and bung eyes infected by the myriad flies. Sometimes she supervised and helped with our correspondence school lessons. All this was mentioned in her diary and she sometimes despaired at getting through the day. Especially with the temperature in the 40's and no air-conditioning.

In May 1945 my brother Melvin was born at the Alice hospital. The birth occured in the middle of the morning shift change, so this time there were people everywhere. All went well, and soon Mother was home nursing him.

Early in September Melvin became ill and began constantly vomiting. The radio transceivers had been confiscated, so the Doctor in Alice Springs could not be called. After a few days without improvement Mother decided that Melvin should be taken to hospital. Father was away, so a man had to be sent out on horseback to find him and pass on the urgent message. Mother, Father, and Melvin eventually got to the Alice by road, where Melvin was operated on immediately.

It was too late. Their fourth baby son did not recover. It appears his gut had twisted and blocked. A bitter blow, a radio call would probably have saved him.

At the age of eight, I must have become accustomed to my brothers dying. I have no special memory of Melvin's passing. However, some forty years later I visited his grave while on a visit to Alice Springs and bawled my eyes out. Mother's diary is blank from the period after Melvin's birth, until April 1947, when my brother Tony was born in the Alice. The memory of Melvin's passing was obviously too painful for her to write about.

Growing up with the aboriginals we naturally learnt to use spears and boomerangs, to hunt animals, find water and other tricks of survival in the desert.

At age three, as described in my Mother's diary, Paul Albrecht, (who was later to become Field Superintendent of the Alice Springs Mission area), and I were throwing kids' spears during an outing to Palm Valley. While fooling around his spear hit me between my right eye and nose. A few millimetres difference and I would have lost the eye! I still bear the scar, and sometimes wonder what my life would have been with one eye.

From an early age all of us kids threw things, not at targets as in hockey or archery but at each other. This sharpened the reflexes and was a prelude to hunting. This illustrates, to me, how seriously the natives regarded survival training. This early grounding in mental attitudes served me well in later life, saving my skin many times.

Our spears were made from oleander shoots, straightened and tempered in hot sand under a fire. Green bamboo was cut to make a woomera or throwing stick, one end being sliced open to accept the spear that butted against the 'stopper' found in all bamboo stalks.

A rather nasty weapon was devised using a whippy young gum-shoot about one metre long, and wet clay. A small handful of clay was pressed on to the thin end of the gum shoot. Whip cracking this stick resulted in the clay 'bullet' flying off, emitting a whistling sound. With practise, reasonable accuracy could be achieved.

A 'killing' hit could not be disguised on the 'whiteys' as bruises remained for several days, evidence of failure to survive an attack. These games were conducted one on one or with as many boys who cared to join the battle.

It was part ritual warfare, part hunting practise.

Our aboriginal friends taught us to hunt in the traditional way. Most of the white kids had a young aboriginal 'boy' companion who came with us when we went on our walkabouts. One of mine was Davey Inkamala, who later became an ordained Pastor in our church. For teaching us to track and kill game, find water, show us which plants were safe to eat and other bushcraft, they shared our lunch. The association probably also conferred some status in their own community.

We caught, cooked and ate lizard, snake, rabbits, fish, birds, witchetty grubs plus native figs, tomatoes and other edible flora. The cooking method for meat, when on walkabout, was quick and uncomplicated. This is what we did:

1. Catch and kill the prey.

2. Get a good fire going, preferably on clean white river sand.

Method:

Fish – push part of the fire aside and make a small hole in the hot sand. Place fish in hole, cover lightly with sand and push fire back over fish. Wait a few minutes (go catch another fish), then retrieve from under fire. Place fish on a rock or green leaves and peel off skin. The lovely moist flesh falls off the bones and into ones mouth. Delicious!

Witchetty Grubs – As for fish.

Birds – finches, budgies, parrots – as for fish but burn off the feathers first.

Lizards, snakes, rabbits – as for fish but remove the stomach and intestines and burn off the fur. Adjust fire size and cooking time to suit animal size and degree of hunger.

It's that simple, and the food tastes wonderfully fresh when cooked in it's own juices. The skin or scales keep the meat clean, while fish gut shrivels. I think it's the only way to eat freshwater bony bream as the flesh does not stick to the hundreds of tiny bones as in most other cooking methods.

The trick in eating witchetty grubs is to grasp the head with finger and thumb, head up, body hanging down, then tilting ones head and lowering the grub into the mouth. Bite lightly just behind the head, and pull upward. The head detaches, taking the gut with it, leaving a mouthful of sweet meat, tasting something like a chicken omelette. Cooking is optional for grubs.

Catching witchetty's entailed serious work. Standing under a gum tree, we looked for a small circular sawdust patch on otherwise smooth bark. Finding this, we climbed the tree, carrying a tomahawk. With luck, a circular bored tunnel is found above the sawdust, eaten out by the grub. When the grub is upstream, it's necessary to hook it out by inserting a forked grass stem and catching the grub on the barb like a fish.

On occasion branches broke and we fell. The tomahawk presented the only danger so it was thrown clear and then we dealt with the descent. If unable to catch another branch, practise enabled us to land on our feet undamaged. We did not pursue the grubs that lived underground in the roots of a witchetty bush. Digging them out was traditionally women's work.

Birds were killed with a slingshot when they came to drink at a waterhole. We sat still in a bush at the waters edge and when a flock of finches or budgies landed we let fly. At Latz's Dam, thousands of budgies came to drink in the mornings and evenings; this being the only water for many kilometres. The flocks were so thick that we just stood on the dam wall and threw a stone in the air when they flew over. One or two budgies invariably fell at our feet, unable to dodge the stone before flying into it and knocking themselves out. Only the parrot family of birds were taken, they being vegetarian.

Rabbits were most easily caught by carefully placing a noose at the entrance to a burrow, which tightened around their necks as they ran in. When successful, the bunny was dragged out and cooked.

Fishing was rewarding when the floodwaters of the Finke River subsided. The previously muddy water became clear and fish traveled upstream between waterholes searching for mates or a new home. We waited for them at shallow patches of flowing water, armed with the wires used for killing snakes in the house. After sighting a school, our wires hit the water heavily, hopefully stunning some fish. We chased the school as they made for deep water, hitting wildly. After the fish escaped, it was time to collect and cook the stunned victims. This was great sport, as the Finke usually only flowed in summer.

At another time bows and arrows became the 'in' weapons. We made them ourselves. Mother's oleander hedge yielded arrow shafts. Saplings were fire tempered and chicken feathers used as flights. With a bit of help from the garage, established to cater for increasing mechanisation, we became young Robin Hoods. This was one weapon we were not allowed to use on each other. Catching game proved elusive, as homemade arrows crafted by a child's labour were rather unpredictable in flight.

Crows were a special hate as they spoiled some of Mother's hard work in the garden. We caught them with a springy two metre long gum or oleander shoot, some string and a piece of meat. One end of the shoot was firmly buried, the other bent over, and using a bit of string, carefully hooked to a previously buried notched stick. The bait and a noose attached to the free end of the gum shoot completed the trap. When a crow pulled on the meat, the 'trigger' mechanism released the tensioned shoot, which usually lassoed the crow while straightening. It was not killed but securely tied upside down on a fence post. Crows don't like this and shout, bringing their friends, who alight on the same post to see what the problem is. The inverted crow locks on to the visiting crow with clawed feet, refusing to let go. After forcibly removing the upper crow, it was dispatched. Usually, three of four crows were caught in this manner before the tribe departed, leaving the one tied to the post to fend for itself. This unfortunate crow was spot painted with any colour other than black and released. The confusion this caused kept crows away for weeks. Some will no doubt condemn our actions but it was either the crows or us that ate.

At around ten years old, I became seriously lost on one walkabout. Having been temporarily lost before, I knew that by avoiding panic, I would eventually recognize my surroundings. This time I was exploring alone in new territory and lost my bearings and landmarks, probably due to inattention. I was in the James Ranges, in a dry rocky area with the sun high in the sky on a warm day. My route had been mainly over bare rock, so back tracking was a waste of time. While climbing the nearest high hill, I fixed in my mind the small valley surrounding me. On arriving at the top of the hill, I could not recognise the landscape. The situation was becoming serious. I had to choose a direction to walk and be prepared to come back to my present position and try again. My first reconnaissance proved fruitless and I returned to the hilltop hot, tired and with an empty water bottle. The sun was now giving me a better hint of direction and I chose a route at 90 degrees to my first foray. This time I was able to travel further before losing my base reference hilltop. To extend my view, I climbed a tree. Imagine my relief as I recognised the black, burnt tree trunk I had passed mid morning. *Careful now, keep your head and line up the best route before rushing off.*

My memorising, identifying topography and navigating skills, developed at an early age, proved invaluable in commercial flying activities on many continents later in my life.

Eventually reaching my beloved Finke, I was parched, but in a dry stretch of river. Using my aboriginal training I chose a likely bend and dug into the

16

hot white sand. Twenty centimetres down the sand became cool. Further digging resulted in water flowing into my hole - salty but drinkable.

I was subdued at dinner that night.

'Are you alright?' asked Mother.

'A bit tired mum, I had a long walk today.'

I would not admit to getting badly lost for fear of restrictions being placed on my freedom.

We instinctively learnt to navigate during our forays with the aboriginals. Years later I read Harold Gatty's book; 'Nature is Your Guide,' printed by Collins in 1958. He wrote that 'primitive' aboriginals in many countries use an entirely different system of navigation than that employed by 'civilised' travellers with compasses. Put simply, modern man relies on knowing where he is now, whereas aboriginals based their travels on knowing where they were in relation to 'home'. The aboriginals' remarkable pathfinding powers used highly developed powers of observation that Gatty, a famed navigator himself, said 'civilised' man has long since lost. For aboriginals, it was a life or death issue, both in finding game and when travelling in featureless and waterless desert areas.

Jared Diamond, the scientist and historical writer, in his book *Guns, Germs and Steel*, has this to say about Australian aboriginal societies:

'As of 40,000 years ago Native Australian societies enjoyed a head start over societies of Europe and the other continents. Native Australians developed some of the earliest known stone tools with ground edges, the earliest stone axe heads mounted on handles and by far the earliest watercraft in the world. Some of the oldest known paintings on rock surfaces come from Australia.'

He also says that 'Stone Age' peoples were on the average probably more intelligent, not less intelligent, than industrialized people.

Diamond mentions studies that show irreversible mental stunting associated with reduced childhood stimulation such as when children are largely entertained by television and radio. Also, in white societies, thanks to modern medicine, regressive genes may be passed on whereas in 'primitive' tribes these genes may not have survived adolescence, and probably only in rare cases were likely to breed. To put it simply, possibly only the intelligent and healthy genes were passed on in so called primitive societies.

As a child I found my aboriginal friends to be very intelligent. My acquaintances spoke two, and in some cases, three languages. They survived in an environment in which whites could not, without assistance from outside. Their society was structured to optimise this, to the extent of not allowing the weaker of twins to live, so the stronger had a chance of survival. All food was shared with the older members of the tribe. For it was they who passed on cultural and hunting skills to the young boys, ensuring continuity of knowledge.

We always went hunting barefoot as shoes cost money and never seemed to fit our wide feet. Some prickles penetrated our thick soles, but worse, during the cold, dry winters, our bare feet suffered. Some mornings, ice could still be found beneath a dripping tap at ten am. The cold ground plus not wearing shoes resulted in our deeply cracked feet bleeding and becoming very painful. I believe treatment with salve was the remedy but it took time for the skin to grow back over the raw fissures.

Conversely, in summer, the sand became so hot that long stretches were covered at speed between patches of shade. In extremis, we sat down and furiously waved feet in the air and hoped they cooled sufficiently before our bottoms were cooked.

During a visit by a group of VIP's, I decided to show off my desert toughness. After finding a few large safety pins, I stuck them through the hide on the soles of my feet. When walking over our flagstone floors, these made a clicking sound.

'Philip, why do your bare feet make that funny sound?' one asked.

'It's the safety pins.'

'What?'

I showed them the soles of my feet and they shook their heads.

I scampered away smiling, leaving them to mutter about the strange habits of these wild Mission kids.

For people and the Mission to survive, every blade of grass and each gallon of water was precious. When possible, any animals we saw that were not our cows or working horses were shot. Kangaroos, emus, turkeys and any other edible game ended up on someone's table. Old or disabled stock horses, having worked all their lives, were not put out to pasture, they were shot as well. I won't attempt to explore the morality of this; it was just considered normal at the time.

Many visitors were keen to try their marksmanship on game such as brumbies (wild horses) and kangaroos. I remember one outing with a tourist keen to shoot anything. We came across a large scrub bull. Unfortunately, his first shot did not disable the beast and the angry wounded bull charged our Land Rover. Dad frantically accelerated while dodging trees, anthills and other obstructions in scrubby bushland. Our visitor shot wildly as we bounced over the rough ground. The beast gained on us, and with the rifle almost up the bull's nostril, another shot sounded and the bull crashed to the ground. It was the last bullet in the magazine. Our visitor, after having such a fright, gave up shooting.

In 1946, Mother, my brother Peter and I went to the airstrip to be filmed as part of a United Nations documentary. The UN team were recording the modern way in which our school lessons traveled. A Connellan Airways De Haviland Rapide aircraft arrived as scheduled. The five man crew who had filmed us for the past week at the Mission, set up the shoot and recorded the handing over of mailbags and freight. On completion, the crew thanked us and boarded the aircraft. We remained to watch the aircraft depart.

It was a hot day and the heavily loaded aircraft barely cleared the mulga trees at the end of the strip. We were horrified to see it fall into the trees and disappear amid the sound of breaking timber, followed by a deathly silence. Thankfully, no smoke or flames appeared and on arriving at the wreckage, we found the passengers and pilot shaken and bruised but otherwise unhurt. The pilot, Cecil Parsons DFC, had put the nose of the aircraft between two trees, which mangled the wings and stopped the aircraft but did not damage the passenger cabin. My mother, as a witness, was required to give evidence to the accident investigators and we backed up her statement.

Strangely, years later, I was a passenger in a Connellan's Cessna which would have crashed in virtually the same place had I not shouted instructions to the inexperienced pilot.

On occasion, American warplanes flying from Darwin to Alice drifted off course and seeing a large airstrip below at around their expected arrival time, landed to find out where they were. These were exciting occasions for us young children, looking at real bombers with guns sticking out. These exposures to aircraft early in my life planted seeds that eventually blossomed.

In April, 1947 Mother went to hospital for another confinement. She wrote that the day before Tony Latz was born she attended the Alice Springs races with the Heenan family. Mr. Casey, the former Governor of Bengal, was also present. On the following day Mr. Casey visited the hospital and met all the new mothers. 'I'm a mother of men' she said, having produced half a dozen. Mother recovered well and soon returned to the Mission. Her diary notes that Tony was a similar type to me and that we got on well. I did not persecute him as I had my first brother, Peter.

On one occasion I was required to make a statement and be prepared to give evidence in the Alice Springs Court. I was eight at the time and had witnessed, from a distance, an adult male aboriginal attempt to sexually assault a young white female as she walked home from a swim in the Finke. I waited in a small bare room with my mother, but was not called to give evidence. After being tried by our system, the aboriginal concerned was dealt with by his elders. The sentence was a public flogging, administered by a shamed relative, and that was the end of it. Painful for the accused, but less severe than a spear through the thigh, a common tribal punishment for such an offence.

That incident meant white girls now had to be accompanied by white males when bathing. Our usual swimming hole was a kilometre away, so this required some coordination. During hot weather, the boys swam frequently, as did a lot of the aboriginal kids. None of us had bathing costumes, and being pre adolescent, we all swam naked stogether. Gender or sex was not considered until one day when a group of us white kids were bathing and someone started the game of 'You show me yours and I'll show you mine.' Innocent, but the awareness of sex began. This episode must have been mentioned to a parent, and after that mixed white bathing was chaperoned by an adult. This did not stop discussions about gender and all the girls said they would rather be boys, as men could pee while standing.

At times, fighting occurred among the aboriginals at the Mission. It often seemed to be among the women who belted each other with their hardwood digging sticks or 'nulla nullas.' These were about 60 centimetres long, pointed, and normally used for digging out bulbs, grubs and honey ants. I remember holding the light while Sister S. Lindner patched up a scalp that looked much like a skinned bleeding pumpkin. While being treated, the injured woman was still jabbering away about how she wanted to kill her opponent.

On another occasion I was Sister Lindner's patient. While being chased, I jumped a fence and landed on a jagged stake, tearing a deep hole in my right thigh. I ran home with blood running down my leg. Mother controlled the bleeding and sent for Sister. I lay on my parents' double bed and read the Chronicle while Sister pulled splinters out of my leg. I suspect she was more nervous than me as it was her first attempt at stitching a wound. Her hands shook while threading the shiny curved needle.

'Is it numb yet?' she asked while prodding my thigh.

I felt sick all over and didn't know how it was to feel numb so thought it best to agree.

Sister was a short slim lass who barely cast a shadow. I felt sorry for her as she struggled to push the needle through my tough muscles. It hurt like hell but I would not cry – it is not the aboriginal tradition. Pain can be ignored, which I had learnt to do to a large extent. Nine stitches were needed and the last few did not hurt much as the local anaesthetic had taken effect. I could not keep still so the scar stretched to two centimetres wide and the stitch marks are still visible 60 years later. When an official form asks for 'any distinguishing marks,' I invariably forget this scar and the barely visible spear wound on the side of my nose.

After recovering from my torn thigh, I resumed walkabouts with my aboriginal mate and badly grazed my shin while chasing game.

'Hey, better you stop that blood,' my friend said.

'How?'

'You piss on it.'

The aboriginals' knew all about survival so I trusted his wisdom. My urine stung a bit but the bleeding stopped. It was a useful trick to know and I have used it many times since. Deeper wounds were filled with mud or sand and we stood still for a few minutes until the blood clotted. It could be properly treated at home an hour or six later but in the meantime the wound would not be allowed to interrupt our days fun.

We climbed anything and scrambled up vertical rock faces using bare fingers and toes, to test our skills and sometimes to get at ripe wild figs. There was no kids' playground; exploring the countryside and playing with spears or whatever was at hand sufficed. I recall getting into trouble once for ripping the bottom out of my shorts on a protruding nail while using our galvanised iron house roof as a slide.

Another game the aboriginals taught us probably prepared me for aerobatics. First we rolled an old truck tyre to the top of a steep-sided hill close to the Mission. Then one of us curled up inside the tyre while another held it upright. Tyre and occupant were launched down the hillside. The winner travelled the greatest distance before falling out of the tyre – up to sixty metres from the bottom of the hill on a good day. This speedy spinning must have either scrambled or strengthened our brains.

Us kids were happiest out in the bush and if a day trip with the men was possible, school was abandoned, lunches demanded and we went off for nature study. Correspondence School could be caught up with on another day. Our supervisor, Miss Mona Kennedy (now Kramer) kept order and organisation among the half dozen white children of school age. Our work was done in a spare room with attached veranda at the Albrecht's house. Three months could elapse from the time we began an assignment until our corrected lessons were returned. By then, my spelling mistakes were ingrained and I continue to have difficulty in this area.

When our radio transceivers were eventually returned we were able to take part in school of the air for several hours on most weekdays. It was an exciting time, enabling us kids to be taught by a 'proper' teacher and to participate with other children we never saw. This contact also brought some of the outside world into our classroom and enabled Mission people to hear recent news.

Occasionally, my parents took a break from their constant workload. Usually, Father drove to a waterhole on the Finke River or Ellery Creek. Us kids would fish, swim, run around and make a lot of noise. After we helped to gather firewood, father lit a fire for cooking and making tea. When the fire had produced a heap of glowing mulga or gum tree coals, the meat could be cooked. Steaks were placed into a coarse wire mesh 'cage' to enable easy handling and then placed directly on the coals. This cage was about thirty centimetres square with a long handle and operated like a waffle iron. Direct contact with the coals imparted subtle, wonderful natural flavours to the seared, lean beef. On a good day, freshly caught fish were added to the menu.

On one of these outings, we had enjoyed lunch and were resting under shady gum trees beside a cool waterhole, when a movement in the water caught my eye. My nine month old brother Tony had been happily playing at the waters edge but was not there now. Then I saw the top of his head appear briefly, before sinking out of sight. As I ran to the pond his head came up and went under again. He was going down for the third time when I reached him. Once back on dry land, Tony coughed, spat out water and then began crawling back to the water's edge. It was a warm day and we kept a close eye on him after that. Mother had lost enough children. Me being the eldest, I felt it my responsibility to help ensure she didn't lose another and assumed the role of a broody hen. I don't recall how any of us kids learnt to swim - it just happened by instinct and watching other, older kids. Safety or flotation devices were unheard of at the Mission.

On another outing us older kids went to Standley Chasm, a popular tourist spot. Reaching our destination someone shouted excitedly, 'Look, paraltye.'

The truck had barely stopped before we were off and running to the adjacent gum trees. Faces and heads disappeared among low-lying branches as we eagerly licked the gum leaves. A busload of tourists, about to embark, stared in amazement. Some wandered over to see what we were doing.

'Why are you all so busy licking leaves?' one asked.

'Lovely grub,' was the muffled reply.

'What?'

'See this white stuff on the leaf, it's sweet and just flakes off on your tongue. It's the easiest way to eat it!'

'Hmm, what about all the dust on the leaves?'

'A bit of dirt won't hurt you!'

The unconvinced tourist shook his head and wandered away while no doubt thinking how native these local white kids had become.

The white flakes we ate, resembling undersized communion wafers, are exuded by a small lerp or scale insect, which feed off the sap in the leaves. I discovered these scientific facts much later from the book 'Bushfires and Bushtucker' written by my brother Peter. We just enjoyed eating free, sweet-tasting food. Our survival instincts overrode any small niceties or decorum.

The tourists were amused and after an explanation realised how well we had adapted to life in our environment.

When I was around ten years old, the environment for all at the mission changed as 240 volt electricity was installed. Machinery had always interested me so I was happy to assist the South Australian volunteer church workers who came to wire us up. I spent many hours as Monty Rieger's spare pair of hands. We crawled about under roofs, running wires above ceilings. A new diesel engine was installed in a purpose built generator and switchboard shed. I learnt the starting and shutdown procedure, as the engine only ran from early morning until ten at night. Naturally, I experimented with electricity and copped a few shocks. Having been heavily warned about playing with live wiring, I did not tell my parents.

The Mission purchased cheap surplus military equipment when the war ended. I believe around £200 ($400-00) was paid for a Bren-gun Carrier - minus the gun of course. Its main use was to pull a scoop to remove sand from cattle waterholes. Previously, we harnessed donkeys for this task. The

Bren was a handy vehicle for learning to drive, being literally bulletproof. My problem was reaching the steering brakes, which needed pressing for other than gentle turns as the steering wheel only disconnected drive to the tracks on one side. I managed to miss a few corners until my legs grew. I figured the trees I flattened would grow again. Initially I only drove this V 8 powered beast in the bush. Later, I graduated to the large four-wheel drive Chevrolet Blitz. It was my favourite vehicle, even though the engine next to my left knee generated considerable heat and noise.

When the Mission purchased a caterpillar D2 dozer to scoop out waterholes and dams I was allowed to drive it, but my training was minimal. I was probably 12 years old at the time. One day, while busy on roadwork, a bank collapsed due to the dozer's weight and I was flung diagonally out of the driver's seat. I managed to kick the clutch lever off while flying through the air and the machine stopped, teetering on a ledge above me. Had it moved forward a few centimetres it would have tipped over and crushed me. A good lesson, and one of my early lives I used up. My guardian angel certainly saved me that day.

Other war surplus materials snapped up, included .303 rifles and ammunition. I don't know how many rifles or tons of ammo came to the Mission, probably enough to equip a small army. It was now far cheaper for us to fire .303 rounds than the tiny .22 bullet.

Our firearms were stored against a kitchen wall, between the kerosene refrigerator and fly-wire covered meat safe. I remember .22, .32, .44 and .303 rifles, and .44 and 12 gauge shotguns completing the ensemble, with duplicates of the more common weapons. As on any cattle property, firearms are a part of working equipment and one, or several, were taken when leaving the house for a journey of any distance. I was taught how to handle these weapons safely at an early age, as were all of us white boys.

The .303 rifle had a strong recoil, but by the age of ten I could just cope with it. The weight of this weapon, 9 lbs. or 4 Kg, was another consideration but we sometimes took a .303 on our walkabouts. I recall Martin Albrecht and I blasting off a packet (twenty rounds) of ammo on target practice one day, as we had not found any game and were bored.

I was always proud of my marksmanship. Another day when Father and I drove out to check waterholes, we sighted a wild brumby family about a hundred metres away. I felled the stallion with a shot through the heart. Mother and foal would not leave without him, so I put the mare down with a shot through the lungs. The small foal was easy picking as Father drove nearer to assure a clean kill. It was a different era; I would not have the heart to shoot harmless animals now.

Toward the end of 1948, mother accompanied her three boys south to her parents' farm. It must have been hell for her on the Ghan, with us running all over the train. At stations, Peter and I disappeared into the countryside. She also had to ensure that one year old Tony didn't fall off the train. Us older boys had done so before, but we could always jump back on. The family did all arrive safely at the farm where mother could recuperate.

When she and my brothers returned to Hermannsburg after the Christmas holidays I remained at my grandparents' to complete my final year of primary school. I was both dismayed and excited at the prospect. Were my correspondence lessons good enough for me to cope at a 'proper' school? Would I be humiliated or bullied, an outsider or an 'ignorant' bushy? My top dog status was left behind at the Mission.

I look back at my early years and consider myself to have been privileged. I had no money, few toys or entertainment other than that which we contrived. We did not even have a radio in our house. But my environment was full of love and care and allowed me to gain physical and mental skills that proved invaluable.

Left, machinery boy, and above, the one that nearly got me.

CHAPTER 2

You start with a bag full of luck and an empty bag of experience.
The trick is to fill the bag of experience before you empty the bag of luck.
~ The Aviators Guide Book

Why was I sent away to do my final year of primary school at my grandparents farm at Appila, 220 kilometres north of Adelaide in South Australia in 1949 at the age of 12? Did mother want to accustom me to living away from home in a 'normal' white Christian society? Perhaps she wanted to prepare me for boarding at a Lutheran high school in Adelaide the following year? I was never told the reason but it certainly meant no more going bush on a whim. Now I had to attend school regularly and help with farm chores.

I attended Pine Creek Lutheran Day School at Appila, conveniently close to my grandparents' farm. Out of thirty-two students, only six were in my class.

After rising at 6 am, farm chores were done, lunch packed and I cycled or walked to school. Lining up in orderly rows for the roll call and saluting the flag were new experiences. Not being a local, I had to watch my back. Neither had I played any form of 'civilised' sport, another source of taunts by the resident bully and his followers. Skill at spear and boomerang throwing did not rate here, but at least I was a killer at 'branders'. A game where a tennis ball is thrown at an opponent – kid stuff compared to the hard objects we used on the Mission. When threatened and outnumbered, I was the only child capable of shinning up smooth gum tree trunks devoid of low branches. A quick sprint and a leap, followed by the busy use of arms and shins had me five metres up, sitting on a tree branch and hurling insults at my tormentors.

'Go and play with your stupid sheep and cows, they can't climb trees either!'

'You just wait Latzy, we'll fix you later. You'll be glad to go back to your monkey tribe.'

Sometimes, to avoid problems, I just sat there until the bell rang for class.

Professor Jack Cross, of Adelaide University, offered the following views at a public lecture. He spoke of his time as a student at Pine Creek during the war, a few years prior to my arrival. Jack and his family were neither Lutherans or of Germanic background so suffered discrimination to a much greater extent than I did.

He stated and I quote; *'Because of the war, the Pine Creek community withdrew into themselves and their past because they were excluded. It was a deeply religious community where all spoke German at home and clipped English with adverbs at the end of sentences, when outside their community.*

Their farms were well organised with rows of pine and fruit trees planted in geometric patterns. Irish farms were chaotic by contrast. School children played in the cemetery and got used to living with the dead but were not let out of the classroom during funerals, a real problem for the teacher. Men and women were separated in church because of the holy kiss. The local people were very serious – happiness was not a legitimate goal. The end of the world was talked about. The men were never to be seen in a public bar. Their pecking order was based on age and Church and school picnics were highly structured. Unmarried people (15 to 60) did folk dancing. Married men played skittles, women played Pin the Tail on the Donkey and prepared food. Cordial and sometimes, purchased carbonated preparations were drunk.

The community was persecuted during both wars, mainly verbally and was ostracised and subject to rumours of all kinds - because of being German speakers. During the depression children wore hand me down clothes, dutifully mended by busy hands.'

Jack, also mentioned that I was not accepted even though I was related to the community – I was still an outsider.

As I remember, his description was largely correct. Years later it was interesting to find that I had not been the only one. The way I was treated prepared me for being regarded as 'different', both at boarding school and when I entered the workforce.

The only other difficulty I recall at this school entailed the mastery of decimals, but I achieved a passing grade. Perhaps decimals were too easy for me, I was proficient at the multiplication and long division of pounds, shillings and pence.

In a letter written to my mother dated September the 4th 1949, I described a church picnic I attended with the rest of the congregation.

'Not long after we got there the races started. I won the tyre race and a few others. When we had finished racing we sang a few hymns and had lunch. We feasted on sponge cakes, cream puffs, meat rolls, lamingtons, tomato and

sausage sandwiches, biscuits, cake and a lot of other things. But somehow they all seemed to look a lot better than they tasted. After lunch we had a treasure hunt and everyone ended up with one and a half chocolate frogs. Then we watched the pillow fighting' (Two men sitting on a slippery rail raised above the ground so their feet were in the air, the object trying to knock each other off).

Later we had supper, which was almost the same as lunch. I won two shillings and eight pence that day.'

I did not mention how this sum was accrued as games of chance were not allowed. The winnings would have bought several packets of cigarettes or a large amount of sweets so no doubt made me feel very happy. Feeling generous, I bought my grandparents a gift of some sort.

I later came to know that their farm was purchased by my great grandparents in September 1872. They bought 148 hectares of land at Appila, near Laura, when gazetted and opened for selection. The purchase price was around three pounds ($6) per acre for this dry farming land. Almondale, our farm, was purchased in the 1880's. In 1908 my grandparents received title to this block; where they established the home where my mother, her four brothers and six sisters grew up. By 1949 the farm comprised 324 hectares; the furthest paddocks being over a kilometre from the house.

My grandparents and resident uncle and aunts treated me very well, but after my year's stay I disliked our staple meat, mutton. Having been spoiled on lean beef at home, fatty mutton or hogget took some swallowing, especially as I have never liked fat of any kind. Money was too scarce to kill a healthy lamb for the table. Almondale is the only place where I have eaten cooked sheep's lung, minced and mixed with spices and rice. Luckily, it was not fatty and tasted good.

Vegetables and fruit were also home grown. As in most mixed farms, cows provided milk, eggs were collected from the farmyard and occasionally a pig was slaughtered.

Dressing a pig involved everyone. Water was boiled for scraping off the bristles, the smokehouse prepared and knives sharpened. After slashing its throat, the pig's blood was saved as an ingredient for making bloodwurst. Even the bladder, after treatment, was used to make self-adhesive pickle jar covers. Only the pig's hair and stomach contents were discarded.

We stuffed sausage meat into washed pig's intestines - after turning them inside out. The latter is a simple procedure when two pairs of hands are available. One end of the intestine is fed into the top of a funnel, passed through the spout, then turned inside out and stretched over

28

the funnel end. Next, water is poured into the funnel and enters the cylindrical space between the walls of the downward facing intestine. The loose end of intestine is then fed into itself as more water is added. The free end snakes across the ground, twisting and turning like a live creature appearing to grow from nowhere. After a thorough washing and soaking in brine overnight, the intestines were stuffed with different prepared fillings such as used to make metwurst, white and black pudding. Cooking and smoking followed.

I found the taste of these traditionally made pork sausages, ham and bacon unequalled by modern techniques, and devouring them was a high point of my time on the farm.

One of my weekly tasks was to collect the mail. Our box was located 3.5 kilometres away on a main road. A pushbike was available; sometimes I rode the riding horse instead, or harnessed the buggy horse and drove it. As Grandpa had not yet bought a tractor, he kept twenty draught horses for ploughing, reaping and hay cutting. We used to harness eight horses to pull the large wagon used for delivering wheat bags to the railhead.

I shared a bedroom with my Uncle Carl, and I recall him rising at 4 am to feed horses before breakfast and beginning a twelve hour workday.

Sundays meant church. The service was in German at 10 am, followed by a large lunch at home. Afterwards the grown-ups' would chat, read, nap and entertain visitors. Children were left to play outside and hopefully leave the adults in peace. Unessential work or any organised sport was frowned upon.

Monday brought the early stoking of coppers, a metre high by half metre circular device containing the copper tub, a chimney and a wood fire underneath to boil the water. Washing went into the tub, and was stirred with a wooden pole while being cooked with homemade soap before being rinsed in water coloured by Reckitt's Blue which purported to whiten and brighten cloth. Good Christians were keen on purging the mind of uncleanliness, and this applied to clothing and linen as well. After this torture by hot water and then sunshine, sheets were squashed in a mangle. Similar to a latter day wringer but larger, the mangle had wooden rollers and a handle for turning, the sheets were pressed between them, resulting in military crisp folds. It seemed a shame to wreck the stiff creases by lying on them but their production was womens' work and part of their duties for mens' benefit. Men made the mess and women cleaned up, that was the attitude I grew up with. Men worked long hours in the fields, 'brought home the bacon,' and women did all the housework and provided a shiny 'nest' for the family. Sex was strictly for procreation and single mothers were ostracised. These attitudes were reinforced from numerous pulpits on Sundays and my attitudes fell in line with the faithfull.

On Saturdays and holidays I helped the men as my strength allowed. Fetching cows, moving the bull from one paddock to another. Picking peaches, apricots, almonds and suchlike from the farm gardens ensured my hands were seldom idle.

'Would you like to help me on the forge today?' Grandpa would ask. 'I have a lot of ploughshares to sharpen.'

'Yes Grandpa, that'll be good.' This invitation was most welcome on a cold winter's day.

The metre wide forge bellows were pumped by hand to keep the coals glowing.

I passed tongs and hammers as hot metal was pounded and shaped on the anvil and tempered in a tub of water. Almost all repairs to the farm machinery were achieved with the clever use of fire and strong arms.

Electric welders were unheard of although the farmhouse featured 32 volt electric lighting powered by a bank of storage batteries. These were charged by a 'Dunlight' wind powered generator atop a twelve metre tower. I remember it making gentle whistling sounds as it worked to keep our lights burning bright.

To cater for my walkabout urges, on occasion I was allowed to go and shoot rabbits. Usually my choice was the Browning .22 automatic rifle from the gun rack. It was light, fitted nicely in my hand, was quickly ready for action and fired eight shots before re-loading. My grandparent's farm backed onto a range of low hills covered in scrubby bush and trees. These forays pleased me immensely and often provided a change from our routine diet of mutton. I remember one occasion when I walked in the rain all day without firing a shot or seeing any game. The bunnies wisely stayed in their burrows. That is often the plight of the hunter, and as I found later in life, can apply to pursuit of the opposite sex.

In June 1949, my grandfather died after a short illness. Mother suffered a renal failure, probably caused by rigours of her life on the Mission and precipitated by her father's death. The Flying Doctor was called to transport her from Hermannsburg to the hospital in Alice Springs, but nobody was flying due to very severe dust storms in Central Australia.

Eddy Connellan, who with Rev. Dr John Flynn O.B.E. and Alf Traeger's radio expertise made the Flying Doctor service possible, heard that my mother was the critically ill patient. Eddy had known our family since his first visit to Central Australia, and was determined to make the flight if it was possible to do so. He probably broke the rules he required his pilots to observe, with regard to visibility on the ground and in flight. This is permitted on mercy flights but Eddy knew the country better than anyone. He collected my mother and flew her to the Alice. She was not expected to survive, so father was hastily bundled on to the aircraft in his dirty working clothes as well. It was his first flight and must have been a nightmare, bouncing around in a raging dust storm, his wife apparently dying beside him. Did he think they were all to die in a crash? In the Australasian POST published on June 30th, 1955, my father is quoted as saying:

'I have never been in such agony of mind as I watched my wife in torture. But the Flying Doctor plane came and got her to Alice in time.'

Mother survived and lived for another 48 years.

Connellan's official flight report stated:

'This flight was carried out under almost impossible flying conditions. A general dust haze reduced visibility to less than a mile (1.6 Km) and actual dust and sand blowing locally gave visibilities from nil to 200 yards (180 M) at Alice and Hermannsburg. Ground winds of 50 miles per hour (80 Km/hr), and higher gusts made taxiing, landing and take-off dangerous.

The flight was made because it was considered the patient would have died if she were not brought in immediately.'

I was not aware of these circumstances until many years later. Apart from the lack of ready communications, children were not told such bad news.

In August our school traveled to Wirrabra, about seven kilometres away to greet the Governor of Australia, Lord Gowrie. I mentioned in a letter to mother that he said he could teach us to ride a horse and camel. I had done that by the age of six. He also asked if anyone wished to speak and some child said 'a holiday?' We were given one on the following Monday.

Some of us examined the Governor's chauffeured car – a large Humber. I noted with awe that fans were fitted under the seats to keep bottoms cool. We were told this luxury limousine was used for HRH the King of England when he visited Australia. Being interested in machinery, this vehicle was a revelation to me. At the age of ten I was once given a book on basic engineering principles. I remember being able to grasp how a car differential worked, and continued to be interested in all things mechanical.

In September, a portable motorised milking machine arrived at the farm. I had never learned how to milk cows by hand, that was considered women's work. But a modern device was of great interest so I listened carefully as the machine was demonstrated.

'Every time, before you use the milker, this oil must be put into the vacuum pump,' the salesman said. I was allowed to hand crank the engine to start the machine and learnt how to fit the suction cups onto cows' teats. I had been fetching the cows, now I often milked them as well.

I didn't travel home to Hermannsburg for Christmas when the school year ended because I was to begin boarding school in Adelaide in early February. Instead, I helped the men bring in the wheat harvest.

At the time, wheat was harvested by using a horse drawn stripper. This machine stripped the heads, leaving just the stalks standing. The heads were then placed in large heaps for winnowing. The winnowing machine removed wheat kernels from their protective chaff. This chaff was called 'cocky chaff' and collected in a wagon for use as animal feed or one of its many other uses such as mattress stuffing. Wheat from the winnowing process was fed into hessian bags, each weighing 80 kilograms when filled. Bags were temporarily left open as stitching the tops shut took weeks, it was more important to get the unprotected wheat kernels off the ground. It was a labour intensive process - one man feeding the machine, another filling bags and the third stacking full bags carefully, fetching empty bags and generally assisting.

My main job at harvest was to evenly spread the cocky chaff being fed into an enclosed wagon. Being light and small, particles of chaff filled the air, creeping into every orifice. Combined with perspiration, it stuck to every part of my body. I used to itch all over, but accepted these discomforts as part of becoming a man.

With all the wheat safely in bags, the tops were stitched shut using curved needles. I remember spending endless days sewing bags while standing shade-less in 38° C heat. They were rammed taut prior to closing, by a special device that pushed in spare wheat. Careful needlework provided two protruding ears at both seam ends to act as 'handles' when moving the bags for transport to market.

Mother's diary proudly mentions that I was paid about £8-00 ($16) for six weeks of work. This sum was probably used for my pocket money at boarding school.

In January 1950, my mother arrived from Central Australia. Preparations were required for my attendance at Immanuel College, the Lutheran boarding school at North Walkerville in Adelaide. We traveled to the city to purchase my uniforms in the required grey melange. It was my first ever suit! The school also required items such as running shoes and football boots – these were luxuries for a boy from the bush. Years later I was amazed to find that listed under 'Other Requirements are: A mattress, pillow, blankets, quilt (blue and white if possible) four sheets, pillow slips, towels (coloured), pyjamas and plain coloured shirts.' However, mattresses could be rented from the college but discrimination applied – the boys cost $1.50 per year, girl boarders only paid $1.00.

The girls were also required to posses a tooth brush, dressing gown, white and navy underwear, umbrella and clothes brush. None of these items were listed under boys' necessities.

The flurry of excitement during this shopping spree was soon replaced by anxiety at the prospect of yet another dislocation from existing friends and relatives. We had no close kin in Adelaide and I knew few of my parents' church friends, I would largely be on my own.

'I'll come and visit next weekend to see how you are getting on', Mother said as she prepared to leave after school opening day.

'I'll be OK Mum, don't you worry.'

Many new boys cried while farewelling their parents but I would not let this occur. As always, I suffered in silence.

The first year students were housed in one long dormitory containing twenty-nine single beds. The main school building was originally a large, gracious, two story colonial house set in spacious grounds in the suburb of North Walkerville. Numerous alterations and additions had been made to cater for the 144 students who attended. Immanuel College was one of the first co-educational boarding schools in Australia and in 1950 the students comprised 79 males and 65 females. Virtually all were boarders.

Females were accommodated in two residential houses several streets away and were required to 'crocodile' or march in formation to and from meals and classes. Our first year dormitory was a prefabricated structure separate from the main house, as was an assembly hall large enough to seat everyone.

House rules were strict and the punishment by our prefects was swift and somewhat harsh. Over the years, I received more than my fair share.

'Latz, you've forgotten to put your slippers away again. Pass me one and bend over.'

Any protest was pointless, so six of the best landed on my backside. They all hurt but I became accustomed to it.

I soon learned that I was no longer an individual, I had to conform like a trained animal. Individuality could only be expressed in essays or on the sporting field. In daily life I had to fit the mould defined by the schools strict rules for junior boys.

Re-reading the 1950 school magazine recently I was amused at an enclosed quotation by George Bernard Shaw, 'The reasonable man adapts himself to the world; the unreasonable one persists in trying to adapt the world to himself. Therefore all progress depends on the unreasonable man.'

My attempts to follow his philosophy earned me time in detention and pain in my backside. At my age and status, I was not allowed to be unreasonable.

Finding a place to smoke without being observed was not easy. My skill at tree climbing and finding seemingly inaccessible parts of the school buildings was useful when I could afford a cigarette. One day a prefect caught me sitting ten metres up a pine tree. Smoking was one way in which I could thumb my nose at the authoritarian regime and get away with it. Over the years it became something of a game for me to outwit the prefects in finding new places to indulge my forbidden pleasure. I was only caught twice in three years. We were not allowed to leave the school grounds without permission except on weekends to play sport and attend church.

After our class settled in, the pecking order established. At home, as a white, I was held to be superior by my aboriginal playmates. At the Mission, I had no white male children of my age to challenge me. Once at school in Appila, I was the outsider and consequently suffered. I was not going to let it happen again.

It was put up or shut up and only several of my classmates put up. John Gniel was one and we had numerous fights. One occurred during our compulsory 6.30 am cold shower before devotions. Hot water was not supplied to the lowly first year students' bathroom, so in the middle of winter a shower took only a few seconds. On one occasion, John and I, both naked, wrestled on the bathroom floor, oblivious to the freezing water pouring over us as no partitions existed between the four shower heads. I don't know what started this fight, or the others that followed. I believe it was to establish top dog status as all other contenders had been eliminated. Our fights continued for several terms and became known to the Masters. They decided that a grudge match should be held to resolve the matter. This contest was held on the front lawn with many of the students watching. Boxing gloves were donned and the sports master refereed.

I was taller than John, but he boxed left-handed which caused me to suffer some heavy blows before I devised a defence. Then, I handed out the punishment.

'Time,' cried the referee.

'What's the verdict?' we asked.

'A draw, so shake hands and no more fighting you two or you'll be in big trouble.'

John and I became good friends and jointly headed the class 'Mafia'. I hope our classmates have forgiven us for any troubles we may have visited upon them.

As in many such authoritarian establishments, new boys were sometimes subjected to ridicule and harassment. Initiation was not sanctioned but one learnt to keep out of the seniors' way. One night our dormitory was raided by a group of older students who tipped over our beds and created mayhem before we chased them out. Then they threw water in the windows. Eventually the seniors retreated to their own dormitory, no doubt having a good joke about the trouble they created.

'Hell, now we've got to clean up this mess before lights out or that horror Roovy will have half of us on detention,' someone said.

'Runt, find a mop quick. Josh, grab some brooms so we can sweep this water out!'

'My bed's all wet through,' wailed someone.

'Too bad, you'll have to get in it till Roovy checks us and turns the lights out.'

Feverish activity soon had the dorm shipshape. The floor remained damp but we hoped Roovy would not notice as he wore thick glasses. It was unthinkable to dob in the seniors - they could make life hell for us and get away with it. Our turn would come next year; in the meantime we had to pass muster.

'The dorm looks a bit untidy tonight,' said Roovy in his usual dour, humourless voice. He was our most feared prefect. 'Just because it's Saturday doesn't mean you can be messy. Don't let it happen again.'

'Yes Sir,' we chorused, thankful to get away so lightly. He must have been in a good mood.

Inevitably I was caught smoking and received a fatigue. This entailed three days filling the coke (similar to coal) buckets that fired the boiler. This stoking was done in what would have been precious free time.

'You on the coke again Latz'y!'

'Yep, building my muscles so I can punch harder.'

'I've never had a fatigue.'

'Well aren't you a goody goody. Your mother will be proud of you.'

'I don't smoke like you.'

'You'll grow up.'

After the first one, fatigues only bothered me because I'd been caught and should have been smarter. Some boys were upset and felt humiliated at this form of punishment, but not me.

At some point a serious offence occurred, resulting in a visit to the headmaster's study. Others had told me of the likely consequences so I assumed a sad, humble and penitent demeanour. As expected, a stern lecture was followed by six strokes of the cane. Naturally I promised not to repeat the offence, and felt suitably chastened, but it didn't change me.

In a letter to my Mother I described a typical weekday at school for the first year boarders.

6.30 am – wake up call by a prefect

7.00 am – private devotions, supervised. Abstaining was not permitted

7.10 am – sweep class dormitory, general houskeeping

7.25 am – breathing exercises on front lawn for all male boarders

7.30 am – breakfast

8.00 am – make beds, brush teeth, polish shoes

8.20 am – assembly in the chapel for all students, bible reading, prayers and public announcements

8.45 am – lessons begin

12.00 noon – lunch followed by some free time (if not on fatigues)

1.00 pm – afternoon classes until 4 pm.

On Monday and Wednesday afternoons training for sport was mandatory. In summer we played cricket and tennis. In winter it was Australian Rules Football.

Tuesdays and Fridays meant working in the school gardens, cleaning our bathrooms and general maintenance.

Gymnastics was practiced on Thursdays. Training on the horizontal bar, parallel bars, tumbling horse and calisthenics were overseen by Mr. Hubble, a wiry professional trainer.

Dinner at 6 pm was followed by supervised homework and study prior to private devotions in the classroom.

At 9 pm we were released to brush teeth and retire. A prefect did an inspection of the dormitory and head count prior to lights out at 9.30. In theory, no talking, noise or tomfoolery was allowed after this. Sometimes we crept into a friend's bed and held whispered conversations before returning to sleep in our own bed.

On Saturday competitive sport was played against other church schools. We struggled to reach any finals, the other schools had greater student numbers to choose from.

Attendance at chapel for the Sunday morning service was mandatory, as was travel to the Lutheran church in the central city area for the evening service. A supposed treat, coffee and cake was provided after arriving home from church. These provisions were usually of dubious quality. Once, most of us threw the 'cake' at a wall where it stuck and quivered before sliding off.

One Sunday evening a group of us were walking back to school from the tram stop when tomfoolery began. My cap somehow ended up being stuck above a street light. While throwing sticks to retrieve my cap the globe was broken. Frightened, we all ran home. I knew I was in big trouble; a broken street light with my name in the school cap above it! Drastic action was necessary - I had to break bounds that night and hope I would not be caught.

I stayed awake until 11 pm, thinking all the prefects must surely be in bed. Heart pounding, I dressed and crept outside. The College was in darkness. Quickly I gained the safety of the street. This was my first deliberate serious offence, other than smoking.

In a few minutes I reached the unlit street lamp and pulled out several sturdy throwing-sticks from under my sweater. I didn't have a favourite projectile, the mini boomerang carved from green gum tree bark, but I reckoned my chosen sticks would fly predictably. One good throw was all it took, my cap fell to the ground. Snoring greeted my return to the dormitory and I went to sleep relieved. Luckily my absence went unnoticed. I had averted another visit to the headmasters study.

Compared to today's vandalism, my unintentional damage was laughable, but Church run private school boys were under close scrutiny by the community and expected to set an example.

My Mission background had not included any of the sports played at College. I had a lot of catching up to do, still being an outsider in that regard. I trained hard but did not represent the school in any sporting events until my second and third years.

On a hot summer's day, during an excursion, the males in our class were allowed to swim in a waterhole. One lad began floundering in the middle of the pool and cried for help. Responding instantly, I quickly reached the half drowned, panic-stricken boy. He climbed on top of me and kept pushing me under. I was now the one in danger of drowning. With no training in water rescues, I did not hit him to gain control. I could not shake him off, only my fitness and strength got us both ashore. I collapsed, utterly drained, spitting water. It had been touch and go for me whereas the other lad just walked away, no doubt embarrassed at getting himself into trouble. I'll let the next one drown, I decided. It's not worth the risk. Martin Albrecht had just let me tow him to the bank when he suffered cramp in Latz's dam a few years earlier. I had expected a similar easy result this time but my trust and lack of training almost did me in.

Term holidays were spent with relatives or at the homes of students in our class whom I befriended. Most were farmers and so an extra hand was always welcomed. For me, it was an opportunity to eat real food again, as the College kitchen only seemed capable of producing tasteless mush. Potatoes, white bread and treacle were about the only unrationed items available to us - not an ideal diet for growing adolescents.

My holiday hosts, in addition to feeding me, often slipped me a five or ten pound note as I left. This bought necessities such as cigarettes or toothpaste. My parents could only provide a minimal amount of pocket money. All Church people knew 'Mission kids' were poor.

First year at the college included religious studies in preparation for our Confirmation. With my upbringing, I was expected to shine at this subject. Among the boys, I gained top marks for Scripture and Science, sometimes opposing disciplines.

Most parents journeyed to the city to attend their children's confirmation, immediately followed by a first communion. It was taken very seriously. Mine could not attend. I remember being in fear and dread that I was not holy enough to be accepted into God's Kingdom and would somehow suffer dreadful humiliation on earth as a result. In a letter to my mother, I asked her forgiveness for all the terrible things I had done. Religion had claimed me, but I reverted to my survival instinct if necessary.

A close classmate, also just confirmed, shocked me a few days later. He was a farmer's son and a bit on the wild side.

'I sneaked out of College after lights out the other night Phil,' he confided.

'You were game. Why?'

'I'm very friendly with one of the girls at the hostel.'

'Did you actually go up to the girls hostel?' I asked.

This was amazing, breaking bounds was bad enough but being found in the company of a female student after lights out could result in them both being expelled!

'Yes, we had arranged a signal and she snuck out as well.'

'And you didn't get caught?'

'No, we had a great time.'

I did not pursue the details; I felt it would be sinful to speak of such things. But it was an eye-opener. I was very naive in romantic and sexual matters and would remain so for many years. Nudity was natural, but feeling up the opposite sex and satisfying lust were something I felt were reserved for courtship and marriage. Of course I had been masturbating for years but that was a different matter.

After our confirmation the final exams were near. A mumps epidemic put paid to those for me, I was confined to an isolation dormitory. I was not badly affected and later relished hearing of the agony my classmates suffered trying to achieve good marks. My good luck continued the next year; I was again isolated during end of year exams, this time with measles.

The seven-weeks long Christmas holidays allowed time for the Central Australian contingent to travel home on 'The Ghan'. This narrow gauge steam train plied the Port Augusta to Alice Springs line and took a nominal three days and two nights to complete the 1,280 kilometre journey.

First we traveled from Adelaide to Port Pirie, a four hour trip. There we changed trains for the short 84 kilometre journey to Port Augusta to board the Ghan.

It ran on lines only 106 centimetres apart, so the 300 centimetre wide carriages rocked and swayed considerably, even when traversing smooth sections of track. Slack couplings between a total of about thirty freight and passenger wagons meant the front of the train moved some distance before its tail followed. This clattering sound was a warning to brace for a sudden jerk as the train came to life, like a row of large dominoes falling.

These different gauges resulted from one Australian state employing a railway engineer from Scotland, and another state an engineer from Ireland. The Scots favoured standard gauge, 4 feet 8 ½ inches, the Irish 5 feet 3 inches. The 3 feet 6 inches narrow gauge was chosen to reduce the cost of the Ghan line to Central Australia. It was considered adequate for the speed trains would travel. In the early days the Ghan managed an average of twelve miles per hour (nineteen km/hr). In 1937, I heard that Port Pirie had the dubious distinction of being the only town in the world served by surface trains running on three different gauges. It took more than 50 years before a single common gauge meant people could travel interstate without changing trains.

Kids from differing religious denominations travelled on the same train north as term dates were identical for all private schools in South Australia. Twice a year the Ghan became 'The School Train' as it took us home in December and back to school in early February. Adult travelers who found themselves on our biannual pilgrimage soon gave up trying to moderate our boisterous activity. We largely had the train to ourselves, as locked doors prevented us from visiting First Class.

Our compartments contained four bunks, two up and two down. During the day the lower beds folded up and provided seating. A corridor along one side of each carriage allowed entry to the cabins and other second class sections of the train. As I remember, each carriage contained eight compartments plus a lavatory at one end and a conductor's room at the other.

I was not afraid of falling out at night, unlike others, so always favoured a top bunk. I could lie there and read or 'accidentally' drop things on people below. It was also easier to defend during the frequent raids on our cabin.

The lavatory featured a large sign which stated 'Not to be used while the train is stopped'. This was because all waste fell directly onto the track below. Too bad if we were parked for hours waiting for an engine changeover or an opposing train to pass.

The second class dining car could not seat all travellers at once so we were allocated to one of the three sittings. We found the food wonderful and attacked everything placed in front of us. Sometimes we were even allowed second helpings.

I remember York Ham being on the menu. While swaying and bouncing through deserted sand hills it seemed incongruous that a pig from England had made it this far to be on my dinner plate.

The crew in the kitchen were the real heroes. With the mercury as high as 49° C in the shade, they slaved over wood or coal burning stoves, cooking for hundreds. The placement of water tanks on the carriages was critical. In the early days it was found that in summer the water would boil - handy for making tea, but rather hot for washing and drinking.

We heard the reputation of the school train was such that errant railway employees were rostered on it as a punishment. I don't remember any vandalism, apart from the spillage during water fights. Being the middle of December, water was cooling and soon evaporated. Air conditioning was an open window, which also admitted soot, hot cinders and dust. Our youthful exuberance at being free and going home after a year away meant little peace for anyone.

I found the history of the Ghan railway interesting. It provided access to the interior of Australia and allowed cattle from Australia's vast inland to be trucked to markets in the south in days instead of months of droving.

Construction of the line to Maree commenced in late 1877. The first freight train arrived there in January 1884 amid a raging dust storm when the temperature in workers' tents stood at 49°C.

As many as 900 workers toiled with pick, shovel and sledge hammer to prepare the track and lay the rails, all done by manual labour amid the heat, dust, flies and isolation. Oodnadatta was reached in 1918.

A small army of men continued to brave the isolation and desolation of the unforgiving desert surroundings and pushed the line northwards. Sandstorms covered newly laid track with huge drifts denying food and equipment to front line workers.

Finally, in August 1929, George Stirling drove the first train into Alice Springs. Unfortunately, the following year, the bridge across the Finke River was washed away by a flood and replaced with a concrete causeway. The old steam trains could cross the causeway with sixty centimetres of water over the line but when diesel electric engines were introduced in June 1954 the maximum was reduced to just 7.6 centimetres. Many delays resulted after the bridge was washed away and George Stirling is quoted as saying that in 22 years the train was held up at the Finke twenty times.

On one of my Ghan journeys I remember the rhythmic clack, clack sounds of our moving train suddenly stopping. Looking out of the window, I saw muddy water drifting by, seemingly just below my eyes. We were crossing the flowing Finke River with the carriage wheels mostly under water

On another trip, I believe we were stuck at the Finke for days. When supplies of meat and vegetables were exhausted some of us went hunting game with a rifle supplied by the guard. I found kangaroo and dingo tracks but it seemed any game had fled the area, so we returned empty-handed.

I was told that the lengthiest train trip between Adelaide and the Alice was around three months. This may be a slight exaggeration but the saying, 'Better On A Camel,' the impolite term for British Overseas Airways Corporation (B.O.A.C.), later to become British Airways, certainly applied to the Ghan on that journey. My favourite train was no hare. We could jump off and stroll beside it, picking flowers and waving to passengers as the engine belched smoke and struggled to climb a hill. Sometimes several attempts were required to pass a crest.

On another occasion, we donned swimsuits as usual, prior to arriving at Coward Springs. Before the train had even stopped, we were off and running to the nearby waterhole. The cool, clear water was wonderfully refreshing and cleansed the dust and soot off our busy bodies. Unknown to us, a railway film crew were travelling in first class. The director, noticing our fun, summoned a cameraman who began to shoot. Normally, our swim lasted five, maybe ten minutes but this time the train was held until shooting concluded. We loved the extra time cavorting. There was no need to worry about the timetable, if the Ghan arrived during its scheduled week that was reasonable and if it made it on the correct day that was fair enough.

Free from the authoritarian rules of boarding school, some of us felt free to indulge our vices.

'How many packets of fags you got Latzy?'

'Enough for me'

'C'mon, you can spare me one'

'Buy your own.'

'I saw you looking at that girl from MLC' (Methodist Ladies College).

'Rubbish. I noticed you talking to Roberta. Do you know she's Catholic, she might let you kiss her. They can do anything if they confess afterwards.'

'I don't want to kiss her. She lives on the next property to us, that's why I know her. I wouldn't touch a Catholic with a bargepole.'

Us Protestants were programmed to view Catholics differently.

Another form of amusement was to goad and embarrass young students of the opposite sex. First, the girls would be enticed out of their compartment. I then climbed outside the train through the window of an adjacent compartment, entering the girls domain via their outside window. After quickly locking the door, I retreated through the window of the moving train and returned inside again.

Now the girls were at our mercy, unable to escape to their compartment. The porter was not amused at being disrupted to use his master key. He berated the girls for their stupidity while no doubt suspecting us boys. We just pulled faces at the girls and mouthed - 'Silly girls, silly girls'.

Meanwhile, the young lasses assured the porter that 'it' would not happen again.

It did, while the girls were having a meal. This time the porter read us the riot act. We tried other tricks. Such as exiting through a window, creeping along the moving carriages and throwing water into the girl's compartment. If we fell off, we rolled along the ground, got up and jumped back on.

If the girls left an outside window unlocked at night, we sneaked into their dark cabin and howled like a dingo before exiting. The trick was to do this and escape without being identified.

During the many lengthy stops when the engine's supplies were replenished, we went looking for something to do. None of the stations had platforms; we just stepped off the carriage onto desert sand. It was rare to travel a kilometre without seeing empty beer bottles and many lay at stops. We held competitions to see who could smash a particular bottle by throwing stones and never thought about a successful result as broken bottles lay everywhere. This target practice made life easy when I fielded in cricket matches and won me prizes at other events.

A retired Reverend from school reminded me at a class reunion forty years later that I had won a weeks pocket money from him. He bet that I could not hit a goal post with a stone. I did, and he said he had never bet since, I had done him a good turn.

We made it home for Christmas where a certain level of decorum and discipline was required. But out of sight of parents we swam naked, fished and hunted as usual. Our joy filled holiday soon passed and then we were on the Ghan again. Behavior on the return trip was less exuberant, the joy of moving up the pecking order at school was muted by the thought of a return to strict discipline.

In 1951, our class size of Sub-Intermediates had reduced. Farming families often considered their children's formal education complete after being confirmed, and at age 14, old enough to work at home. In our second year at college the dormitory was smaller and hot water flowed in the bathroom. The prefects also allowed us a little more latitude.

I began to rebel against the awful lunchtime food. I stopped attending but was caught so my class master began searching for me. After that, I made a point of greeting him on entering the dining room, then positioned myself in the centre of the six metre long table, which he headed. As everyone sat down after grace, I continued downwards and slid under the table. This disappearing strategy worked for some time until I became bored and tied some shoelaces together. During the ensuing confusion after lunch I was sprung again.

Our Master now kept a close watch to ensure I was present and also eating my lunch. I deviously worked out another ploy. After placing something on my plate I pretended to eat while pushing bits of so called food off my plate and onto the napkin, from where it mysteriously fell to the floor. At some point I was caught again and forced to sit next to the Master, resulting in a stalemate.

'Latz, you will eat this nourishment, given to us by the Grace of God.'

'Yes Sir,' I replied, my hands remaining motionless.

Minutes elapsed without a morsel passing my lips.

'Latz, you and I will remain here until you eat your food!'.

'Yes Sir.'

Grace was said and everyone else departed. We sat down again in stony silence.

Kitchen staff eyed us curiously while clearing tables. The Master began to plead with me but I would not budge. Eventually he realised this and said, 'I will have to take this matter further but you may go now.'

'Thank you Sir.' 'I would eat it if it was real food Sir.'

'Yes, yes,' he muttered.

I wondered what this rebellion would cost me. Nothing happened and I was left to either eat or not. The staff must have decided I had a case that could not be reasonably challenged. I have eaten snake, lizards, flora and fauna that other people would not touch let alone eat, but I could not force myself to swallow evil tasting, re-constituted and often re-heated, mush. To survive, I stole bread and if possible, butter from the staff table, but had to be quick. I became very adept at carrying concealed items under my armpits, as removing food from the dining room was forbidden. Bread was toasted on a bar heater and if butter was not available, eaten dry. Many times I found myself desperately hungry in our land of plenty, but I suppose the kitchen was operating on a very tight budget and relied on students being well fed when at home.

Years later I discovered Matron consistently underutilised her annual food budget. I also found a copy of the menu, repeated every week. It listed items such as mince meat (often green when served), scrambled eggs (preserved, also green or black), liver (indigestible rubber), stew and pressed meat (butchers floor sweepings). Saveloys (full of carcinogenic nitrides), sago (*frogs eggs*), custard (cow curd), bread and butter pudding (without the butter) and other such delights that rarely passed my stomach.

Notwithstanding my fasting, I managed to train hard, and was chosen to play in the school's under 15's football team. During one match I jumped to catch the ball and misjudged. The ball hit the little finger on my left hand. Nothing seemed amiss until I noticed my hand covered in blood. Looking closely, I saw a white bone protruding from the blood around my finger. Thinking it dislocated, I pressed on the bone and clicked it back into place, then continued to run after the ball.

When the coach noticed my bloody hand he called me off the field. He drove me to casualty at a hospital to have my finger attended. I felt bad about climbing onto clean white sheets wearing my muddy shorts and football boots but was told to do so. Seven stitches repaired my finger, but no painkillers were given to me so a sleepless night followed.

For one school term, I was elected as Vice Chairman of the class Social Club. At these structured and supervised Saturday night events we were actually allowed to mingle and speak to our female classmates. During these evenings, films and slides were shown, guest speakers entertained us and debates held. Definitely no form of dancing was allowed.

Again, I escaped the end of year exams due to contracting measles. Then it was home on the school train for our usual Christmas festivities, hunting, fishing and swimming.

In 1952 Immanuel College enrolled eighty girls and eighty-one boys, mostly boarders. Twelve full time teachers and three part time music tutors provided our academic education. Some teachers doubled as sports coaches and a specialist gymnastics instructor appeared.

In our third year we hardly bothered to speak to first year students. A new entrant to our class was naturally un-bonded and so subject to some bullying. For example, if we found him snoring, toothpaste was squeezed up his nostrils and into his mouth. It must have been hell for him, being an effeminate, non-sporting, intellectual type who never complained. I suppose he was eventually accepted but our behaviour to him was shameful.

I joined the school choir so I could mingle and whisper to the girl choristers. My election as Chairman of the class Social Club during the second term conferred status in our dormitory. The ignorant 'bush boy,' naturally accorded leadership among aboriginals at home, was exhibiting these qualities in his new environment.

I was selected to train for the State gymnastics team until flying off the horizontal bar and landing on my head. My head was undamaged but not so my spine. Matron 'Tut, tutted' unsympathetically, even though I couldn't bend my back for almost a week. I had no examination or X-rays. Years later when my mother finally heard of the incident, a chiropractor remedied the damage to my spine.

This accident did not stop me playing football and I graduated to the A team making the best players' list in four out of seven matches. I still recall playing Rostrevor College on their home ground. The dark robed and white dog collared coaching priests shouted encouragement to their team and abuse at us. The priests' use of swearing and undignified actions betrayed their holy orders, greatly upsetting our team.

Due to the small numbers at our school, on the football field I usually found myself pitted against young men several years my senior in age and experience but this only increased my determination to match their skill.

John Gniel, my previous enemy but now good friend, and I became interested in making explosives. Conducting boring experiments to measure the amount of reduction in certain elements was of no interest. To pass our chemistry practical tests John and I worked backwards through the logarithmic tables, starting with a number just off the correct answer. This produced very good marks and allowed us time to get on with making explosives. Mr Hebart, our chemistry teacher, was astounded when I told him of our shenanigans years later. He had no idea of our deceit or other experiments.

One day, having made what we thought was a good brew, John and I decided to explode it on the sports field. The chemicals were in a capped metal tin, which I was swinging in my hand as we walked. When the tin began to expand, I immediately let go. It exploded in mid air and set our trousers on fire. We both jumped into a nearby fish pond, extinguishing the flames. It was a sheepish pair that crept upstairs to our dormitory; removing evidence of our unauthorised and dangerous activity. Luckily for us this episode passed unnoticed but black nitrate flecks emerged from my numbed hand for weeks afterward.

We reverted to more predictable explosions such as merging sodium and water. One such was set off in a toilet bowl and it blew a manhole cover metres into the air and flushed other toilet bowls upwards. The unfortunate school handyman, a dour, unpopular person, happened to be sitting on a toilet during the explosion. The bowl emptied itself on him! This prank really soured his view of younger students. John and I were adept at not getting caught, so all the Headmaster could do was issue yet another warning during general assembly.

As the end of the school year approached, I hoped that I would not be quarantined again as we were to sit the State Intermediate exams. Our class settled into serious revision and silly pranks were forgotten. I completed papers in English, German, Maths One and Two, Science and History and was confident about passing all except German. I had never bothered to learn the complicated grammar rules and found the written exam difficult, although I breezed through the oral test.

The school break-up was a bittersweet day for myself and others who would not be returning. The intimate friendships we had forged in adversity would now change forever.

This year, Robert Arnold, a classmate and friend was coming home with me for a visit. Once at home I mostly helped fixing vehicles. I also rescued my Missionary Uncle, the Reverend Herman Pech when his truck broke down. My diary mentions that I hit a tree with the Blitz in the process but no damage occurred and we arrived home at midnight. These responsibilities fell easily on my shoulders at fifteen years of age. My driving was only on Mission property so I did not need a licence.

This holiday ended my financial dependence on others. I was about to begin a five year apprenticeship as a motor mechanic in Adelaide. As the secular working world was totally new to me, I was apprehensive about succeeding. Also, I would have to survive on a pittance and make new friends. My confidence at succeeding in adapting to 'civilisation' was threatened by facing another new world.

But first I had to get there, as heavy rains were making travel south of the Alice difficult.

The 'Blitz'

Immanuel College main building.

CHAPTER 3

A 'good' landing is one from which you can walk away.
A 'great' landing is one where they can use the plane again.
~ *The Aviators Guide Book*

Robert Arnold and I flew to Adelaide from Alice Springs in January, 1953. It would ensure I arrived in time to begin my first job. Flight was a new and exciting experience for us. Early in the day we eagerly boarded the piston engined, twenty eight passenger DC 3 plane. I had seen inside other aircraft, but this one was much bigger and made of gleaming metal. I was impressed, examining the inside carefully. The plane was almost full and very hot inside. I didn't care one bit and watched in fascination as we took off and the trees got smaller.

Being summer, the air was turbulent and soon the aircraft began to bounce. As the day progressed the ride became distinctly rough. I have since learnt that the slow and un-pressurised DC 3 could not legally cruise above the turbulent air. We made several landings to embark people. Many of the passengers were sick, including Robert. I decided that throwing up would not spoil my thrilling trip. When the hostess arrived with lunch Robert took one look and again reached for his sick bag. I just got stuck into the food, with great enjoyment. Very few others were eating. The hostess returned and saw my polished plate.

'Would you like another steak?' 'There are plenty left over'.

'Yes, it was great'.

Robert shuddered at the thought of more food and threw up again. My diary mentions that he was sick five times during the day-long series of flights. I managed to demolish four steaks before I conceded defeat, regardless of the vomiting around me - much to others chagrin.

My first flight was a wonderful adventure preceding my entry into the working world. For years, aircraft had been a vital part of outback life, but the experience of flying excited me and no doubt planted another seed in my brain.

Robert took himself off to travel to his family on York Peninsula and

I caught a tram to the boarding house that would be my home for some years. Arriving at 8 pm, I was too late for dinner but the steaks I had eaten would tide me over until breakfast.

At the tender age of 15, I awoke to a new day and new life. My apprenticeship was arranged by church connections as Sidney Crawford, the Managing Director of Commercial Motor Vehicles (C.M.V.) was a supporter of the Mission and their people.

Having been told to visit the company personnel officer in the city, I dressed in a white shirt and long trousers. After a hurried breakfast, I cycled to Franklin St., on the fringe of the Adelaide C.B.D. and reported to Frank Holland. He assigned me to the Commer truck and David Brown tractor assembly division. I was excited to be starting 'men's' work, even if it was at Overingham, an industrial suburb, some distance away.

I began work in the truck assembly area where my white shirt soon became filthy. The world of industry was completely new to me, so I had a steep learning curve during the first few weeks. Though hardly a sissy, I was astounded at the vulgarity and language used by some of my workmates. I discovered that generally, religion had no place in their lives, so I certainly did not admit to being a 'Mission' kid. Having lived entirely in Lutheran circles, I had never met these sorts of people before. Their worlds seemed to revolve around sex, drink and sport, all of which were freely discussed as our department consisted entirely of male workers.

My survival instincts quickly rationalised the situation and I began to live two lives - one during working hours and the other aligned to church activities. I had to hide my shock at hearing workmates discussing their love lives and how they 'used' some women. This talk sometimes distracted me so much I made stupid mistakes. I was both horrified and titillated, being a regular churchgoer and committed Christian. My hormones were raging and I dared to think that one day I might sample some of the intimate pleasures possible with girls, so casually discussed by my fellow workers. After fifty years I still remember one saying he preferred women with small breasts and big stiff nipples as these felt good on his bare chest. Would I ever experience this, I wondered? My conscience warned it should only happen in wedlock.

I wore dirty white shirts for three days before coveralls arrived, these were set off against my pay. For the twenty kilometre round trip to work my bicycle was essential; I could not afford bus or tram fares. First year apprentice pay amounted to £3-10 shillings ($7-00) while board and lodgings alone cost me £2-15 shillings ($5-50) per week. At work,

I could rarely afford lunch. A few times, I had no money to repair my bicycle, so walked the twenty kilometre round trip to work. Luckily this only happened occasionally. I did celebrate on hearing I'd passed all seven subjects in my year 10 State exams, buying a packet of 10 cigarettes that cost 24 cents. They lasted for a week.

It was not an easy time for me. My parents were far away, but I met with a few friends still at College. This contact helped keep my spirits up. I began to make new friends near my age at church.

My lodgings were owned and run by a strict Christian spinster, Miss Tilly Lohemeyer. A middle-aged lady with a generous figure but often sharp tongue. She boarded nine of us, seven males and two females, in her three bedroom suburban brick house at No. 12 Morcombe St., Maylands.

I shared a bedroom with two other males. We could just walk around the three beds. It was still a vast improvement over my crowded dormitory at school. The women slept in an enclosed veranda known as a sleep-out. Tilly was a tireless worker, cooked tasty, nutritious meals seven days a week, washed our clothes and vacuumed busily. However, we feared her tongue if the strict house rules were broken.

Arriving late for the evening meal without prior warning was not acceptable. Working or indulging in any sport or frivolous activities on Sundays was unthinkable, and arriving home after midnight was a sign of total degradation. We endured these restrictions as the quality and value of her establishment were unrivalled. I believe the female boarders paid less in exchange for domestic duties.

Lack of finance meant I was frequently home alone on Friday and Saturday evenings. Tilly attended weekly choir practice, and other church events. After the constant bustle at school, I felt lonely and deprived while others were out having fun. I was again at the bottom of the heap. With so much time on my hands I read the Bible from cover to cover.

One evening during Tilly's absence I overhauled her broken decorative chiming clock. I was bored and thought it a pleasant surprise for her. It ticked happily on the mantelpiece after my attention.

Next morning learnt that I had almost killed Tilly. She returned after 11.30, and was almost asleep when the clock chimed twelve times. Tilly thought she had died, gone to hell and the devil was claiming her. A good deed gone slightly awry.

Saint Stephens Lutheran church in Wakefield St., adjacent to the C.B.D., became the focal point for my social activities. Singing in the choir was free and as the female choristers sat in front of us at a lower level, sometimes I could even look down the front of their dresses. My hormones screamed, even in church. I also attended many of the free Young Peoples Society's functions and during summer played tennis with the church team.

I still fancied a girl from our class at Immanuel. Ruth still attended college, but as a senior was allowed more freedom. We chatted briefly after church once. Exchanging letters was the only way to communicate freely. An unchaperoned meeting was arranged. Planned to be after church on a Sunday evening in a park near her quarters at Immanuel. I arrived early on my bicycle, palms sweaty and full of trepidation. What should I do or say that would endear her to me? I had received no training in matters of courtship.

Ruth arrived in civilian clothing. I managed to hide my nervousness as we talked about our daily lives. I was too inexperienced to compliment her on her lovely dark hair or form fitting dress. We stood chatting under a tree and I managed to move closer to her in the darkness. I was too shy to place my arm around her, even though I was aching to feel a part of her body against mine.

She glanced at her watch. 'Goodness, 'I have to go, otherwise I'm sure I'll be missed!'

This was the moment. She let me kiss her and I was so afraid I withdrew after a second or two. It was the first time I had kissed a female on the lips. No great sparks flew during that brief touch.

'Goodnight Ruth, I'll write soon.' I watched her disappear into the night.

Then I discovered my bicycle had a flat tyre and I had a five kilometre walk home. I didn't mind, I was walking on cloud nine. I'd kissed my first girlfriend!

As an apprentice, I attended Technical College for a weekly evening in the classroom plus one full days practical work, every fortnight. Having passed in math's and science at College, I was not stretched to achieve high marks. Many of my fellow apprentices resented having to work all day and then attend school at night. I was happy to do so as lack of money prevented the pursuit of other interests. Besides, the other lads lived at home and were presumably better off financially.

After turning sixteen in February I passed a simple theory exam and was issued a driving licence. The process took less than half an hour. Now I could legally ride or drive any motorised vehicle of any tonnage or number of wheels. Due to previous experience, at work I drove various company cars, trucks, tractors and also operated the mobile crane. Little, if any, specific training was given, even on the crane. I was expected to use my common sense and learn on the job. This approach worked, I don't remember any damage or accidents occurring.

I submitted a simple cost saving idea to management and received $2.00 – almost a third of my weekly pay. Seeing another opportunity at work, I conducted a search and filed a provisional patent for my invention. Unfortunately, I lacked the business acumen and modest finance to take it further. I was peeved to find my idea being sold in the marketplace a short time after my provisional patent expired and had no idea that it would spread worldwide. My patent was just a simple hinge. It was added to an electric welding mask to allow the dark protective glass to be flicked open for clear vision, instead of moving or removing the whole mask. My forays into the world of original ideas would continue over many years.

That winter, when the Aussie Rules Football season began, I joined Ross Garrett, a roommate, in training with South Adelaide. After playing with them, I discovered a transfer from Norwood was required, living in that team's area. They refused this, so I began training with Norwood (after being disciplined for unknowingly playing illegally for South Adelaide). More lessons on life in the real world. Footy was short lived. After a few matches I was hit from behind, developed back problems and decided to give up playing competitively.

At work I got to know a sincere man, Jack Conquest, a keen spearfisherman. Me being a Piscean, the sport appealed, it had to do with water. Also, it was healthy and other people didn't try to hurt you. The fish might suffer, but at least I could get a feed.

At the time spear guns were not available in Adelaide; it was necessary to make your own. Jack supplied me with the plans and contacts for material purchases. I used my spare time at work, and the facilities at school, to began cutting and filing non-ferrous metals. Stainless steel was expensive, so I forewent more lunches to enable the purchase of materials I could not scrounge from a waste bin. The 1.5 metre long stainless tube that housed the spear propulsion spring cost $4.00 and a custom spring, $1.75. Expensive items that took some time to afford. I fashioned the trigger and spear release mechanism from the top of a worn out piston. My diary mentions I was given a pair of flippers, saving me $5.00. I managed to buy my mask and snorkel for $3.70. I fashioned a lethal shark knife by carefully grinding an old file, tempering it, then chrome plating, and finally attaching a wooden handle. Rubber from a discarded truck tube, cut to size and riveted to shape, formed the sheath.

I tried out my new weapon at a secluded beach south of Adelaide, hoping my inexperience would not be evident. The beach was completely deserted.

After swimming to a reef several hundred metres offshore where I hoped to spear a fish, I inevitably missed with my first shot. Reloading had to be done while bobbing around in the waves. Somehow, the line from gun to spear became tangled around my legs, then my arms and snorkel before the spear tried to penetrate my backside. It had all gone horribly wrong. I would have thrown the gun away, but it was still attached to me. Little did I know, I had broken a cardinal rule of diving - never go out on your own. I swallowed a lot of water before finally getting untangled. Eventually, I made it back to shore. After recovering, I practised reloading in shallow water.

The following weekend I returned to the same location and tried again. Fish were elusive, and a teething problem saw me heading home.

By chance, the Australian spearfishing championships were held at 'my' beach a few weeks later. I attended to see the experts at work. Many big fish were brought ashore, before shouting and distress signals came from the reef. Then, a casualty was brought in; his chest and abdomen torn open. The feared white pointer shark had mauled a spearfisherman. His life was saved only by expert medical assistance being on the beach.

I shuddered, thank God I had not managed to spear a fish and put blood into the water during my solitary outings at that reef. It seems my guardian angel knew how to swim.

I never went out on my own again, and after more practise, caught my dinner.

Another interest, aviation, led me to investigate the Government sponsored Air Training Corps (A.T.C.). That organisation accepted suitable males under the age of eighteen. Also, in 1953, compulsory national service was still in force and I had no desire to spend three months footslogging in the Army. I hoped that by joining the A.T.C. and perhaps later the Citizens Air Force, I'd escape the Army.

The A.T.C. accepted me, and after training, I was issued with a uniform, which I proudly wore. This began my formal association with aviation. But before learning anything about aircraft we were taught the most important thing – how, and who to salute. Lectures were given on radio communications, aircraft recognition (it's not good to shoot down your own planes), and much time was spent on the parade ground. We never went near an aircraft but some of the lectures gave me the opportunity to learn more about aviation.

My relationship with Ruth faded as I got to know other ladies in our church group. Square dancing was becoming popular and the church allowed this slight contact with females.

Square dancing became a feature at our church socials and a group of us became so proficient we provided demonstrations at other churches social events. On one such outing I was very envious of Jim after he confided to me that he had got to number seven with a girl on the bus trip home. I can't remember what this meant but it was certainly much more than kissing. Number ten was the ultimate experience (only allowed after marriage) so Jim did well, even if he was in the rearmost seat of our dark bus. I was still too afraid and shy to dream of trying to feel under a woman's clothing.

In December my exams were over and at the technical school wind-up I won dux of Maths and Science. My overall average for the compulsory five subjects studied was 89% which was gratifying.

With holidays due, I caught the Ghan, arriving home before Christmas. Rev. Gross's daughters from the Mission, Ruth and Margaret were also travelling so I chaperoned them. Though not of legal age, I bought a bottle of beer at Maree. It was a boring trip as the 'school train' had run a week earlier.

It was great being home and not having to punch time clocks. Religious duties remained and my diary notes I attended church six times between December 25th and January 3rd. In between, I shot seven crows in the vegetable garden one day. I began teaching Marie Gross to drive the big Chevrolet four-wheel drive Blitz. It was not thought strange that a 16-year-old should teach another of similar age to drive a truck. After all, I was a licensed driver.

Marie's sister accompanied us. Double de-clutching was necessary in the days before synchromesh gearboxes and while Marie concentrated on de-clutching we ran off the road. She was unable to control the heavy steering with one hand and then we hit soggy mud, becoming hopelessly bogged. I left Marie and her sister, walking five kilometres home in the heat of summer. We towed the Blitz out with another truck. I gave up teaching girls to drive after that. Instead I installed lights at the hospital, fixed vehicles and made household items for Mother. Also finding time to swim and do some shooting.

At Maree, on the return trip to Adelaide, I was brave enough (and I thought big enough) to breast the bar and drink beer with the men.

While walking back to the Ghan after the second whistle, I saw one fellow crawling rapidly through the dirt on his hands and knees toward the train. He must have remembered the fence between himself and the train. The guards usually assisted alcoholic stragglers to climb the moving step after long stops at stations with hotels. At these places the engine driver blew two whistles before pulling out. After the first one, there was a mad rush to order and drink another beer before the second whistle, a few minutes later. After this trip I calculated that I had travelled over 25,000 kilometres or 16,000 miles by train during the first 16 years of my life.

Back at work in Adelaide, in 1954, my second year apprentice pay permitted more social activity. Diary entries were full of involvement with the church; their Young Men's Club, Young Peoples Society, tennis and choir. In addition, I involved myself with the Automotive Apprentices Association, Air Training Corps and Commercial Motors socials, football games and spearfishing in the summer.

School attendance was still mandatory and serious study was necessary to retain my top dog status. At year's end I achieved a first class pass with an average of 86% but did not win a prize.

In February 1955, I was honourably discharged from the Air Training Corps on reaching eighteen years of age. After passing the Armed Services trade test I signed up with the Citizens Air Force as an engine fitter. Our fortnightly weekend camps meant travelling to the air base at Mallala aerodrome, fifty-seven kilometres north of Adelaide. This aerodrome has been decommissioned and is now a car-racing venue.

The regular Air Force personnel called us 'weekend warriors' and other less polite terms, but we were tolerated and useful for doing dirty or unappealing jobs, such as peeling potatoes in the Officers' Mess. While scrubbing vegetables I heard tales of some Officers of both sexes drunken behavior. It almost curled my hair but gave me another insight into how some people lived.

Other tasks that we weekend warriors were allowed to do included guarding the Base's main entrance. Late one Saturday night I was reading, my feet up on the desk in the guardhouse, when a vehicle approached. Recognising the Commanding Officers car, I dashed outside, smartly opened the gate and threw the boss a snappy salute. He responded, drove away, I closed the gate and re-entered the guardhouse. Shock, horror – my hat sat on the desk. Saluting an officer while bareheaded is an offence - and I had done it to the C.O. I expected to hear a Military Policeman's vehicle skid to a halt outside, then have my ears blasted, but the boss must have been in a good mood as I heard nothing further.

I was also allowed to assist in maintenance on the squadrons Wirraway and Mustang aircraft. The Stang's were inspiring; although almost outdated as fighters, they could severely bite overambitious aviators. They killed several of our weekend warrior pilots. I remember being amazed that a Stang could gouge a ten metre deep hole after hitting the ground at high speed. Ejection seats were not fitted to these aircraft (they came later in jet fighters).

On another weekend, we were dropped off into the country around Gawler late in the day to try and catch our Officers who were simulating escaping from a POW prison camp. They had been dispersed, penniless, in full uniform, behind our positions and were attempting to sneak through our lines to their pick-up point without being caught. I heard that some of our lot stopped a passenger train and held it for checking. Don't know what story they told the driver, but there were repercussions - that sort of action was not acceptable during peacetime exercises.

As the night wore on I became bored sitting in my concealed position. A solitary farm shed stood nearby, so I thought I'd check if an officer hid inside. Walking quietly along the barn wall I reached the open end, swung around to face the interior, and switched on my torch. A blood-curdling snarl pierced my soul as long, white, sharp teeth lunged for my throat. Miraculously the teeth jarred to an abrupt halt less than an arms length from my face as the large ferocious guard dog reached the end of its chain. The sudden attack momentarily rooted me to the spot, but a half-second later adrenaline kicked in and I took off, all thoughts of stealth forgotten. Had I taken another step into the barn I could have had my head ripped off. Few animals scare me but killer dogs are another matter. It took some time for my pulse to return to normal. Eventually I was collected and we all returned to barracks. Lucky for me, that dog was my nearest brush with danger while in the military.

The day arrived for our flying display. Being the only Air Force Squadron in S.A., a visiting Sabre jet fighter stole the show by breaking the sound barrier several times. As the sonic boom was aimed directly at the crowd, we were hit with a massive whip cracking sound, like a huge pane of glass being shattered close to our ears. We instinctively jerked, to avoid being hit by 'something'. It was a first for many people.

We lay in the grass in front of the numerous spectators. Then a Tiger Moth flew crazily past, a metre above the ground. I was horrified to see its lower wing strike a glider launch crewman sitting on his open tow truck.

Fortunately, the man saw the approaching aircraft at the last moment, ducked his head, was struck on the shoulder and sent sprawling onto the grass. He was lucky not to have had his head severed, instead, the glancing blow bruised his back.

A Vulcan bomber arrived to strut its stuff. After a very low, slow, pass, full power was applied as the aircraft rotated to climb vertically. The ensuing jet blast that hit us was horrific; our fingers frantically dug into the ground to prevent us being blown hundreds of metres across the airfield. The ground seemed to shake and the thunder of the engines hammered our chests as we struggled to hold on to the earth. When the danger passed, we all rolled over, shook clenched fists and swore at the pilot who had almost blown us away like plastic bags on a freeway.

On another weekend, General Grant, the WW II hero, visited. I found myself, rifle in hand, locked in a dimly lit hanger to ensure that no rats or snakes tried to hitch a ride on the Generals' plane. Like many before me, I found military duties involved long periods of mindless boredom, but at least we were paid for it. Thankfully, technical people like me had minimal formal parades, but participated in marches on Anzac day and other ceremonial events.

The Air Force didn't reward me very well, but thanks to annual pay rises, I now earned six pounds and three shillings per week, ($12.30), almost double my first year wage. The rise enabled me to buy a second hand 250 cc BSA motorcycle for £5 - $10. Being cheap, it was not very reliable until I overhauled worn out parts. I needed the motorised transport, now being out almost every night of the week. In addition to playing competitive tennis, table tennis and badminton for our church team, I began learning to roller and ice skate. The old scholars association elected me to their committee and I also began to date girls.

On one date I rode to collect my partner for a formal social evening with our church group. She appeared in a lovely long white gown and while assisting her onto the pillion seat I warned her about the dangers of motorcycle chains and loose clothing. We rode off but some time later she cried, 'Phil, please stop.'

It was too late. Much of the lower part of her gown was mangled, a mess of shredded black rags.

'I don't think you pulled your skirt up high enough.'

'I was afraid of looking indecent.'

'You wear shorts don't you?'

'Yes.'

'Why were you afraid to show your knees. You have lovely legs, you should be proud to show them off!'

She hung her head in embarrassment.

'Lets see how bad it is, perhaps we can cut the bottom off.'

She pulled at the skirt to check and it ripped to above her stocking tops.

'It's no good Phil, I can't go in this,' she wailed.

We did not attend the function, but instead found a quiet park and I consoled her with kisses and cuddles until it was time to go home. I thought this unplanned incident a good outcome for me, I didn't have to worry about the ruined dress.

One lass I dated took me home to meet her mother after only a few outings. Mother thought I was a lovely young fellow. So did her daughter, but it was the wrong ploy for me. This bush boy still had ambitions to fulfill and a humdrum suburban life raising good Lutherans was not one of them. I was after more of everything, including sex education, before a family came into my picture. I never asked that girl out again, I did not want to be answerable to mothers at this stage.

One of my ex college friends, John Gniel, invited me to attend a country dance in the Barrossa wine growing area. To avoid disturbing the peace, dance halls were located well outside town. Our carload purchased flagons of cheap fortified wine on the way. I was an interested spectator but drank little.

On arrival at the hall, a typical scene greeted us. A band was positioned on the stage, opposite the entrance. Rows of chairs, occupied by expectant girls displaying their finery, were seated adjacent to one wall. Opposite them stood unoccupied chairs, but the males huddled in groups around the entrance. It was some time before any dancers took to the floor. Single males spoke with forced gaiety while sneaking furtive glances at the gossiping ladies.

'I fancy that one in the pink dress, hope she'll dance with me.'

'That's Joe's sister, she'll go with anyone. Watch out, she could be pregnant and looking for a husband to make it legal.'

'Well, I don't fancy her that much, perhaps I'll try the one in blue.'

Such conversations were academic to me, I couldn't dance, even if my church allowed it. My faith kept me within fairly strict bounds of social behavior, though bush survival instincts bent the rules on occasion. Some of the Lutheran community, I suspect, ignored the ban and danced with their wives or girlfriends.

In those days, the consumption of alcohol was not allowed within two hundred metres of a dance hall, presumably to protect females from being corrupted by the drink. We piled into the car, drove a safe distance down the road, parked, and began emptying flagons.

And so the evening passed, drinking being interspersed with trips to the hall to see who was dancing with whom and evaluating the possibility of finding a stray to take home. We never thought about what female in her right mind would want to be escorted by a bunch of inebriated males who had not even bothered to dance. It was a pathetically lost cause.

I came to grief at one of the first country weddings I attended. The Barrossa Pearl - a cheap carbonated Champagne imitation - flowed freely and I overindulged, becoming violently sick. I vowed that this would never happen again. Inevitably it did, many years later.

A rather tragic and bizarre event one of my work-mates experienced reinforced my early respect for the effects of alcohol. Jack was driving a small truck on a sealed road in the country. A sedan approached, weaving all over the road. Jack swerved to avoid the car but as it passed, without apparent contact, he heard a thud. The other vehicle continued but Jack stopped to investigate and found a complete arm lying on the road. Jack's vehicle appeared unmarked. He grabbed the arm, and hurriedly drove after the sedan. Catching up with it, he persuaded the driver to stop. The intoxicated mans right arm was missing, and incredibly he was not aware of it even though blood covered his right side. A hospital was nearby and Jack took him there, saving his life.

One day at technical school, the headmaster approached me about applying for the Apprentice of the Year competition.

This contest was open to all third year apprentices of any trade.

I filled out some forms and forgot about them. Several months later I was asked to do an interview. More time passed and I was told I had made it to the best twelve in the state. A final interview would determine the winner.

The suit and tie interrogation was held in the Bank of Adelaide's boardroom. A panel of judges asked me questions covering a wide range of subjects. A week later, the finalists, of which I was the only motor mechanic, were treated to an official luncheon. After this, the Deputy Director of Education announced the winner.

It was not me. I realise now that my view of the world was too limited and clouded by religious bias. Most of the extra curricular activities on my data sheet given to the judges also fell under the same hat. I was not bothered by the outcome; I was enjoying life and still had a lot to learn.

Later that year, a woman more sophisticated than I, befriended me. We had many mutual friends, but Rose was also emotionally much wiser than I. What she saw in me I can only guess. Perhaps my different background, innocence, unbridled curiosity, willingness to learn and a zest for life?

We both attended the same church. She had her own bedroom which I sometimes visited. We talked, kissed and cuddled in her small private space. Once we contrived to spend a whole night on her bed, however, remained clothed throughout. Perhaps she expected me to seduce her but I was too afraid to attempt any removal of her garments. My Christian morals prevented any drifting of hands below the waist, even though our mutual passion was screaming for release. I didn't sleep a wink that night, the anticipation was overwhelming. However, this torture did mean I could attend church and communion with a clear conscience.

We sometimes visited a particular cafe for coffee after church. When becoming known to the owners, we ordered Special White Coffee. It was not on the menu, the contents being illegal on Sundays due to strict licensing laws. We received white wine in a coffee cup, an almost laughable offence in the present context of available drugs.

When the school term ended I spent many evenings with my Rose. Just before I left to travel home for Christmas we attended church together. After the service, a group of us watched a performance of Carols by Candlelight near the Torrens River. From our position on the north bank the view showed reflections in the water, and the fountain shooting colours into the sky. Opposite stood the sound stage, choir, and waves of candles, which seemed to flicker in time with the rhythm of harmonious voices. The soft warmth of the summer night and hopeful visions of peace on earth stroked one's soul and left a rosy glow.

After the show, Rose and I somehow found ourselves alone among some bushes and stopped to kiss. It seemed there was a melding of minds and then bodies as we fell to the ground and were almost immediately joined, as if the heat of passion melted our clothing.

It was a spontaneous, feverish, almost spiritual experience when our pent up desires were expressed in the fusing of our bodies. It was the first time a woman had allowed me to give myself completely to her. The final burst of exquisite pleasure, was for me, a monumental explosion from the depths of my soul. It coursed through my entire body and left me utterly drained but feeling a touch of heaven on earth. This was far beyond any emotional or religious experience I had known.

All too soon, I returned to earth and noticed a stick jabbing my elbow. Rose was, I suspect, more experienced than I but left no doubt that she had wanted me.

These were pre-pill days and so I practised what was quaintly termed coitus interruptus - no doubt her upraised skirt was badly stained. We didn't linger among the leaves and twigs. I could hardly believe what had happened as I fell into bed that night. My groin still twinged with feelings of pleasure.

The experience was so wonderful I didn't feel any guilt or shame and went to sleep smiling. I had finally tasted the forbidden apple and now knew the full extent of spiritual bonding and sensuous enjoyment two people could share. I suspect my hormones overrode any guilty religious feelings. Besides, Rose was my mentor. I allowed her to guide me in life and sexual matters.

I suspect that Tilly would have thrown me out of her house if she knew what I had been up to, but at the time I certainly didn't care.

God heard from me, asking forgiveness for my sins, but I didn't mention my loss of virginity to anyone else for many years.

There was little time to reflect on my becoming a man as a few days later I boarded the train for the Alice. My only diary entry for this journey notes that I rode in the Ghan's engine between two stops. This made me appreciate the driver and fireman's arduous labours. The day was not hot, but the sweat poured off them continuously as dust, cinders and soot swirled around in the fierce heat radiating from the firebox. I had seen crews change shifts at dusk; often the two heading for the brake-van were black from head to toe with only the whites of their eyes visible.

Arriving back at the Mission, I found myself involved in the usual maintenance activities. I worked on vehicles, equipment, and did odd jobs such as helping scoop sand out of waterholes so cattle could drink. I gave my parents their first radio set for Christmas; they couldn't afford to buy this luxury item. Now we could listen to the news on Radio Australia's short wave service.

Once back in Adelaide, I attended evening classes for two nights each week. The subject studied was equivalent to year 12 maths. Being three years since I had studied maths at year 10, I found the going tough after a hard day's work. Another night was spent on homework, which made a severe dent in my social life. I persevered, to maintain the scholarship I'd been awarded the previous year.

In 1956 my diary was blank until March, the extra curricular load was so high due to study and other commitments. I decided to give up the maths as I saw little chance of achieving a passing grade. Instead, I elected to do industry specialities - automotive electrical and diesel courses over two years. Now I was able to cope, with only one night a week at school, I could maintain my social life.

I dated a few females but was too busy to give any serious attention to them. I saw Rose occasionally, but our lives were on different paths, so contact was sparse. Sadly we were not intimate again. During those pre-pill days, probably only prostitutes or married women had contraceptive means readily available. So the timing of any intimacy was very important and it was hardly fair to ask a woman to make a date only during her infertile period. My religious beliefs forbade me from buying or carrying condoms, although I knew many of my workmates did. I was now being torn between religious and secular social mores, wanting more sexual experience, but not prepared to begin a serious relationship. I settled for kisses and cuddles and had no idea how to unfasten a bra.

My cheaply purchased motorcycle was becoming increasingly unreliable so I sold it and bought a KSS Velocette. This was a 'hot' bike which could be tuned for racing and featured an overhead camshaft with hunting tooth timing. For the technically minded, this meant the two sets of gears driving the camshaft had irregularly numbered teeth to prevent sympathetic wear caused by constantly engaging the same teeth. Using the equipment at technical school I did a complete overhaul which included re-boring the cylinder and cam-grinding the piston, normally a specialist job. My steed now did 160 kph, faster than most cars of the day.

The company I worked for was large and prosperous, selling and servicing everything from farm tractors (Case and David Brown), small to large trucks (Commer), plus a complete range of economy to luxury cars from the then Rootes Group ie, Hillman, Humber and Sunbeam Talbot. Panel beating, bus body manufacturing, breakdown and farm service divisions completed the diversity of services.

Apprentices rotated through all the departments to increase their skills. We were fortunate to have this opportunity. By the fourth year most had settled in one division. I liked the truck department. It was proper work, not having to deal with irate owners complaining about silly squeaks, rattles or crooked floor mats.

At some point the Company obtained a contract to install turning indicator lights on the top four corners of public transport buses. This work was performed in a large shed at a depot in Hakney. A long six metre high rear wall at our workplace backed onto parkland. One day, we watched in amazement as the regular workers dropped their tools, ran to the rear of our shed, and glued their faces to the corrugated iron wall. We followed and asked what was going on.

'Find a peep hole and take a look,' someone said quietly.

Finding one, I saw the attraction. About six metres away, a young couple were standing and embracing, the girl with her back against a large tree trunk. The males' trousers covered his shoes and the girl's skirt was rucked up around her waist. Their lovemaking was brisk and vigorous. When he withdrew, someone standing on the roof threw a bucket of water at them, most of which missed. Immediately, the men began pounding on the tin wall and shouting comments.

'Lousy bugger, can't you afford a hotel.'

'Bet she's someone else's wife.'

'Glad I've got a bigger one than you.' Other ribald remarks followed.

The poor couple ran in terror. The female got away smartly, her panties flapping from one ankle. In shock, the man forgot his trousers were down, immediately fell over and had to suffer further insults before hitching them up and escaping. I felt very sorry for the lovers, and no doubt it was an episode they would never forget.

'It happens quite often,' said a veteran worker. 'That's why we've all got our peepholes. Reg likes to get up on the roof with his bucket of water. He gets a better view from there, he says.'

We finished our contract work after a few weeks but sadly did not see a repeat performance.

While working in the car department I made a tactical error. Returning from lunch, Bob Adey, the foreman, called me.

'Phil, I want you to do a valve grind on this Hillman.'

'OK, any other problems to fix?'

'No, but it has to be finished tonight. You are the only one who is free to start now.'

'But I've got a date.'

'Give her a call, tell her you'll be late.'

'Not that easy, never mind.' I knew she would be difficult to contact so ruled that out.

I set to, worked fast and didn't waste a second. This job could take seven hours, but working feverishly, I finished after only four. The vehicle road tested perfectly and after that I copped the same task for weeks.

SOS, I thought, same old shit, don't stick your head out of the trenches without expecting repercussions.

One evening after working late, I walked out of the shop into drizzling rain. While stepping onto the footpath in Franklin Street in the C.B.D. a loud bang and flash of blue light erupted above me. I jumped forward, turned and saw a high-tension electricity line sparking and dancing on the footpath where I had been standing. Had it fallen a second earlier, it would have draped itself over me. I shuddered and gave thanks that my Angel was still around.

In June, I was called to the manager's office. *Why does he want to see me, the foreman usually passes on instructions. What have I done wrong?*

'Got a surprise for you Phil,' Stan said when I entered his office. 'How would you like to go to Melbourne this weekend and bring back a new truck for us?'

'That would be nice. When do I have to be back?'

'The usual time Monday. You'll get the standard allowance for a night away but we won't pay any weekend overtime.'

'That's fine. Thanks for giving me this trip.'

'I think you have earned it,' he said graciously and provided details.

A unionized employee might have claimed all sorts of allowances but cheap labour apprentices did jobs like these at very little cost to the Company.

My fellow boarders were rather envious. Australia was hosting the 1956 Olympics in Melbourne so I hoped I could get into the stadium on Saturday before driving back slowly on Sunday.

After flying to Melbourne in a DC 3 early on Saturday morning, I collected the truck and then drove straight to the games. It cost me 13 shillings and 6 pence ($1.70), or the price of a few packets of cigarettes to enter the stand up section of the Melbourne Cricket Ground where the athletics finals were being held.

The stadium was full, the games were almost over, with many finals being decided. The atmosphere inside was electric. I was excited and elated to be one of the fortunate Australians present. Especially as I could not have afforded that privilege without the Company providing my transport.

Notwithstanding the capacity crowd, at times one could almost hear a pin drop - for example when a pole-vaulter began a run in to jump. Followed by a chest thumping roar or groan as the bar was either cleared or fell. It was certainly worth standing to see the worlds best athletes perform. Now, major events are available at the click of a remote control, which I feel often devalues the performers efforts.

The afternoon passed quickly. Drained of emotion at the conclusion of this memorable day, I found my way to the suburbs to spend the night with my Uncle, Reverend Herman Pech. He had previously worked as a missionary at Haast's Bluff, at the time an outstation of Hermannsburg, so we reminisced about missionary life. Once I had driven to his rescue when his Mission truck broke down.

Next day I had the boring task of driving slowly back to Adelaide, 'running in' the new truck. This took most of the day, but it was worth it to have seen the Olympics.

By chance, 30 years later, I happened to be touring Universal Studios in Los Angeles when it was announced that Sydney would host the 2000 games. Cheering erupted. After asking any Australians to identify themselves, many hands went up, but I was the only one present who attended the 1956 Melbourne games.

In August 1956, Cyril Kleinig, a fellow boarder and I drove his almost new Volkswagen Beetle to the Alice. In those days, after leaving Port Augusta, one had to camp out as no facilities existed apart from isolated petrol stations. The main road was basically a rough bush track, scratched over by an occasional grader. Along the way we saw numerous abandoned vehicles and caravans, the latter with shattered suspensions which could not handle the rough road and constant corrugations. It was rare to meet other traffic, but we met a few travellers camped beside their broken down vehicles, awaiting the arrival of spare parts. Assistance was given to complete strangers; indeed, survival depended on it. We gave what water we could spare to various stranded people.

On our way north, we deviated by 500 kilometres to visit Ayers Rock (now called Uluru). I heard a story about the making of this road. It seems the Governor of Australia, or one of the States, expressed a wish to visit the Rock. This posed a problem - it would require a lengthy camel journey, hardly fitting for an eminent public figure. A gazetted, large expenditure of taxpayers money to accommodate one persons wishes could hardly be justified. It seems a secret plan was devised. A trusted grader driver was told to go out and get lost and in the process end up finding himself at the Rock. The Governor's desires were satisfied and a tourist trade began to develop.

I was driving when we left the main road and headed west. We had not seen another vehicle for hours. On a smooth section of continuously curving road flanked by two metre high bushes, I saw a large ex Army four wheel drive Blitz coming towards us. We were both driving quickly and he was positioned in the centre of the narrow road. The other driver, sitting high above the ground, gazed sideward over the tops of the low bushes. A head on collision was imminent. Only one course of defence was available to me. I jumped the Volks over the half metre high bank fringing the road, flattening bushes as the Blitz raced by. I just had time to jump the car back onto the road before hitting a tree. It was all over in a few seconds and then I brought us to a halt.

We thought the other vehicle should have seen us go off the road and return to see if we were OK. In the meantime I checked the Volks for damage, finding only a few scratches. We were very lucky not to have rolled over when twice clearing the bank and also to have found space between trees. My extensive experience driving on dirt saved us. I shuddered to think of being injured in this isolated place with a disabled vehicle - it could be hours or days before anyone passed by.

The Blitz did not return, so we carried on, arriving at the Rock. It was deserted. We were awed by its towering presence in the empty landscape. We inspected Maggi Springs, topped up our water supplies, then visited the Olga's (Tjuta). These huge lumps of conglomerate rock, hundreds of metres high, appear something like rounded blobs of cake mix dumped on the flat desert floor.

The following day we began climbing the rock, but Cyril only made it a short distance before chickening out. The steep, bald surface without handholds or terraces defeated him. One slip can result in bouncing down hundreds of metres to the ground. Once beginning to fall, it is impossible to arrest the descent and several deaths have been recorded. Now handrails are available on steep sections of the climb and painted lines help tourists stay on the safest route.

In recent years aboriginal custodians discourage climbers because of Uluru's spiritual significance. Park Rangers also disallow climbs when dangerous conditions exist.

After the arduous ascent I added my name to the book at the cairn situated on one of the highest ridges. Next morning, after sunrise photos, we drove to the Alice.

I took Cyril to the tourist sites around Alice and eventually drove to the Mission. I managed to borrow a Land Rover and we visited Palm Valley. Forewarned, and as a civic duty, we painted over tourists names on Battleship rock, a much photographed feature. It is sad to think graffiti was about, even in 1956.

Cyril visited other beauty spots while I worked in the garage before we had to head south again. It took us three and a half long days of daytime driving to reach Adelaide, indicative of the state of the main road at that time. Travelling at night was not advisable as hidden washaways could rip the suspension off your car and hitting a kangaroo was more likely.

Toward the end of the year, an opportunity arose for me to board with another family. Mrs Brown was a widow and her only child Len, an ex Immanuel student, was now at university.

'Phil, if you come to stay with us you will be treated as one of the family and can have your own room,' she said. 'I work night shifts a lot so you would have to get your own breakfast.'

' I'm sure that won't be a problem.'

'Good, you can move in when you are ready.'

While Tilly Lohemeyer provided excellent food and accommodation at budget prices, her strict rules and sharing a room with two others was becoming irksome. The midnight 'curfew' was interfering with my social life and Tilly's rigid meal times made for problems when I worked overtime.

I moved in with the Browns and enjoyed leaving years of restrictive rules behind.

Having been home to the Mission in August I worked through the Christmas and New Year period. Boxing Day saw me watching the Davis Cup tennis finals at Memorial Drive. Another exciting experience, watching the world's top players perform, and seeing Australia defeat America.

In 1957 I attended school on Monday and Friday nights to complete my Electrician and Diesel Certificates. Now as a rare fifth year student, almost all my original classmates having left after completing their mandatory third year. I still recall the evening at school when we rushed outside to see Sputnic, the first satellite, fly through the night sky. It was an event of similar significance to Robert Kennedy's assassination.

My Church, social, sport and Air Force commitments resulted in me usually being home only one evening a week to recover and study. Also, having established myself in the truck division, at times it became almost obligatory to work overtime and finish a job. Commercial operators needed their vehicles on the road to stay in business.

Later in the year, during an Air Force camp at Mallala, I found a 1936 SS Jaguar sitting on blocks under a carport in the Officers Married Quarters. I paid a paltry £95-00 ($190) for it, and after some repairs managed to drive my first car home. These rare cars can now sell for a million dollars.

The previous owner was a fighter pilot and had installed aircraft switches all over the dashboard. They looked impressive, but many were unnecessary and would cause me problems later. My Jag, of which there were only three registered in the State, had an eye-catching appearance. Bright red, it was long and low. Large prominent chrome plated headlights protruded from the narrow 107 centimetre (3.5 foot) long centrally hinged bonnet with louvered sides. The sweeping rakish mudguards flowed in almost continuous curves from front to rear and formed a central running board or footstep area. Large wire wheels with chrome plated spokes were splined to their axles and held on by a single central nut which only required a hammer blow to spin off or tighten. At the rear of my Jag, a spare wheel sat on the box shaped boot above the shiny ornate bumper bar. A sunroof was fitted along with very comfortable leather bucket seats front and rear. These seemed just centimetres above the road and required some agility to access and exit.

The previous owner said the original four-cylinder Jaguar engine had self-destructed and instead a six-cylinder Holden engine now lived under the commodious bonnet. The power was great for going fast but stopping was another matter. The mechanical brakes used rods and levers attached to each wheel and required frequent careful adjustment or the car would jump sideways when applying the brakes. My alternative was to brake very gently. I had some interesting moments until time permitted a complete overhaul of the braking system. With modern cars hydraulic pressure is automatically applied to each wheel. Many cars now have anti-skid systems, first developed for braking aircraft after landing.

Few spare parts were available, which made my task much more difficult, but eventually the brakes worked properly. I modified the front passenger seat so it folded rearwards to a horizontal position to join the rear seat, forming a comfortable narrow bed. Now I could sally forth and show off my skirt catcher with confidence.

Whenever I parked in a shopping area, almost all the passing pedestrians paused to look at my rare, beautiful beast. Some checked the registration disk to ascertain the make of the vehicle and on seeing Jaguar body, Holden engine, the enthusiasts begged me to open the bonnet to look at my hybrid vehicle. As for the girls, few would decline a ride around the block. Some were more forward, offering to help me polish the car or commenting that they would like to experience a longer, faster drive sometime. Being so low to the ground, the Jag could corner at speeds that shocked or exhilarated passengers. All very good for one's ego but I was still a respectable Church going lad and didn't play fast and loose - I sure could have with that skirt catcher.

Occasionally, for laughs, I donned a smart cloth cap, trailed a scarf from my neck, stuck a pipe in my mouth and slowly drove around with the sun roof open and watched people staring at me. It was also a good trick at a time when female hitchhikers were rarely at risk and happy to climb into a stranger's vehicle.

One of my girlfriends caused herself a mischief one wet evening. After dropping her off she discovered that part of her long voluminous skirt had hung outside the passenger door and swept the road. This happens easily in low slung cars. Unlike the motorcycle chain occasion, this ladies skirt would probably recover after a good wash and repositioning of the hemline.

On another occasion I took the same girlfriend to a drive-in movie theatre. While selecting a parking spot, I was amazed to see a car similar to mine already parked, with a vacant space beside it. It was one of the two others in South Australia. The male driver jumped out when I parked beside him and we were soon deep in conversation. It was decided that the men would sit in one car, our lady companions could then use the front seats in the other vehicle, as the movie screen was not easily seen from the rear seats. The girls grumpily accepted this arrangement. They had no choice if they wanted to watch the film. Our discussion about rare vehicles was much more interesting than the film and unlikely to be repeated. Little conversation took place in my vehicle as we drove home. I didn't even get a kiss from my partner that evening.

My car still had a few tricks up its sleeve. One evening, about 800 metres from home I suffered a puncture. No problem, one nut to undo and shove on the spare. The spare refused to fully slide on to its hub. I pushed and kicked, to no avail. Disgusted, I slowly drove away with the wheel unsecured. About a 100 metres from home it fell off. The Easter holiday was beginning and I was without wheels, literally. My beautiful beast crouched in the gutter on only three of its four feet. Most unhappily, I rolled the spare home.

It took most of the following day to fix the problem - bent splines in the spare wheel hub that prevented it from slipping on fully. Previous owners never tell you about such problems.

Another evening when I slid into my car to drive home after work, the starter briefly operated, but the engine would not turn over. I had forgotten to turn off the electric fuel pump that morning. The previous owner's love of switches, and my slip up, resulted in the pump flooding the carburettor and eventually filling several cylinders with petrol. This created a hydraulic lock that prevented the pistons moving.

I removed all the spark plugs so the petrol could be blown out of the affected cylinders by using the starter motor. In my haste, and disgust at the delay I omitted to disconnect the ignition system. When the petrol blew out a spark ignited it. Now I had a fire in the engine compartment. This was going from silly to stupid and worse. No fire extinguisher was accessible. I stood on cinders in the parking lot, scooped up handfulls and threw them into the flames until the fire was extinguished. Now I had flung cinders and dirt into the cylinders through the open spark plug holes.

I drove out ten minutes later, vowing to re-wire the fuel pump to operate only with the ignition on. To hell with the fancy array of switches.

Few of my dates would consent to utilising my fully reclining seat modification. One did, and after the movies, I parked in a dark area close to her home. Being summer, I opened the sunroof, dropped the seat down and lay next to my partner. We were kissing and cuddling, fully clothed, when a strong light hit us and a uniformed head appeared above the sunroof.

'What are you up to?'

'Nothing Officer, we're just being friendly.'

'Well don't get too friendly or you'll be breaking the law. This is a public place you know and being indecent is not allowed.'

'We won't be doing anything like that officer.' *She wouldn't let me anyway.*

'I'll go but mind you behave properly.'

He switched off his torch and walked away but the romantic mood was shattered, there would be no hanky panky tonight. Unusual or sporty cars attracted the police. It was a disadvantage I had not previously encountered. At the time, it seemed policemen considered themselves serious guardians of public morality.

My Jag began to have gearbox problems. Complete disassembly became necessary, which I did in the backyard of the Brown's house. Pride in my beautiful beast turned to dismay when I discovered one of its superior features included the use of herringbone patterned gear teeth in the gearbox, one of which was damaged beyond repair. This type of gear made for silent running but presented a major problem to replace.

It cost me two weeks wages to have one made. A third of what I paid for my vehicle, and a serious blow to my budget. I now knew that exclusivity came at a price.

According to my diary, in 1957 I dated ten different females. I don't know if they knew this was occurring. Some certainly should have, most attending the same church as I did. Perhaps each hoped they would win my heart in the end. Rose came back into my life again for some months before she left on an overseas trip. We made love once prior to her departure but it was a hurried, mechanical coupling, unlike our earlier spiritual experience. At an age of almost 21, I had experienced intercourse twice and despite it being considered very sinful, somehow it did not seem wrong to me. How conveniently hormones can colour ones indoctrination.

Rose's departure unsettled me, rekindling my childhood walkabout urges. It was time for a change; I had been in Adelaide for nearly eight years. I was still indentured to my employer for some months, having previously agreed to stay with them for another two years after my five year stint. This was because they allowed me a fortnightly day at Tech school to complete my optional 4th and 5th years practical school work.

The matter was resolved by my secondment to the company's affiliate in Mount Gambier. It was a smaller workshop and only employed five mechanics to service the complete range of Rootes Group vehicles. Plus Annie, the receptionist/secretary/typist, a lovely girl, engaged to Gordon, our car specialist mechanic. She kindly baked a cake for my 21st birthday – it was the only social recognition of this milestone in my life. Lack of a party did not bother me; I was happy, healthy and beginning to find my way in life, or so I thought. With regard to the opposite sex, I was still very immature. Work was interesting and varied and I now had enough experience to handle difficult jobs.

One day the Company car salesman said, 'Who wants to come to the Australian Grand Prix in Melbourne this week-end?'

'Sure, I'll be in on that,' I replied.

Leaving early, it was a five-hour dash for Albert Park. We positioned ourselves at a strategic corner on the racetrack and saw cars crash spectacularly before Stirling Moss won the Grand Prix. Driving home, our salesman, perhaps inspired by Stirling, flew off a corner at speed, but managed to aim the car directly at a thin metal dropper post on the approaching paddock fence. This folded when we hit, taking the four fence wires down with it. We streaked over the lot, into the paddock and our vehicle only suffered a few scratches. After slowing down, 'Stirling' turned around and drove back to the fence. He had to stop as the wires had bounced up. Producing wire cutters from a handy door pocket, 'Stirling' hopped out, cut all four wires and drove out of the field.

This episode took less than a minute; at one point disaster loomed as we left the road, yet in almost a blink of an eye, we were back on the road as though the excursion through a fence had not occurred. Our driver just grinned when asked how often he had performed this manoeuvre. The tires continued to squeal so I leaned back, closed my eyes and trusted my angel to see me home.

My qualifications came to the notice of the Education Department and I was persuaded to teach first year apprentices at the local Tech school one night a week. With no teaching qualifications or experience, this proved to be an arduous, thankless task. My class of unruly 16-year-olds seemed only interested in fast cars and women, and I had trouble controlling them. By contrast, my Adult Education class persons were there by choice and eager to learn about basic car maintenance. Many of these were women but I didn't socialise with any.

My interest in aviation led me to join the Mt Gambier Aero Club. It was a branch of the Royal Victorian Aero Club, based at Moorabbin Airport, Melbourne and I became member number 128 of that renowned establishment. In March 1958, I found myself strapped into an open cockpit Tiger Moth behind Roger Collins, the instructor, to begin my first flying lesson. Other sorties soon followed as finances permitted.

Meanwhile, I found Mr and Mrs Smith in Wehl Street, who boarded me. They were a middle aged, conservative Australian couple with married children living away from home. I was treated like a son and fussed over by the matronly Mrs. Smith.

My tenure with the education department was short lived. It was demanding and paid poorly. I opted out as I was eager to learn to fly. The overtime necessary to pay for this expensive hobby took increasing time and effort.

My first solo flight took place after only nine hours of instruction. That first trip, alone in the sky, generated a healthy mix of fear and exhilaration in me. Would I bounce all over the airport when trying to land? Playing it safe, I didn't try a three pointer, but put the main wheels on first and then let the tail settle onto the ground.

I understand that now a minimum of ten hours are required in aircraft which are much easier to fly than the Tiger biplane, with its narrow undercarriage, no brakes and only a tail skid to steer with on the ground. On occasion, I had to quickly stop the engine, jump out and grab a wingtip before the wind blew the aircraft into a hanger or other obstruction as the tail skid had little steering effect on tarmac.

After nine months of training, I passed all the theoretical examinations, medicals and the practical flight test conducted by a Departmental Examiner of Airmen. It was my first aviation licence and allowed me to fly non-paying passengers, and hopefully not kill them in the process. This nearly happened some months later when I allowed a passenger to fly the Tiger. It was a club rule that only instructors were allowed to carry unlicensed passengers when dual controls were fitted to the front seat. But it was known that a short length of broomstick could be smuggled aboard and placed in the socket as a substitute for the normal control stick. I allowed my passenger, ensconced out of sight in the front cockpit, to do this when we were at a safe height.

'OK Brian, put your stick in and have a go,' I shouted through the gossport speaking tube.

He did so, and after a few uncoordinated turns and vertical wobbles, the Tiger started to dive at the ground.

'Pull the stick back,' I shouted.

'I can't, it's jammed behind the instrument panel.'

Bloody marvelous. Here we were, going down fast with the controls jammed! There was only one thing I could try and it had to be done quickly.

'Brian, I'll push the stick forward and you get the bloody broomstick out. Quickly.' He knew we would die if this maneuver didn't work.

I pushed forward; we were now in a vertical dive with the trees rapidly increasing in size.

'It's out,' Brian shouted.

I pulled back on the stick gently, careful not to stall the Tiger at our low height. That could also prove fatal. We cleared the trees by a few hundred feet before gaining altitude. Just a few seconds difference between life and death.

'Throw the bloody broomstick out, Brian.'

He did, it fell into the trees. That short bit of wood could have done for both of us. Murphy is always waiting to catch someone out, and this was an important lesson for me. I learned that there are various interpretations of Murphy's law but it basically means 'If anything can go wrong it will,' so a defence against this should always be in place, especially in critical situations.

I sold my Jaguar after completely repainting it in spare time. It was traded for a boringly practical, almost new Humber Hawk sedan, which didn't require intensive maintenance to keep on the road. A few months later, a young apprentice was relieving me at the wheel on a trip to Adelaide when he hit a telephone pole. We were unhurt, but the car was badly damaged. I traded down to a smaller Austin with less onerous repayment schedules.

To cater for my expenditure on flying I frequently worked overtime for twenty-four hours straight – from 8 am Saturday until 8 or 9 am Sunday. Then I went home and slept until Monday morning. The extra money earned went into flying lessons on Monday afternoon. Roger taught me aerobatics and I reveled in being upside down in the sky with nothing but a shoulder harness preventing me from falling out.

One young, high-spirited lass I took up said she'd like to experience aerobatics but I doubted whether she would enjoy it. Surprisingly, she did, so I gave her the works including loops, barrel rolls and spinning, which would have had most men crying for mercy. Fearless women can be found.

Devotion to flying began to replace church activities, though I continued with some community work for my fellow Lutherans. Now I was mixing with different kinds of young women, those without a religious bias to life. Some allowed, or even encouraged, upper items of clothing to be undone for mutual enjoyment. But I abstained from intercourse for fear of the possible consequences. An unmarried mother would not trap me.

The separation from Rose seemed to deepen our friendship and we corresponded. Both of us were in a new environment, among strangers. It was then I discovered I could communicate with her telepathically. Having grown up with this occurring among the aboriginals, I considered it normal but had not consciously tried it. I found Rose answered my significant unwritten queries and feelings in her letters. This occurred too frequently to be considered coincidental. I remembered entries in mother's diary and other events in my childhood.

Spiritually aware people, black or white, sometimes 'see' events occurring in their minds. Twice, while in hospital on confinements, Mother wrote that she 'knew' her husband had visited the hospital late at night, having driven for five hours after a days work, to inquire at the desk about her condition. Sure enough, he would turn up next morning and confirm her 'vision'. She used the word telepathy and we saw the aboriginals at Hermannsburg demonstrate this many times. When women in the aboriginal camp began wailing, Mother asked a house girl what the problem was.

'Missus, man he die.'

'Who was it?'

'Me think Joshua.'

'But Joshua is out in the stock camp. No truck has come in.'

'Yes missus, soon he come.'

Sure enough, the truck arrived with a casualty. The vehicle was the only method of communication but the women had 'heard' about the accident as it happened.

I lost my telepathic ability in 1960, after separating from Pamela, my first soul mate. It returned forty years later, when I began meditating.

The sewerage system in Mount Gambier was intriguing. Homeowners just dug a hole in their back yard into which wastewater and toilets were plumbed. The effluent all disappeared. The area is known for its limestone caves, presumably the subsurface is sponge like. It's also well known that a large stream of water flows under the town, into the famous Blue Lake, and continues to the sea at Port MacDonnell, some 26 kilometres distant. To complete the circle, the town water supply is drawn from the Blue Lake where it ends up back in the toilets again, hopefully filtered by the underground limestone. I didn't suffer any stomach upsets so the system worked while I was there.

At work, by 1959 I had established a reputation as a troubleshooter, able to think outside the box. This was reinforced when a desperate truck owner brought his vehicle to us. Nobody, including the manufacturer's agents, had been able to get his Perkins R6 diesel truck engine to pull a full load properly. The usual fixes had been tried, none working. A new approach was needed. It was tedious, took time, effort and maths but finally I knew I had found the problem. Somehow a rogue camshaft had passed the manufacturer's quality control and was fitted to this engine. My findings were not believed, it just could not happen!

After I fitted a new camshaft, the engine pulled properly. The truck owner hailed me a hero and I suppose told others; I had vindicated his disputed assertions. In some situations it's wise to remember the old adage 'trust no-one and take nothing for granted.'

I was now regarded as something of a truck doctor and sent out to fix broken vehicles all over the countryside. I worked at all hours, grateful for the overtime, unlike most married men who sensibly joined their families at night.

As so often happens, a fall from grace occurred. It was late and I hurried to finish a job. We were missing a special tool and I had to work without it. I was sure the locking ring necessary to secure the rear wheels of a semi-trailer were properly tabbed, finished the job and left. Some days later, the truck lost a set of driving wheels, causing much damage. The semi was stranded in the Adelaide Hills for weeks. The loss of income, plus the cost of repairs, lost the owner his truck and livelihood. I was partly to blame but luckily not penalised, management knew the risk of not buying the special tool. However, it was a large dent to my professional pride.

Polishing skills in the air revived my sprits. Our locally based Tiger Moth flew to Moorabbin, Melbourne's then secondary airport, for its routine inspections. I was allowed to fly it there. It was my first trip to a capital city. I was exited and anxious about this new responsibility, carefully drawing lines on maps. Roger briefed me fully. The trip took three and a half-hours flying each way and an overnight stop in Melbourne. It was winter and my steed had no heater, radios or navigation instruments other than a compass and dubious clock. I remember the rain running down my helmet and goggles, dripping off my nose, onto my chin and slowly seeping down into my boots. I was so cold and stiff at Warrnambool, I could barely move the controls properly to land for refueling. *And this was supposed to be fun.*

All went well until I overflew the Moorabbin airport, a standard procedure prior to landing in those days. Mayhem erupted! Aircraft flew everywhere instead of the tidy stream I had been told to expect. Did I cause this confusion, I wondered, until I saw the puff of smoke by the tower. It meant the wind direction had changed and with it the landing path. There were no radios to co-ordinate the milling aircraft, just eyeballs and standard procedures.

Us pilots sorted out the mess and then it was my turn to get a green light from the tower. I landed on smooth grass and managed a credible three point touchdown. It didn't rain the next day so I was able to enjoy the trip home over familiar territory.

A different Aero Club aircraft became available to us. The Chipmunk DHC1 was over 15 years old, but an all-metal, aerobatic training plane, previously used by the Air Force. It featured an overhead Perspex canopy and a radio so we could speak to air traffic control towers. To use this, a Radio Operators License was necessary, entailing another exam. An electric starter meant we didn't have to hand swing the propeller. The Chipmunk was a delightful aerobatics aircraft and great fun to throw around the sky. Its engine had more power than the Tiger so height was not lost when correctly looping the loop or doing barrel rolls. I could just flow from one such manoeuvre to another, performing an aerial three-dimensional dance, all the while imagining shooting down 'enemy' aircraft.

The Chipmunk also had brakes and a tail wheel, enabling the use of tarmac runways. The Tiger Moth had to land directly into wind in anything other than a gentle breeze. The 'Chippys' sliding canopy meant I didn't get wet on rainy days, and it could be opened for air conditioning while on the ground. In short, a great fun aircraft, a sports car of the air. At the time the 'Chippy' was among the best aerobatic plane in Australia that non-military pilots could fly. It made me feel like a World War II 'ace', and I took great delight in throwing it around the sky. With my limited experience of complete intimacy with ladies, well performed aerobatic sequences thrilled me more than sex. Besides, my church did not ban unmarried aerobatics.

We were invited to join the Warrnambool club in a day of flying competitions. The first event was streamer cutting. This involved throwing a toilet roll out of the cockpit and cutting it with the wing three times as it unraveled, in the shortest possible time. All events had a safety pilot in the competing aircraft to ensure it was not unraveled as well. I won the streamer cutting event by using a little known trick – instead of going to full throttle to increase speed, I pulled the throttle off to make a tighter turn at low speed which takes less time than going fast around a larger circle. An old hand had passed on this knowledge to me. To add insult to good fortune, I also won the flour bag bombing – my childhood games of throwing things at moving targets groomed me for this event.

Despite, or perhaps because of such small triumphs in the air, I began to feel the need to go walkabout again. The seemingly continuous cold, damp weather was getting to me. It was in Mt. Gambier I first heard the saying, 'If you can see the Mount, it's a sign of rain. If you can't see it, it is bloody well raining!'

News reached me that a Lutheran pilot, Ray Jaensch, was flying in support of the church's Mission activities in Papua New Guinea. I wrote to Ray about the possibilities of obtaining a maintenance job, with a view to continuing on to a pilot's position. Other friends and relatives were working in P.N.G. Missions so I thought perhaps I should join them in the noble task. I knew my parents would applaud such a decision. Had I known of the difficulties faced by early aviators in P.N.G. I would have thought twice. Even twenty-five years later, on returning to P.N.G as an experienced helicopter pilot, I only flew the Company aeroplane occasionally. Then only when the weather was good, over routes I knew well.

Ray replied to my rather naïve letter pointing out the long, hard road necessary to qualify for the demanding job. This idea went on the back burner and I continued gaining as much flying experience as I could afford.

The thought occurred as to my good fortune in life – I had been to the Davis Cup Finals, the Olympics and had attended a Grand Prix. Notwithstanding humble beginnings, I had been blessed in many ways. But it was time to move on to new experiences. I recalled a recent party. Most guests were locals; their future would be woven into the area's history. I knew this place was not for me in the long term; I could not identify with it. Leaving the party mid-evening, I collected my sleeping bag, drove to a quiet country area and slept under the stars. In the morning I awoke renewed, surrounded by curious cows. Other people thought it crazy to forego a warm, comfortable bed but I just followed my feelings and the need to get close to nature.

My walkabout urges re-surfaced strongly. The obligation to my employer was almost completed, I had learnt to fly and fix almost any vehicle, but felt the need for a new challenge. Having no strong attachment to the area or its people, leaving would not entail emotional hardship. Climatically, I was too far south and needed to head north, closer to my tribal country.

On my last flight there, I said good-bye to the town from the air. The wind, as often, was strong that day. At a safe height, I slowed the Tiger to just above the stalling speed with power full on. The wind was stronger than our ground speed, so we flew slowly across the town backwards. Had the wind been as strong at ground level, I could have landed from a hover. Was this a portend of things to come - I was not even aware of helicopters then.

Naturally, I was sorry to leave the friends I had made during almost two years in Mt. Gambier and promised to keep in touch. My toolbox, clothes and few possessions easily fitted into my small four-seater Austin. It was June 1959, wet and cold as usual. Pleasant, nostalgic memories flowed as I drove past the grassy aerodrome on my way to Adelaide. I had no idea what I would do next, but I did know that finding a job somewhere would be easy thanks to my references and contacts. After almost seven formative years of being tied to an employer I was at last free to make my own choice of employment.

CHAPTER 4

When in doubt, hold on to your altitude. No-one has ever collided with the sky. ~ *The Aviators Guide Book*

I spent a few lazy weeks in Adelaide, visiting friends, flying at Parafield and looking at job advertisements. An opening as a maintenance fitter at Radium Hill was advertised. This seemed a challenge so I applied and was accepted. I left Adelaide in high spirits, early in July 1959 and drove north along the main road to Port Pirie. Radium Hill was the world's second commercial uranium mine, located 48 kilometres west of Broken Hill, just over the border in South Australia. Douglas Mawson, best known for his work in Antarctica, first surveyed the area in 1906 with the mine opening in November 1954.

Beyond Port Pirie, the road was unsealed with no evidence of human habitation. The countryside showed little sign of any winter rain. Drab stunted mallee soon gave way to saltbush amid the dry red sand. This was not of any concern to me, it was my sort of country. A knocking sound from the engine did concern me – I had completely overhauled it before leaving Mount Gambier. To avoid potential damage, I stopped, about eighty kilometres short of my destination. Not having seen a vehicle since turning off the main road, I expected a long wait, but my luck turned and I soon got a lift with a mineworker.

Radium Hill was a purpose built town to house mining and associated employees. The Mines Department of South Australia ran the entire enterprise. Almost everyone there being government employed.

'You will be sharing a hut with Fred,' said the personnel officer. 'It's number 37. Here's your key'.

I carried my bag to a fibro box perched on metre high wooden legs; one amongst over a hundred similar planted in the red sand. Inside, I found two metal framed beds, small wardrobes, a table and chair. My billet was hot in summer and cold in winter, not a nest to treasure. An ablutions block squatted thirty metres away, the mess hall requiring several minutes walk to reach. About half of the three hundred single workers could be fed at one sitting.

I caught the company bus to the mine site, several kilometres away, to begin my first days work. James, the young, bustling boss introduced me to my workmates. He enjoyed salary status and lived with his wife in married quarters housing. I found the other four maintenance fitters in our gang were single, hourly paid men like me.

Our duties were to maintain the compressors which supplied high pressure air to the miners working up to four hundred metres underground. In addition we serviced the ore crushers and mechanical parts of the winding gear. The latter moved uranium ore out and men and equipment to and from the surface. One man, called a 'winder driver' controlled the electric motors which wound the cables attached to special ore buckets, called 'skips'. While one skip full of ore traveled up, its partner went down to the 'loading station'. The skips were filled manually at various loading 'shute gates' but tipped automatically when reaching the unloading shute on the large gantry where wheels are seen above mine shafts.

Another winder driver drove the cage, or lift for persons and equipment. A 'cage man' determined the movement of the cage. He normally always rode the cage continuously and signaled its next destination to the winder driver by pulling on a cord, which rang a bell close to the winder driver. The number of bell rings indicated the cages next desired destination.

Our gang also maintained the below ground water pumps. Even in this patch of semi desert, ground water continuously seeped into the shafts, which would eventually flood the mine if not removed. Checking the pumps entailed going far underground, a potentially dangerous arena.

'You are new, so you will be working with Steve as he knows the ropes,' said James on my first day. 'Also, you will have to join the union'.

His wry smile meant nothing to me. He was staff and didn't have to join any of the half dozen different unions represented at the mine. Unions were new to me but I came to realise what this meant when I almost shut the mine down completely by doing an electrician's job. I waited hours for a sparky to repair a lead and eventualy reconnected the broken wire. My automotive electrical licence did not cover the mine, I was not in the electrical union and my action, when discovered, caused furor. I was let off due to my 'ignorance' and a general strike averted but received a stiff lecture about job demarcation.

'If you do this again Phil, the union will black you which means you lose your job. Understand?' demanded the Union steward in a thick Pommy accent.

80

I apologised for my transgression and indicated my willingness to toe the union line. I didn't want to lose my job, although the inefficiency and waste caused by union rules constantly grated against my natural instincts. Again, I worked in a different world.

During the next few weeks, Steve, a portly, genial forty-ish emigrant from somewhere in Europe led me through the maze of new machines and procedures.

On my first weekend a workmate drove me to collect my abandoned car. I found a blockage in the oil supply, rectified it, and all was well. Little, if any, damage had ensued.

On the job I learned fast, was keen to please and soon able to work without supervision.

'You can go and check the pumps today Phil,' said Steve at our 8 am job review. 'See you after lunch.'

Actually checking our three sets of pumps took twenty minutes. Each was on a different level underground, and the cage only ran to every level on the hour. The mine had ten levels carved into hard rock, descending to 400 metres below ground. But the cage could be shuttling between a few different levels for long periods. We could not 'order' the cage like a normal lift. At 8.10 am, after logging in, collecting my miner's lamp, helmet and battery I waited until 9 am to reach my first destination, three levels down. After taking ten minutes to look over the pumps, my head was in a book until 10.00 am when I dropped to my next destination. This is why twenty minutes work took four hours.

To shortcut this procedure and show I was keen, I decided to use the ladders between levels instead of waiting for the cage.

At Radium Hill the main vertical shaft servicing the mine consisted of four columns. The first contained the ore haulage skips. The personnel and freight cage travelled up and down the next vertical tube. Another shaft contained the counterweight that balanced the weight of the cage – when one went up, the other went down, requiring less power to raise an upcoming cage and less braking on the way down. Between these two columns a narrow space held ladders which reached from the bottom of the mine to the surface. The ten metre high, almost vertical steps zigzagged from one landing to another. This long thin chute, black as the inside of a ink bottle, rattled with scraping sounds as the skips and cage rushed past. Any lighting had long since failed; a well-charged miner's lamp was essential.

One morning, fed up with waiting, I found myself cheerfully descending a ladder into the depths of the earth when a rumbling noise came from above. It sounded like a large boulder was falling. *Was it in the ladder shaft?* In theory all of them were separated by a wire mesh barrier to prevent falling objects penetrating another shaft. Unfortunately, rusted mesh was not replaced as profits plummeted due to competition from new open cut mines.

I was many metres from a landing that might have provided protection. The rumble came closer - a loud crash and thump above me pounded my ears as the intruder bounced from one wall to another. I froze on the ladder and craned my neck upward. The lamp seemed dim and showed only dust moving in the darkness above. Timing was crucial, if a boulder knocked me off the ladder I would fall to my death in the darkness, my final scream unheard. I had to wait and judge its trajectory after the nearest bounce. Another crash sounded and I saw the lump of ore approaching fast, several metres above me. Lunging behind the ladder, my feet dangling in space, my lamp showed a lump of rock half my size flashing past. The crashing noises diminished, replaced by the sound of gravel bouncing off my helmet. Heart pounding, I swung around again, my feet scrabbling to regain the ladder rungs. My legs pumped furiously as I scrambled down to the next level and left the ladders for the security of a horizontal shaft with solid rock above my head.

Where did these large boulders come from? They fell off the top of overfilled skips carrying ore to the surface. Why were they overfilled? Simple, the skip loaders were contract staff paid by the tonnage delivered to the surface.

Normally, personnel were not in the ladder shafts unless the cage was inoperative and underground workers were forced to climb to the surface at the end of their shift. If so, the skips would not be hauling ore. It seems my Guardian Angel had followed me underground.

One Monday morning, I found few others eating breakfast. Perhaps the golf tournament on Saturday, followed by a sweaty football game on Sunday caused the lack of interest in food. The bleary eyes and lack of conversation when we assembled to start work reinforced my suspicion.

I had not taken part in any of these games and associated festivities. Getting drunk with the boys at a sporting event was not my idea of a good time. With only about six single female residents to entertain the 300 unattached males, socialising with the opposite sex was confined to a few privileged males. Instead I continued my love affair with motorised metal that could legally fly inverted.

Broken Hill had an active Aero Club and I became member No. 191. Having been certified as fit to play with their aerobatic Chipmunk aircraft I spent my money hanging upside down in the sky. After driving 48 kilometres to Broken Hill, my Sunday afternoon had been spent 'beating up' fair weather cumulus clouds that provided safe hills and valleys for me to zoom up, dive into and draw patterns on their vertical faces in sheer indulgent joy. Having the earth spin around and jump into view above one's head is thrilling and provided me with great satisfaction when I completed these manoeuvres perfectly. Sometimes I flew for many kilometres in a straight line while continuously rolling the aircraft – all I saw was the world constantly rotating around me. This fun kept my flying skills honed, and built hours towards a Commercial Pilots Licence.

The downside was the rapid erosion of my pay cheque. I preferred flying rather than giving my money to a publican and so it appeared I was the only worker not suffering from Monday blues.

'Come on boys, get the rope inspection done,' said the boss. 'You know it's always the first job today.'

I grabbed heavy-duty gloves and Rupert and Franc followed me to the mine pithead. The wire rope or steel cable supporting the cage was a single length of woven wires about five centimetres in diameter and almost half a kilometre in length. It could not be patched or joined – if any section frayed the entire length was replaced.

Movement of the cage was controlled by the winder driver who sat in the Winding House, over thirty metres away from the pithead or main vertical mine shaft. He moved levers to control large electric motors with brakes three metres in diameter. As mentioned, the driver was signaled by bell rings. He could not see the cage, but a pointer moving over a dial roughly updated its position.

To conduct a rope inspection an empty cage was sent to the bottom of the mine. Control of the signal bell was transferred to us workers, using a bell pull next to the pithead. After the wire rope stopped moving down we dropped a strong steel mesh rectangular platform over part of the gaping mine shaft. This door shaped device was hinged at its bottom edge. Its only purpose was to cover almost half the 400 metre deep hole so I could walk on it and reach the rope in the middle of the void. When not in use the platform stood vertically against a solid concrete wall next to the pithead.

'Right let her go Franc,' I said.

The platform swung down with a clang and extended almost to the cable. I stepped onto the mesh floor and placed my gloved hand on the stationary rope with fingers up. If a frayed wire strand caught my glove it would hopefully only take my glove and not me with it.

I nodded to Rupert 'OK, lets go.'

He pulled on the cord, bells rang and the rope began to move under my glove. I peered into the depths below my feet, seeing nothing but a black hole. Typical, the senior man watching, the next waiting with his hand on the bell pull, with the new boy in the hot spot.

We watched and waited as the rope slid rapidly upward. The cage rushed into view, coming to the surface far too fast. Rupert reacted slowly, only one pull being required to signal the cage to stop. The driver was also slow applying the brakes. I had no time to jump before the cage hit the platform, folding it up against the concrete wall with me squashed in between. My hard hat shattered and pushed into my head - the cage stopped. I stared at the heavy steel mesh, a centimetre away from my face, trying not to think about it crushing my head. I saw Rupert's ashen face, his body seemed frozen rigid.

Trapped, I said, 'Just make sure you give him a down bell.'

The cage inched down and freed me. Had it travelled up another ten centimetres I would have been minced through the heavy steel mesh like sausage meat.

I stepped out uninjured. *Another near thing, I've used up two lives here already – how many do I have left? I knew underground mining could be dangerous, humans were out of their natural element as when airborne. I'd have to learn quickly to dodge the different hostile arrows here.*

'Rupert you broke my bloody hat!' The banal remark broke the tension hanging in the air after a near fatal occurrence due to negligence. But Rupert couldn't look at me while mumbling 'I buy you a beer tonight Phil.'

It wasn't entirely his fault; the winder driver approached the surface too fast and was slow reacting to the bell. He bought me a beer as well. I mentally shared one with my Guardian Angel.

I thought that Monday mornings was not a good time to conduct inspections, with so many people hung over. But it was traditional. Random alcohol testing is now routine for drivers and commercial pilots. Will it be extended to workers operating machinery in crucial situations?

On another day a man was killed while performing maintenance in the counterweight shaft. Such are the dangers of everyday mine work.

Whenever men were maintaining the main or counterweight shafts, a large sign was placed inside the cage, another facing the winder driver. These reminded both to avoid running the cage or counterweight through the level being worked. Notwithstanding those precautions, the counterweight swatted a man to his death.

Occasionally we performed a rope inspection, caused by a winder driver's inattention. If the cage approached the top of the gantry (where the big wheels are on a pit head structure as seen on TV or the movies), or the bottom of the mineshaft too rapidly, override governors automatically slammed on the brakes. This prevented a potential disaster if the driver became incapacitated.

Sometimes, the winder driver approached the bottom of the shaft too fast, causing the brakes to clamp hard. Five hundred metres of rope stretched before the cage stopped, then tension in the rope snatched the cage upward. It's not widely known that almost all lifts and mine cages have automatic 'grabbers' that immediately stop a lift if the hoisting cable breaks or goes slack. These grabbers are spring tensioned to bite into guide rails secured to the shaft walls.

In the event of a mine cage leaping upward after a sudden 'stop', the rope becoming slack causes the grabbers to bite, stopping the cage instantly, preventing it falling. Any people or equipment in the cage had a rough ride, first a very sudden stop, then being launched into mid air only to fall to the floor again. After such incidents shaken passengers took themselves off for first aid, while we completed a rope and cage inspection. The winder driver's pride suffered severely and usually his beer money disappeared as well.

Some weeks after arriving at Radium Hill, I heard of the local Amateur Drama Group and went to their meeting. It was rumoured that most of the young single girls were involved and this was a chance to meet them. Especially as Rose had just written me a 'Dear John' letter saying she had met another man and they planned to become engaged. This upset me, even though I had been out with other girls to 'pass the time'. I was ripe for a new romance.

'Welcome Phil,' said John when I arrived at the Drama Groups venue. 'We are always short of men. Have you been in theatre before?'

'Sort of. I've been on stage in short skits and that type of thing, nothing serious.'

'We'll be glad to have you. Come and meet the rest of the gang.'

'What sort of work do you do?' asked Lorraine.

'I'm a maintenance fitter at the compressor house.'

'So you work for James.'

'Yes, we get on well.'

'Are you going to be in our next play?'

'I haven't been asked yet.'

'You will be.'

I learned that Lorraine was a secretary in administration. Except for the nurse, all the single girls worked in various offices.

Being part of the drama group, I became one of the select few males invited to parties where one could dance with single girls. My intent was to find one, have an affair if possible, and move on. Working on an isolated mine, I had decided, was only one step in my career path.

'Would you like to dance with me?' asked Pamela. She was a well-proportioned brunette with a lovely disposition and ready laugh. Later, I heard she had once been the Miss Australia entrant for Radium Hill.

'I don't know how to dance,' I replied. 'My church did not allow it.'

'Poor you. Come on. I'll show you, just hang on and follow me.'

I did, and this led to cuddles and kisses. Our relationship deepened over the following weeks, but Pamela was a practicing Catholic and I discovered that her knickers would stay on until a priest's blessing and gold band were in place. Her's was a mining family, like many of the others living in married quarters. These families breadwinners specialised qualifications often resulted in a lifetime spent in isolated mining communities.

This did not deter me, I had fallen in love. How or why this happened I do not know. I had previously rejected females wishing to form a permanent attachment. Our relationship began with my intent to seduce a fair lady, notwithstanding the competition for her favours. Having left behind the enclosing wings of the church, I gained my own metal ones and ventured forth into the unrestricted secular world. But my heart, it seems, was ready for a new experience.

It was a gradual process, speeded by the isolation of our community and consequent daily bonding. Pamela's vibrant personality, loving nature and good humour won me over completely. Being a traditional hunter, was I subconsciously seeing this chase through to the end?

She did represent the traditional enemy of the Lutheran faith; however, our love would surmount these dogmatic obstacles. We were inseparable and nothing would prevent us from living happily ever after. How wonderful to believe life was so simple!

In the meantime, the Engine Drivers went on strike and only two of our group could be spared to do their job in the compressor house. We monitored hundreds of gauges to ensure that the mine was supplied with compressed air and electricity. The miners relied on pressurised air to operate their equipment while the electricity was essential for lighting, ventilation and to prevent the mine flooding. With so many safety issues involved, we were not black banned from doing someone else's job in this instance.

'I'm glad you have volunteered to do these twelve hour shifts Phil,' said James. 'But Rupert is senior to you so you'll have the graveyard shift – 8 pm to 8 am, OK?'

'I think I can handle it.'

'Good, now I'll take you around and show you how to start the emergency power plants. You know what to do first when the power goes off?'

'Yep, run like hell,' I replied, having been briefed on the possible hair-raising consequences of a power failure.

If the power supply was momentarily interrupted the simultaneous start-up of the stalled machinery overloaded our system. We had to manually switch off many high loads before the main high-tension supply was re-energised, otherwise our circuit breakers in the compressor house could trip. Under these circumstances, the large circuit breakers had been known to explode, showering our workplace with boiling oil and molten metal. That's why I'd been told to run.

Reduced activity during my graveyard shifts made it easier to keep all the gauges in the green. After the first few nervous evenings passed uneventfully, controlling the nerve centre became routine and I phoned Pamela and chatted at length.

One evening, loud banging on the control room door interrupted our conversation.

'What the hell is going on here?' queried an angry voice. 'We ain't got no air!'

Being deep in conversation with Pamela, I had forgotten to monitor the large master pressure gauge. It was down to 70 P.S.I. – it should have been 100.

'Sorry mate, had another matter to sort out, I'll get your air up now.'

'Couldn't get you on the bloody phone either.'

'I know, don't worry, we're all sorted.'

Low air pressure meant the miner's machines worked much slower, reducing their ore production. They were paid by the ton so this was no laughing matter. I hurriedly switched on more compressors, being careful not to cause an overload and lose the lot.

After two weeks the engine drivers had finished their self imposed holiday. I suspect some strikes by various trades broke out for no other reason than to relieve the monotony of working constant shifts. The majority of men had limited off duty entertainment or social contact, except with similarly occupied males. The regular drivers return was none too soon for me. Sleeping during the day, in noisy quarters, with the temperature in my hut above 32° C was difficult.

Perhaps due to the small closed community, unsocial behaviour was uncommon but did occur. Bill, a Pom and eight-year veteran at the mine site was the only person who insisted on having the same seat in the mess at every meal - most people just chose an unoccupied space among the eighteen dining tables. I inadvertently sat in Bill's seat once and was told 'That's Bills chair.' I moved. On another night, after being told, the fella said 'So what' and stayed put. Then Bill arrived.

Without warning, the table was overturned, broken crockery sliding across the concrete floor. Pandemonium broke out as other diners joined in. More tables went over with cups, saucers and plates flying through the air. I grabbed my plate, rushed outside and watched through a window as the battle raged. Grown men crouched behind overturned tables like school kids, hurling projectiles at others crouching behind 'enemy' lines. The cooks slammed down the shutters above the servery to prevent the kitchen area being bombarded. The 'war' was over when there was nothing left to smash – taking all of five minutes. Everyone left before the lone policeman, who lived on site, arrived.

A lot of men went hungry that night but most said it was worth it. Just men being boys I guess.

Meanwhile, I was busy rehearsing with the Drama Group during the evenings. The book, We Were Radium Hill, compiled by Mr M. Harrington and Mr K. Kaloschke, mentions that Pamela and myself were cast in the play "A Pound on Demand". I have no recollection of how the performance was received but Pamela and I certainly spent most of our free time together. The pool and drive in theatre were popular and sometimes barbeques were organised in the nearby dry Olary creek-bed. Two young people in love need little formal entertainment – just being together was enough.

Before thinking of a formal engagement the matter of our differing religious faiths had to be resolved.

'Phil, my family would be devastated if we were not married in a Catholic

Church.'

'That's fine. My family would expect a church wedding too.'

'But we can't unless you become a Catholic, that's the problem.'

'Well I guess I'll have to look into changing. How about you becoming a Lutheran?'

'Phil, much as I love you, my faith comes first. I could not do that!'

Catholics seem so sure of themselves. Perhaps they were not the anti-Christ as religious leaders in our church had told me. It was written that Martin Luther led the Reformation because of his revulsion at the selling of 'Indulgences'. These, he felt, enabled people to 'buy' redemption for their sins. Since paying cash to absolve their sins was stopped, they could just go to confession and say a few 'Hail Mary's' instead. My childhood indoctrination had led me to feel disgust and distrust of any Catholics. Now, I would have to revise my feelings to follow my heart.

A meeting was arranged with Father Shiel. He welcomed us wearing shorts and a casual shirt. After greeting Pam and shaking my hand he indicated comfortable chairs.

'Pamela said you are thinking of joining us. I am very happy to help you. And I must congratulate you on your friendship with Pamela, having known her for some time. She is a fine young Christian girl.'

'Yes,' I said, 'perhaps you could tell me what is required for us to marry?'

He produced various booklets for me to take away and study. While discussing general matters I was struck by his genial friendliness and good humour. I was more accustomed to the 'holier than thou' aura normally surrounding our Lutheran Reverends.

'What did you think of Father Shiel?' asked Pam after we left.

'Great guy, nothing wrong with him. It's the Pope I'm worried about.'

'Don't think you'll see him out this way.'

'You mean he's not coming to convert me?'

We laughed and went off in my car for a kiss and cuddle in the bush. Problems with church rules and dogma were easily forgotten, they could be dealt with tomorrow.

Christmas was near when Pamela and her family went away on holidays. The mine was shut down over this period with only a skeleton crew on site. Being unable to see Pamela, I elected to remain at work.

Without her happy presence, I wrestled with the problem of either leaving my religion or losing Pamela. My conditioning from birth and at church schools was not easy to shake off. Another major problem was that any of our children would automatically be Catholic. I would have no say in their choice of religion.

During this quiet holiday period, I was free to roam from the uppermost structures to the bottom of the mine. Four hundred metres below the surface the silence was eerie, often I was the only person below ground. The sound of my heart thumping and blood rushing through my arteries seemed deafening at first - until I realised it was normal. Few people get to experience this sensation while some even panic when deprived of all external sound. I enjoyed the feeling of solitude and uniqueness of being alone in my underground world. It reminded me of the remoteness and peace to be found in outback deserts.

With most of the lighting switched off, extra care was essential. I remember walking along a tunnel, turning my helmet lamp downward to illuminate the path and seeing nothing but a seemingly bottomless gaping black hole adjacent to the rail line. It was an ore chute leading down to a loading station. An inadvertent fall into this was not survivable; my body would lie undiscovered until mining resumed. I should not have been exploring deserted shafts but the desire to go walkabout was irresistible.

We were not required to be on duty for Christmas or Boxing Day so I asked the Chief Engineer if I could leave the mine and visit my grandparents at Apilla, 200 kilometres away.

'Sure,' he said, 'might as well go, nothing happening here.'

Going to church with my relatives over Christmas made me earnestly assess my situation with Pamela. I realised that becoming a Catholic would break Mother's heart. She and my father would be judged as failing in the most important area of life on this earth if their firstborn left the mother church. Especially to marry the archenemy.

Once back at Radium Hill, my ears were assailed by tales of woe from everyone. Where was I when they needed me? It seems the power had failed on Christmas Day, just as the turkeys were to go into the oven.

The Chief had to start the emergency diesels, but due to his inexperience, it took him four hours to restore power to the town.

Being missed by the townspeople was very gratifying but didn't solve my situation with Pamela. With her being away, I looked hard and deep into my heart and head. Our union would be fraught with practical and emotional problems. After many sleepless nights I finally gave Steve my resignation, to apply soon after Pamela returned. He was both surprised and disappointed. I can't remember what reason I gave for leaving.

The frustration and hurt during my final days at Radium Hill were so severe that I have little recollection of this period. Likewise, I remember little of the three day drive home. I can remember crying for long periods while on the road and not caring if I arrived or not. Luckily I did not die in an accident. It seems my guardian Angel guided me home.

Pamela was likewise devastated and told me later that she cried for hours after I drove away. Why had obedience to the same God caused such pain to both of us?

I was an emotional mess on arriving in the Alice. My parents had moved to town some years earlier due to father's failing health. They lived in a modest house of their own on the Mission block. I was warmly welcomed back home. My folks were unaware of my inner turmoil and I didn't confess

my thwarted love for a Catholic girl. It would just cause more pain. I explained that my troubled composure was due to fatigue.

My younger brother and sister slept in enclosed rooms on the front verandah. The spare bedroom became my hiding place. After moping for several weeks I figured I had to stop feeling sorry for myself and find a job.

Pamela and I at a party

CHAPTER 5

*The three most useless things to a pilot are the altitude above you,
the runway behind you, and half a second ago.*
~ The Aviators Guide Book

A friend of the family, Eddy Connellan, offered me immediate
work. In retrospect, my mother probably arranged this, as she had my
apprenticeship. Eddy, a pioneer airman, operated a fleet of small aircraft
over much of northern Australia. After the few weeks recovering from
the loss of Pamela, my toolbox and I arrived at his hanger. It was located
at the Townside Airport, on the fringe of settlement, next to the cemetery
where my brother Melvin was buried. Being in love with aviation, I hoped
Connellans would be a new and exciting challenge.

It was a steep learning curve, working on delicate aircraft instead of
massive lumps of mining equipment; at least females were not a distraction.
The pain of parting with Pamela haunted me. I found I could hardly look at
another woman, let alone touch one, except of course in a formal manner
as required in polite society. Just the thought of embracing another woman
in a loving or lustful way was abhorrent.

I poured all my energy and time into learning new skills. My objective
was to become a Licensed Aircraft Maintenance Engineer so I could certify
aircraft fit for flight after maintenance or rectification of defects. Apart
from the supervised, practical experience required, I had to pass many
examinations. Knowledge of diverse subjects such as metallurgy, plastics,
properties of timbers and metals, linen, fabric stitches and air law was
required. I also had to pass written exams on each different engine and
aircraft type.

My work and qualifications in the motor trade earned credits for the
five years experience required before gaining a license. After just seven
months with Connellans I was issued with my first license to sign out an
aircraft engine following maintenance.

Job-wise I was doing well but my heart was still in a mess. I couldn't rid
myself of my love for Pamela and phoned her several times. For her next

holidays she arranged to visit the Alice. I told Mother about this and our background.

'Philip,' she said, 'I am sorry but I cannot allow a Catholic in this house.'

I was stunned. I couldn't fight against Mother's religious sensibilities or what she considered was best for her son. She always seemed to be the voice for my parents. Her refusal of Pamela shook me to the core. I loved Mother dearly; she had sacrificed so much for us and yet would not allow her eldest son to accommodate his true love in the family home.

I began to resent my mother and our religion for the pain it caused me. My life had been based on Lutheran Protestant doctrines but now I began to seriously question those principles. The age old dilemma between differing faiths and philosophies had finally come to roost in my life. Why did a merciful God cause such misery in Pamela's and my lives? In essence, I again lived a double life. A dutiful, church going, religious son in harmony with his Mission worker parents at home and an ordinary secular male in the workplace. I was repeating my situation in Adelaide when first beginning work, but now felt religion had betrayed me instead of providing comfort.

My parents' house sat on Mission property, I lived in the thick of religious activity and observant eyes. A few hectares had been acquired many years earlier to house stores destined for Hermannsburg. Subsequently, a church, Manse, various storerooms and hall were added adjacent to our home. Work was my only saviour, and I assuaged part of my guilt at turning against religion by modernising my parents' home. I installed power points, painted, re-plumbed and refurbished the only bathroom. I was recruited to teach Sunday school to white children from our church. Several times with the Minister away, I even conducted church services as the lay reader. All this was terribly hypocritical, I went through with it for the sake of appearances.

Many years later my brother researched the origins of our family name and concluded that almost certainly our forebears, on the male side, were Jews. It is a matter of record that many Latzs from Western Germany were gassed during WW II. My father's family line originated in Poland, in an area later becoming part of Eastern Germany. It's likely that hundreds of Latzs from there suffered the same fate as those in the West. Our branch of the family came from the East but left Hamburg in 1859, escaping Hitler's pogrom. In view of this, I wondered if my forebears were originally Jews who decided to change after arriving in a devout, predominantly Lutheran community in South Australia to avoid the discrimination they left behind in Europe.

I also wonder how I would have felt had I known of our possible Jewish heritage, and what Martin Luther said about them – we had never been told of his views during years of religious instruction. I quote his writings below:

'Oh adored Christ, and make no mistake, that aside from the devil, you have no enemy more venomous, more desperate, more bitter, than a true Jew who seeks to be a Jew. Now whoever wishes to accept venomous serpents, desperate enemies of the Lord, and to honour them to let himself be robbed, pillaged, corrupted, and cursed by them, need only turn to the Jews.'

And Luther's remedies to the Jewish problem?

'First, their synagogues should be set on fire and what ever does not burn up should be covered or spread over with dirt so that no one may ever be able to see a cinder or stone of it. And this ought to be done for the honour of God and of Christianity in order that God may see that we are Christians, and that we have not willingly, tolerated or approved of such public lying, cursing and blaspheming of his son and his Christians. Secondly, their homes should likewise be broken down and destroyed...Thirdly, they should be deprived of their prayer books....Fourthly, their rabbis must be forbidden under threat of death to teach anymore.....To sum up, dear princes and nobles who have Jews in your domains, if this advice of mine does not suit you, then find a better one so that you may all be free of this insufferable devilish burden – the Jews.'

Quoted by Martin Luther, Von Dem Juden und inhren Lugern, (On the Jews and their lies), Wittenburg, 1543.

Would my forebears have adopted his faith if they were aware of Luther's feelings? If we are of Jewish descent there is certainly some irony in my growing up on a Lutheran mission and becoming a lay preacher. It's as well that this information was unknown to me then, I had enough turbulence in my head to deal with.

After I'd been home for nine months, one of our aircraft needed specialised repairs in Melbourne. It was scheduled to refuel in Broken Hill. Here was a chance for me to see Pamela again.

I was granted unpaid leave for the few days away. The boss agreed that it could be beneficial to have an engineer travelling with the aircraft for most of the journey.

I phoned Pamela and made arrangements. She was working, but able to see me at night. I told Mother it was necessary for me to go with the aircraft but made no mention of seeing 'the Catholic girl'. It was easier to hide the truth than upset her again.

After arriving in Broken Hill, I did a flight check with the Club instructor in the Piper aircraft I had previously flown. Then I flew to Radium Hill and collected Pamela after she finished work and we returned to Broken Hill.

I could barely contain my excitement and concentrate on flying the plane back. We were like a honeymoon couple who had bypassed a journey to the altar. It seemed that possibility remained as distant as ever, but for that one night I was in heaven, just being with Pamela.

After dinner, we spent our first night together in nine months, at the Royal Exchange Hotel. We kissed and cuddled for most of the night. I didn't expect anything more than this; it was enough for me to have seen and touched her again. Pamela told me she had asked her father's permission to go away with me. He must have trusted us. Respectable, unmarried girls simply did not overnight with men in those days. Our liaison caused quite a stir at Radium Hill, but Pamela's reputation was not impugned.

Early next morning I flew her back to work. That was it, a spiritual reunion but still with no future. I can't recall my feelings during the half-hour flight back to Broken Hill after dropping her off. My logbook states I did a flight check in the Club's Chipmunk aircraft I knew so well. After that, I took off and threw my metal steed all over the sky. Watching the earth revolve outside the cockpit was a good way to clear my head.

My transport to Alice arrived, and it was back to the daily grind.

I can't find diaries for this period of my life, perhaps because of my emotional difficulties. I had to put Pamela from my mind and move on. To get away from home and the church, I became involved with an amateur Drama Group. A shortage of men resulted in my portraying Nigel in an Agatha Christie crime mystery. This was followed by another play in which I took a lead role as a murderer. I began to be known as a thespian in our small community. Lucky for me, again in a male dominated town, the drama group was well supported by single, female schoolteachers. Slowly my reluctance to socialise with girls diminished. *I will not, I reminded myself, have a repeat of the Pamela scenario with another woman from a drama group.*

I need not have worried; my heart was locked away from emotional contact yet my persona was that of a considerate, sober, eligible male. After a few months I allowed a slim, attractive brunette into my life. After rehearsals Deirdre and I began to return to her quarters on Todd Street.

She was a schoolteacher and we conversed easily. Weeks went by before we kissed. More time went by and many evenings were spent on the bed in her small windowless dormitory room, talking and cuddling.

A thin wall separated Deirdre's room from that of her friend next door. Josie, an extroverted, gregarious lass sometimes spoke to us through the thin fibro wall. One night she asked, 'Why are you two so quiet? What are you up to?'

We lay silent.

'Come on, I just want to be sure you are OK in there.'

Further silence, we tested Josie to see if she would cease her interrogation.

'Alright, alright, so you don't want to talk, even if I'm feeling lonely.' She muttered to herself.

Deirdre whispered, 'She can be a bit melodramatic at times, don't take any notice.'

A loud crash occurred just above our heads as a two metre long aboriginal hunting spear smashed through the wall and embedded itself into a chair across the room.

'God I'm sorry, are you alright?' shouted Josie. 'I didn't think the spear would go through the wall. I just wanted to make a sudden noise to see if you responded.'

Josie joined us. She helped pick up fibro before leaving. We laughed about her spear chucking, but she knew it was lucky her impulsive throw didn't result in injury.

After the hurt caused by Mother and Pamela, I regained my ability to touch females. One night, perhaps to discover if I was impotent, Deirdre encouraged me to undress her. I found myself responding and we made love. This was only the second woman I had penetrated. At the age of 24 I was still very naive and inexperienced in sexual matters, yet very conscious of the consequences of an unwanted pregnancy. In 1961 abortion was still illegal, so a marriage was expected. This greatly tempered spontaneous lovemaking. Many girls would not take the risk, prior to formal engagement. We made love again, but I was still living at home so my behaviour was always discreet and I didn't stay out late.

There I was, teaching Sunday school, an occasional lay reader at church services, and bedding females. A hypocrite and morally bankrupt, yet still passing as a pillar of society. It was a mentally conflicting time.

As our church seemed to cater largely for the town's aboriginal community I also attended the John Flynn Uniting church where I found other single people in my age group. Some of us played tennis at night. Due to the small population in Northern Territory towns, many members of sports clubs drove long distances to find a competition. One long weekend we found ourselves driving to Darwin to play tennis. This meant a round-trip of over 3000 kilometres, just for a game. Flying was far too expensive.

Meanwhile, I was studying, passing exams and gaining qualifications. Though the youngest employee on the shop floor, I was amazed and a little apprehensive when promoted to being a shift boss. It was a challenge but I had the necessary academic qualifications and tact to avoid confrontations with older men who had been in the industry for many years. We all worked under considerable pressure to complete maintenance requirements. Connellans being a scheduled airline, the aircraft had to be ready to fly at specified times. I ran the night shift, which meant we worked until the aircraft were finished and ready for flight, regardless of the hour. Added pressure required one aircraft to be ready at a moment's notice for Flying Doctor flights.

One afternoon, an ambulance arrived and the medivac aircraft landed soon after. The pilot and ambulance men were talking on the tarmac when a cry came from the Cessna. The aboriginal woman patient had given birth while they were chatting about her condition. The mother and child were fine, but left a mess for us to clean up.

On another trip, an injured worker was being flown in from some distance away. The patient was losing blood at a rate greater than the supply on board. He was expected to die in flight. We launched another aircraft with more plasma, the two met at a convenient airstrip, and yet another patient's life was saved.

The following is quoted from an official report, on medivac flight number 43; it illustrates how tough the desert aboriginals were in those early days of the service.

'Dr Riley flew out in the aircraft to bring in a young aboriginal girl whose kidney fat had been removed by her brother. It would be a 5 hour plus round trip to the isolated location. The brother wanted to commit a murder, and in accordance with tribal beliefs believed if he took his sister's kidney fat it would give him the strength to carry out his plans.

He cut a 20 cm gash in his sister's back, pulled her kidney out and removed the fat, which he cooked and ate.

Dr Riley considered that any white person would have been dead long before, but the girl was flown back to the Alice and recovered completely.'

Little wonder why outback people swore by, relied on, and held the greatest respect for the Flying Doctor network.

One day a new cleaner, David, arrived to begin duty at Connellans. Atypically for a cleaner, he wore a suit and tie. After lunch David's broom stood unattended and we eventually found him asleep in a corner of the hangar. His breath reeked of alcohol, whereupon he was unceremoniously slung into a vehicle, driven to town and dumped onto the footpath. That's him gone we thought. Next morning he arrived in his coat and tie and began sweeping as though nothing unusual had occurred. After lunch we again found him sleeping off the effects of alcohol. He had obtained pure alcohol from our store. We used it for cleaning critical parts. I told the storeman not to hand anything to David without express permission from a superior. We thought the problem solved, but some days later David was found asleep again. This time he was driven some distance out of town and dumped on the roadside. Would he would get the message and leave town? Wrong again. He turned up and managed to work for a few days before his after lunch snooze. Investigation found he had been drinking aircraft hydraulic fluid. In addition to highly toxic liquids, it contained some alcohol. Drinking this cocktail would kill most people, but apparently it just sent David to sleep.

This was too much for the company. To avoid dealing with a casualty, the boss bought a ticket on the Gahn. We made sure David was on that train to Adelaide. That was the last we saw of him, but rumours said he had been the headmaster of an exclusive boy's school in England before falling off his perch.

I was lucky enough to witness a helicopter landing behind our hanger. I had heard of these strange machines, but had never seen one. The way it came down almost vertically between our rear hanger wall and adjacent rocky hill amazed me. I was hooked by their apparent versatility. It was like having an exotic sports car, one that could go up and down as well. I knew that some day I would have to work on these strange looking aircraft, with their clear bubble cockpit and tubular tail boom with a propeller at the end.

The helicopter crew worked on their machine for a few days, then flew away to survey the Simpson Desert. Several weeks later the chopper broke down and the isolated party was in trouble. Could we fly out, locate the base camp and drop spare parts and water? Not an easy task in the featureless, unending sand dunes that stretched for hundreds of kilometres. Maps of the area indicated 'relief data unreliable'. The location of the camp could only be estimated. George Taylor, our Chief Pilot, had to rely on dead reckoning and sharp eyes to find it.

Meanwhile, tyre inner tubes were filled with water, these usually don't burst when dropped from an aircraft. Our Beech 18 aircraft's fuel tanks were topped to the brim and when the parts arrived we set off. I had volunteered, along with several others, to provide assistance on the drop. The aircraft's only door was removed, it could not be opened sufficiently in flight to jettison our vital cargo.

The trip out took hours, then the search began. Eventually the camp was found and a successful drop made. Most of the return journey was in darkness. The aircraft and pilot were not licensed to fly at night, but this did not present a problem for George. He had flown the Atlantic Ocean at night in Super Fortress bombers. We did have to land at the main airport, the only one equipped with runway lights, but that was a minor inconvenience.

An amazing story was later revealed. It involved an experienced surveyor's actions while the helicopter was grounded. This man had been dropped in the desert 48 kilometres away from the base camp with a limited supply of food and water. When the chopper failed to collect him he had to make a difficult decision. Not knowing when the chopper might return, should he stay and possibly perish; or try walking back to camp? He trusted his skill and compass, deciding to walk. To keep a straight bearing and climb hundreds of featureless sand hills was amazing. He survived because he found the base camp.

I continued to socialise with Diedre. She was great company but I thought we were only good friends. The drama group was the main interest we shared. Diedre had never been to our house; I did not want her or Mother to think our relationship might become permanent. I was licking my wounds; my heart still locked. Apart from the several times we made love, a clothed kiss and cuddle was it.

I planned to drive to Adelaide for holidays. A friend from my Adelaide church group and her girlfriend, both teachers, were flying up to the Alice for their break. They asked if could I give them a lift back. I accepted as it would provide company on the boring drive and might lead to romance. My only problem was to tell my girlfriend of six months about this arrangement. Cowardly, I waited until the day before the other girls were to arrive. Because my heart was closed, I didn't notice or ask about Diedre's feelings for me. I knew so little about the female psyche.

She was quietly inconsolable when told of my departure. Especially as she was about to begin her holidays. I didn't have any idea of the depth of her feelings for me. She had given me no clue or perhaps I was not perceptive enough to notice any. I wished she had ranted and raved and called me names. I would have agreed with her. Instead, I didn't know what to do in the face of an unending flood of sobs and tears. After many hours of attempted consolation, I gave up and left. It seemed there was nothing I could do to ease her grief.

I soon forgot Deirdre after setting out with Ruth and Jane in my Holden utility. Our long-range fuel tank would allow us to drive to Hermannsburg, Haast's Bluff and then via a back road to Ayers Rock (Uluru). My two brunette passengers were shapely, intelligent and around my age. I fancied Ruth; I had watched her play netball for our church and square danced with her during my apprenticeship in Adelaide. Mother had no qualms about me going off camping with the girls; they were from known Lutheran families.

Neither having done any serious camping before, both girls happily rolled out their borrowed bedrolls on either side of mine for added security. At some point during our first night under the stars, I noticed Jane wasn't in her swag. Sensing something amiss I investigated, finding her sitting in the ute.

'Why are you in here, aren't you cold?'

'I heard funny noises and got frightened.'

'Why didn't you wake me. There's nothing here to be afraid of.'

'Listen, there it is again.'

I cocked my ear and laughed.

'There must be horses around. That was one snorting.'

'They were much closer before. What are they doing here?'

'There's a waterhole close by and the horses are curious about the smell of humans. They won't come close, neither will any other animals be a bother'. To lighten the mood I said, 'Just shake out your shoes before you put them on in case a scorpion is inside.'

I persuaded Jane to return to her bedroll. She had reminded me that fear of the unknown can be a powerful force.

The girls soon settled down to the camping routine and began to enjoy the sights, sounds and smell of the desert. I taught them to cook over an open fire. Beyond the Bluff, on the rarely traveled back road to Uluru, careful driving was required as we were not in a brutish four-wheel drive. This dirt track was infrequently maintained and washouts across the road could rip the suspension off if hit at speed. After leaving the Alice, I would drive in excess of 1,500 kilometres before reaching a sealed road again at Port Augusta.

After climbing Uluru and exploring the Olga's came the long, boring, three-day drive to Adelaide. I made no headway flirting with Ruth. She was very friendly but gave no hint of wanting a holiday romance.

When dropping the city girls off in Adelaide after the weeks sightseeing they said it had been an exciting, memorable trip. For me, it was just a change to have female company on that route.

Just before leaving Adelaide, I visited Jane one evening. We drank wine and it soon became apparent that she was open to my advances. Her room was not private so we found a secluded corner in a nearby park and feverishly indulged our passion into the early hours. What a waste, I could have had a great time on the trip but had been barking up the wrong tree. It seems she thought of me as some sort of outback hero.

Testosterone was now overruling my fear of women but I trod very warily for fear of being hurt, or causing hurt again. Back in the Alice, I began to socialise with girls from the Uniting Church and nursing sisters at the hospital. I was not game to rejoin the drama group or show my face in the teachers quarters after what I had unwittingly done to Diedre.

I arranged an afternoon picnic with a nurse and we drove south of the Alice for a change of scenery. After thirty kilometres, I left the main road and headed into the bush and somehow found a patch of bulldust, becoming hopelessly bogged. The properties of bulldust are unique; it looks like firm sand but is actually mostly air, similar to the head on a glass of beer. Vehicles just settle in it, until supported by bodywork or reaching a firm base below.

I needed to be towed out, not having a winch. While pondering the best way to get help I recognised a rumbling sound. It could be a train heading for the Alice. The line must be near. Quickly getting my bearings we ran east to intercept the train and found the railway line. As the engine approached I waved my arms. The driver acknowledged with a toot and applied his brakes to slow the Ghan to a walking pace. As the passenger carriages passed we jumped aboard and a guard soon arrived.

'G'day, your vehicle broken down?'

'No, I got bogged in bulldust and need to get a tow.'

'Yeah, hard to get out of that stuff. You want a lift in to Alice?'

'Could you drop us off at the airport? It'll save me driving back out.'

'Sure, I'll tell the driver to slow down as we go past.'

There was never any suggestion of paying a fare; it was just the outback philosophy of helping people in trouble. The Ghan slowed as promised and we jumped off.

My friends were rather amused at our story; flagging down the Ghan was something they had never heard of before. We retrieved my vehicle. The picnic had not gone as planned, but it had been an interesting day nevertheless.

I began to challenge the influence my parents and religion had on my life. The charade I was enacting at home needed a sanity preserving safety valve. I needed to engage socially with people outside strict religious circles. A fellow workmate suggested joining the Returned Services League (R. S. L.) Memorial Club.

Mention of my membership caused a minor crisis at home as good Lutherans should not be found at a bar, even one restricted to members or 'respectable' guests. I was resolute and over 21. Gradually the issue subsided. It seems a leering devil could not be seen sitting on my shoulder. On Saturday nights at the club I began dancing with ladies again.

To further emphasize my emancipation, after knocking off work on Friday nights I joined my fellow workers at a hotel in town. Six o'clock closing was in force so between 5.15 and 6 pm we all shouted a round. On a heavy night up to a dozen beers had to be drunk before we were thrown out at six. This was known as the six o'clock swill. Luckily, breathalysers had not been invented yet.

On return from another holiday I found several of my work mates were the proud owners of a Tiger Moth. One of our pilots and his brother Peter, bought it cheaply, although it was in a bad state of repair. I was disappointed at missing out on a share of the purchase, it would have meant much cheaper flying for me. Still, I helped Peter to completely overhaul the Tiger, including hundreds of hours spent stitching new linen over its four wings, some of which entailed using needles thirty centimetres long.

After months of late night labour 'our' bird flew again, in sparkling new livery. The hard work was rewarded by leaving the earth, and our cares, behind. I spent many happy summer hours aloft wearing just a helmet, shoes and shorts. When lightly clothed, it was wonderful to feel the elements. Problems with religion or romances were blown away by the wind passing through the open cockpit. Possibly, skiers, sailors, and other sportspeople feel the same when alone in their element. Being detached from earth and prolonged flying in several dimensions simultaneously is a feeling only pilots know. Being upside down, held only by a shoulder harness, was especially thrilling as we didn't have parachutes. All this fun meant I kept my license current and was able to take friends and family flying.

The Alice had an active gliding club, which operated from the Townside Airport on weekends. Peter, my friend and co-worker, was an instructor with the club. The Tiger Moth also earned revenue for its owners by towing gliders to a greater height than a winch launch.

One Sunday, Peter and his student had reached a height of about 200 feet (60 m) in the glider, with the student flying, when disaster struck. Perhaps the pupil was frightened by the rocky terrain below. For whatever reason, he flew the glider too high above the towing Tiger Moth, which caused it to power stall. Perhaps the Tigers pilot, Peter's brother, delayed releasing his tow because of the inhospitable surroundings the glider faced if released?

That hesitation cost him his life. The Tiger exploded into the ground from a vertical dive induced by the power stall. Peter took control of the glider and somehow landed it undamaged in an incredibly small area of level ground, adjacent to where his brother lay in the burning Tiger Moth. No one could fathom how he managed this feat, especially after the stress of seeing his brother crash. Peter's gallant rescue attempt was doomed; nothing could be done to save his brother from the fierce fire that engulfed the mangled wreckage.

I only heard of the tragedy the following day as I was out of town camping. Not only relatives, but the company and our town's close knit community were affected. It was fortunate that I had not invested in the purchase of the Tiger, being uninsured with the remains now virtually worthless. Losing a friend in this tragic way shocked me. It again emphasized the absolute care necessary when operating out of our natural element. Perhaps I was being hardened. In the future I would lose many more friends and co-workers. My angel had protected me from physical harm, and in this case, financial as well.

I became more involved with nurses. I didn't want to bring them home, but men were banned from their new two-story dormitory or 'bulk store' as unattached men called it. Males were only allowed as far as the downstairs common room. Were nurses and sisters considered inclined to licentious behaviour? Or was it that work stresses might cause them to become relaxed morally and be easy marks? Matrons were obliged to protect young, vulnerable, nurses from sexual exploitation. However, could not the older, trained sisters be allowed more latitude, as applied to teachers?

One hot day I drove to the sisters quarters and asked if anyone felt like a swim.

Soon, three nurses piled into my vehicle and we drove to a cool secluded waterhole outside the Alice.

On arrival, the girls walked left to change into bathing costumes, and I went behind some bushes on the right. I only took a minute to change and return to the vehicle. The silence was shattered when a nurse erupted from the foliage, screaming while tearing off her costume.

'Help me Phil,' she cried. 'I'm being bitten to death.'

Her naked body was covered with large biting ants.

'Jump into the pool,'

I ran to lead the way and she followed, arms flailing and bosoms bouncing, before jumping into the pool

'Do you need any help?' I asked hopefully as she swiped ants off her intimate parts.

'Yes. Can you get rid of the ones on my back?'

The other girls arrived and I regretfully suggested they attend to the task.

'How on earth did you get all these ants on you?' I asked when everyone had settled down.

'I must have put my costume on their nest. When I pulled it on they got really angry at being squashed inside and attacked me!'

'How do you feel now?'

'The bites sting, I think I should go home and put cream on them.'

We retrieved her costume and returned to town.

That was the end of the outing but it led to me swimming nude in the waterhole with one of the girls after a few more dates. Much kissing and cuddling was allowed but sadly none of those nursing friends would allow anything more.

I rarely brought a girlfriend home. Mother immediately assessed her suitability as a daughter-in-law, which I found embarrassing. As for taking one into my room for a cuddle, that was out of the question! Any intimacy occurred elsewhere.

Jody, my latest girlfriend, had a room on the first floor of the sisters' dormitory. I was determined to get into her room so carefully surveyed the premises during daylight. I found a way of getting in - I shinned up a corner drainpipe like a monkey, crawled to my left along a narrow ledge, then climbed into her room through a conveniently open window.

After one heavy night of kissing and groping, Jody and I fell asleep, only to wake at six am. A departure down the drainpipe in full view may have implied larceny, so I elected to walk out the front door. As I hurried downstairs, the starched, middle aged Matron entered.

'Good morning,' I said, while passing.

She reciprocated the greeting before realising with a shock that an unauthorised male had left sacred ground. I swiftly disappeared. Having no idea whose room I had come from, all nursing staff subsequently copped a stiff lecture about the dire consequences of allowing males to access them, or the premises. After that experience we always set the alarm whenever I visited.

Time busily slid by. I passed more exams and was licensed to sign off engines, airframes, electrics and instruments on all of Connellans Beech, Cessna and De Haviland single, twin and four engined aircraft. I also worked on transient machines, including a beat-up Piper Tri Pacer that needed attention. She was piloted by Bryce Killen from N.S.W. I volunteered to stay back, fix his aircraft, then drop him off at his accommodation.

'I'll be flying through again in a few months,' Bryce said after thanking me. 'I hope you can service my plane when I arrive.'

'I'd be happy to.'

After several more visits, I asked Bryce for a favour.

'I don't suppose there is any chance of letting me do a few circuits in your Piper? My licence is coming up for renewal and I need some flying time.'

'Sure. How about first thing tomorrow?'

'Great. I'll pick you up.'

My willingness to help was paying off handsomely, otherwise it meant a trip to Adelaide to keep my licence legal. I was elated at my lucky break.

'Phil,' Bryce said as we flew around next morning, 'I have an interest in a helicopter company in Sydney. You should come and work with us.'

'I'd love to, but first I need more aviation experience. Also, I want to get my Commercial Licence.'

'You do that and when ready, give us a shout. I'll talk to Bill Williams, the boss in Sydney.'

During a tea break, I was daydreaming about working on helicopters when a problem occurred with an aircraft at Innisvale and I was flown up to fix it.

It was a three hour flight to the cattle station, west of Katherine. On arrival, I found the engines of the Beechcraft Travel Air didn't produce full power. It was strange for both to be similarly affected. Investigation found the fuel filters almost completely blocked by a fibrous material, restricting the flow. Further checking, determined that the contamination must have been introduced during re-fuelling at Tennant Creek. To avoid a possible fatal accident I contacted the Civil Aviation authorities by radio. I told them to ground all aircraft that had recently uplifted fuel from Tennant until they'd been checked. It was the first time I played at being God.

Inspectors eventually found the source of contaminant in the fuel tanker at Tennant, and my action was applauded.

A Cessna developed the same problem at Hermannsburg and I was sent to fix it. After cleaning the blocked filter, I asked the rookie pilot to try an aborted takeoff to confirm that the engine was behaving normally. Becoming airborne, at a height of five metres, the pilot fiddled about, then decided to land when we had almost reached the end of the strip. My mind flashed back to when I had seen Connellans Raphide crash in exactly the same place. We couldn't stop before hitting the trees so I shouted at him to take off. He slammed the throttle open and we only just cleared the hardwood at the end of the runway. I had beaten the jinx. I believe Murphy had tried but my guardian angel was still looking after me. When I flew myself into my 'home' airstrip years later I took extra care, it would not be third time unlucky.

I was enjoying my work with Connellans, had been promoted and was not aware of having caused any trouble when Eddie called me to his office.

'How would you like to go and work for us in Darwin?' he asked.

'Sure, I'd like the change.'

'The Department of Civil Aviation will provide you with a room in their mess at Parap. Would you be happy with that?'

'Sounds OK by me.'

'Good, I'll get back to you.'

I was happy to be moving on and spreading my wings. There were just too many constraints imposed at home. Especially now that I had all but rejected my parents' faith. I fully respected their sacrifices, lifelong dedication and unshaken belief, notwithstanding the extreme duress they suffered without complaint, especially during the early Mission days. It was time for me to begin living without pretence as a normal secular person and get away from having to again live two lives. I felt I couldn't bring a woman home unless she had church affiliations and that was something I wished to break away from. My parents' home had been a safe port to weather my storm with Pamela, but the waters had calmed and it was time to set sail again.

I had long wanted a four-wheel drive and traded up to a second-hand long wheel base Land Rover. At that time no other choice of marque existed. This acquisition easily accommodated my belongings and company equipment for the move to Darwin, where I began work in October 1961.

Our small northern operation didn't have use of a hangar, so I serviced the aircraft on hot asphalt. The pre-wet season weather, both hot and humid, was horrific. I felt weak and dizzy after just 20 minutes working in the sun. Salt tablets became essential, swilled down with large amounts of water. Plus ten minutes sitting in the shade every hour enabled me to continue working. Most Westerners don't realise Darwin is the city closest to the equator inhabited predominantly by Europeans. In those pre-air conditioning days it was said the climate was fit only for blacks and idiots.

In July 1962, I moved to Katherine due to schedule changes and a company aircraft being based there. I rented a room at the Civil Aviation Department Mess on the airport. Only primitive cooking facilities existed so I drove several kilometres to town to eat, soon coming to an arrangement with Ma Peterson, who operated a popular café in town. She supplied me with set meals for a reasonable charge.

One day during lunch Ma asked me, 'Know anyone going to Darwin? That girl over there is looking for a lift.'

'I don't know of anyone going by road, but Jim will be coming through on his scheduled flight later on. If there is a spare seat I'm sure he'll take her.'

'OK, I'll let her know.'

I finished my meal and before leaving asked Ma, 'Does that bird want a lift to the airport?'

'Don't think so. She said she was a smart city girl and wouldn't be taken in by a dumb come on line like that from a country bumpkin.'

'Well, that's up to her. If she wants to bounce around in the heat for six hours in a smelly truck instead of an hour in the air,' I said loud enough for her to hear.

I left and soon after Jim flew in to refuel and drop off his passengers. He left for Darwin with an empty aircraft and would have been delighted to have a young girl up front with him. Smart city slicker indeed, as they say – when in Rome. It seems some people are just too clever for their own good.

This incident reminded me of an occasion when I had bummed a ride from the Alice to Darwin with T.A.A. – later, absorbed by QANTAS. On receiving news of the problem up north, time was so short that I leapt out of my transport on reaching the airport and ran straight onto the apron.

Ground staff were pulling the boarding ladder away from the four-engined Viscount propjet as I sprinted up and jumped across the gap between it and the aircraft cabin. I had no booking, no ticket, was not manifested or on the weight and balance sheet; I just arrived on board and a hostess calmly closed the door behind me. Because I worked for Connellans they treated me as crew and I was welcome aboard. Imagine trying that with a major airline today.

Working and living on the airport, I soon got to know the pilots flying the daily TAA Fokker Friendship 'milk run' services from Adelaide to Darwin. Connellans had a partnership with TAA and so I often bummed rides from Katherine to Darwin and back. The thunderstorm season had begun and on one trip we were suddenly struck by severe turbulence. Lucky for me, even in my early flying days, I always wore my seatbelt. Many aboard did not, and in an instant, adults and children were flung out of their seats. I remember smaller children bouncing off the cabin ceiling. Instant pandemonium, but fortunately no severe injuries were suffered and the flight concluded normally.

That incident taught me a valuable lesson and since then I have always asked the person(s) sitting by me to fasten their belts at all times when seated.

Trusting the crew up front they usually said, 'Why? The light isn't on.'

'If we suddenly hit turbulence and you break your neck on the ceiling that is your prerogative. But can you guarantee you won't cause injury to me, when you fall back down?'

This retort was usually enough to achieve a result, if not, I tried changing seats.

On another flight from the Alice to Darwin, this time in a four-engined propjet Viscount, the aircraft was struck by lightning. The strike melted the end of the HF radio antenna wire, leaving the remainder banging on the side of the fuselage. I suspect it also disabled some of the aircraft's navigation equipment as the flight took much longer than usual.

I was sitting at the rear of the cabin; statistically it's the safest place to be.

From there I could see the end of the antenna wire whipping a cabin window. Quite unconcerned, a passenger sat next to the window. I was alarmed and spoke to a hostess.

'Don't you think you should move that passenger, or at least get him to wear his seatbelt?'

'Why?' she asked.

'Well, if that window breaks from the wire banging on it, the passenger might be sucked out as the cabin de-pressurises.'

She looked at me with shock and said, 'Goodness, I'll ask him to move.'

He quickly did after the hostess spoke to him.

I knew that the external window was not structural and it could break without us losing cabin pressure, but the wire might then attack the inner window, which was a different matter. It didn't happen, we eventually arrived safely, but who knows when Murphy is ready to strike.

My Guardian Angel was sorely tested again on an approach to Katherine. I was sitting in a left window seat of a Friendship carrying almost a full load of passengers.

As required by law, the aircraft had overflown the single sealed runway, then began its descent and started turning onto the final approach path. It was a clear, sunny day except for a small, heavy rain shower positioned in line with our approach path. We had to fly through it briefly on the final turn lining up with the runway. When we hit the shower, the aircraft nose dropped and the bank angle increased. I think the crew must have been looking forwards out of the cockpit and not at the instruments. They seemed unaware of the deteriorating situation as it's possible to see downwards in heavy rain, but not forwards. The aircraft continued to roll and dive towards the trees. I thought I had a few seconds to live – certainly not enough time to warn the pilots. At the last moment someone up front saw the trees. We straightened up, and the engines roared. I don't know how the top branches were cleared; it felt I could reach out and touch them. The horrified airport manager, watching the approaching aircraft, later told me he had his finger on the airport crash siren and was about to press it just before we recovered.

It was a very subdued flight crew who attended to turning the aircraft around. I had disembarked and noticed the aircraft spent minutes sitting on the runway prior to departure. No doubt the pilots were discussing how it had almost gone terribly wrong. They very nearly killed us all - and on such a nice day.

My friend, Bryce Killen, turned up at Katherine during the summer of 1963. He had purchased Willero Cattle Station, located 130 kilometres west of town. The lucky sod had also upgraded to a much faster and more comfortable aircraft. His Beechcraft Baron V tail Bonanza, fitted with long range wing-tip tanks was a smart, expensive, powerful single engined machine. I had no inkling that in the future I would fly it myself.

My long wheel-base Land Rover couldn't fly, but being extensively modified it certainly impressed the nurses at the Katherine Hospital. I replaced the standard canvas rear canopy with shiny aluminium weatherproof sheets, installed a water tank, an extra battery, and also an aircraft converter, which produced 240 Volt AC current. This meant I could use my electric razor while driving or operate other common household appliances such as my record player. Next came a small refrigerator, which operated on gas or electricity, and a shower. Of course my trusty rifle was included which sat handily above the dashboard, ready for immediate use. I had additional winch wire wound around the bull bar, which also held a shovel and axe. The axe head was wedged into the open end of a large buffalo horn, the combination looked like the 'Grim Reapers' scythe. It was a true R.V. unit well before the term was coined. I could even sleep snugly in the back if so inclined.

Newly arrived nurses were quite blown away by listening to Beethoven, drinking cold wine, with lights and a shower available while parked beside a pristine waterhole, only accessible by four wheel drive. In the 60's they had never seen anything like it. Unluckily for me, the female contraceptive pill had only just become available and so my advances were not fully consummated.

Apart from the nurses and the odd schoolteacher, few young single girls were to be found in the area. I didn't frequent hotels but heard of an attractive policeman's wife who was known for making interesting suggestions to men new to the town. She then led the punter out to a quiet spot for an 'intimate' drink whereupon her husband appeared and beat up the poor male. It seems they both got off on this act. Obviously the victim did not complain – it would be his word against that of a policeman and his wife.

There was a buzz around town when a new doctor arrived at the hospital in Katherine. Roz had been transferred from the Alice, she was familiar with the outback. Amazingly, she was young, voluptuous, and most importantly, single. We also learned from a nurse that she drank beer. The summer temperatures had probably converted her to this method of restoring fluid balance. This made it easy for us to organize a piss-up to welcome her.

We invited all the medical staff to our grounds for the shindig as the hospital was located just a stones throw from the airport.

I was one of many males to court our new unattached guest at our party. Roz was a great catch. She was allocated a doctor's house, unlike the nurses who lived in matronly run quarters. After many beers and much verbal jousting with other determined men, she chose me to drive her home.

We were both inebriated and somehow a friendly goodnight kiss triggered uninhibited passion. We coupled on the entrance lobby floor. Hardly romantic but I could not believe my luck.

It was the beginning of a very intense sexual relationship. We both aroused deep passion in each other.

Roz was well versed in all the finer things in life. Ten years my senior, she was sensuous and sexually unhampered by religious strictures. She became my pleasure mentor and finally released me from guilty feelings about enjoying sex. We talked about philosophy, art, and our differing worlds, while she taught me to uninhibitedly enjoy the pleasures of food, wine and bed. I began to re-think my view of the world and the behavior of people in it. The ground was set for a relationship that would immediately flame whenever we met.

Roz was the best thing that happened to me in years. Unfortunately, after a few brief months she was transferred to Darwin. This prompted me to examine my future. I had not reached my career goals and following her north would be a retrograde step in that regard. Until Connellans bought new, larger aircraft, I was in a stagnant work situation in Katherine. I felt it was time for another career move and was ready for the challenge of maintaining helicopters. I spoke to a friend in Darwin, Gordon Anderson, an engineer with the only helicopter operator in Australia. He assured me I would not be disappointed if accepted by his company.

I wrote to Helicopter Utilities in Sydney, with whom my friend Bryce was associated, and was offered a job. Cheekily, I said I would like to accept but my starting pay was too low. Promised an increase, I handed my notice to Connellans and prepared for another move. Gordon said I could board with him and his mother in Guilford, near Bankstown Airport, where the company was based.

My replacement engineer, Paul, arrived in Katherine for briefing several days before I was due to leave. He saw me taxi our twin engined Beechcraft Baron to the refueling point – I held a pilots licence but don't know if he was authorised to do this. It was not for me to tell him how to do his job.

On the morning of my planned departure I lay peacefully in bed when I heard the aircraft's engines start, then abruptly stop.

Moments later Paul appeared by my bedside.

'Phil,' he said in his Pommy North Country accent, 'A've fooked oop the Baron.'

'What have you done?' I asked sleepily.

'It boogerd orf while Oi were startin the hengines!'

After pulling on a pair of shorts and heading outside I saw with dismay that our sleek aircraft now had a buckled left wing astride the stout fence close to the terminal building. The left propeller blades were also badly bent.

I'll never get away from here I thought, as we inspected the mess.

'How did you manage to do this?'.

'Oi forgo do re-sit the parkin broike.'

It was a known trap on these aircraft that the parking brake pressure bled off overnight. Paul had started the first engine and then, due to the noise, watched the cockpit gauges when starting the second one. With both running normally he looked outside and saw the fence approaching fast. He instinctively stomped on the brakes but they had no effect. Paul remembered his omission too late to prevent expensive damage. The parking brake knob must first be pushed off which then allows pressure to operate the wheel brakes.

I stayed to help repair the aircraft and eventually left a week late. Life in the reputedly 'sin city' of Sydney would be a new adventure, but first I had a slow journey to complete.

It sure was boring driving the mostly straight road from Katherine to the Alice alone. To avoid straining my Land Rover with its oversized tires I traveled at around 70 kilometres per hour. Hours passed without seeing another vehicle. Sometimes I set the hand throttle and sat there trying to stay awake. For increased comfort I placed a pillow in the corner of the cab to rest my head on. I discovered I could doze while driving and when my vehicle slowly veered off the tarmac onto either side of the road, the change in sound woke me sufficiently to steer back to the bitumen. On occasion, I had no recollection of covering over 60 kilometres.

With traffic so rare, sometimes for amusement I sat on the passenger side of the cab steering with my foot and playing my guitar as a vehicle passed. I also found I could crouch on the floor and peer through the narrow ventilation slats just above the dash. To the oncoming driver it seemed the vehicle was unoccupied! The other vehicle invariably left the road to give me a wide berth and I often wonder what the occupants thought of a Land Rover apparently travelling by itself. I wouldn't attempt these silly tricks nowadays.

Roz managed to join me for a few days after I reached the Alice. To escape my mother's watchful eye, we took off into the bush and spent a bacchanalian weekend at a secluded waterhole on the Finke River. Sadly

I found I could not make love in the open during daylight because of a subconscious fear of Mother's omniscient eye watching us. After this blissful break, Roz flew back to Darwin and I set off to face an unknown future in Sydney.

Top: *The Torture Chamber,' Hermannsburg church interior.*
Above: *My family, all at home in 'The Alice,' 1958.*

CHAPTER 6

There are old pilots and there are bold pilots. There are, however,
no old bold pilots. ~ *The Aviators Guide Book*

After the slow drive across Australia, I found my way to the western
outskirts of Sydney. It was a relief to arrive; now I began to worry about
getting lost. My Northern Territory number plates proclaimed me to be
a country boy. Would my ignorance result in me falling into the hands of
criminals in this city reputedly full of prostitutes and gangsters? I somehow
felt they were waiting for me to arrive. Such thoughts troubled me as I
looked for road signs.

My friend Gordon had explained how to find his mother's house. I
just hoped my lumbering vehicle would not cause traffic problems. Being
anxious made matters worse. My heady excitement at getting into the 'big
time' had long since evaporated, replaced by fear of the unknown.

Relief flooded over me when I found 'my' street in Guilford after several
wrong turns. Gordon's mother welcomed me warmly and said there was
plenty of parking space in her back yard, which also held the traditional
outside loo. My new home was comfortable; the first hurdle had been
cleared. Though hardly ever there, I would use this address as my base for
the next year.

In April 1963, traffic was not a problem, and Bankstown Airport was
not difficult to find. Another relief. Reporting for duty at Helicopter
Utilities office in a small hanger, I found the boss, Bill Williams, and an office
girl were the only people there. I was again a new boy, with much to learn
but now more confident of succeeding. Bill told me that all the other
pilots and engineers were out in the field, somewhere in Australia, and I
would soon be flying to Queensland.

The next day I found myself on a flight to Winton, in the centre of the
state. I was there to maintain two examples of one of the first commercial
model helicopters as featured in the M.A.S.H. TV series, Bell D I's. With
no helicopter maintenance experience I carefully approached my charges.
The engines were familiar, but for the rest of the whirling bits I had to rely

on the maintenance manual. It was a bit crazy, I'd barely seen a chopper before and now I was supposed to keep two beat up examples flying, on my own!

Our task was to help a Mines Department survey record the pull of the earth's gravity at thousands of locations. This was measured from far western Queensland to the sea and islands off the central coast. A mammoth task, taking months. Minute differences in gravity readings, combined with surface geology might indicate valuable minerals.

Our accommodation was a simple tent, which I shared with a pilot. I cooked our very basic meals as no refrigeration was provided. The pilots didn't mind – they were away flying all day. It was a busy, steep learning curve on the realities of helicopter operations, especially with no one to provide advice on keeping them in the air.

'My' two machines had been hurriedly imported from New Zealand for this particular job and unfortunately were in a sad condition. The company had insufficient time to overhaul them before being pressed into service. I found myself in many different country garages fixing major components, as well as continuously ordering expensive parts from head office. On one occasion, when a long distance from any town, I needed to use a gas welder so we found a road repair gang and landed. They were happy to allow me to use their unit for nothing. My experience in roadside fixing as a motor mechanic was paying off. I had to be resourceful to keep my machines flying.

Our helicopters were underpowered for the task expected of them, so the pilots deliberately over-revved the engines to obtain enough lift for takeoff. I only discovered this years later. This explained why some of the main bolts holding the engine together (crank-case thru-bolts) broke and dropped out in-flight. Such were the travails of the early days of the helicopter industry in Australia.

Following the book while conducting a hundred hour inspection, after disconnecting it I barely had the strength to turn the rotating part of the swashplate. This was a serious fault, if the bearing seized in flight, probably all aboard would perish with the machine becoming uncontrollable. Even with my inexperience I was able to prevent a possible disaster. Amazingly, when changing the vital, fearfully expensive bearing, I discovered incorrect assembly of the original caused the problem – it had never been able to receive grease as was regularly required. I had one chance at fitting the new bearing – while frozen it had to be correctly placed into its heated housing! This meant first finding a country garage or restaurant with a freezer and gas welder or an oven. My learning curve was going almost vertical. Some of the jobs I did were technically illegal but I knew enough so as not to endanger anyone.

Then one helicopter's engine began backfiring and losing power. I tried everything to solve the problem but it only became worse. By chance, a strike stopped all trains while we were conducting test runs in a field next to the railway station. Stranded, interested passengers came to look at our helicopter. We offered some attractive girls a ride. Soon after lifting to a hover the engine backfired and the helicopter fluttered to the ground. They thought it had been a normal, if short, flight and thanked us profusely.

Just on dark, Russ Weatherstone, did another test. Our Chief Engineer had flown in to see if he could help solve the problem. We had loaded ballast on the machine to prevent it leaving the ground. Russ applied power and after backfiring, twilight was lit by a long, bright orange flame from an engine exhaust as a piston self-destructed, blowing out a stream of burning embers.

'Fire' I shouted and had barely closed my mouth when Russ stood beside me. First having snapped the throttle shut, switched off the ignition, battery and undone his seat belt in one flowing motion.

'Guess it's an engine change now,' I said.

'Sure thing. That's solved our problem.'

Mine had just begun. The stricken machine had to be towed, skidding down the main street of the small country town to a garage, as I didn't have a set of detachable wheels. Their workshop had a hoist attached to roof beams. It would make changing the engine much easier, the rotor blades and heavy transmission having to be removed first. Although handy, there is a limit to the use of a 200 litre drum-top as a workshop. I replaced the engine and over the next few weeks my workload decreased due to the major components I had fixed or changed. This made it easier for me to cook, clean, erect and dismantle our camp and support equipment every few days. Usually I drove a vehicle carrying our gear as well.

It was a continuous, fourteen hour plus working day apprenticeship, without refrigeration or any fresh food to enjoy in the evening. Cooking was over a campfire. I was amazed to hear that the military flew in half a dozen men in a DC 3 to conduct a routine inspection on a single similar helicopter they operated. There was just me to do the same task on my two machines.

After a month, the survey reached the Queensland coast. What a joy it was to stay at South Molle Island tourist resort at company expense for several days before accompanying our machines on the flight to Sydney.

I enjoyed a few days off before my next assignment. After clearing extensive Commonwealth security checks, the pilot, Pat Long, and myself began working with the army mapping corps in the Woomera Prohibited Area. Six years earlier atom bombs had been detonated there but it was now deemed safe for us to enter. We collected our Bell 47 G2 in Adelaide and ferried it north.

I remember one bomb site, where six of the Mustang fighters I had worked on at Mallala years before were parked at varying distances from ground zero. It broke my heart to see them derelict and unloved, so I thought to carry away a small useful part for posterity. Their voltage regulators unclipped easily and were common to many aircraft. Several were removed, rather than let them languish in the desert. Quite unaware that these items were still radioactive.

Many years later the 'nuked' aircraft were sold to private owners. I heard that one Mustang was flown out of a makeshift strip to Adelaide after only minor work, not a full overhaul as was required by law. It proved to me how well built these planes were.

We drove through places such as Dingo Flat clay plan, and along Len Bedell's Gunbarrel Highway. After weeks of dreadful army provisions we yearned for fresh meat. A dingo proof fence, twenty kilometres away, enclosed thousands of sheep. Surely, one would not be missed. Using the chopper, no telltale vehicle tracks would be left. Pat was despatched to catch live meat, which he did late in the day. We tethered 'Molly' to a tree as it was too late to butcher her. Next day a horrendous dust storm blew up and we were confined to our tent. Then a General came to visit, and Molly was hidden. Without warning, word came through to move camp. Molly could not be butchered in time. We weren't going to leave her to the dingoes, so she had another helicopter ride over the fence, back to her friends. So much for our fresh meat but can you imagine what Molly told her friends?

Then the helicopter needed a new carburettor. The machine stood motionless while we sat in our tent for a week waiting for it to arrive from Sydney. Being on the end of a 350 kilometre supply line over rough bush tracks resulted in water rationing to the extent that we could only wash once a week. Underwear was rinsed in the small amount of water first used for cleaning plates. Other clothes went unwashed. Ted's army issue long trousers literally stood unsupported beside his camp bed overnight.

We hoped our fighting troops would be better provisioned if Australia were invaded!

Thankfully, the survey was almost over. To rejoin the world, Geoff, the official army driver and myself had to drive two beat up Land Rovers across trackless sandhills to the main Adelaide to Alice Springs road that lay an unknown distance to our east. The army's organisation was such that no maps were supplied to us. The standing joke was that we had Latz and Long (Pat and my names = latitude and longitude) so we should know where we were.

Geoff and I set off on a compass heading early one day while Pat and Ted, the army surveyor, departed in the helicopter. We planned to meet at a bore on the main road, noted on Pat's aeronautical map. It was hard work traversing the 15 to 30 metre high sandhills. I was towing a trailer with supplies, making my task more difficult. While traversing a flat bushy area, Geoff staked one tire, then another, so we had no spare. And he was supposed to be a professional driver.

We needed maximum speed when approaching sandhills to reach the top before drowning in sand. Sometimes the ridges fell away unexpectedly on the unseen far side and our vehicles became airborne. It makes for interesting driving, but on one such flight Geoff landed on a small tree, wrecking his vehicle. After transferring valuable instruments and the remaining fuel to my vehicle, I continued to battle the terrain. We left the trailer to be collected later. It took all my driving skills but eventually, late in the day, we drove onto a scrubby plain and soon after found a bush track. I dipped the fuel tank – only a few litres remained.

Now I drove with my foot off the accelerator when possible, to conserve fuel. After dark, we finally reached the main road. What joy, but which way to turn? My homing instincts urged me to head north, which I did, but before long the engine coughed. We knew it would stop soon. When it did, with the last of our momentum, we crested a hill and saw lights below. My angel had helped me to perform a near miracle – this sort of thing only happened in the movies. After coasting into their yard, we found the lights shone from a station homestead. An amazing stroke of good fortune.

Next day we borrowed fuel and found the helicopter. Pat and I ferried it to Alice Springs. We left it there and flew back to Sydney. My introduction to helicopters had not been dull.

After those months of living rough, I intended to make the most of my break. Roz flew in from Darwin and met me at the Hampton Court Hotel in Kings Cross. She insisted, for the sake of propriety, to register a room in her name, next to mine. Her bathroom and bedroom linen remained unsoiled, which seemed rather a waste of money but I didn't question her motives. As usual we quickly came together in mind and body. After a few days of great happiness in each other's company, I had my first brush with out of this world ecstasy.

We began the day with a bout of lovemaking followed by a lavish brunch with wine. An art gallery was visited, then we prepared for more exquisite cuisine and wine. After a leisurely dinner, we fell into my bed and slowly began undressing each other.

As our passion increased, my fingers, lips, tongue, nipples and even my pubic hair seemed charged with electricity as I slowly kissed, licked, touched and stroked all over her body. Fusing into the ultimate intimacy of mutual contact, the electric charge between us increased ever higher as the tempo of our lovemaking built. Finally, the voltage was sufficient for a huge spark, which shocked me into a different world. My climax triggered a series of uncontrollable spasms, each one increasing the strength of my orgasm to greater heights. The convulsions shook me off the bed and onto the carpeted floor where I continued to writhe in ecstasy. My mind was out of this world, my body thrashing like a demented beast. Roz became concerned about my state, but I was experiencing blissfully exquisite visions transporting my consciousness to an indescribably beautiful place. Time ceased as I floated, becoming a rainbow of light. I momentarily returned to reality to placate Roz, but was experiencing something like a near death encounter.

Eventually, I climbed back into bed and fell into a dreamless coma in the arms of my lover. Our union had caused, in me at least, an incredible transformation, one I somewhat feared to replicate. I thought it could prove fatal if the same intensity was reached again, the strain on my heart might be too much.

Needless to say, our lovemaking during the following days was exquisite but not on the same level.

In January 1964, I was sent to Papua New Guinea (PNG) for the first time. The country was still under Australian administration, which continued until Gough Whitlam forced it to become independent in 1975. Many locals told me that independence occurred against the wishes of the majority and I believe supporting the country has since proven costly for

Australian taxpayers.

A task I remember took place in the Western Highlands when we flew Government Officials into Lake Copiago, to celebrate the area being de-restricted. This meant white people were allowed in without a permit or police escort. Basically, the locals promised not to kill or eat visitors. Long pig (people) it seemed, was off the menu.

At the welcoming ceremony the Chief greeting us was dressed in modern gear instead of the traditional belt of plaited creeper with leaves hanging from it, covering his genitals and backside, known as arse grass. Instead, he only wore three red, used, shotgun shells – one screwed onto the end of his penis and one stuck in each ear. An up-market fashion statement to show he was 'with it'.

My next stint saw John Hurrell and I working on a Government contract in the northern part of the country, staying at the Madang Hotel. A pleasant place, situated close to the sea. One morning, John was summoned to the phone, interrupting our breakfast.

'Bad news?' I asked when he returned.

'Afraid so. George (Nature Boy) and Wally Rivers are upside down on top of Mt Otto. We have to leave immediately and get them off before the weather closes in. Seems George was doing a high altitude check on Wally, without dual controls mind you, and Wal blew it. Fortunately the radio still worked so they were able to contact Madang immediately.'

'Are they hurt?'

'Not sure, lets go.'

We grabbed our bags, and headed for the airport.

Fortunately, the 12,000 foot (3,660 m) high Mt. Otto was still clear of cloud when John arrived. He rescued the pilots and took them to Goroka, the nearest town.

George had cut his right calf but otherwise both pilots were OK. Due to the crash we now had only one working helicopter in PNG, so John was kept busy. I'm sure he flew extra carefully, knowing that if he bent his machine he'd have to walk out.

The problem George encountered with Wally arose because few pilots were trained on high altitude mountain top operations. The helicopters capable of safely doing so had only just become available and were in short supply. These new turbo-charged machines were able to carry a reasonable payload to landings above 10,000 feet (3,000 metres). They were being used to set up telephone relay towers on mountaintops.

George was under extreme pressure to show an otherwise experienced pilot how to handle this work. He must have thought it could be done safely without dual controls. George had exceptional skills, perhaps he thought others were of the same standard. After a demonstration and coaching, George changed seats on top of Mt Otto, leaving Wally with the only set of controls. Before becoming properly airborne, Wally managed to roll the machine over resulting in expensive metal being badly bent, in a very inaccessible location.

The wreck was salvageable so early next morning John dropped me off on the mountaintop. Moving from sea level to 3,660 metres in the thin tropical air, I moved slowly to avoid breathlessness while unloading my gear off the chopper.

'I'll be back in 20 minutes with your two helpers,' shouted John before departing on a rapid descent of 1,800 metres to Goroka, deep in the valley below.

I surveyed my new habitat. It was a bald mountaintop, about a thirty metre square of soggy, decaying, undulating grass, that fell away on the northern side. Cautiously approaching the edge I looked down and saw bare rock plunging almost vertically for hundreds of meters before it met the jungle where it tapered to meet the base of the Ramu Valley 3,000 m below. I shuddered, thinking that this was no place for sleepwalkers. My view extended for fifty to a hundred kilometres to the Finnistere Ranges and the Pacific Ocean beyond. I noted that the southwest part of my new home sloped away gently before reaching jungle in the distance. Beyond that sat the town of Goroka, hidden from view by intervening ridges. The only sounds I could hear were my boots squelching in soggy moss.

After another glance at the inverted chopper lying beside the central level area, I selected a patch of high ground on which to pitch my two-man tent. Testing the spot with my boots, it felt secure. I'd heard these mountains received over five and a half metres of rainfall per annum so camping in a sheltered hollow was not wise.

While erecting the tent I was dismayed to see clouds forming around me. There was no sound of a chopper, so it seemed I'd be on my own. John mentioned that these mountaintops could remain shrouded for days, sometimes weeks.

He didn't return, but I was not concerned. I had shelter and plenty of tinned food. Rain was common and my aboriginal friends had taught me that I could survive on water for over three weeks. Dismantling the wreck without help would be difficult, but I was determined to try. On this damp, bleak and cold location, sitting in the middle of clouds, there was nothing else to do.

I concentrated on establishing my campsite. I had only been in New Guinea for three weeks and was not experienced in tropical rainforest survival, but basic bush camping skills apply anywhere. The tent must be secure as thunderstorms can produce strong winds and torrential rain. I set up the inside of my domicile by unfolding the bed frame and arranging my sleeping bag, blankets and waterproof cover. The Primus went inside the tent fly so I could heat food and water regardless of the weather. Food cartons formed a table and the bed doubled as a seat. By 7.30 am I was ready for work and carried my toolbox to the wreck.

My first task was to disconnect the battery to avoid a spark igniting fuel or other combustible material. Then I checked for fuel leaks. None were apparent but a little fuel remained in the tanks, which I saved for lighting fires. While assessing my battle plan I saw deep gouges in the damp ground and surmised that the main rotor blades cut these. The chopper probably drifted sideways, settled, and when the skids contacted the ground, the machine tipped enough for the blades to hit the ground. When a rotor blade hits a solid object at over 400 kilometres per hour, it invariably flips a helicopter. In this case it came to rest almost completely upside down.

As I began to strip the wreck light rain started to fall. It continued all day. Soon I was standing in ankle deep mud. It was necessary to limit the maximum weight of individual pieces or bundles of parts to around 200 kgs, the maximum John could lift in the thin air.

My lunch of tinned ham, cheese, butter and pickles on fresh bread was a welcome break. It would take time to boil water, so I settled for a drink from the container collecting rain from the tent fly.

Well before dark I prepared for the night. My torch and spare batteries would be saved for contingencies. Lighting the Primus stove for warmth, I exchanged wet clothing for dry woollies and warmed my hands. Being isolated and alone on this cold, wet night in the middle of the sky without any means of contacting the world did not bother me. I was being paid for this adventure. I had previously spent many nights alone, miles from habitation, albeit in familiar territory. While waiting for my stew to heat I tuned my transistor to Radio Australia. My after dinner coffee could be drunk just off the boil. Water boiled at much lower temperatures due to the low atmospheric pressure at this altitude. It was still raining as I drifted off to sleep, warm and cozy in my cocoon.

Dawn revealed another overcast sky. John wouldn't try flying up today, so I'd get no help. It rained all day but I managed to shake the 150 kilogram engine out of its twisted mounting frame. It took a few choice swear words, rests between heavy exertion, and many hammer blows before I succeeded. With that done, I soon finished the remaining work and all the pieces of helicopter were ready to be lifted out to Goroka. My promised helpers were unnecessary.

After dinner that evening a storm raged around me. I attempted to listen to Australia playing a cricket test match against England in the U.K. The thunder and pounding of heavy rain on my tent made it pointless attempting sleep. It felt like I was inside the bowels of a monster with a violent stomach problem. Peering out of the tent fly between bouts of torrential rain I saw shaft lightening shooting by, striking the ranges below. I thought that with any luck the metal frame of the chopper would attract a strike if we were to be hit. The lightening did hit my mountaintop, causing my hair to almost stand on end and my ears to suffer. I was very thankful when the sound and fury subsided and I slept. I didn't ever want to be so far inside the middle of a storm again.

Next morning the view amazed me. It seemed I could see the whole country spread out below. The storm had swept all before it and brilliant sunshine burned my eyes. I packed up and prepared for John's appearance, my first task complete. All I had left to do was load the chopper when John appeared. The heavy items would be slung out.

As the sun climbed I realised it would not be today. John was probably busy elsewhere. The inactivity was boring and I looked again to the southwest. A path from the summit led in that direction and I knew Goroka was only about ten kilometres away as the crow flies. It should be a simple downhill stroll through the bush. I could be there for lunch, saving John a trip to get me. The wreckage could be retrieved later, when convenient, without upsetting our customers.

Before leaving I chose a piece of wrecked aluminium tubing as a staff. This decision would save my life. The sun was shining as I walked off the top of my mountain, along a path fringed with grassy tussocks. After a half-kilometre the path led into jungle and I happily continued on downhill. Further on, the trail forked. I had a decision to make. Tall jungle trees and clouds obscured the sun so I couldn't judge direction. Stupidly I had left the chopper's small compass behind. I decided to keep heading downhill. Soon the downhill grade increased, followed by a steep uphill climb and more forks in the trail. These climbs and descents were repeated continuously while the wet mud underfoot had me constantly slipping and falling.

After several hours, I seriously considered retracing my steps to the mountaintop but wasn't sure of finding it. I was completely lost. My bush walking in Australia had always allowed me to see for some distance and walk in straight lines if necessary. In this secondary jungle, with dense undergrowth from ground level up to the limit of my vision I was confined to a foliage tunnel that snaked up and down to some unknown destination. Had I crawled a metre to the side and been able to stand, the tunnel would be lost to view. When stopping to catch my breath, the silence around me was frightening. I continued, fighting the terrain. Hearing a roaring sound, I came to a torrent of water cascading down a swollen stream. I was dismayed at the thought of having to cross but there was no option. A solid green wall faced me on the other side.

Taking a deep breath, I launched into the cataract and was immediately swept away as I lost my footing on unseen slippery rocks. By flailing my arms and jumping off rocks I made the crossing, but then faced the arduous task of finding my tunnel again or being stranded at the water's edge. Careful not to be swept away, I repeatedly parted the green wall while moving upstream. If my search for the concealed tunnel was unsuccessful I realised I could be lost forever. It seemed hours, and my heart was pounding before my staff displaced a branch and revealed the escape route. I rejoined the tunnel and while leaning on a tree to regain my composure, was startled by an almighty crashing sound, followed by a piercing shriek. I spun around to face the unknown, staff upraised, nerves and muscles tense and ready for action. Not a leaf moved. I ran in a state of blind panic until exhaustion overtook me and I collapsed on the muddy path. My brain went into overdrive, telling me I might as well curl up and die, I would never find my way out of this nightmare. It seemed pointless to continue. It's one of the hardest things I have ever done, fighting my way back to a semblance of sanity and logical thinking. I forced myself to believe the sound I heard came from a wild pig upsetting a native bird and not a man-eating crocodiles meal.

Back home I knew of people who had perished, naked in the sun, having thrown off their clothing for no apparent reason while a vehicle full of food and water was nearby. Tourists confronted with a simple dilemma such as getting bogged in sand, on a hot day, in the loneliness of the outback, can lose all reason when a problem arises in unfamiliar territory and help is not readily to hand

I lay in the mud until my breathing and pulse rates dropped. The locals live here and walk these trails, so I must eventually find a way out to a village I kept telling myself. Just keep going and don't give in to panic or it will kill you. I have no idea of the number of times I was swept down various streams. I just had to keep going. My strength and determination were badly sapped when I reached a fast moving, wide, boulder-strewn stream. A tree had been dropped across the banks, so this crossing should have been easy. Fatigued, I slipped and fell into the turbulent water. I was bounced from one boulder to another while being driven downstream. Battered and winded I gave up. I had no fight left in me and didn't care any more. Thoughts of my fraught drive to the Alice after leaving Pamela flashed through my head. Where would I end up this time – heaven or hell?

Then the staff, somehow still clenched in one fist, jammed between two boulders and the torture stopped. I had just enough strength to climb onto a rock above water level where I lay for a long time recovering. Amazingly, sunshine bathed me. Slowly I became aware of a thundering sound.

Cautiously standing, I saw the torrent of water disappear from view some ten metres downstream. *The raging sound must come from a waterfall.* I shivered with the realisation that my guardian angel was still with me. I would be all right, it was not my judgement day yet! Luckily I had been carried almost to the far bank of the stream. Fascination compelled me to investigate. Carefully gaining the bank I maneuvered my way downstream. Soon, a picture perfect view greeted me. The waterfall dropped probably eighty metres, before exploding onto solid rock and boiling downstream. The surrounding spray and mist, sparkling with halo like rainbows in the sunshine was lovely to see. I shuddered; it could have been red with my blood. I'd been spared but still had the difficult task of getting upstream to the log bridge.

Eventually I regained the path. The trail seemed all downhill now and was easy going. The jungle thinned and I walked into a semi-cleared area. Hooray, I must be nearing a village. A little further, a vegetable garden appeared. I had definitely made it. A native appeared, jabbering furiously in a strange language. He held a machete in his right hand and wore traditional arse grass. In moments he was joined by a dozen similarly attired adults and naked children of both sexes. They stood before me, chattering and showing excited body language. A command was issued. Silence fell and the whole group bowed to me. I smiled, said 'Hello, Hello' and moved forward with my right arm extended. Shrieks followed and they all rushed to shake my hand. I could not understand a word they said but eventually asked 'Goroka where?'

'Ha, Goroka,' with much furious pointing and follow me gestures. I trailed along with the mob as they danced, sang and chanted around me. We passed other villages and the mob swelled. I couldn't understand the reason for their excitement; I just went with the flow. It seemed no time passed before we reached the outskirts of Goroka where I led the mob to the Talair hanger we used as a base.

Soon, I was surrounded by expats.

'You walked off Mt Otto on your own?'

'Yep, can't say I would do it again though.'

'You're bloody crazy.'

Eventually I was told why the natives made such a fuss of me. An interpreter said they thought I was a God descending from the mountain as no normal white person would consider walking on patrol without a myriad of carriers, servants and police. The natives also believed in a 'Cargo Cult' whereby a 'God or Big Man' would appear and dispense largesse to them. They were sure the whites had a secret that would be passed to them by this 'God' and then aeroplanes full of cargo for natives would arrive. Perhaps they thought I was to be their saviour?

Bad luck for them, after a shower I was off to the pub to celebrate my survival. I could not buy a beer in the hotel that night, everyone wanted to hear my story. It was a boozy, late night and it must have been exhaustion that caused me to stagger home.

John flew in a few days later and said 'You stupid bugger, I was coming to get you. Then the office phoned and said you had walked off. Now you have to go up again anyway to sling up the loads for me to fly out.'

We achieved this early next morning, and I must admit to great relief as my camp and I left on the last trip. It took all of seven minutes to come down the mountain, compared to my eight-hour ordeal. Soon after this episode my tour of duty was completed and I caught a flight to Brisbane to begin my time off.

It happened that my friend Bryce Killen had flown into Brisbane in his Beech Bonanza. I believe he had invested considerably in our company and was now Chairman. He must have been happy with my efforts in PNG as he flew me to Coolangatta. After a pleasant day on the beach, we flew back to town. Bryce would continue to appear in my life for years to come. After a few more days recuperating I flew back to Sydney.

I had arranged to spend my month's leave with Roz, who still worked in Darwin. She lived in a small flat supplied by the Health Department. Hers was adjacent to three others, occupied by senior female nursing staff. They were not amused when I moved in with Roz, it was meant to be an all-female residence. We ignored their veiled hostility. Strangely, years later after Roz had left me; I bedded one of these women while visiting Darwin. She had changed her outlook. In the meantime, Roz and I enjoyed each other's company and spent a lot of the time in her bed. On one occasion when we were making love, a previous boyfriend rang her from interstate. Perversely, I continued, while she spoke to him in a strange voice. He soon hung up.

Too soon I was back at work. My next tour found me in the harsh light and stony ground of central Western Australia. It was back to rough living, long working hours and celibacy in a male only camp.

On returning to Sydney, I received a letter from Eddy Connellan asking me to be his Station Engineer in Darwin. This would entail my supervising a staff of five and maintaining four-engined De Haviland Heron aircraft. I would also fly as second pilot on that aircraft. It was an attractive proposition; it would provide me with a base to complete my flying training for a commercial pilots licence. I already had sufficient experience to obtain my helicopter engineers licence, adding another string to my bow.

I resigned and prepared for the slow drive to Darwin via Adelaide.

To my great regret Roz also handed in her resignation to me in the form of a 'Dear John' letter. She must have realised I was not ready for marriage and returned to her home state where I believe she married a previous boyfriend. It left me without a partner but I could hardly blame her. I can but hope she found as much bliss in her new union as she gave me.

*My faithfull
Land Rover*

127

CHAPTER 7

Keep looking around; there is always something you have missed.
~ The Aviators Guide Book

I drove to Darwin via Melbourne. While visiting the Aero Club at Moorabbin airport I was surprised by Russ Weatherstone, a diminutive helicopter pilot who I had worked with in the NT and Queensland.

'What are you doing here?' he asked.

'I'm just visiting a girlfriend before I go up north. How did you know I was here?

I might have been anywhere in Australia. In those days, within the helicopter community, almost everyone knew each other but I had not seen Russ for months since he left Helicopter Utilities.

'Well, I was flying past, saw your Land Rover, landed and here I am.'

We caught up on gossip and then Russ left. It struck me that I couldn't go anywhere in Australia without people knowing where I was. My shiny Land Rover was so distinctive!

Once, a policeman on point duty in the main intersection in Kings Cross, on seeing my vehicle approaching, stopped all traffic. He left his post in the middle of the road and strode to my door. I feared the worst, wondering what I had done wrong.

'What's that strange black thing on your bull bar?' he asked.

Much relieved, I replied, 'Sir, it's a buffalo horn holding my axe.'

'I've never seen one of those before. Have a good trip.'

He resumed his post, smiled, waved me through, then continued directing other traffic.

One evening in Melbourne, I drove my girlfriend to a party. It seemed that most of the other guests were brain surgeons, famous writers, painters and suchlike. None of them knew me, so when asked what I did, I decided to play the bushy and replied in my broadest possible OZ accent 'I'm a camel trader mate.'

In fact, a friend of mine bought and sold wild camels to the Middle East at the time.

'Oh, how fascinating,' was a frequent reply. This was usually delivered in a condescending tone, followed by an abrupt, 'Sorry, must see if I can find a drink.'

However, some of the aforementioned males' girlfriends, mistresses, daughters or whatever, took a different view. They were fascinated and wanted a ride in my Land Rover. I became the flavour of the night with them. I drove around the block many times with various lovely ladies. This did nothing to enhance my standing amongst the other males at the party.

By April, 1964 I was back in Darwin. Though designated as the capital of the Northern Territory it was comparable to an isolated country town. A rough, tough, Wild West place with more than its fair share of no-hopers and misfits. One of the first questions sympathetically asked of any professional new to town was - 'Did you go bust down south or are you running away from your wife?' No stigma was attached, regardless of the answer, Darwin accepted anybody.

The town's four hotels were well patronised and a fight could be had at any time of the day. Rental accommodation was expensive and difficult to find. Often such establishments were converted military barracks, a corridor with rows of rooms on either side with thin walls constructed of fibrolite to avoid being eaten by white ants.

I recall one such dormitory, certainly not for its facilities, but for the young heterosexual couple next door.

One evening, while reading in bed, their voices became heated. Then my door flew open and my neighbour burst in and flung herself down next to me. She wore only a skimpy bra and panties. It was a warm night and I was naked.

'Save me Phil, he's going to beat me up.'

'Take it easy,' I said while gently pushing her off my bed and stepping into a pair of shorts. I savoured her body briefly before saying, 'It'll be worse if he finds you in here. Do you want me to call the police?'

'No, but if you hear me shout will you come and rescue me?'

After a few minutes, only hearing muttered voices next door, I left the building and went for a drive. Attractive, white females were in short supply in Darwin, they numbered about three per thousand males, but I knew well enough to stay out of domestic disputes. Here, virtually any fair skinned woman could change 'husbands' in minutes if threatened. With so few available women in town, some were very busy socially.

Meanwhile, as co-pilot on the thirteen passenger Heron, I flew numerous trips from Darwin to Mount Isa via various outposts. This aircraft, thanks to its four piston engines, could safely land and take off on short bush airstrips. It was very maintenance intensive compared to today's aircraft. I carried my toolbox plus essential spares on long trips.

We overnighted at Mt Isa every week, which was in the throes of a long running miners strike. After months of idleness and agitation the town became polarised. On entering a hotel bar, as strangers, we didn't dare look left or right or speak to others for fear of accidentally provoking a fight.

Another of our overnight stops on the weekly milk run around the top end was Wyndham. This provincial port was more isolated than Borroloola, with access only by air or sea. When the meat workers hit town for the abattoirs killing season, violence among them was common. We stayed at the Wyndham Hotel, the other hostelry being infamous for all night revelry and worse. I heard of one fight where a man's head was smashed to pulp with a rock, only metres outside the hotel. Afterward, the mob involved returned to the bar.

It was worlds apart from my previous cosy, nine to five work routine and church outings. I was still learning how some people lived and played, and how to disguise my shock when confronted with their behaviour. Even at the Wyndham Hotel, it was difficult to sleep before the early hours. Leaving at 5 am, I usually saw the footpath and gutters outside the barroom covered in dried blood, a memento to the night's disagreements.

One summer, a croc was shot in the town reservoir and the carcass polluted the only water supply. Boiling presumably rendered the water safe to drink, but the taste and smell was such that few did. As a result the town's population rushed onboard visiting vessels, begging for a drink of water. The crew must have thought they had gone mad. Even hardened drinkers said beer with breakfast, lunch and dinner was a bit much after a few weeks.

The local airline pilots also knew how to drink. I remember a barbecue outside Halls Creek, attended by passengers and crew of Western Australia's premier airline at the time. We ate and drank copiously until after midnight. The captain and co-pilot jokingly tossed a coin to decide who would perform the early morning takeoff. A rather haggard group attended the airport next morning, but we all arrived at our destination safely. One can imagine the outcry if this occurred in public now.

Years later I had occasion to land my helicopter near the top of the high, steep-sided, stony hill behind Wyndham town. It was difficult for me to determine how much the ground sloped, so after my passengers exited, I carefully placed one foot outside the helicopter and slowly transferred my weight. As my machine began to fall on its tail I hastily jumped back inside and moved it to a safer landing spot. Had I shut down the engine and blithely jumped out, the helicopter could have fallen backwards and likely rolled all the way down the hill to end up a tangled mess, just behind the Wyndham Hotel. This result might have amused some, but would not have made my day.

Interestingly, I heard that one enterprising individual in Wyndham designed and built his own helicopter and illegally flew it. It's surprising what one finds in the most unlikely places.

Back in Darwin, during the suicide season from November until the wet starts in December, the high temperature and humidity combine to make life very miserable for humans. Before air-conditioning arrived, this sometimes sent people over the edge. Once, after playing squash at Darwin's only court, I visited the Victoria Hotel in the main street and downed pints of shandy to quench my raging thirst. While breasting the bar, I saw a man begin to climb up the tall water tower that stood at the rear of the hotel grounds.

'Betcha he jumps,' said someone.

'Nah, Rusty'll come back down, just wants to work up another thirst.'

'Yer got ten quid?'

'Sure.'

'OK, you're on!'

More bets flew around the bar. As word spread people carried their beer to the back verandah to watch Rusty climb and then stand wobbling on the top platform next to the water tank, a good fifteen metres above the ground.

'Jump ya bastard,' shouted someone, 'I've got money on yer.'

'Come on down Rusty and I'll buy yer beer all arvy,' came another cry.

I didn't wait to see the outcome of this episode but Rusty's death was reported in next day's paper. It appears that quite a few people jumped from that tower over the years.

Paul, a Navy surgeon, who played A grade in our squash team, told us the military had de-restricted an area on West Point Arm which housed the fifteen inch (35 centimeter) gun stations installed to protect Darwin during W W II. We decided it would be fun to have a barbecue on this previously restricted site – especially with its ocean view. While enjoying our steak and wine the Naval Police arrived.

'This is a prohibited area and you are trespassing. I will have to report you all to the Base Commander,' said the smartly uniformed sergeant in his best authoritarian voice.

'I wouldn't do that if I were you,' Paul said quietly. 'You see, the area has just been de-restricted and besides, the commander's daughter is enjoying our company.'

It was the ultimate riposte; the Sergeant gave an embarrassed cough as he recognised Paul and Jan.

'Sorry sir, I'll be going now. Enjoy your evening.' The poor chap had dumped himself right into it and the private accompanying him suppressed a smirk. That story would be doing the rounds of military mess halls for weeks.

Back at the airport, my aircraft cleaner was due for leave so I advertised for a causal worker. Some rather questionable individuals turned up for interviews and I eventually settled on a failed student enjoying a break from Sydney University. He was a stocky fellow who wore thick glasses. I hoped he could see well enough to clean properly. Not having a phone, meant driving to his address to ask him to start work on Monday.

He lived in rooms under a large house on stilts but was not at home. I sat down at a table to write him a note. While doing so, giggling sounds came from one of the rooms. A door opened and a young woman emerged, walking towards me, still laughing and looking into the room behind her. She was naked except for a toothbrush in her mouth. As her black, hairy bush advanced I coughed discretely and after seeing me, she fled into a room and slammed the door. I finished my message and left without further distractions.

A few days later, during an idle moment I said to our temporary cleaner, 'You've got some nice looking girls staying at your house.'

'Yeah, they're OK. A bunch of lessies.'

In Darwin lesbian relationships went unremarked, in that era most other towns were not so accepting.

'Interesting, what's it like living with them?'

'Great. They cook, wash, sew and look after me really well. They often invite new girls around to party and some of them decide they prefer men so I get looked after in bed too.'

I could see why this young lad was not rushing back to Sydney to continue his studies. My education in relationships was continuing, although I had no intention of experimenting with a same sex partner, even with the dire shortage of single ladies.

At the newly built, now air-conditioned, squash courts, I met Mike. He was the chemist and second in charge of the Swan brewery in Darwin.

Also building a sleek wooden fifteen foot ski boat in his spare time. I agreed to help him. Construction took place inside the brewery grounds after working hours. I left the woodworking to Mike and fitted the big V8 engine, propeller drive, steering controls, fuel and electrical systems. No wiring looms were available so I designed one, purchased the bits and installed it.

When darkness ended our work, we adjourned to the open-air smoko area where a sink was affixed to the wall. Above this sink stood two taps, one dispensed cold water, the other beer. I didn't drink Swan by choice, but being free, managed to force some down.

Our boat was christened at Vesteys Beach. Mike was first up on the ski with me driving and watching for teething troubles. The boat handled well and I was up to a good speed with Mike sashaying behind when the engine stopped dead. Moments later the acrid smell of burnt insulation hit me. We had lost all electrics as the earth return wire was burnt out - it was not large enough to handle the load and cooked. My fault, I was accustomed to metal vehicles and aircraft structures that provide sufficient conduction for return current flow.

We were stuck out in the bay and had to bum a tow back to the beach. Instead of a day on the water I was buried under the dashboard unraveling burnt wiring.

By chance the current Miss Australia beauty queen visited Darwin soon after this. As the only bachelor in the Rotary Club, Mike escorted her to social events. I feverishly rewired the boat so we could take the Miss out on the water and see her in a swimsuit. All went as planned and we powered away from the beach amid the envious eyes of onlookers.

The sea was a bit rough but Mike was keen to show off the speed and performance of his craft. The hull handled the pounding for a minute, then I heard a loud crash and we were immediately engulfed in petrol fumes.

'Switch off the engine,' I shouted.

Again we bobbed silently in the water without propulsion. I could just see the headlines, 'Miss Australia in horrible boating accident, disfigured for life by burns.'

'Seems I didn't make the fuel tank mounting strong enough,' said Mike.

We didn't catch fire and again were ignominiously towed back to the beach. This time it was not my fault. Our VIP passenger was untroubled, she probably didn't realise how dangerous the situation had been. She went off in another boat as we trailered our crippled toy back to the brewery. At least we had salivated over her swimsuited company for a short time.

After the second fix we enjoyed many happy days skiing and entertaining ladies.

Evening events often involved barbecues. For large parties I sometimes provided the meat. It came from Wildman River station where the manager shot a buffalo. I flew the Aero Club aircraft there to collect a full load of freshly butchered meat. On one of these trips, trying to leave, the strip was so boggy I couldn't gain flying speed. On my second attempt a buffalo walked out onto the strip in front of me. It was third time lucky. My previous attempts had compacted the mud and this time the animals stayed away.

Due to the company's flying schedules we performed major maintenance on the Heron aircraft overnight. The inspections were required every hundred flying hours - probably every three weeks. A hangar, constructed by the airport authorities, was now available. When our smaller aircraft required servicing, I often taxied them in, chopping the engines just before reaching the hanger, which saved a lot of sweaty pushing. This infuriated the unpopular airport manager, Mr. B., being against regulations. If he saw anyone breaching the rules, he jumped into his official vehicle and with lights and sirens flashing, raced over to catch the perpetrator. We disappeared, which infuriated him even more as he couldn't find a culprit to prosecute.

One calm afternoon our hanger started to rattle and shake. It was my second earthquake and more violent than the small wobble I felt in Adelaide. After racing outside to safety we were astonished to see parked cars bouncing up and down. The shake caused no major damage but it gave everyone a fright.

The Australian Air Force maintained a major presence on the airport. One day a Sabre jet fighter fell into Darwin Harbour just short of the runway. The pilot bailed out and was rescued. When the Navy divers arrived to salvage the wreckage they found a civilian diver already sitting on it. It was the late Karl Atkinson, a well-known character around town. I don't think he was allowed to claim salvage rights to a military jet but he tried. The story goes that he cleaned out valuables from ships in the harbour, sunk when the Japs bombed Darwin during WW II.

Karl always seemed to have a young curvaceous blond sitting next to him in his modern, convertible sports car. I was invited to his house on one occasion. Perched on a steep cliff overlooking Darwin Harbour, what impressed me most, apart from the million-dollar view, was the electric winch he had installed. It lowered kegs of beer from the street level entrance to the lower entertainment area of his house. At that time Darwin was renowned as the beer drinking capital of the world and Karl kept up the good work.

In contrast I imported wines from Western Australia and held tasting nights for friends. The sea freight from Perth was far cheaper than surface transport from South Australia so I didn't buy wine from my friends and relatives in the Barossa Valley. The latter, and Roz, had piqued my interest in the grape. Ladies appreciated my knowledge of food and wine. I had stopped buying bottles locally; it was often undrinkable due to poor storage before the days of air-conditioning. When I complained about wine being stored standing upright in a tin shed, I was told that if laid down, the corks blew out.

Meanwhile I continued flying training, amassing more flight hours and gained my license to sign out helicopters after maintenance, which helped pay for the flying. I was authorised to sign out the Australian registration documents for two imported helicopters. I cleared the first one for flight on the condition that the single big nut (called the Jesus Nut) that secured the hub and rotor blades was re-tightened and locked after an imminent test flight. The importing company's engineer agreed to do this, it was normal procedure.

We were returning from Mt Isa when I heard a radio call from this helicopter. They had just left Darwin for an offshore island to begin work. I contacted the chopper, asking them to confirm tightening and locking the Jesus Nut. Silence, then, 'No I think we forgot in the rush to get away.'

'Get back to Darwin right away. You are grounded until I inspect the machine.'

Bloody marvelous, it's my signature on all the documentation. What if the helicopter disappears into the sea on its first flight in Australia after the rotor blades fly off? It probably wouldn't have happened, but was an unacceptable risk. You never know when an unsecured nut will undo in flight. A very chastened engineer met me after we arrived – he had abused my trust.

As an eligible, 'respectable,' male with a responsible job in aviation, I found myself invited to the nurses quarters along with a few other 'proper' single men such as teachers. We were allowed to use their swimming pool and I surprised the ladies by preparing sumptuous food in the adjacent recreation hut. Few men cooked in those days. Now, I had a selection of girls to choose from.

Janice, a theatre sister was a slim, good-natured brunette with a very photogenic face. She became my regular girlfriend but like many other specialists, was often on call at night. Once, halfway through dinner at Darwin's best restaurant she was called away to assist in a caesarian section. I drove her to the hospital, discovering the anesthetist was a friend whose aircraft I maintained. He invited me to put on a mask and gown and watch the operation, which I did. Somewhat unethical but this was Darwin. Several times while watching movies at the drive-in theatre, Janice's name was flashed across the screen. It meant we had to leave and race to the hospital.

My small room in shared premises was not conducive to romance so I searched for more private quarters. These were expensive and not easily found. Eventually a single room under Clive Keetley's elevated house became available. Clive operated a taxi service that was still thriving when I last visited Darwin. My room was private; I could come and go as I pleased, so entertaining Janice was not a problem.

At the time Darwin had no maintenance organisation to cater for itinerant and local charter aircraft. I registered a business name and made myself available to provide this service when not working on Connellans aircraft.

Ozzie Osgood, a long time Darwin resident and out of work pilot, happened to meet an heir to the Guinness Stout and Beer empire from the U.K. who was driving around Australia. Ozzy convinced him to invest in an aircraft and begin a charter business in Darwin. Naturally with Ozzy as the pilot.

With finance arranged, they began operations with a Cessna 210. This service was only viable because my engineers and I provided maintenance on their aircraft. Being the only charter operator in town their business flourished. They bought another aircraft, providing more work for me in addition to my normal duties. Being the only independent man on the spot, I was also commissioned by Lloyds of London to survey a damaged aircraft for insurance purposes.

To satisfy the increasing demand, I frequently worked for twenty hours a day, sometimes for weeks on end. I learned to fall asleep at any opportunity, anywhere, anytime, even if only for five or ten minutes. Over the years this 'power snooze' has proved very useful.

Janice was seeing little of me due to my work commitments but I was determined to take her out on a particular Saturday night. A problem arose with the Heron late that day, so I tried a shortcut. My time saver resulted in the nose-wheel retracting as I was sitting next to it, dumping the front of the aircraft onto the ground. When it began to fall I had both my arms in the nose-wheel bay, snatching them out a split second before the nose-wheel and strut arrived to occupy the cramped space, otherwise both my arms would have been chopped off.

I still had my limbs but my night out was now shot to pieces with our aircraft's tail high in the air. At least the airport manager was not around to further harass, humiliate and require me to fill out numerous forms. We eventually got the aircraft back on its three wheels and it flew next day as scheduled. Two small circular dimples in the aircraft outer nose skin, where it fell on my knees, remained as testament to the night when I almost lost my arms. My guardian angel was certainly busy.

To log my necessary night flying hours, I had to go round and round doing landings and takeoffs at Darwin airport. I took Janice along for one two-hour session. It was a lovely calm moonlight evening, with the lights of the city and harbour providing a twinkling, multicoloured, fairyland backdrop. Becoming bored, I suggested Janice try her hand at flying. Hesitant at first, but relaxed and entranced by the beauty of the night, she agreed. I coached her and after some time, she accomplished very credible landings and takeoffs. The only airspeed indicator being on my side of the cockpit, made it difficult for her to polish her newfound skill. We changed seats while flying straight and level on the downwind leg, she was now in the captain's position. By the time my sortie was completed, Janice flew the aircraft perfectly without any coaching. Emergencies aside, she could have gone solo - circumstances sure accelerate learning.

I still shiver to think what I almost did to her less than a week later. We flew out to Wildman River station, where she relinquished her front seat to the manager. It gave him a better view during a survey of his property. Janice chose to sit behind me on the left. On completion, I landed to drop off the manager. Janice jumped out to rejoin me in the right hand front seat and ran forward, close to the cabin. I had not shut down the engine as we were heading straight back to Darwin. She passed my window and was about to run into the almost invisibly turning propeller when I shouted '**Stop!**'

She froze, centimetres away from being seriously maimed, or most likely killed. Even if I had immediately switched off the engine, the slowing propeller would have injured her badly.

We were a shaken pair that returned to the city that day – it was a very near miss and one I have always been mindful of.

A Beech Bonanza aircraft became based at our airport. It belonged to an ex RAAF driver who had won a lottery. A rough, knockabout sort of person, he lived with an aboriginal woman somewhere on the outskirts of Darwin. To keep them in beer and rum he illegally shot crocodiles and sold the skins. To find crocs, he landed his aircraft next to a likely river. He must have been a skilful pilot to cope with off field landings and takeoffs in unknown rough terrain.

I asked him if I could pay to fly his aircraft to obtain another Type on my license. The club instructor was to fly with me but before we went the owner said; 'Don't retract the undercarriage, it may not come down again. And don't touch the propeller pitch control or it may do strange things.' He mentioned other items not to be touched and we wondered how our flight would go. I knew the aircraft had seen little maintenance but it was structurally sound. No responsible engineer would have anything to do with it, yet I was desperate to obtain this flying qualification. It was a great relief when we completed my check without any disasters.

Years after leaving Darwin I heard that this individual killed himself in the aircraft. We knew this would happen and just hoped he didn't take anyone with him. The authorities tried to ground him many times but he very craftily evaded them and continued flying.

In 1965 the Diocese of Carpenteria held their bishops' conference on Thursday Island. To collect and transport these Reverends they chartered our Heron. I traveled on the trip to ensure the continuing serviceability of the aircraft. It was an interesting jaunt with one overnight stop at a station in Cape York where we went fishing and caught dozens of large barramundi.

We landed at Horn Island (T.I.'s airport) with one engine cowling covered in oil. The problem was a blown cylinder. I had a spare in the baggage compartment and next day fixed the engine so we were ready to fly again.

The pilot and myself had almost a week with nothing to do until the conference finished. I discovered a dentist and had my teeth checked. The poor man had virtually no other customers so kept me for hours, talking his head off while polishing and picking at every tooth. This went on for days and my fangs received a complete overhaul for very little cost.

Thursday Island was in the grip of a drought so the hotel had no running water. To wash ourselves, we dipped into an open drum and carried a bucket to the room. It was amusing to see a bishop in flowing robes carrying a bucket to the only usable toilet in the hotel backyard. The Reverends were surprised to find an ex 'Mission' boy helping crew their aircraft. I applauded their good work in health and education but didn't mention my own disillusionment with religion.

Just before we left I was annoyed to discover that the local nurses were dying to meet single white men. It seems only one unattached gentleman lived on the island and he was elderly. Such is life, but the restful days and nights were a tonic.

Janice and I did manage to attend some social events – one being the Aviation Ball. We happened to be on the floor when she was chosen as the 'Belle of the Ball.' The prize was generous - a return ticket to Adelaide, worth a month's salary.

In July 1965, several government examiners of airmen arrived in Darwin to conduct bi-annual flight tests. I was desperate to complete my commercial fixed wing pilot's license and move on in my career. I had only one theory exam and several flight tests to pass. Gaining this qualification would be a passport to fly helicopters, my longstanding dream.

Eric, my flight examiner, notwithstanding his easygoing banter, was renowned to be strict but fair. In those days we feared the Department of Civil Aviation head office administration. They ruled with an iron fist and showed no mercy. It was safest not to make any jokes – I had learned this from the engineering side of officialdom.

My first check flight had to be repeated because my instructor didn't show me a particular maneuver, so I didn't know what to demonstrate. The examiner was not allowed to explain. After landing, I was given the necessary information and becoming airborne again, easily performed the missing routine. Such was the pedantic approach. They were leaving Darwin after another days testing so I was desperate to finish my check flights. I had to complete the required flight and theory tests or start from scratch as my overall time limit was expiring in a few months. It could take years to redo all five theory subjects again as a new syllabus was being introduced. This meant paying for updated school courses and much additional study.

The following day I had to fly a cross-country trip, the latter part of the route only being disclosed after our departure. This did not bother me; I knew the Territory well but was suffering a bout of diarrhea at the time and did not feel fully fit.

After climbing to 8,000 feet out of Darwin I leveled off to cruise to our first turning point. Soon after, the engine began to run rough and threatened to stop at any moment. Murphy had given me a genuine emergency, not simulated or instigated by my examiner.

My eyes and hands were everywhere - mixture full rich, fuel selected to both tanks - as I turned toward nearby Bachelor airstrip, which I hoped was within gliding distance if the worst occurred. I checked the engine response to throttle but it just continued to run rough at low RPM. We continued to lose revs and height.

'What are you going to do?' asked Eric.

I knew I should have declared an emergency and landed at the nearest suitable airstrip. To make matters worse, my signature was on the maintenance release as certifying the aircraft had been properly maintained and fit for flight. A correct decision now was vital to my future career and possibly our health if we were forced to land in the rough country below. My diarrhea threatened to erupt at any second.

'I'm almost certain I know what the problem is,' I replied. The engine should run normally very soon.'

As if on cue, the engine picked up and ran smoothly.

My examiner looked at me with raised eyebrows.

I opened and closed the throttle and the engine responded perfectly. Our next leg was to be flown at low level. If the motor stopped, we would have little time or height to find anywhere to land. I somehow remembered the saying 'fortune favours the brave'.

I answered Eric's unasked question.

'You see Sir, this engine and aircraft are almost new and not fully run in. The pistons are fitted tightly. Until they wear in, the cylinders can shrink and nip them when suddenly cooled, like when we just leveled out after climbing. When the piston temperatures equalise, the engine runs normally.'

'I hope for our sake you are correct. What is your decision?'

I was very confident about my diagnosis of the problem so didn't seriously consider turning back. Completing the test was so important to me. I felt my angel would not abandon me now.

'I see no reason for not continuing the planned flight.'

Eric could have overruled me at any time and taken over if he decided the situation was unsafe. Thankfully he let me continue. I breathed a sigh of relief and concentrated on completing the tasks at hand flawlessly.

As we taxied in to the parking area at Darwin Eric spoke.

'Are you going to check the engine after what happened today?'

'Definitely. I'll pull the plugs right away. You can have a look in the cylinders yourself.'

'I'll be interested to see if your diagnosis was correct.'

Upon inspection, we found the telltale scratch marks inside the cylinders. Nothing else in the engine or fuel system was amiss.

Subsequently, I was notified that I had passed all my check flights and could see the finish line to a new career. Only one theory exam remained. I was elated, threw a small party and booked myself into a week's full-time class in Adelaide to prepare for the last hurdle. It was time to think about my future direction and goals.

I thought hard about setting myself up in business. The opportunity for a full-time maintenance organisation in Darwin beckoned. It would mean long hours and take many years to make it worthwhile. I talked myself out of it. What is the use of being rich when the best years of your life have gone? I needed to experience more of the world after all my years hiding behind work and study. Besides, Darwin was still a backwater. Instead of starting my own business, I gave notice to Eddy Connellan again. Unfortunately for him, most of my close-knit maintenance team did so as well.

I was off to Sydney where a job with Helicopter Utilities was waiting.

Before leaving, my anesthetist friend asked me to ferry his Chipmunk aircraft down to Adelaide so he could sell it. I agreed to this knowing I could use half of Janice's ticket, won at the ball, to fly back to Darwin. In return, I'd drive her to Adelaide and she could use the other half of the ticket to return to her job in Darwin. I'm sure, like Roz, she realised I would not be a marriage prospect for some time so was prepared to leave me and try her luck elsewhere. Ladies of Janice's age were expected to be raising children, social pressure was far greater then.

The ferry to Adelaide took almost three days, due to frequent refueling stops. The flight proceeded as planned until near Barrow Creek. Looking south, I was dismayed to see a very high, apparently solid, wall of dust extending to the left and right a great distance. I buzzed the hotel, landed and was tying the aircraft down when the storm hit. A Connellan's Cessna appeared out of the brown sky, attempting to land. He missed on the first attempt as a wall of sand blew through, but then made it safely down on the short strip. The pilot was Col Prichard flying the scheduled run from Mt Isa to the Alice. His passengers were a Hollywood film star and her female attendants. They were supposed to feature at a meeting in the Alice that night. Due to the massive storm, we would only be going as far as the nearby hotel.

Being the only building of substance in a bleak, dry landscape, it was a strange gathering of locals and high profile guests who sat in the bar watching the dust settle at this barren outpost. An interesting evening followed, where I flirted outrageously with the attractive starlets.

Next day I flew south in clear skies, pausing briefly in Alice Springs to phone my parents and explain why I had not arrived last evening. The light was fading as I landed at William Creek, where aircraft parked at the back door of the hotel.

Entering a small bar, I asked the lone barman if a room was available for the night. Without answering, he turned and reached a shaking hand for the Scotch bottle. He poured himself a generous slug, swallowed it, and then faced me.

'Bu – bu, but you can't stay tonight. It's the Annual Ball. We always close the hotel and go. It's the only night of the year we have off. Now you turn up and we can't.'

A man standing at the bar spoke.

'Look, you've got Bill all shook up. Why don't you come to the ball as well? There'll be spare beds in the wool shed I'm sure.'

'Where is it being held?'

'The homestead is a few kilometres to the west. They have an airstrip.'

'OK, close the pub. I've got just enough time to fly over before it gets dark.'

I had a blast. People drove hundreds of kilometres for the annual races and ball. Even cattlemen from Alice Springs had driven down, so I didn't feel like a complete stranger. During the evening, one young chap pestered me continuously for a ride in my aircraft. Finally I relented, 'OK if you're at the airstrip at six in the morning I'll take you for a flight.'

I didn't expect him to be there.

Arising next morning, amid much snoring, I was interested to note the position and number of feet protruding from beds in what was supposedly an all-male dormitory. In those days, gays did not survive in the outback.

Arriving at the strip, I was surprised to find an eager passenger waiting for me. I strapped him in tightly, he was going to get the works. I threw us all over the sky. After landing he thanked me profusely, told me it was his first flight and that he enjoyed it immensely. Poor chap – he got out and vomited. I left him to his heaving stomach.

South of Oodnadatta, the engine developed a strange erratic vibration. I was not anxious, but flew high enough to find a landing area if it stopped. It didn't, so after landing at Parafield, Adelaide's secondary airport, I handed the aircraft over to a maintenance organisation. They were to complete an overhaul before the aircraft was sold.

Next day someone rang me and asked where the additional aircraft records were to be found. I told them there were no others I knew of and had previously chided the owner regarding this.

I heard that the propeller and magnetos had to be thrown away, along with other less critical parts. It's hardly surprising I experienced vibration from the engine.

The commercial flight back to the Darwin was rather tame compared to my trip down.

After I packed up in Darwin, Janice and I headed down the track in my faithful Land Rover. We planned to spend a week relaxing at Edith Falls, just north of Katherine. A magnificent, unspoiled location, where I had previously taken other ladies.

I set up camp a few metres from the sparkling freshwater pool. Being October it was pleasantly warm and dry during the day. During our idyllic week we saw nobody and rarely wore clothes. After rolling out of our swag in the morning, we dived straight into the pool for a swim before breakfast. Another honeymoon without the wedding. My travelling fridge was well stocked with luxuries and naturally I had sufficient wine to stir the soul. A holiday I long remembered.

I'm not sure how we spent our time but with a lovely naked lady constantly in attendance I don't remember being bored for a moment.

One day, upstream in the gorge, we sat on a ledge with our backs being massaged by a waterfall while our legs dangled in the pool below. Soon, a dozen metre long Johnston crocodiles appeared only centimetres away from our feet. It seemed they liked the waterfall washing into their mouths. They hung vertically in the pool with only long open jaws above the surface. An interesting display of myriad needle sharp teeth. I was tempted to put a finger into this array of fangs but thought better of it and tried a stick. The croc, annoyed, just moved away from the intrusion and continued cleaning his teeth.

After our blissful interlude, it was a dreary drive to the Alice where Mother inspected Janice very carefully. We only stayed a few days before leaving for Adelaide. Mother was extremely concerned that only one bedroll was in evidence. I explained to her that the other one still had to be made up. Doubt showed in her face but she managed a smile as we left.

I don't know what I said to Janice as I waved goodbye after our 'this is the end of the road' drive to Adelaide. She had been a loving regular partner after I helped her overcome a bad relationship. But my emotions and feelings were still kept in check by the barrier raised to protect me from being hurt again. Reinforced by a mental fight with religious beliefs and focus on my career path, which did not allow another person to claim me.

We both sensed it was the end of our relationship. I did stay in contact and took her out for dinner in Canberra some months later. Years later when visiting London for the first time, I slept on the floor in her bedroom. She was engaged to a man she subsequently married.

After Janice left I stayed in Adelaide, attending classes prior to sitting the last exam required for my commercial license. A few weeks later **the** letter arrived – I had passed and could be issued with my Commercial Licence.

For Christmas 1965, I was in Sydney. Immediately after starting work with Helicopter Utilities I was sent straight to Port Moresby where I spent New Year's Eve. The company intended to use my engineering skills before slotting me into pilot training. Qualified engineers were more difficult to

find than pilots, the latter being in the limelight. Also, pilots did not have to lug a heavy toolbox around the world.

On the flight to Moresby I wondered when I would begin another apprenticeship as a fledgling pilot. Hopefully it would be my last one. My new career would be both exhilarating and frightening. At last I'd achieve my dream, but was also greatly aware that I could easily become a statistic. Many pilots did so during the early days of helicopter work in Australia. Did I have what it takes?

'The Belle' and I

CHAPTER 8

It's always a good idea to keep the pointy end going forward.
~ The Aviators Guide Book

Early in 1966, George and I stood in the international airport terminal at Port Moresby waiting for the showdown. A contingent of Australia's top military brass had just arrived on an official visit as Papua New Guinea was still a UN Mandated Territory, administered by Australia.

I first met George in 1962 at Katherine Airport when I worked with Connellan Airways. One day a helicopter flew in and landed in front of the Airport Terminal. After shutting down a naked man stepped out of the pilot's seat. Even from a distance his penis looked huge. George reached into the bubble, found a pair of shorts, stepped into them and walked toward the terminal building.

'G'day,' I said approaching him. 'Anything I can do to help?'

I was very interested in any helicopters – they were rarely seen in those days. The size of his member may have caused envy in some, but was only of academic interest to me.

'Hullo, I'm George. Can you fix me up with some fuel?'

'Speak to the Civil Aviation guy inside, he'll get Shell for you.'

George ordered fuel and we chatted while waiting for the Shell tanker to arrive. After refueling, George removed his shorts, got into the chopper and departed. I didn't see him again for a year, until I moved to Sydney in 1963 to work for Helicopter Utilities.

Within the company, and later in Asia, George was known as Nature Boy because he disliked wearing clothes. Of any kind. A tall, gentle man, he was regarded as a natural pilot. How he endured his days in the Royal Australian Air Force I don't know. He appeared to be a loner and to my knowledge never married. It's unlikely a woman could have successfully competed with his love of aviation, snow skiing and nudist camps. When not flying helicopters, most of his time off seemed to be spent chasing powder snow in some part of the world. Nature Boy was also sometimes referred to as 'Allcock and Brown' – these being famous Australian pioneer aviators who had flown together – George won the title for his appendage and all over tan.

One day our Operations Manager received a complaint about George from a client. They praised his piloting skills and compatibility with the team, but his habit of flying in the nude was a little disconcerting to some passengers. Eventually a compromise was reached regarding the one eyed trouser snake – instead of putting a sock in it, it was put in a sock. Our client was happy and George maintained his overall tan except for the disturbing appendage. How the sock was held up I don't know, perhaps he tied a knot in the whole thing?

The Moresby terminal became filled with Generals' Stars, colour flashes, decorations of every description and gold stripes up to the armpits. Personal Aide de Corps twittered about nervously like birds before a storm. One of our helicopters had been booked to start the contingent on their grand tour of the country. Schedules planned with military precision had been promulgated and distributed to cover their week long visit. Our helicopter was the first vital key to beginning their hectic inspection tour of the country.

But we had a problem – the turbocharger had failed meaning our bird could not fly. The nearest spare was in Australia and of the few other helicopters in PNG, none were available.

George informed the 'Brass' that their elaborate schedules could be torn up. In deference to the occasion he was fully dressed – shorts, thongs and a faded ex Air Force fatigue shirt with the top three or four buttons undone. He leant against a pillar while the pot boiled around him and the bad news was digested.

'I'm sorry General but we can't fly today,' he said to the chest full of medals confronting him.

'When will you have it fixed?'

'Not sure, if the part gets on tomorrow's flight from Australia, probably the day after.'

'Totally unacceptable, why is there not a spare machine available?'

'You did not agree to pay for one.'

The General glanced at his Aide, who tried to avoid the accusing eyes but was forced to meet the General's stare. George had explained all this to the Aide but the General thought he could use his authority to sort out this troublesome civilian.

'Is that so,' the General turned to face his Aide. 'Whose decision was that?'

'The General Accounts Office, Sir. You countersigned for all the expenses.'

'But that was over twenty pages, I don't have time to look at all that detail.'

'Yes Sir.' The aides eyes were downcast.

'We'll be in touch with your head office,' was the General's parting shot as he led his entourage away.

'And the best of British,' murmured George under his breath as we left.

On my next job I worked with Bill Wallace. He was trained by the Royal Air Force in the U.K. and flew front line fighters until an explosive decompression in the cockpit burst both eardrums. After medical treatment, I'm told that hearing is not usually impaired but it's inadvisable to risk further ruptures, so in peacetime injured pilots are barred from commanding pressurised fighters. Bill was given the opportunity to fly military helicopters. After leaving the Air Force and seeking new adventures, he joined Helicopter Utilities, where I joined him in Papua New Guinea.

He was respected by all as a true gentleman, seldom seen without a smile. Bill was a joy to work with, his quick mind and wit enlivening the day. A rotund, jovial ball of energy, always ready to party and a very skillful card player.

We left Moresby and headed for the island of New Britain in March 1966 to begin a contract with the Government Forestry Department. We were helping to map the flora of the western part of the island, beginning from Kandrian and working around the coast clockwise to the Talasea area. The predominantly Australian foresters had already been positioned by Government workboat.

The camp was primitive. No electricity for luxuries such as refrigeration or even fans to stir the hot humid air. A small generator charged the battery for an essential H.F. radio transceiver – our only speedy means of contacting the outside world if the chopper radio failed.

Most of our food came from cans plus whatever edible local produce could be purchased. Tinned Bully Beef, corned beef, leg ham and sardines combined with canned vegetables and dry biscuits hardly provoke a rush of saliva at meal times. I still find it difficult to eat canned baked beans or spaghetti. The local cow-cow, cassava or taro should be left for cows to eat. The native pigs were expensive, tough, full of worms and god knows what else.

Our beds were a canvas sheet stretched between two poles supported by several A frame local timbers, with the inevitable mosquito net suspended above. A constant stream of perspiration, except for an hour or two before dawn, meant it was normal to sleep in a damp, smelly confine. After a while body's start to rot unless great care is taken to prevent ulcers.

The days were filled with hard, sweaty work. To relieve the evening boredom we played card games. The stakes were kept low to avoid trouble - ten pence (ten cents) being the maximum bet allowed except when doubling.

'How much are you going to win tonight Bill?' I asked as we walked to the mess tent.

'An easy night I think. Make it twenty pence. I don't want to put people off by winning too much.'

To my knowledge Bill never lost a card game.

Night after night I saw him collect his previously nominated (only to me) winnings.

Whenever we hit a town it was open slather — all the expats on the Island tried to take Bill on. All lost to him. I never partook in these serious games, but was surprised at how many Catholic Priests arrived with a bottle and reasonable sums to put on the table.

Our task was to move the Foresters into the jungle and back again when their surveys were complete. One problem common to all helicopter operations is caused by people attempting to carry lengthy freight on their shoulders. It can so easily strike revolving rotor blades when quickly loading or removing long cargo from the choppers outside litters. Our locally hired labourers, known as bush kanakas, were rigorously drilled, in their own language and 'pigin english', on safety matters.

Even so, we all kept a sharp lookout whenever long objects were to be flown and literally flattened an offender before any damage was done. A helicopter is invariably grounded if a hard object strikes the blades. A replacement could take days or even weeks to arrive. In the meantime people are stuck in the bush, perhaps without adequate food, and work stops.

'Masta, mi loose im tink-tink' (Boss, my brain deserted me), a common excuse was not tolerated.

Bill's punishment for carrying anything above head height near a chopper was simple and effective. He grabbed the culprit, shoved him into the helicopter and flew to an uninhabited jungle pad five minutes away, landed, and threw the man out. If the offender wanted to keep his job, he had to walk back to camp, if not, good riddance.

I recall one such unfortunate local who took two days to return. On arrival, after eating copious amounts, he sheepishly reported to sick bay and was treated for numerous cuts and abrasions after negotiating crocodile infested rivers and difficult terrain. This treatment was harsh but achieved the desired result.

With Bill away flying, I found myself maintaining the outboard motor used to power Forestry's three-metre aluminium workboat. To test it we water-skied. The natives, never having seen people walk or run on water before, watched with great interest. One day while at speed on a fast sweeping turn, my slalom ski stopped dead. Instinctively letting go of the rope and curling into a ball, I rolled along the top of a coral reef for over ten metres. The natives watching from a nearby jetty started howling, convinced I'd had it. I managed to stand up on the reef in barely ankle deep water, blood pouring down my arms and legs. Nothing seemed broken. The coral had inflicted hundreds of small cuts. I stumbled to the edge of the reef where the shaken driver collected the ski and me. The fin on the ski was almost torn off.

My angel had been busy again; I was lucky to be whole. After this episode, water areas were carefully checked for reefs before skiing began.

Now I had to prevent the worst of my lacerations becoming severely infected. One cut on my foot developed an ulcer that grew to almost a centimetre deep. It did not heal, despite constant attention, until I returned to Australia a month later.

When our camps were set up adjacent to the shoreline, our lavatory utilised nature's daily million litre flushes. The local labour pushed piles into the seabed or reef and a walkway was constructed from shore to the 'little house', made from branches, vines and bark hacked from the jungle. Pollution didn't occur as every time we sat down hundreds of fish rushed to position themselves directly below. The fish could be observed through gaps between uneven tree branches laid to form a floor of sorts. Any solid matter was fought over and quickly eaten, the tide disposed of the remainder.

Our helicopter developed a power loss problem. I decided that all six pistons and cylinders needed replacement. Not a simple job in a bush camp, normally special tools were used for this major overhaul. When the parts arrived, the top of a 44 gallon (200 lit) drum became my workshop. Even without power tools or lighting, Bill was flying again with the loss of only half a day, in addition to his scheduled day off.

At Cape Gloucester we stayed at the Government Station. The

Resident Officer in Charge of Government Administration in the area, called Kiaps in PNG, was the only white expatriate in the area. He was so happy to speak English again that he threw a party when we arrived.

Many mute sore heads appeared for breakfast next morning. We were served by House Marys - all native females were then, and some perhaps still are, called Marys. I sat awaiting food when suddenly a plate of scrambled eggs was dumped in front of me. I turned my head to thank the waitress and almost stuck my nose into a large nipple protruding from a perfectly formed naked breast. I resisted the impulse to gently bite the nipple and smiled a Tenk Yu as she returned to the kitchen. An interesting way to start the day, being served by a statuesque topless young female.

The Kiap was complemented on his choice of young titter to do the housework. Marys with large, un-drooping breasts were called young titters.

'Well, she's my House Mary and wife as well. I bought her from the local tribe last year.'

'Nice looking girl,' commented an envious male.

'For the moment, yeah. She'll probably last a few years and then I'll get rid of her and buy another one.'

'How many have you had so far.'

'A few.'

I was surprised by this revelation. As I heard more stories from old hands in the Territory I realised the isolation and lack of contact with normal society resulted in some white bachelors taking advantage of being all powerful in their areas. No doubt the father of the bride was happy to sell her for hard cash. The bride became a privileged person and was unlikely to disagree to the arrangement.

Other stories came out regarding House Boys. Many expats utilised male domestic servants as tribal tensions could arise with a female being in the Masta's house at all hours. Especially if the Masta (Boss) was single - usually the case. Having a House Boy avoided this problem but training natives to observe European standards of hygiene in the early days presented some challenges.

One tale I heard involved a Masta waiting for his breakfast. He checked the kitchen and found his House Boy seated comfortably in front of the fire, a slice of bread clutched between his big toe and adjacent digit.

'Maski, Maski, yu no ken wokim kai kai long mi dispella wey!' (No, No, this is not how you prepare my food!). 'Yu mus puttim kai kai long spia na kukim.' (You must put the food on a spear and cook it).

150

'Masta, spia bilong kai kai em e brok' (But the food spear is broken).

My personal experience was once being brought milk covered with a green slime and sugar contained hundreds or angry looking ants. I gave up using either.

After we moved to Linga Linga plantation, I was surprised to find the manager there had flown the Mustangs I worked on in 24 Squadron. He was dismissed after destroying his fighter while beating up the airfield.

I was recalled to assist at our base in Port Moresby when the forestry survey finished. Bill was allocated a different engineer on his next job.

In 1966, life in Port Moresby could be difficult for white women. Prior to Independence, many were employed as teachers and nurses to train locals and provide professional services for the large expat population. Some of these single girls were housed in six bedroom quarters with a communal kitchen and toilet facilities.

It was common for them to board a trusted male in a spare bedroom for protection from the local 'Rascals,' the unsociable elements of the population. In those days razor wire was not used, instead, a two-metre high mesh fence around the compound was meant to discourage night prowlers.

Bill Wallace's girl friend lived in one of these quarters. I was allowed to board in this house whenever in Moresby, being beneficial to all parties. Bill's girl friend kept me posted on his adventures. He had a few mechanical problems with his machine over the years in PNG. Once Bill suffered a complete tail rotor failure, requiring the engine to be shut off or the machine spins uncontrollably. He managed to glide to a dry riverbed and landed between high surrounding trees without further damage. His skillful piloting and a bit of luck saved him from death or injury.

Some time later he suffered an engine failure and was forced to land in thick jungle. I was in Madang, over 400 kilometres away when this occurred. To speed up the search effort it was decided to dismantle the machine I was maintaining, load it into the hold of a Bristol Freighter, then fly both to an airstrip not far from the crash area. I slaved all night to get my machine stripped, after which it was carried into the aircraft hold by rice power (a term used to describe the application of force by many native workers). Exhausted, I climbed into the freighter with my toolbox just before dawn, the first part of my job done. We taxied to the end of the airstrip and my heart sank as I heard one engine backfire during the run-up. That was it, the aircraft was grounded pending repair.

I could do nothing more except hope Bill was not badly injured and awaiting rescue. Another of our choppers was sent to the area. I went to bed and slept until after lunch. Then we heard that Bill survived the crash and walked out to a nearby village. After taking leave he was back flying. His luck did run out some months later while airborne. I heard he was flying from Lae to a camp late in the day, crashed again, and this time paid the ultimate price. He was one of many good people I came to know in aviation who died violently while doing what they loved to do. I don't know the cause of Bill's crash but mechanical failure caused many deaths in the early days of helicopter operations.

One of our expat staff based in Moresby retaliated after his wife experienced several frightening attempts to get at her while he was away. 'Boy wire', strong steel mesh, covered all the windows of his house. He decided to connect the upstairs bedroom window mesh to the house wiring at night. Additionally, he hammered nails through small wooden boards so they protruded several centimetres. These foot-sized beds of nails were placed at ground level, under the upstairs bedroom windows, pointy side up.

A few days after these preparations, a scream and a thump was heard as a Rascal fell after climbing onto the electrified boy wire. This was rapidly followed by a diminishing clacking sound as the intruder departed with his feet still nailed to the wooden blocks.

His wife was not troubled again.

In time, more helicopters were needed in PNG and a resident manager was employed. John, or 'Smiling Jack,' as he was usually called, lived in Port Moresby with his wife. He coordinated operations and flew us crew around the country. As an ex QANTAS Catalina and DC3 captain in PNG, he knew it well. John had also worked for Connellan Airways so we had that in common.

I remember John for the excellent food and wine provided to guests at their company house in Port Moresby. They had a magnificent view of the town and harbour below.

John frequently flew me around New Guinea in the company Piper Aztec aircraft when I sat in for our PNG chief engineer during his leave. (*Have you still got that half inch / nine sixteenth SAE spanner of mine Herby?*) This resulted in an almost continuous round of hotel rooms in different towns after fixing machines in the field. One night in Lae, the only accommodation available was in a condemned, elevated section of the old

Cecil Hotel where less than half the floorboards remained. Stumbling out of my bed on the wrong side during the night would have resulted in me falling four metres to the ground. The manager was reluctant to let us sleep in the decrepit building but we insisted, the alternative was to sit up all night in the lounge.

John was to come into my life again years later, in Singapore and Hong Kong as we both weathered the vagaries of our industry.

During my long tour of duty in PNG, I pushed to return to Australia and begin my flying training. Constant travelling, being 'a helicopter doctor' made for social life on the run. Fortunately the perceived glamour associated with helicopters gave me a great advantage in competing for the small number of single white females in PNG. I was not shy in bestowing my attention and money on any personable member of the opposite sex.

Eventually, escaping PNG, I was still being used as a troubleshooting and engineering 'fix it person' all over Australia. The company gave me an airline credit card to facilitate my ad hoc travels.

I managed to arrange a girlfriend in every major port, and one, an airline hostie, travelled as I did. The hostess and I crossed paths in various cities, sometimes just for a night together. The devil associated with fornication was truly banished from my life. I was a cad, but deceit was unnecessary – I made no promises.

Was I still rebounding from a thwarted love and my mother's rejection of Pamela? It was probably just hormones and my determination to progress my career without emotional complications. Relationships were on my terms. My continuing nomadic life made a 'normal' relationship difficult so I spread myself around and enjoyed the variety and challenge this entailed. Aboriginal survival and hunting instincts were directed to winning fair ladies.

For example, soon after beginning flying training in Sydney in June 1966, I was sent to Wittenoom in central WA for a few days to fix an aircraft, then spent a night in Perth. Before returning to Sydney, I enjoyed one night in Adelaide with my hostie and another with a lady in Melbourne. I don't know what these girls thought of my occasional visits to their beds. Maybe they hoped I would eventually settle down with them. Back then; if unmarried and childless at age thirty, it seemed society judged ladies to be a failure. The pressure was great to achieve rings on the third finger.

The girls at head office in Sydney told me I received almost as much mail as that arriving for the Company. Maintaining my relationships meant much letter writing as interstate phone calls were far too expensive.

Nowadays, I'm told young people think nothing of bed hopping but back then it took hard work.

During this period many hours were spent waiting at airports and travelling on airlines. Sometimes I read a book every day and to cater for this consumption rate, joined the Mary Martin book club in Adelaide, which sold remaindered, or passed in books, very cheaply. I read philosophy, history, many religious tomes including Buddhism, the nature of the universe, and remember digesting an interesting 300-page volume on ants.

At that time I professed atheist or agnostic views, depending on the situation, and was into humanism. Sometimes I found myself sitting next to a clergyman on an airline flight. In those days, most churches were intolerant of other faiths. My conversations with reverends revealed they knew little of other doctrines, faiths or details of the so-called heathen eastern religions. As an intellectual exercise these captive travelers were fair game. It was somewhat cruel to expose the extent to which they had been dogmatically preprogrammed, as I had, but they had not 'escaped' to view the world in a different light. It seems that having faith is the only answer to explain the unexplainable. I had lost my faith with regard to Western Religion but not my belief in an aboriginal type of spirituality and connection with the universe.

My disjointed life coincided with a census during yet another overnight flight from Sydney to Wittenoom Gorge. On the DC 3 flight north out of Perth, over a boiled egg breakfast, I read the official document. Apart from my name and date of birth, the form had no validity for me. I had no fixed address, had not worked in one place for more that a few days, ditto for place of abode and didn't even know which Australian State I was in at midnight on census night. On arrival at Wittenoom, I saw a male leaning on the bonnet of his station wagon. He also seemed to be having trouble with the census form. There was a mattress in the back of his vehicle, which wore interstate plates. As least he knew where he spent the night.

In July 1966, I was again engineering in Port Moresby; in August I was propositioned by a native male in Rabaul. In September I began snow skiing at Thredbo where to my delight I found sophisticated, sexually active, single professional women. I was soon bitten by the snow skiing bug so joined a ski lodge to minimise costs. These diversions were integrated with flying training as my instructor now spent more time with me.

Transport wise, my faithful old Land Rover wasn't ideal for Sydney traffic and expensive to run. It had served me well and facilitated some unforgettable memories but my recreation was now city oriented. It was time for a new image. Regretfully, I traded it for a near new, white, MG-B sports car. I decided to rent a flat of my own as my mobile 'home' had gone. I found a long narrow upstairs attic in Randwick at the rear of a large house. It was probably once coachman's quarters with stables below. These now housed my 'horse' - the MG-B. My dolls-house was not posh, I could only stand upright in the centre half, but it was close to the airport and the rent was only $12.60 a week. Visiting ladies described it as 'cute'.

With the beach just down the hill, life was perfect. The ignorant boy from the bush was becoming a city slicker frequenting the best restaurants in all Australian capital cities.

The single office girls were amazingly attentive, helpful and complained about not having dates, knowing I could overhear their conversations. However, I was not going to play where my movements could be closely monitored.

Another young lady I politely ignored lived in the house in front of my new quarters. She often disported her shapely young body, clad only in a white bikini, in the small courtyard leading to my attic. She was too close to home to touch and I didn't even learn her name.

I found myself in Cairns again, fixing helicopters. That done, I accompanied Ted on a ferry flight to Darwin. On the way I hitched a ride to Normanton in a DC 3 freighter and left Ted to trail behind. That evening, in Normanton, while having a drink, I noticed a framed photograph of a very large crocodile on the wall behind the bar.

'That's a huge croc in the photo, what's the story?' I asked the barman.

'It's a bit sad. That mongrel ate three children from one family. They used to ride on the same horse to school and one day didn't get there. We found the tracks where the croc spooked the horse and then grabbed all the kids when they fell off. Took awhile, but we eventually shot that killer in the photo.'

'Now I'm glad I grew up in the desert.'

Next morning a scruffy looking individual dressed only in ragged shorts and thongs offered to drive me to the airport in his battered, stripped down, topless Land Rover. The only taxi was out bush somewhere. During the slow drive, dodging deep potholes, a few casual, chatty questions revealed that my driver was a cattle station and mine owner, no doubt a multi millionaire. I had long ago learned to treat these unknown, apparently 'hick' bush characters with respect and as equals, you never knew who or what they might turn out to be.

While hanging around Sydney, waiting to fly, my weekends were spent in the snow and on many weeknights, wining and dining lady friends. And I was being paid to do this. My life could not be bettered. But I knew that after obtaining my license, I'd be living rough and tough again.

In October 1966, social distractions were minimised as I concentrated on a final burst of flying training. I flew 27 sorties, all requiring intense concentration and some physical effort as my Bell 47 D1 training machine did not have hydraulic boost. The control stick constantly shook, and if the friction dampers were worn, rubbed the skin off my knees when trying to stop its excessive dancing.

This time, my first solo was just a routine effort and the helicopter theory exam easily passed. But further training continued to be demanding. I was very conscious of having to achieve a good result, even though I didn't have to fund my flying. Reverting to full time fixing was not on my calendar.

Too soon, I felt, my instructor booked the government examiner to test me for my licence. Peter said I was up to scratch. I hoped he was correct and that this flight would not seriously test my judgment, as had the emergency during my first official aeroplane check flights.

City Slicker – my car and I 'gone bush'

CHAPTER 9

The ONLY time you have too much fuel is when you are on fire.
~ The Aviators Guide Book

On a sunny November morning in 1966, I waited nervously at Sydney's Mascot Airport, hearing bird song between the thunder of arriving and departing jets.

'Good morning Phil.' John said as he shook my hand.

'Morning John,' I replied with a nervous smile.

I was meeting John, the one and only Helicopter Examiner of Airman for the Department of Civil Aviation in Australia. His initials were J.C. It was rumoured, he was not averse to being regarded as a latter day incarnation of the original mentor of high standards.

I was tense with apprehension and wondered if I'd pass my Commercial Helicopter Pilot's flying test. My personal reputation and future prospects were on the line again. If I failed, would I be relegated to just fixing choppers? It's unlikely they would fire me, having invested so much time and money on my flight training. But after working so hard to reach this point, it would be a massive blow to my ego and confidence.

We soon got down to business.

'You've done the flight plan?' John asked.

'Yes, for the training area, not to fly above 1500 feet. ETD 1030 local time.'

'Good, I'll brief you now. Then we'll do the pre-flight inspection.'

A standard briefing followed – procedure for simulated emergencies, radio routine, when and who was to manipulate the flying controls. It's important to know who is flying the aircraft if both pilots are on the controls, one might think the other is doing so when in fact neither is, or else one fights the other. This type of confusion has caused crashes.

When we checked the aircraft before the flight, John hardly quizzed me. He knew I was a licensed maintenance engineer and probably knew more about the nuts and bolts than he did.

As we strapped in, the knot in my stomach eased somewhat but I still felt like a groom at the altar waiting for my bride to appear. The stage was set but I still had a lot to say and do before the paperwork was signed.

The helicopter we sat in was a Bell 47 D1, Serial No. 28. The same model as used in the M.A.S.H. television series. I'm told Serial No 32 is on display in the Smithsonian Museum in the U.S.A., as an example of early helicopters used in commercial operations. This machine was of simple construction, low-powered and difficult to fly. It was good for training as students had little margin for error.

I obtained a start clearance from Mascot tower. Soon we were at 500 feet (150 metres) and following the beach past Brighton Le Sands heading for our training area at Botany, west of the oil refinery.

The sun still shone, and a gentle breeze washed the waves ashore. The traffic on the roads below was congested, as usual, but my whole being was concentrating on keeping our inherently unstable lump of metal positioned exactly in its allocated bit of sky.

On entering the training area just south of Botany Bay John said, 'See that brown patch of sand surrounded by grass? Do a normal approach and land there.' I did and we began working our way through the prescribed test procedures. I was not aware of having blundered when John asked.

'Mind if I take over?'

'Go ahead, you have control.' I was happy to have a break.

'I don't get much chance to practice my auto's (landings with the engine off) so I'd like to try one or two.'

Now I became the observer. When I saw that I could do auto's, a difficult manoeuvre, better than J.C. my remaining tension evaporated. I didn't become complacent but the remainder of the test flowed naturally and I thought it went OK. This was later confirmed at the debrief when John complimented me on my performance. My marriage to noisy, vibrating, sky-going fling wings was sealed if not yet fully consummated.

My first revenue earning flight with a passenger aboard occurred a week later. I was given the job of flying the original 'Eye in the Sky' helicopter traffic patrol. I flew over Sydney every weekday morning from 8 am until 9 am. After the first few nervous white knuckle trips this became a cushy number as my working day was often over by 10 am. During this period, Peter also trained me to fly underslung loads and land in confined areas. Throughout my career, training never stopped, new equipment and specialised uses for helicopters were constantly found.

One hazy morning over the North Shore, I had just finished a position report to Sydney Tower when the near sky completely filled with birds.

'Fuck off,' I said instinctively only to realise my finger was still pressing the radio transmit button. All aircraft approaching Sydney at this busy time heard my transmission. The feathered friends vanished as quickly as they appeared.

Sydney Tower called, 'Uniform Tango Delta, what was that?'

Profanities are forbidden in radio transmissions, and chat on the air is not appreciated, especially close to busy major airports.

'Sorry, I almost collected a flock of birds.'

'You OK now?'

'Yes, no actual bird strike.'

A British Airways 747 crewmember, using a terribly proper voice, then called asking for the location of my problem. However I could almost sense that 'they' were far too civilised to hit uncouth colonial birds!

One sunny Sydney Saturday I took the owner of the service station fuelling our Company cars for a joy ride. Jack brought a Qantas hostie with him and it was a fun trip around the harbour. During the flight I mentioned I was delivering Santa to a Northern Suburbs party that afternoon.

Later, after dropping Santa, I sensed tension in the Tower's radio communications. It seemed something had upset the operators.

When I landed next to our office and hanger complex at 11th Street, Mascot Airport, a lot of people rushed outside.

One of the engineers ran up to me and said, 'You're dead, didn't you know!'

'Well, I didn't think I looked that bad'. I wondered what all the fuss was about.

Fred explained why they were not expecting me to return. The only other, far smaller, helicopter operator in Sydney at that time was flying a film crew around the harbour when the tail rotor assembly separated from the tail boom. The loss of weight and lack of thrust from the rear caused the machine to enter an uncontrollably steep spinning dive. The cameraman continued to film until hitting the roof of Goldfields House in Circular Quay. All on board perished.

I had flown past the area just before this happened. Our Company was the best known helicopter operator and a popular radio station incorrectly broadcast that our machine had crashed, killing all aboard. Hence the peculiar reception when I returned from the dead. This was my first time to be reported dead by the media. Funnily enough, it would happen again.

Late the following morning my home phone rang.

'Is that Phil?' asked a female voice.

'Yes.'

'You bastard. I've got a dreadful hangover because of you!'

A great way to introduce yourself I thought.

'You took Jack and me up on that lovely flight yesterday morning, and then I heard on the radio that you died in the crash so I went out and got pissed. You seemed like a nice guy and too young to die like that.'

I felt I should console her, plus she *was* a vivacious and attractive hostie. We spent a comfortable afternoon chatting and I took her home after dinner. If I remember correctly, it was a great night as well. Coming back from the dead can have its reward, but I had to come back to earth after spending a short while in heaven.

About a week before Christmas in 1966, I was sent to Cairns to ferry a machine back to Sydney. Junior pilots generally copped these long ferry flights to build flight hours and experience. Before departing, my sporty MG-B went in for a service. I wanted it to be ready for my holidays.

For this festive season I had reserved a place, along with many other single people, at the Young Adults Country Club north of Sydney. The management assured me that I would find many attractive females there during my ten day stay.

I collected the helicopter in Cairns and followed the coast south at an airspeed of 110 kilometres per hour. A scenic flight, with a few setbacks due to weather and having to land on a beach and clean fouled spark plugs several times when the engine ran rough.

These delays meant I'd reach Sydney late on Christmas Eve. As a precaution I phoned the office and asked for my car to be delivered there from the garage. After passing Gosford I decided to drop in to the Young Adults Club and check it out. The road access had been provided when I made my booking but I had to find that route on my aeronautical map and hope to identify the Club. I did locate it in an isolated rural setting with stables and adjacent river. After landing next to the largest building, people rushed out like angry ants around a disturbed nest.

'First time we've had a chopper land here,' said the manager as he treated me to cucumber sandwiches and tea on the front lawn. I was an instant celebrity.

'And you will be back as a guest tonight – wonderful.'

I knew my unusual arrival wouldn't hurt my chances with the ladies either.

Curious eyes watched as I departed.

160

My happy anticipation of a festive Christmas was soon shattered. My car was not at the office. A taxi took me to the workshop in Bondi but it was locked. It was after 5 pm and Australia was effectively shut down for the next three weeks. I found a public phone and dialed the garage after hours number. An angry woman answered and told me to F-off as that bastard had run away with a bimbo. Several other calls went no better.

Time was passing and I felt the surrounding grey walls and locked doors closing in on me like a prison – police, yes, I'll try them.

They said 'Try the Fire Brigade.'

After telling a good story they arrived and let me in to the workshop. Luckily the key was in my car. The firemen didn't want any money and wished me a Merry Christmas. The traffic was heavy out of Sydney but I managed not to dent the car in my haste and arrived back at the Club just in time for dinner.

The food was average, but true to their word, the available women were not. To my amazement I bedded one that night, and another the following. I had never had such quick success before. Being 'the' helicopter pilot had made my nights.

I will never forget the second girl who allowed me to sleep with her – even though I cannot remember her name. We only got together once, on the floor of a garden shed as we slept in segregated dormitories. I experienced another orgasm of massive proportions. Similar to the one with Roz but not as intense. She also thought I was in my death throes. I did go to my blindingly beautiful world but eventually came back to earth with the hard cement floor under my back.

I explained what had happened but the surroundings soon drove us to our beds. Next, Julie targeted me and would not let me out of her sight. In a way it was a relief, at least I didn't have to make any more choices. We swam, water-skied, rode horses, played tennis and found secluded corners in which to indulge ourselves. I was keen to have as much passion as possible, having a lot of catching up to do. Plus much time in rough, male only bush camps to look forward to.

After ten days of hedonism, once back in Sydney, Julie jumped heavily into my life. My previous girlfriend, having a key to my flat, arrived one day to see why I had not contacted her. She let herself in, and on opening the door was confronted with the sight of Julie and I in the throes of intercourse. She gasped and left. I did feel guilty about the way in which that relationship ended. *Was I still getting back at my mother?*

At work I flew odd jobs and got lumbered with trying to teach newly employed, experienced, American helicopter pilots how to navigate. With few roads or railways to follow in Australia's wide-open spaces they simply got lost. I flew these Americans out of Mascot in the boss's Beech Bonanza, much cheaper than using a helicopter. Daunting at first, following large airliners to the departure runway in our four-seater ship. I doubt this would be allowed now.

After a few trips with the Americans I told Peter I was wasting my time; basic ground school was needed before these guys could hack it.

Months later I was sent out to save a contract in outback WA as the American pilot kept getting lost. This was particularity galling for me. There I was, a junior pilot, making less than a third of the import who could not do the job. I certainly earned the Company the cost of my flying training. At least my low paid three-year employment contract meant I gained valuable experience. That lack, and the inability to get it, stymies many aspiring pilots.

In January 1967 I began my first 'serious' task with a helicopter in western NSW. We were chasing grasshoppers, or more precisely, plague locusts. I was excited, but very conscious of my inexperience. I could so easily come to grief in the low-powered Bell 47 D1 machine I had to fly. The first few hundred hours are known as a particularly dangerous time for helicopter pilots – fixed wing guys mostly just have to follow the book to avoid trouble. Aerodromes are surveyed so dimensions are known but us rotary wing drivers have to judge if an area is safe, or large enough to land and take off. I was determined to stay within my capabilities and perform well, justifying the company's faith in giving me a chance.

I began inauspiciously when an airline flight was diverted to look for me. I had forgotten a scheduled radio call when unexpectedly asked to land for a quick discussion with fellow workers. It became a long-winded affair and involved my input, which made me forget to check in. When a Fokker F27 roared overhead I realised my omission and quickly reassured the pilots that all was well, which they relayed to Sydney. Only a few words were necessary on the radio, but my please explain paperwork (the dreaded Form no. 225) would have to follow promptly. I was slapped on the wrist for this stuff-up but allowed to continue.

That decision was vindicated when Reg, the locust expert and I, devised a new procedure for using the helicopter to count locusts, assessing the plague potential. In target areas, it entailed flying slowly at a metre above the ground, hopping over fences and scuttling under power-lines. Our downwash flushed out the hoppers as we approached while Reg identified and counted those in a marked area on our bubble. The marks represented a metre wide strip on the ground and I was able to fly a known distance by timing our run. This information gave a locust count for the area.

Our technique was so successful that the plague locust breeding area was surveyed in a few weeks, not the three months it normally took. We were featured on a television program and I believe the procedure was adopted overseas. Sadly, the pilot who flew the next evaluation hit a powerline and crashed. The machine caught fire and Ian was burnt so badly that he spent months in hospital.

When management decided to base a helicopter in Perth, I was chosen to be the pilot. I would be marketing, flying and maintaining the machine. The company paid for my relocation so I took my MG-B on the transcontinental railway from South Australia to Perth. I traveled first-class – a new experience for me.

I entrained at Port Pirie and discovered that the cast of the musical comedy *Funny Girl* occupied most of the first-class section of the train except for the principal, Jill Perryman, who flew over.

The two day journey became one long party with a few pauses to rest. The piano in the club car must have sighed with relief when we departed, likewise the springs that kept the carriage from jumping off the rails. It reminded me of a sophisticated, adult version of the Ghan school train. Two dignified older ladies, the only other first-class passengers, were outraged by the frivolity. They locked themselves into their cabins and were rarely seen except at mealtimes.

I settled into a motel in Perth and it was natural for me to invite Jill, the star, for a helicopter flight. It would provide good publicity for her show and our company, as television cameras were on hand to film the flight for the evening news. In return, I received a complimentary ticket. The show was particularly amusing, having seen the cast perform an uninhibited, outrageous cameo version.

The exposure resulted in me being interviewed by a popular radio station but little local work resulted. Our machine was just too expensive, specialised applications take time to mature. Meanwhile, I had a great time squiring females; in 1967 I was the only single male in Perth with a sports car and a helicopter. Perth girls were considered the most attractive in Australia, but frustratingly kept their legs firmly crossed and would not be bedded.

For the Easter holiday weekend I flew to the nearby tourist resort of Rottnest Island and conducted joyrides. The financial return was dismal, though I did have a great time. Sadly we were just too expensive for the general public as well.

Exploration for iron ore was booming up North. All too soon I was back amid the dust and flies of a bush camp far from the city lights. Drilling for oil on the North West Shelf accelerated. Apart from a few breaks, I would spend fifteen months in the area. It was rough, tough, men's country. I remember a time when things were so wild at the Port Headland hotel that the solitary airline hostess, who I barely knew, asked me if she could sleep in the spare bed in my hotel room. The locals knew her room number and would have harassed her throughout the night, but she felt safe with me.

I fitted floats to my machine at Bristow Helicopters hanger adjacent to Dampier, where I met Ian Clark for the first time. He would be my boss in Sumatra nine years later when I was Bristow's chief pilot there.

Just outside Dampier, I remember dropping into the local service station for air. This was to inflate leaking float bags on my helicopter; it was much easier and quicker than using a hand pump. The other patrons seemed not to mind my covering their cars in dust as I arrived and departed. The floats were fitted so I could fly offshore to Barrow and Monte Bello Islands.

I seemed to be stuck in W.A. as my next job was with B.H.P., based at Kalumburu Mission, west of Wyndham, in the Kimberley Ranges. This Mission could only be easily reached by air. Our party set up camp on the gravel airstrip and we were invited to the Mission for drinks. A priest showed me a map found on a prospector who walked into Kalumburu in a very sad state and died soon after arriving. A large number of good-sized diamonds were found in his possession. I made a sketch of the map. While flying, I kept a sharp lookout for the features shown, to no avail. I often wonder if the source of those diamonds has been found.

Meanwhile, the geologists I transported discovered large bauxite deposits. I found it necessary to carry a chainsaw to speed up and extend their search. After landing in a small clearing I cut down trees to enable us to take off again with a full load. We were lucky to be paid to view, what I consider, some of the most spectacular scenery in Australia - the ruggedly beautiful river gorges leading to the Timor Sea. They appeared similar to the pictures I had seen of New Zealand or Scandinavian fiords. But a bronze coloured, starker, sharper edged, mostly bare rock defined version with stepped vertical walls to the waters edge. I suppose, apart from the water, they reminded me of my 'tribal' country. Thirty years later, specialist tourist boats and even scenic helicopter flights serve the area.

I had been on duty continuously for six months and needed a break and some female company. I was given three weeks off. First flying to Perth and selling my MG-B. Then I flew to Adelaide for a day, Sydney for a week and went skiing in Thredbo for a fortnight.

I was away for over five months, with only a week off in Sydney during my next tour of duty in the top end of Australia. During one visit to head office, I noticed a particularly stunning secretary. I could not resist making a play, even buying her a dress, but she politely evaded my overtures. Just as well, I discovered she was the general manager's 'Lady'.

Twenty years later I was told that some of the office girls steamed open and read letters from my many girlfriends. They probably knew weeks in advance what my plans were or how close I was to a particular girlfriend. That knowledge proved futile, I didn't allow any of them to become too friendly.

In October 1967 I began a contract with the Northern Territory Lands and Survey Department in eastern Arnhem Land. It was in an uninhabited area of the aboriginal reserve and north of any existing roads. This survey was the final link to establish the position of the east coast so new maps could be accurately drawn. Moving the surveyors in stages over this 170 kilometre route was my responsibility. Vehicles had already transported the crew to our starting point, the abandoned Bulman mine site, about 280 kilometres north west of Katherine.

I flew my machine from Darwin and found most of the gang down with diarrhea. Government Survey Camps could be spartan, and in this case only vehicles and camp gear for their staff were supplied, certainly not refrigerators or fresh food. The workforce was paid a daily allowance and left to fend for themselves. I suspect only a little of this money had been used to buy food prior to arriving in our isolated camp.

I asked the boss, 'What's the problem?'

'I think the meat has gone off.'

'Well, lets get some fresh stuff.'

'How. Ain't no shops around, and we can't chase anything with our vehicle in this rough country.'

'You got any good shots?'

'Sure, Joe can drop a bullock in full flight from a moving vehicle.'

'OK, go and get him and we'll go for a trip.'

'You can't do that, chopper time is too expensive.'

'Who's to know. Anyway, what about the cost of everyone sitting around not working? Besides, I have to eat and nothing will happen if I am sick and can't fly.'

'I suppose you're right.'

'Hey Joe,' I shouted, 'we are going for a fly.'

Joe was part aboriginal and proved to be a great guy. I briefed him carefully. I knew we would be turning steeply to stay with our quarry but I couldn't have him shooting holes in our 'invisible' rotor blades.

Once airborne, we found a good looking bullock who took off, twisting and turning through the trees. Joe missed several times. It was difficult shooting, he but finally put the beast down. In theory, the animal belonged to the Queen, being an unbranded cleanskin on Crown land. I'm sure she would not have minded us eating her wild cow.

I landed and Joe grabbed his sharp knives. We butchered a few hundred kilos of the best beef, the remainder was left for the crows and dingoes.

Back at camp, a large fire burned, providing a heap of glowing coals onto which complete beef rib bones were placed. Soon we were tearing meat off bones with our teeth. Caveman stuff and superb food. Most meat should be hung before eating, but ribs are an exception I'm told. Joe and I were heroes that day and from then on we shot a cow or buffalo whenever meat was required. Stomach problems soon disappeared and the crew were happy to be eating free fresh meat.

The tree cover north of our camp was such that I couldn't find clear landing spots. Many gaps existed between trees but none as large as our rotor diameter. In the end I had to chop my way down through the foliage using the main rotor blades as a mower. The blades were constructed of aluminium with a stainless steel leading edge. The tips, travelling at over 480 kilometres per hour, easily demolished the small outer twigs and branches in their path. My passengers first experience of being inside an airborne mower with the sky full of shredded leaves and twigs invariably left their knuckles white. They eagerly chopped down trees after these initial landings. While spectacular, this tree pruning had no noticeable effect on the rotor blades. In contrast, landings in sharp desert sand completely wears away the blade skin over time.

After reaching the coast we backtracked and 'shot' the angles and distances between our line of sight locations. The surveyors did this at night to minimise the possible errors caused by 'bending' of light which can occur from the heat differential between hot surface air and cooler air above, especially during daytime. In those days, angles were measured with a theodolite, and the distances calculated by using a Telurometer. This machine transmitted radio waves to a similar device at the other location. It was very accurate in comparison to observing the transit times of certain stars as had occurred during my survey with the Army, previously mentioned.

I camped out with the lads doing the measurements and one night we were sitting on a hilltop when lightning started a bushfire nearby. The flames burnt furiously and headed straight for us. My machine had no cockpit or landing lights, it was far too dangerous for me to take-off into the dark, smoky sky. An anxious half-hour followed as we furiously cleared dead branches and nearby foliage around our perimeter. Luckily the wind changed and the danger receded. We were not equipped for a long walk home, and it's a huge loss of face for a helicopter pilot to have to walk.

I awoke several times during that night to check on the bushfire, the last time just before dawn. In the half-light, I noticed the ground next to my stretcher seemed to be moving. Curious, I swung my legs over the side of my wooden folding camp bed and sat up to investigate. I heard the sound of wood cracking as the stretcher collapsed under me. It had been eaten out by white ants overnight and I witnessed them leaving. With my body lying prone, the ants had finely judged the strength of the structure they were eating but with my weight concentrated in a small area, the woodwork folded. This was adding insult to injury, first my helicopter almost being burnt to the ground and then having my bed eaten, it was time to go home.

On another survey, late in the afternoon I began to shiver and shake uncontrollably. The weather had been warm so we flew without doors on our bubble type helicopter. During the afternoon a cold front blew in and I got wet. This sudden change brought on a bout of malarial fever. We were working in an isolated part of the Northern Territory and I had two geologist passengers with me. Somehow I had to fly over rough country, to our base camp at a government run aboriginal settlement.

I knew I was technically and physically unfit to fly but we had to get home. If I radioed Darwin and declared an emergency, it could be days before we were found. From past experience I was confident that my body would respond to this crisis. I controlled my shaking sufficiently to fly back and land at our camp. On this occasion I didn't have quinine tablets with me. Amazingly, the government nurse managed to find some, enabling me to recover overnight instead of being bedridden for days. I had caught malaria in East Timor during a free trip and two hour tour of Dilly. Even though taking quinine pills before and after the brief visit. My attacks were rare, which is why I didn't take pills with me.

Another contract I will always remember was with a geological survey crew in the then unpopulated Hamersley Range area. Several geologists plus support personnel were to search for mineral anomalies in their company's prospect area. I was providing the transport to rugged trackless areas, my vehicle again being a two passenger Bell 'bubble' type helicopter.

Soon after commencing work, it was decided to explore the distant reaches of the survey area, about forty-five minutes flying time from our isolated camp. Having stopped to check several other locations along the way, it was well after lunch before we reached the distant site. Before the two geologists disappeared to crack rocks open, I reminded them of our departure time.

They both set off in different directions and were soon lost to sight. As usual, I checked my machine, and satisfied all was well, continued to read a book. Later, as the shadows lengthened, I began to watch for my passengers. John appeared on time, but we could not see or hear David. This posed the usual dilemma - to go, or wait and be stuck out overnight.

'We'll give him a few more minutes and hope he hasn't got lost,' I said.

We began calling but without result.

David finally turned up when the sun was just above the horizon and immediately began to apologize.

'Just get in so we can go,' I interrupted.

Geologists are often so absorbed in their work that they lose all track of time. It was a constant problem.

We set off with little hope of reaching our camp before nightfall. I would have to make the difficult choice between landing somewhere before full darkness, or carrying on if our campfire or Land Rover lights were visible from the air. At that time, my experience of night flying was limited to fixed wing aircraft with full instrumentation. In those days, on short contracts, it was rare to have any radio communication from the aircraft to the camp.

As twilight darkened we were still miles from home with no sign of any terrestrial lights below. A Perth controller called on the long distance H.F. radio wanting to know if I had landed and was I canceling my S.A.R., (search and rescue watch) i.e., their responsibility to search for me if I went missing. We aviators were fearful of the Aviation Authotity, so I cancelled my radio watch with Perth rather than get into trouble for flying after dark. Besides, I was thinking we had to land as I still couldn't see the lights of our camp. It was a stupid move; any problems and we would not be searched for until people at our camp raised the alarm.

A few minutes went by as I had to change frequencies and manually re-tune the antenna so Perth understood my transmission. When my attention returned to getting us down, I was shocked to find the valley below in darkness.

My option of landing safely on the rocky hills had passed. Now I had to either find our camp, or attempt a controlled descent onto unseen rough terrain. To make matters worse, I had noted a strong headwind arising with the fading light. As the aircraft had no landing, instrument or cabin lighting whatsoever, the instruments and compass were now unreadable. We never carried a torch - it was just extra weight. I didn't even want to think about the engine failing.

Sitting in the dark, I steered by dim starlight and hoped the strong wind would not blow us far off course. A black velvet carpet seemed to stretch below but we knew it concealed rocky hills several hundred meters high.

The geologist sitting next to me struck matches to illuminate the instruments until I asked him how many remained.

'Three,' he said after counting.

I asked him to save them until later. Hopefully, this was reassuring to my passengers.

Conversation ceased, we all knew ours was a precarious situation. It could only be resolved in one of two ways, big trouble and possibly death, or a happy ending after finding and landing back at camp.

The minutes crawled by and I could feel the primeval fear coming from my passengers. They were confined to a small dark cave hanging in the sky, the only external reality being the stars ahead and the growl of the engine behind. There was nothing they could do. They were reliant on my recovering us from my mistake of not landing while we could see the ground.

I concentrated on holding my course and attempting to keep our height constant relative to the position of the stars. This was not the way I had been taught to avoid crashing into rocks. I knew a mountain range was waiting to snare us if the wind blew us off course. Our future literally depended on the stars not being obscured. It was crazy to be reduced to this.

'Hey, I think I see something!' John shouted excitedly.

There appeared to be a dull red glow ahead. I begged God to let it be our camp and not a bushfire. As we crawled towards it, still battling the headwind, the light brightened. It seemed to fall below the horizon of stars and was joined by a white glow.

'It must be the camp' was a hopeful comment.

'About time it came up,' I said, full of false confidence. 'The strong headwind really slowed us down.'

I asked for a match to illuminate the fuel gauge and the first one didn't catch. The next match showed that about an eighth of our fuel remained, it should be enough but the gauge was notoriously unreliable. I always used a dipstick to measure remaining fuel levels and noted our airborne times to be sure of not having the engine stop for lack of gas. Due to our rushed departure I had not noted the time accurately and to make it even worse, could barely read the luminous dial on my wristwatch.

We made it. It was our campfire, with the helipad lit by Land Rover headlamps. I carefully noted the wind direction by observing flames and smoke from the fire before commencing my landing approach, to avoid a crash landing. Most of the usual pre-landing checklist was meaningless; I could not see the instruments. I had to guage the vital rotor revolutions by ear when reducing power to descend. Touchdown was never so sweet. I had pushed the odds to the limit, but my Guardian Angel had seen me through yet again.

The authorities never heard of my serious breach of the regulations, so I was not grounded or otherwise disciplined. I had flown illegally at night as neither the aircraft or I were licensed to do so. I had also flown without Search and Rescue coverage, which broke another rule. The client did not complain, so I avoided a please explain from the Operations Manager but I vowed never again to stretch my neck so far. Funnily enough, I had no trouble with tardy geologists for the remainder of the survey.

My extended work schedule resulted in much juggling of my logbook to stay legal and meant I was owed considerable leave. All commercial pilots are restricted to a maximum number of flying hours per week, month and year. The maximum time on duty, per day, week and month are also stipulated. Many other restrictions can apply, such as the minimum time between imbibing alcohol and commencing duty.

When able to take time off, I spent Christmas 1967 with my Melbourne girlfriend before flying to Zurich on a months skiing holiday. I had been told to go to Zurs in Austria, but met some ladies on the Arlberg Express and missed the stop. I got off with them at St Anton instead and fetched up in a four-star hotel, finding that cheaper places were already full.

A cool move I discovered in this hotel was to open a window, break off a small icicle hanging from the eaves and drop it into my glass of duty free Scotch. I felt I had the world at my feet. The gauche, scrawny, broke Mission kid had been left behind. Transformed, I felt, into a sophisticated

International jet setter. All I needed now was female company to make it perfect. Then, the sudden climate change brought on a heavy bout of malaria, which laid me out for several days.

After recovering, I hit the slopes and had a rude shock. In Australia I could ski any of the steepest slopes easily, while here some of the black runs, the most difficult, appeared suicidal. I barely made the intermediate competence level at this resort. Luckily, I met experts on the snow who helped me progress. There was Aussie Pete, busty Barbara (American), fireman George (Canadian), Ronnie the mad Swede, Kiwi Annie plus Doc Snow, an 80 year old American MD who carefully slid down the easy runs, and others.

The last stop on the run home was a bar cum restaurant called the Crazy Kangaroo, located about sixty metres above the village. It was part owned and run by, naturally, an Australian.

We sometimes visited the Crazy Kangaroo, accessible by taxi, to party at night knowing getting back down the hill was easy. We just fell off a low retaining wall outside the back door, landed in the snow and slid down on our backs, feet in the air, usually giggling drunkenly.

On one such wild night my dual time Rolex wristwatch became detached while sliding home.

Someone suggested trying the police.

I thought it a waste of time but duly filled out a small form at the local Constabulary describing my lost item. Its value was requested, and I nominated a goodly sum, thinking of insurance claims.

'Please wait,' said the policewoman as I handed her the paperwork. In moments she returned with a Rolex.

'Is this your watch?'

'Yes, it is. I'm amazed it was found.'

'That will be 1,500 shillings (A$100) or 10% of the value as reward for the finder. Do you have it with you?'

'Yes, I think so.'

'Good, I will give you a receipt and you can have your watch back.'

No wonder my Rolex was turned in to the cops. It taught me not to inflate insurance claims.

Naturally I tried to get close to the ladies for a holiday romance. I was dating a personable Australian lass, Ingrid from Melbourne, when I stopped to say hello to a young English girl on the piste one day. Mary was friendly and extroverted. We skied down together and she accepted an invitation to meet later. During dinner I learned she was almost ten years younger than I. She was skiing the whole season on a pittance and worked at any available part-time jobs. To minimise costs, Mary slept in a cold, semi-converted barn with rudimentary facilities and several families of mice. We became good friends and had a wonderful time together with our gang.

The Bahnhoff or railway station café was our favourite watering hole. The beer and food was the cheapest in town. One crazy night, I wore shorts, stood on the table and played a digereedoo made from a rolled piece of cardboard. This amused the locals no end.

We always farewelled members of our gang at the Bahnhoff. The departee had to down schnapps until empty glasses placed on top of each other fell over. This practise resulted in the Mad Swede travelling two countries too far in the wrong direction after falling asleep on the express train. I don't remember my farewell – except I did manage to catch my flight out of Zurich.

My last day of skiing that season was magical. The snow and weather were perfect and I managed three runs from Valuga top station, at 3,500 metres, to the village before lunch. I also enjoyed the challenge of the fearsome Schindlerkar run, a slope so steep it wasn't safe to walk down in ski boots. If you fell at the top, a bone breaking descent of over 200 metres followed, a fall could not be stopped. On this run, the icy sides of the moguls stood vertical. I saw one unfortunate male tumble down from halfway. He lay in the snow at the bottom until carted off in a stretcher by the ski patrol.

I sadly left my newfound friends after three weeks and visited London for the first time. Mary saw me off and said she would write. I didn't take her words seriously but my view proved to be quite wrong.

On the flight to Heathrow I chatted up a hostess and subsequently took her out to dinner at the revolving restaurant topping the GPO Tower. The evening was not a success and cost me plenty. Then I caught up with my ex-girlfriend Janice and slept on the floor of her small room in Earls Court. She was nursing in London and engaged to an Englishman whom she subsequently married. After seeing the city sights and no doubt being overcharged by wily locals, I returned to Sydney in February 1968, via Bermuda, Acapulco and Tahiti on a QANTAS flight. I didn't have time to stop off, but thought the pink marble terminal in Acapulco rather decadent.

Just a few days after leaving the cold London winter smog, I found myself working back in steamy Darwin. I was to collect a two passenger

Bell G2 and fly it from Kununurra, W.A., to the Company workshops in Sydney. It would be a slow, weeklong, ferry flight. On-route, I was to stop off at Ayers Rock to fly a filming contract. My machine and its engine were overdue for a complete overhaul but the company had received permission to allow me to continue to fly the helicopter. They knew I could nurse the machine back to Sydney.

A minor cyclone in Darwin delayed my departure, but did not prevent me enjoying some bed-time at the nursing quarters. In the tail of the cyclone I ferried the replacement helicopter to Kununurra where the Company had a rice-spraying contract. Early next morning I set off for Alice Springs in the other, tired machine.

In those days, I believe I was the only helicopter pilot to fly these slow machines direct from Victoria River Downs to Tennant Creek, across the uninhabited northern section of the Tanami desert. This shortcut saved hours of flying time but required a landing in featureless desert to top up the fuel tanks from onboard jerry cans. I also had to stop at the only service station in Elliot where I bought ten gallons (25 litres) of standard petrol. This amount, mixed with the avgas remaining in my tanks, got me to the airport in Tennant Creek. Even with the shortcut, the flight from Kununurra to Tennant took seven hours flying time.

Next day I made the Alice and took my mother and young sister for a short flight - their first helicopter ride. Mother said she was so proud of me and enjoyed the expansive views through the bubble. It was also a thrill for me to land at Connellan's hanger, where I had seen my first chopper. I could remember that day almost ten years before, and how I had dreamed of one day piloting these strange looking beasts.

Next day, I flew my machine to Uluru, or Ayers Rock, as it was then known. I parked at the back of the Redline Motel where the film crew were staying. They had flown from Sydney direct to the Alice in a chartered jet. Then continuing to the rock in two Cessna's which were able to cope with the short dirt airstrip.

After dinner, we retired to the bar area where Smithy, who managed the local charter company, bought Beverly a beer and took her away to a private table. She was the slim, dark haired model featuring in our film shoot. I stayed with the group at the bar and watched with amusement to see how Smithy fared. The motel facilities were basic but adequate, quite palatial in comparison to camping out. Considering we were hundreds of kilometers from anywhere, four walls and a tin roof would have been welcome.

Smithy appeared to be working hard on Beverly and bought more beers.

Soon after 9 pm, Bob the director, snapped his fingers and addressed her.

'Bedtime, off we go Bev. Got to have you looking gorgeous tomorrow, OK.'

She dutifully got up and left the room.

'But you can't go just like that,' Smithy said to her retreating figure. 'Christ, I bought her two beers and she just up and left!'

Most of the remaining film crew soon departed.

'That's film stars for you,' I said. I had been around models before and knew it was pointless trying to score with them. They had the world at their feet and when working were at the director's beck and call.

The TV commercial we were to shoot was to be shown worldwide as the 'piece de resistance' for a major multinational company. The aim was to open with a scene showing a silhouette of Ayers Rock on the horizon. Then, less than thirty seconds later, to zoom in to a bikini clad Beverly, listening to a transistor radio while standing alone on top of the rock. I thought it doubtful her radio could have received much apart from hissing short wave programs, but that was not the point. The implication being that the advertised brand of transistor provided entertainment in the most isolated places in the world. It was hoped viewers worldwide would recognize Uluru from the opening shot.

Next morning, having reconnoitered the top of the rock, my first task was to drop off Beverly and Bob on location. They chose to be placed above a feature known as 'the brain', well away from any tourists visiting the cairn at the western end of the monolith. I flew many kilometres to the north before Boris, the cameraman, could capture the full outline of the rock. My old model helicopter, even at its maximum horizontal speed, could not fly from this position to Beverly quickly enough without large gaps in the shoot. I tried every trick to give Boris the film sequence he wanted. Sadly they were not good enough.

'Well,' I said to Boris, 'there is one other way.'

'What's that?'

'How about climbing up high and rapidly dropping down on Beverly?'

'Let's do it.'

I climbed up to 8,000 feet (2,440 meters) while positioning for a run into the prevailing easterly wind. After selecting carburetor heat and rolling the throttle to idle I began a rapid descent at a slow forward speed. On the way down I revved the engine several times to prevent the spark plugs from oiling up. Just when I was about to recover from our rapid descent, the controller in Alice called me to pass on traffic information. With hindsight, I should have told him to stand by, but instead, dutifully listened, which distracted me from the task at hand at a crucial time. I applied full power and pulled the nose up to slow our speed to zero but the rock came up too fast. I saw we could not stop in time so banked left to parallel the slope. Then we hit the ten metre high ridge Beverly was standing on. The right landing gear crumpled, the rotor blades disintegrated on hitting rock, and both Boris and I blacked out. One of the last things I remember before unconsciousness was that the rotor revs were at maximum, vital if the engine was to develop full power and give us maximum lift.

When I awoke, the only sound was the wind whispering. Scrambling out of the cabin, I woke Boris and walked him away from the wreckage. Petrol was dripping from a cracked fuel tank onto a hot exhaust and I was afraid of fire. There was no sign of Beverly or Bob. I found both crouched in a hollow, terrified. No doubt they imagined us both mangled and were very relieved to find us alive. The sound of our impact and breaking rotor blades must have been horrifying. I retrieved the first aid kit from the wreck and attended to Boris' cut shin.

Fortunately the leaking fuel tank did not result in a fire. I recovered the aircraft documentation, while other party members took photographs of the wreck. There was nothing else to do except to grab my water bag, Boris' expensive camera, and begin walking off the rock. Our walky-talky had been in the helicopter; now it didn't work.

The distance to the tourist cairn was not great but a continuous series of ridges up to fifteen metres high along our path made for strenuous climbs and descents.

After about forty five minutes we reached the cairn and the marked trail down to the plain below. It was a relief after the seemingly endless rows of ridges we had traversed. At about this time Smithy flew over, saw us, and we pointed towards the wreck. He reported the crash to Alice Springs Air Traffic Control.

The local radio station soon heard the news and broadcast that everyone in the helicopter was deceased. Fortunately, Mother did not hear this early transmission.

The midday sun heated the rock and when Beverly's flimsy sandals gave up, her feet were slowly cooked. Although her bikini was covered with a brief shift, her arms and legs became sunburnt. Boris also suffered discomfort from his cut shin. Our only salvation was to clamber down.

I encouraged and helped as much as possible, knowing how dangerous the descent could be. There were no handrails to grasp on the steep sections then.

It was a slow journey with the others probably suffering shock. The descent did not bother me, I had done it twice before.

Eventually, everybody collapsed into a waiting bus. At some point, we all received a stern lecture from the park ranger for not checking in with him on arrival. To emphasize his authority, he threatened to fine me $500 for hurling missiles and a further $500 for littering.

Beverly and Bob returned to the motel while Boris and I were transported to the Alice Springs hospital in the flying doctor aircraft. After being examined, I went home to my relieved family while Boris was held for observation.

I had to complete an accident report for the authorities and as per company policy, refused to make any statement to the press. An erroneous account of the crash appeared on the front page of some national and the local newspapers.

Two days after the event, Connellan Airways chief pilot flew Stan Cooper, from the Aviation Authority, and myself to the Rock to investigate the crash site. I climbed the rock for the third time.

At the crash site, I searched for clues to determine why it all went wrong. The wind was blowing much the same as the day we filmed and I noted it produced roll turbulence in the area of my approach. Using a handkerchief, I saw that during gusts, the wind direction could change almost 180 degrees while producing significant downdrafts. Straight away I was sure of what had caused our downfall. To my mind, three factors had crucially aligned. These were:

1. The radio call which delayed my recovery from a high rate of descent

2. The headwind changing to a tailwind accompanied by a downdraft

3. The engine not achieving full power, due to being overdue for overhaul.

This knowledge made me feel better; knowing I had been dealt a cruel hand. It was a hard lesson and one I have never forgotten. Thankfully my angel had saved me from injury.

This accident would be the first and only time I knowingly damaged an aircraft in forty years of flying.

Once Stan completed his investigation, we collected the aircraft radios and flew back to the Alice. Am I the only person ever to have walked up the Rock three times and down four? Sometimes I wonder if I will forever be known as the only person to crash onto Uluru? This unflattering record may stand, because the only flights allowed close to the rock, or permitted to land there now are for medical evacuations, training for this contingency or possibly if for a resulting cultural benefit.

Next day I saw Boris off to Sydney and then I joined the boss's Beech Bonanza on its way to Mascot. More paperwork was required at head office but in those days I didn't even have to do a post accident medical or flight check.

I was surprised when Bryce Killen, our Chairman of the Board, invited all participants in the crash to his luxurious offices on the 20th floor of a building in Australia Square, in the heart of Sydney, for pre lunch drinks. It was a festive occasion, we were glad to be alive and enjoying life in swinging Sydney town.

'Phil,' Bryce said to me, 'why don't you take these good people to lunch at the Summit. Here's my credit card, use it to settle the bill.'

'That is very good of you.'

'Just order whatever you want, don't worry about the cost.'

The first Summit restaurant, near Circular Quay, was reputed to be one of Sydney's best. We certainly enjoyed superb food and wines before reluctantly leaving in mid afternoon.

A few weeks later Beverly sold her story to the Woman's Weekly and I appeared in a photo next to the wreckage on page three. The accompanying article stretched credibility but I suppose artistic licence was applied to make it a good read. I heard that someone in our party also sold pictures of the event to Time/Life.

My boss was happy too. I had written off an old helicopter on which he received a full insurance payout. The wrecked machine was later lifted off the rock by one of the Company's large helicopters and rebuilt. The engineers told me it was the worst bent Bell 47 airframe among the many they had seen. Over time, it was rebuilt, and flew again.

After several weeks recuperating in Sydney, it was back to working in the Darwin area, this time for Water Resources. Notwithstanding my misadventure, I was not apprehensive about this routine task. I flew Dave to service the Department's water recorders in Arnhem Land, between Darwin and Borroloola. Our transport was another Bell 3-seater helicopter, with several days' food supply and camping gear strapped to litters on both sides.

After leaving Darwin our route took us over virtually uninhabited areas. Radio contact could be maintained with the outside world but apart from that we were on our own. Fuel for these inspection flights was previously positioned on a few tracks in the area.

The water level recording towers were situated on major rivers or flood plains. Our trip was before the beginning of the wet season so the recorders were easily accessible. In contrast, during the wet, helicopters wore floats and we often had to land in deep water. It was necessary for the technician to swim to the tower towing his tools and spare batteries on a float. Then do battle with the many poisonous water snakes that slept in the tower, before beginning work.

We didn't carry sea anchors so always stayed with the machine when floating as a breeze could push us to a tree lined shore. Starting required a clear space as the helicopter spun uncontrollably up to four times before the tail rotor could stop the rotation. Water didn't provide enough friction to counter the reaction to increasing the main and tail rotor revs. Even with prior briefing, this out of control spinning always startled passengers initially.

On our safari, well before dark we found a suitable camping spot next to a lagoon, first ensuring no crocodiles or tracks were visible. Then it was time to catch our dinner; a decent barramundi was always landed within a few minutes of our lure hitting the water. These inaccessible lagoons may never have been fished before by whites, but there was little point in catching more than we could eat. Potatoes baked in the campfire and tinned vegetables accompanied our catch, leaving us feeling at peace with the world and ready for bed.

One night I was woken by a strange snuffling sound outside the mosquito net. Lying still as my eyes focussed in the dim light, I saw a pair of horns above the end of my stretcher. These wickedly pointed, scythe-like appendages stretched far wider than my bed. Behind them loomed a ton of buffalo. I soon realised the beast was sniffing my toes through the mosquito net. I lay motionless and watched, unperturbed. Contrary to popular myth, I knew these creatures were harmless unless defending their calves, or were otherwise provoked. After a few minutes, curiosity satisfied, the large creature quietly left my bedside and I slept undisturbed.

We completed our task and after overnighting at Borroloola, flew to Katherine. My task there was to fly construction materials to the water recording station in the Katherine Gorge. I moved the gear from the end of the road direct to the site. It was a scenic job and before the days of tourist boats, so I flew at a low height for the short flights.

During this shuttling I noticed a vehicle arrive and park by the river. Two couples appeared and admired the scenery. Later, the vehicle departed leaving the two ladies behind.

Completing my task, I flew back to Katherine along the road and noticed the girls walking back to town. The day was warm and their trek would have been exhausting, possibly dangerous, as they seemed to carry no water. The girls still had over twenty kilometres to walk, so, being a considerate chap, I landed on the road. Leaving my machine and strolling towards them, I instinctively grabbed for a cigarette. Then, reaching the girls, I politely proffered the open pack.

Immediately, both doubled up with laughter, unable to speak.

Hello, I thought, what have we here - a pair of loonies? Is this why the men left them?

'Is anything wrong?' I asked.

Recovering, one said, 'Are you the Marlboro man?'

'No. Who is he?'

'Haven't you seen the TV ad where he gets out of a chopper and offers somebody a Marlboro? We can't believe this has happened to us out here in the boondocks!'

'No I haven't seen the ad, and sorry, although I smoke them, I am not the Marlboro man. But I can give you a lift back to town.'

'That would be marvellous, it's getting bloody hot.'

The girls enjoyed the chopper ride and I enjoyed spending that evening with them as well.

On another occasion I was flying alone between two isolated towns in outback western Queensland. Following the road was always a good idea in case we had a problem. Seeing a female standing on an isolated stretch, I presumed she was waiting to hitch a ride. Naturally I landed and offered her one. They never refused a lift, and another friendship was made. It was all too easy to pick up girls.

In the late '60's the search for different base metals seemed to change almost as quickly as fashions, now the rush was to find uranium. One problem is that uranium is not visible like copper or iron. An instrument, such as a scintilometer, is needed to find traces of radioactivity, possibly indicating the presence of that valuable metal. I happened to fly one of the early, airborne scintilometers over an area east of Darwin. While this new technology device was being fitted to my helicopter I learned it contained a large man-made crystal, worth many times my annual salary. In the event of a problem - for example the engine stopping - resulting in a crash landing, the most important item aboard was that crystal. In practical terms, it could not be replaced. Whereas, it was inferred, the helicopter and the two of us could be. Good to know where one stands in the scheme of things.

Soon after reaching the search area our expensive box came alive and then went back to sleep. We continued and the same thing happened again. Then I twigged – it was my H. F. radio calls that set it off. Nothing else did and I was happy to say goodbye to that crystal next day.

In August 1968 I began my first overseas posting as a pilot flying for C.R.A. (Con-zinc Rio of Australia, now Rio Tinto). I was based at their camp on the East Coast of Bougainville Island, in PNG. I had agreed to do a six-month tour of duty, take leave, then work another three-month period. I also agreed to maintain the helicopter on my weekly pilot's day off. For saving an engineer's salary I was paid an additional miserly sum of $40 per month on top of my annual salary of roughly $5000.

It made sense to give up my flat in Sydney and park my stuff with friends, being away for almost a year. Temporary homes and cars could be rented when in Australia.

Bougainville was peaceful in that pre-mining period and the nearby town of Kieta was a sleepy backwater. A primitive port and airstrip were the major infrastructure. In an interesting twist, a Japanese WW II submarine had been stripped internally and was used as a bulk fuel tanker. The sub's inside was filled with fuel so it just floated, then a tugboat towed it from the busy port of Rabaul to Kieta.

A large helicopter lay on its side next to our helipad near town, which faced Arawa Bay. The wreck did not inspire confidence in visitors about to fly with me. This Sikorsky S58 had been backed into the hanger structure in flight. Its tail rotor flew off and the S58 spun, rolled over, and beat itself to death. I stripped the remaining useful bits off the wreck, attached an old rope, and my two passenger Bell G3-B1 just managed to lift the cabin section of the larger machine into the air. It gave me great pleasure to deliberately drop this load to its final resting place in the middle of the bay. I was told it greatly improved the fishing.

I soon became acquainted with most aspects of the construction plans for this billion-dollar mine. Defining the orebody was ongoing work but major de-forestation, road works, a new port facility and town site had to be planned and land acquired. I was the tour guide for engineers and scientists from all over the world and could usually answer their queries as we flew around the area.

Sir Maurice Mawby, the Managing Director of CRA, was a regular passenger. I also took his wife and daughter to Buka to buy the villagers' famed baskets. Returning, we resembled a market stall, many baskets being tied securely outside with the inside of the bubble already packed full.

My accommodation was a small one room detached hut standing on metre high stilts and constructed of local wooden materials. Special roofing leaves folded around sturdy sticks kept the tropical rain out perfectly. But on a dry day, if a gust of wind blew up the roof slope, the leaves and mounting sticks pivoted upward and much blue sky appeared before the leaves fell down.

Bougainville Island is on the Pacific Ring of Fire, an area of active volcanism, and shook regularly. It was also home to one active volcano and another that steamed quietly out of a small vent. It was common place to see my coffee climbing the sides of a cup sitting on the bedside table. We paid no heed to tremors, while these occurred regularly a major shake was unlikely.

I was very kindly invited to share lunch with an Australian family in Kieta on Christmas Day, 1968. I am still mortified to think that I forgot to take them a present and was too embarrassed to make amends later.

Most expats working on/off schedules returned to Australia for leave. Some men elected to relax in a native village not far from Rabaul, where a baby farm had been set up. I was surprised to hear the reason for this venture.

The tribe involved was known as the smartest in the area, to the extent of not being challenged in warfare as they defeated everyone. The clever tribe members noticed that white men must have been even smarter. Whites had guns, vehicles, aircraft and much cargo of every kind. The story goes that the wise men reasoned a white skin was needed to find the secret to possession of all this cargo. Their radical new approach resulted in a baby farm being set up as the first step. I doubt the females involved had any say in this decision. Returning visitors told me that young attractive girls were provided for enjoyment, primarily to be impregnated. Everything apart from alcohol was free. The men I spoke to, returning from their local leave, grinned from ear to ear. They said the girls also enjoyed the indolent lifestyle as opposed to toiling in the family garden. Since the war in Bougainville, it seems one result of this experiment required the redskins, as the mixed race people were called, to return to their own island.

One day a drilling crew told me not to pick them up, saying they'd walk home from their jungle pad. That decision was regrettable, one perished on the half-kilometre stroll. Crossing a stream on the way home, a large tree crashed down, close to their trail. Two of three drillers chose to jump forward, one stepped back. The latter was hit by the falling tree and pinned down in less than thirty centimetres of water. His mates were unable to save him from drowning despite frantic efforts; the tree was too heavy to move.

It made me question why he was meant to die in this freakish manner. I had faced difficult odds and braved threatening elements many times and survived. Did I have a superior angel? Was my number still to come up? The ebb and flow of life-giving, subtle and raw energy in the universe holds many mysteries.

Soon after this accident, I jumped into the helicopter and started the engine but the rotor blades didn't turn. Something was horribly wrong. Investigation showed that the engine and transmission were full of metal bits – something in the transmission had broken and caused it to jam. Moments before, I had been flying over thick jungle. Such are the twists of 'fate'; my angel had saved me again.

A crane carried my machine into CRA's workshop and I found myself working amid heavy machinery. I was the butt of good-natured humour and great interest was shown on aircraft maintenance practices when I disclosed my past qualifications. Later, with some help, I built a makeshift hanger on our new mine-site helipad so I could service my machine when it was raining.

With a large workforce of single males the half dozen females on site had a large choice of company. One evening a female tried to arouse my passion but I pretended to be asleep because of drinking too much beer. She was obviously after me as a husband and getting pregnant was the first step. I avoided giving her the option of feeling rejected. After that she backed off, for reasons only known to her.

I was surprised when Mary wrote to me and we began corresponding regularly. I thought we had just enjoyed a holiday romance. As males often are, I was wrong. She decided to fly out to Australia, arriving in March 1968. I was looking forward to her arrival so did not get involved elsewhere.

A moment's loss of concentration on my last day before leave, almost caused me to crash and roll the machine into a ball. I recovered just in time. It was a sobering finale before handing over to another pilot.

Having worked for six months with hardly a day off, the flight to Sydney was like escaping from jail. Then Mary arrived and I showed her around Sydney. She had her first experience of the traditional Australian lavatory situated in the back yard at one older home where we stayed with friends. The 'dunny' housed the usual compliment of red-back spiders which didn't impress.

I took her to meet my parents and friends in Adelaide and quizzed one close mate about her suitability as a wife. I was ready to choose a partner at the ripe old age of 32. Many of my friends and colleagues had ten year old children. Mother was bemoaning the lack of grandchildren. Social pressure was mounting.

Seeking to impress, I took Mary flying in the Company Bonanza that had just been quickly serviced. After queuing behind heavy jets at Mascot we took off and immediately the radios failed. I followed procedure and flew out of the area to Hoxton Park, at that time, a quiet airfield to the west of Sydney. I managed to get the radios working again, and proceeded to practice circuits. After a few landings and takeoffs, the undercarriage stuck halfway. Mary was not amused when told she might have to turn the small emergency handle fifty times to get our wheels down. Fortunately the undercarriage went down and locked normally but it was time to give up and have the aircraft checked before anything worse happened. Then, while taxiing off the runway, one brake failed. I could only turn sharply to the left and the parking area was uphill on the right. We described a few circles before managing to leave the runway, park, and phone for an earthbound lift home. A bystander probably thought I was intoxicated.

I was under the influence of having an attractive, personable lady constantly in attendance. Permanency in a partner began to seem an attractive proposition and I was beginning to feel some of the emotion I had totally suppressed after my enforced parting from Pamela. I felt I could let a woman into my psyche again.

My departure was a tearful event; I still had another three-month stint to complete in Bougainville as part of my agreement. Mary found employment in the ski fields while I was away.

Back in Kieta we now had two machines flying for CRA. I also had an assistant to help me with maintenance. His name was Rick Howell. He later completed his flying training and flew the ABC news helicopter for many years.

Tony Karas also joined me and I showed him around. He was an experienced pilot, but new to the area. I was not to know that sixteen years later he would be my employer.

Sir Maurice flew up with his retinue and as usual we collected them from the airstrip. I got into the mine site camp with Sir Maurice, while

Tony was stuck on the other side of the range, due to cloud covering the mountains. Unfortunately his passengers had to resort to an arduous road journey. Tony was astounded that I had made it to the mine-site. I used my local knowledge - a detailed three-dimensional map in my head, knowing which 'tunnel' below the clouds to enter, among the dozens of seemingly alike steep green valleys heading inland. And being certain of the way to turn at forks in the gorges to avoid hitting a dead end.

I also enjoyed the advantage of maintaining my own machine, knowing its every nuance, both on the ground and in the air, like a finely tuned instrument. Aircraft are called 'she' for good reasons as they have distinct personalities and often respond differently to different pilots. Helicopters particularly so, having many more moving parts requiring careful adjustment to ensure smooth flight. Although, I feel, with modern technology some stiff wings are so boring and alike, perhaps the masculine gender could be applied.

The scale of the future mine in Bougainville was brought home to me when chatting with senior managers. It was mentioned that only two people in the world were known to have the skills and experience to bring this mega project into successful production. One would have to be headhunted, whatever the cost.

I would not be there to see the mining begin, it was time to go after nine months on the job. Rick and I left on the same flight, finding only one room available at the solitary hotel in Rabaul. We had to share a double bed. However, had that bed contained a land mine in the middle, neither if us would have been in danger.

Once back in Sydney I proposed marriage and Mary accepted. We celebrated this major event by joining our friends at 'my' lodge in Thredbo. It was fitting, having first met in the snow. After only three weeks off, I went back to work in the Kimberley. Our parting was again very emotional; we had made a commitment to each other.

The uranium boom was still on. Again we searched for invisible ore but now the geologists carried hand-held scintilometres. This job was a first for me in that I had a helicopter and the Company Beech Bonanza to fly, while maintaining both. The Bonanza was used for collecting our supplies from Darwin.

After a long hot day, while flying home, one of the geologists suddenly pointed and said, 'Phil, can we land on that large outcrop below?'

'I'm sure we can.'

It proved to be a massive hill of iron ore. Because the geologists were after an invisible mineral, the iron ore-body had not registered previously

184

although we had flown over it many times. In most developed countries, finding such high-grade ore would have been hailed a great commercial success. In the isolated, roadless Kimberley, it was only of academic interest. Australia is very fortunate in containing so many natural resources.

After three weeks I had to officially stop flying, I was on the legal monthly limit. Not one to just sit around a bush camp, I noticed that a large Caterpillar bulldozer was idle.

'Hey Fred, you got something for me to do with the D7?'

'Sure, can you drive it?'

'No problem.'

'Well, we need some ground cleared and leveled for drill sites.'

'Great, I'll have a go at that.'

For over a week I played with another 'toy'. I flew the short distance to the drill sites and started the dozer while my chopper was idling for five minutes to cool the turbo. After shutting down my aircraft, the dozer had warmed up and I started ripping boulders and pushing dirt. The reverse procedure applied at the end of the day. The field crew were most impressed. They said it was the first time they had seen a pilot maintain his own aircraft, let alone work a dozer. It was a great job, rarely a moment of boredom. On my official day off I flew several of us to a nearby pristine river where we swam and caught fish.

After seven weeks away, I enjoyed a two week break with Mary. As a treat, I rented a Halvorsen thirty foot (9m) cruiser on the Hawkesbury River for a week. This luxury vessel could sleep six but we were the only occupants.

With appropriate supplies on board we set off up river to enjoy a week of cruising. Halvorsen's private buoys along the rivers' reaches ensured mooring without fear of the anchor dragging overnight.

After some days the ice in the cooler melted so we docked at Wisemans Ferry for supplies. Carrying a new block of ice aboard, it slid out of my cold hands, heading for the river below. I lunged to recapture it, but in the process my backside went through a plate glass cabin window behind me. My rear end suffered no damage but sharp broken glass shards had spread throughout the cabin and were very tedious to clean up. Fortunately it didn't rain so the missing window caused no problems.

When I handed the luxury cruiser back after our glorious, secluded time on the water, the bill for the smashed window cost me $50 as opposed to a dollar for a block of ice.

Too soon, my next tour saw me in Darwin again. The nursing quarters did not see me this time. My initial task was learning to operate my first turbine engined helicopter - a four passenger Bell 206A. I had previously turned down that opportunity as the early engines fitted were unreliable and many failed in flight. First I completed a generic turbine engine course in Sydney. Another exam was required to operate the engine in the aircraft. The company wished me to complete a much longer engineering course. I refused. It was becoming too specialised for me to properly maintain these new engines, in addition to flying full-time. I wished to leave my toolbox at home, though over the years I came to know many turbine engines almost as well as the people who maintained them. I wished to help my angel as much as possible by recognizing problems before they tried to kill me.

The great advantage of turbines was their greater power output for less engine weight. The disadvantages were the high initial cost; greater fuel consumption and difficulty in starting due to the large amount of energy required to spin them up before lighting their fire. They made the pilot's life much easier because the engine governor kept the rotor speed correct without the pilot having to carefully manipulate the throttle. However, most early turbines fitted to helicopters could be burned out during a starting attempt, or almost destroyed by a pilot demanding excessive power. As usual with any machinery, increased complication and automation usually meant different problems arising.

With my flying training complete, I traveled to Broome by airline. Another B 206 A needed ferrying to the opposite side of Australia – to our offshore operations based in Sale, Victoria. This time I had a machine that cruised at 185 kilometres per hour through the air, almost double the speed of my previous mounts.

After traversing over 1,600 kilometres of arid inland Western Australia I began the boring 1,200 kilometre flight across the Nullarbor Plain. A few hundred kilometres north west of Ceduna I landed in the middle of nowhere to refuel from jerry cans. On restarting, the engine didn't respond to the throttle and immediately oversped uncontrollably. It had to be shut down. I tried starting again, with the same result.

Now I faced a serious dilemma The battery likely only provided one more starting attempt. If that proved unsuccessful, a search would be necessary to find me in the flat, featureless terrain. Nowadays, using the Global Positioning System (GPS) it's a snap, but back then, a rescue mission could have taken days and incurred great expense.

I readied the cockpit, myself , and began another start. I was prepared to become airborne to load the engine and possibly prevent the overspeed, just a few seconds after releasing the starter. I didn't know if this would work and had to be ready for the engine dying while becoming airborne. It was a calculated risk, I hoped the engine would behave normally if I did get into the air, otherwise I'd have to switch it off and land without power. In the worst case, I could easily roll the chopper over while trying to do everything at once.

As the engine roared and the revs raced toward the red line I pulled pitch and we became airborne. The revs stabilised; I flew off and gained a safe height before tidying up the cockpit.

Over an hour later I heaved a sigh of relief as Ceduna airport came into view. My problems weren't over yet; I couldn't land normally due to the engine overspeeding and so had to turn it off to get down to earth. I knew allowing the engine to overspeed uncontrollably could result in its destruction and shedding of my rotor blades. Pilots train for these situations but this was the only time I have ever had to completely shut down the engine so I could regain terra firma. I was able to do this while hovering just above the ground in the parking area, so it was not a difficult task to flutter gently to the ground.

Many people are not aware that if a helicopter's single engine stops, immediate correct action by the pilot results in a controlled, steep glide to earth. Washing off the forward speed and using the inertia in the spinning rotor blades results in a soft landing if the tricky manoeuvre is correctly performed. Practise is the key to getting it right every time.

A new engine fuel control solved my problem and after overnighting in Adelaide my brother Peter came along for the ride to Melbourne.

Mary was not happy about my long absences as she had few friends in Australia. I had no option as base jobs were reserved for senior pilots and I was still earning my spurs.

A few weeks after the ferry trip, I found myself on the mainland in New Guinea, at Wewak. I was flying a two passenger Bell for a survey team at Frieda River searching for copper. One of our engineers, Barry, flew out with me. We were laden with camp supplies for this two hour plus flight. It was totally new territory for me, so I constantly referred to my map. About half an hour out, the map perched on my left knee, blew out of the window. In outback Australia this is not necessarily a problem as we circle to see where it lands, do likewise and retrieve it. I had no chance here with solid jungle below. What to do? We were urgently required back at camp, it was mid afternoon and to turn back would mean most of another day lost.

'Barry, you've been at the camp for weeks, can you direct me to it?'

'Sure, no problem.'

'You reckon we can find it okay?'

'Yeah, yeah, let's carry on.'

We found Ambunti on the wide, muddy, Sepik River without trouble, and after refueling continued upriver. Large storm clouds sat on the 3,500 metre high mountain range which stretches for hundreds of kilometers along the central spine of the country. Clouds also obscured the many valleys leading down to flat country and lightning could be seen flashing in the dark clouds ahead. We needed to find the correct valley, our camp was located some distance along it, in steep foothills leading up to the main range. I began to feel apprehensive as fading light, coupled with worsening weather and not knowing where we were, caused my stomach to knot. After flying for more than an hour over dense jungle and passing many entrances to the high mountains, Barry said 'It's up that valley on the left.'

'Good, I was hoping you'd see it soon.'

Ten minutes later he said, 'Sorry Phil, I don't think we've got the right one, must be the next valley.'

We retraced our route and continued flying west to the next entrance into the cloud shrouded mountains. My heart was sinking as quickly as the fuel gauge.

'See the camp yet?' I asked, controlling my rising fear.

'No, it's not this valley either.'

What a situation! I had relied on another person and consequently we were lost with solid jungle below, storm clouds ahead, low on fuel and limited daylight. My mouth was dry with tension and my knuckles were white on the controls.

'Barry, this is getting serious. You better think carefully about recognising the correct valley entrance. So far I haven't even seen anywhere to land when it gets dark, let alone if we run out of fuel.'

Barry sighed and knitted his brow in concentration.

'I'm quite sure we haven't passed our valley yet so it must still be ahead. The one we are coming to now looks like it.'

'I doubt we have enough fuel to check any more after this. Let's just hope there is somewhere to land safely if it's not the right one. I don't fancy having to fall into the tall timber around here. And you know we can't give anybody an accurate position if they have to look for us.'

He knew how vital this information was. At that time, most crashed aircraft were not found for days, weeks, or sometimes never, unless the location was known or survivors walked out. The jungle simply swallowed them up. Locator beacons in small aircraft would only be introduced years later.

The minutes crawled by in tense silence as we entered another steep sided valley. There was nothing left to say. We could both see the fuel gauge hovering over empty in the dim light under the dark solid overcast.

'This looks familiar, keep going Phil.' Barry leaned forward, as if to get a better view.

'This is it, see the track down to the river. That's where we collect supplies from the canoes when the river level is low. The camp should be another few miles up on the right.'

Soon we saw smoke from a fire. At least someone was in the unending greenery below.

'The camp,' Barry squealed, 'up there on the right. See it?'

'Yes, thank heavens.'

After landing, I dipped the fuel tanks. Less than five minutes of fuel remained.

It was another near miss and taught me to be extremely sceptical of other people's well meaning assurances, especially if it could affect my livelihood or health. It was my life and license at stake. I figured if I kept myself alive, then my passengers should survive, even if I ignored their advice.

Apart from the search for copper, another major project was taking place not far from our camp. An airstrip was being constructed in dense jungle next to the river, using only local labour and hand tools. I was told the original preferred alignment had to be changed due to one massive hardwood tree, which alone could have taken months to demolish by hand. It took thousands of man-hours, using axes and shovels, before several small dozers were shipped in on a specially made barge, after which rapid progress was made. Even so, the 640 metre long strip took several years to construct. It was a common endeavour in the early days in New Guinea where so many places were accessible only by helicopter or walking.

My tour at Frieda was completed at the end of November and I handed over to Alan Guest-Smith. Several years later he would replace me as the resident manager in Fiji.

On returning to Sydney I worked out of Mascot for a week. Mary had already returned to England to arrange our wedding. I paid $3,132 for a new, duty-free Alfa Romeo GTV coupe, to be collected in London, for our use in Europe. After holidaying, we intended to export this car to Fiji as I had applied for, and been awarded, one of the two pilot positions available at the company's new outpost. Many staff sought this posting as it promised working mainly from home. The country's warm climate was another attraction. Mary was ecstatic; I would not be away for long tours. The disadvantages were that I was flying older model helicopters and still being involved with maintenance. Career wise, it was a step up, being second in charge of operations in the country.

In mid-December 1969, I stopped off in Fiji on my way to England to obtain a local pilot's licence.

Top: *The Ambunti trade store in 1969*
Above: *Typical drillsite pad, PNG*

190

*more from
the album*

Clockwise from top:

*My parents and I admiring
a 11kg cabbage.*

*Our house and front garden,
Hermannsburg.*

*Our house-girl and myself,
taken in1938.*

*Myself in front of our house
at age three.*

Left: *Off to my first job and my first flight.*

Below: *Wearing my Air Force uniform.*

Below left: *My waxed mustache period.*

Right: *My home on Bougainville Island for almost a year.*

Centre: *Myself performing at a CRA mine site concert.*

Bottom: *Some of our St Anton 'gang.' I'm second from the left.*

CHAPTER 10

Good judgement comes from experience. Unfortunately, experience usually comes from bad judgement. ~ *The Aviators Guide Book*

While boarding the B.O.A.C.VC 10 jet at Nandi airport in Fiji, I thought this was the beginning of my new life. My thirty four hour journey was scheduled to arrive at London Heathrow, after landings at Honolulu, Los Angeles and New York. The flight entailed travelling exactly half way around the world and included a six hour stopover in L.A., due to the curfew at Kennedy Airport. During this break, the airline provided free accommodation, but involved the hassle of customs and immigration while entering and leaving America.

Inside the cabin, the hostess said - 'Your seat is right at the back.'

I found myself sitting next to two of the four engines fitted close to the fuselage. Soon, an attractive young lady arrived and took the seat next to mine.

'I guess you're travelling sub-load as well' she said. 'They always put us next to the engines.'

In the days before discounted fares, subject to load (sub-load), stand-by fares were available to airline and associated companies employees at varying discount rates and priorities. In my case, I only paid 25% of the economy fare.

After take-off, drinks arrived and we chatted amicably for much of the long flight across the Pacific Ocean. She was an American, a hostess with one of the airlines there. I sensed she was making a discrete play for me.

'Phil,' I've still got a week's leave. Why don't y'all get off in L.A. and I'll show you the sights. There's plenty of room for you to stay in my apartment.'

'I don't think my fiancé would be too impressed if I did that. I have to spend three weeks in England prior to our wedding or they won't issue a marriage certificate. It's something to do with Pom's marrying a foreigner like me; it can't happen at short notice. I'll just make the three weeks

more from the album

Top: *My crash on Ayers Rock (Uluru). Boris is wearing a black shirt.*
Below: *Our rented house in Kota Kinabalu, Gavin in the foreground. Our shared boat at an uninhabited island with Mt Kinabalu in the background.*

Top: *Our overnight huts on Mt Kinabalu, middle left of picture.*

Centre: *Up 4100 metres on my legs, instead of pulling a lever to get there!*

Below, left to right: *The back patio at our first Singapore house, in Changi. Our house inside Seletar airport grounds, showing the added platypus racing patio.*

Top: *Gavin, our dog and car in front of our Rochester Park ex Colonel's quarters.*

Centre: *Our pool at Rochester Park, viewed from the upstairs balcony.*

Below left: *Gavin in front of our townhouse in Cheltenham, England*

Below right: *Our pet Sumatran owl in his quarters above the bar in the 'House Wind,' inside Shell's compound near Pallembang.*

Top: *The standard clearings made for Parker Drilling's helirig operations, in Central Sumatra.*

Centre: *The rig derrick being assembled after living quarters, tractors in pieces etc were flown in.*

Right: *The famed, illegal, 'Dance of The Flaming Arseholes' performed by two servicemen above the public toilets at the original Bugis Street, Singapore.*

Above: *WW II fort covering the road through a high mountain pass between France and Italy.*

Above: *The entrance to the Sultans Palace in Kuwait, built with imported sand.* Below: *A normal road scene in a Bengali city or town.*

From the top: *My machine parked, just outside the war zone boundary in the Arabian Gulf.*

In PNG, regular landslides take out main roads for weeks.

Part of a radio tower I positioned on the 3800 metre high Hagen Range.

Above: *One of my friends oil wells, on their property near Fort Worth, Texas*

Top: *Site preparation prior to flying in an oil drilling rig into a typical location, in the Southern Highlands of PNG.*

Centre: *The Mt Kare valley prior to the gold rush.*
The same valley view a few months later.

This page, clockwise from top: *Billowing smoke from the blast I witnessed, after the explosives storage containers at Porgera detonated. A 'little hill,' over 3400 metres high in the Porgera valley, just a few km from the airstrip, town, helipads and mine.*
A typical Huli tribes-man's fancy hairdo – keeps his head dry!

Opposite page from top: *My two-bedroom company house and car in Mt. Hagen, behind the swimming pool – one of three in our guarded compound. The Hagen market where I bought my vegetables.*
The bar named after me on the bow of MV Marella.

This page, from top:
Glowing tons of gold on Rangoon's largest temple dome, in Burma.
People celebrating a young Burmese boy's coming of age in the temple grounds.

Opposite page, clockwise from top: *Positioning PNG soldiers close to the Indonesian border.*
Unloading the Mil at Moro's future airstrip site.
The Russian Kamov Ka 32.
The Mil Mi 26, flying a 16,000 kg underslung load in PNG.

This page, from top: *'Arse Grass' costumes and body paint on display. Village men in the Sepic area wearing penis gourds.*

Opposite page, clockwise from top left: *Tribal costume worn at the Mt Hagen show. A Show 'Belle' displaying multi-coloured Bird of Paradise feathers. Tribes persons with drums at the show.*

Top: *Myself in a flak jacket, next to one of our Cambodia based aircraft.*

Right: *Water filled bomb craters scarring the Cambodian countryside.*

Top: *The family skiing somewhere in Europe.*

Centre: *Myself enjoying time off from nursing Russian crews.*

Right: *Gavin in flight over the town of Verbier, Switzerland.*

Above: *Re-visiting my birthplace after sixty years – the A.I.M. Hostel, next to the John Flynn Church in Alice Springs.*

Below: *The sun leaving our peaceful valley.*

residential requirement as it is, so have to decline your offer.'

'That's too bad. I should have known a nice guy like you would be taken.'

Why didn't I get these offers when I was flying overseas and available. Was the devil tempting me? There was no chance I would accept her invitation, being committed to Mary.

It was a dreary cold winter's morning when I arrived at Heathrow's Terminal three. Mary and Tony, a family friend, collected me and we took the A40 for Cheltenham.

My mother and sister flew over to represent our side of the family. Paul, my squash playing naval surgeon friend from Darwin was my best man, presently working toward his specialist's degree in radiology at a Birmingham hospital.

Our wedding was a church affair with over a hundred guests. I don't know what my mother thought about my marriage to a Church of England lady. Mother was probably just grateful I was getting hitched at last, and to a non-Catholic. Besides, Mary's father was the town's eye specialist so the family must all be 'proper', respectable, people. Mary and I did not much discuss religion though I suppose we thought it good to sanctify births, weddings and deaths.

Having discarded organised faiths, a church wedding was just a formality for me, to be endured for the benefit of the bride. Perhaps also an opportunity for families to make a statement about their social standing. Happily, Mary and her parents had organised the event so I was largely along for the ride. I caught a train to London, returning with our duty free getaway transport.

The usual panic and pandemonium occurred on the day but thankfully the ceremony went off without any problems. The weather was cold but at least it didn't rain.

Mother shed a few tears during the church service. Afterwards, I noticed one guest in full military rig, wearing golden sashes and a dangling sword. In my wildest dreams this bush boy had never imagined getting married wearing a top hat and tails or giving a speech to society people who spoke with an upper class English accent. The British class system still existed but it seemed Australians were tolerated as curiosities. Rolf Harris and friends had seen to that.

After dinner and speeches at an upmarket reception centre, Mary and I departed for London in our new, bright yellow Alfa Romeo coupe. We were exhausted and wanted to get away to a peaceful night at the

Dorchester Hotel in London.

It was a harrowing drive as much of the winding A40 in Gloucestershire was shrouded in thick spooky fog that swirled around the gnarled tree trunks guarding the roadsides. I wouldn't have been surprised to see a ghost or goblin flit through the mist. It was close to midnight when we reached the hotel. I couldn't believe my luck at finding a parking space almost opposite the entrance. We checked in and found our room contained two single beds bolted to the floor.

'Your request for a double bed must have been mislaid,' said the clerk. 'Sorry, we don't have any other rooms available.'

Too tired to make a fuss I went to collect bags from the car. To my amazement I found it unlocked, with the small triangular side window forced open. In a few minutes our car had been broken into and my briefcase stolen. All my traveler's cheques, ferry tickets, driver's and pilot's licences, passport – my identity had gone. Fortunately I had one credit card in my pocket which would keep us afloat.

At one in the morning, on our wedding night, Mary and I sat on single beds providing details to two policemen. They asked why I hadn't used the secure car park under the building.

'I will, now I know it's there!'

'Don't worry Sir,' said one Bobbie. 'We'll have your briefcase back in a few days I'm sure. All they usually take are convertible notes like traveler's cheques and then they throw the bag into the gutter. Someone will bring it to us.'

'I sure hope so.'

'She'll be right mate,' said a cop, trying out his Australian accent. 'You sleep easy now and leave it to us.'

We were too exhausted to do otherwise.

Next day we checked out of our expensive hotel and went looking for a cheap place that accepted credit cards. It seemed the two were mutually exclusive. We eventually found a room next to a noisy boiler and when I sat on the bed, one of its legs fell off. A few London telephone directories sorted out the bed, American Express replaced the traveler's cheques, and our ferry booking to Oostende in Belgium was cancelled. The Alfa garage did a quick fix on the car's jammed window so we were ready to roll if and when my papers were returned.

True to their word, on the third day the police recovered my briefcase. My documents were intact, with only the traveler's cheques missing. It was an enormous relief, we could now begin to relax and enjoy our honeymoon.

The strain of hanging in limbo had not been conducive to romance.

Several days late, we crossed the channel and found the sign posts from the ferry port into and out of Oostende sadly lacking and well hidden. This, combined with driving on the right in a right hand drive vehicle, made for many anxious moments and much horn blowing around us. We kept heading east and hoped. It was a great relief to reach the German autobahn.

We took an exit off the autobahn, but being unsure if it was correct, I parked at the tip of a V junction. While Mary was correlating road signs with maps, a police car arrived, sirens blaring. A large policeman accosted us in a belligerent manner.

'You fools, what are you doing? Here you cannot park!' he said, speaking loudly in German.

'I'm sorry, we can't understand you,' I lied - we could both speak German - while pointing at the map. 'How do we get to Austria?'

'Eenglees dumkopf. To Austria,' he said and pointed to the right, 'You go, schnell!'

We did, amazed at how speedily the law had arrived.

We crossed the Alps, reaching St Anton late in the afternoon. It was like a homecoming as many of our gang were on the streets. Invitations to three parties that night followed, before reaching Herr Schmidt's pension – cheap B & B accommodation – where we were booked to stay for almost a month.

'Wilcommen, aber Sie sindt ganz spaet.' (welcome, but aren't you a little late) said a beaming Herr Schmidt. He did not speak English.

'Ya, wie hatten ein kleiner problem.' (we had a small problem) The explanation followed as he accepted us into the household again.

We settled into a hard skiing and partying routine with our friends.

My mother and sister flew to Austria on their way home and spent a few days in Innsbruck. We drove there and joined them. The twisting, narrow road clung to one side of a steep valley and afforded spectacular views. I missed most of it as my eyes were firmly on the bitumen avoiding ice. A skid on this menace could result in us crashing hundreds of metres into the freezing river below.

We took my family to a nearby ski resort. My sister enrolled into a beginners ski school. Mother watched, reveling in the cosmopolitan atmosphere, poodles and all, while talking her head off in German. Mary and I skied on what had been a winter Olympics downhill run and were not impressed - it was nowhere near as challenging as various ones we enjoyed at St Anton.

My family left to continue their European adventure while we drove to Liechtenstein to ski with some other Australian friends.

With three weeks of skiing over, I discovered the wheels of the Alfa were frozen into an ice-block on the ground. Much swearing, chipping of ice and boiling water eventually freed our transport. Due to heavy snowfalls, the Fern Pass, our shortest route out of Austria, was only open to vehicles equipped with chains. We didn't have these for our fast sporty car as chains damage radial tyres. An alternative was to fit snow tyres, an expensive exercise just for this trip. We decided to try the Fern Pass regardless and hoped that a costly rescue would not be necessary. Being foreigners, perhaps we could plead ignorance if becoming stuck.

I drove with intense concentration heading up the mountain, ready to execute a 180-degree spin at any time if traction was lost. I used the handbrake several times to prevent one rear wheel spinning, to maintain upward momentum. We were skating on thin ice. I avoided looking at the deep snowdrifts lining the narrow, snow-ploughed strip of road. Sliding into one of those would undoubtedly mean missing our ferry.

Getting over that pass was one of my most anxious drives. What a relief to begin heading downhill. Once back on the German autobahn, I drove 544 kilometres in four hours, including a stop for fuel and coffee. Travelling at 160 kilometres per hour was comfortable, yet other vehicles still passed us, including trucks with trailers.

While boarding the ferry we learned that severe sea conditions existed for our crossing to Dover. Neither of us suffered from motion sickness so we weren't bothered.

After leaving the sheltered harbour people began throwing up. We decided to have a decent meal on board to celebrate the end of our skiing holiday. The dining room was deserted.

'Can you serve a meal with the ship pitching and rolling like this?' I asked a waiter.

'Certainly Sir, I'll bring you a menu.'

We both chose to have steak, not having eaten any in Austria. It was too expensive as European cattle have to be hand fed and housed during long winter months.

'Be careful or your plates could slide off the table,' said the waiter as he placed our meals on the white linen tablecloth.

'Don't worry, we won't let them get away. Haven't had steak for ages.'

The meat was tender, tasty and soon disappeared. Without warning, Mary threw up. Her meal reappeared, this time all over the white linen cloth.

'Oh dear, are you all right?'

'Damn, I enjoyed that steak. Think I need a glass of water.'

The waiter was sympathetic and said it had happened before.

'Any refund for returning the meal?' I joked.

'Sorry Sir, you have to send it back before it's eaten.'

We spent four extra hours at sea. It was too rough for the ferry to berth. Eventually, gray and haggard passengers were thankful to wobble ashore. I had enjoyed the wildness of the wind and waves; at least it was not a boring, routine voyage.

In just a few days we boarded a flight to Sydney to prepare for our posting in Fiji. I was looking forward to the new experience of having a wife to come home to. On my stopover in Fiji, I had noted that our new Alfa could not be properly maintained there and would soon rust away on the coral based dirt roads. Reluctantly, it was left behind to be sold.

It was early February, 1970, when we landed in Sydney. Before even packing a shirt, I was sent to Alice Springs to fly a four passenger Bell Jetranger on a nickel survey for a large Australian mining company.

It was a shock to move from the below freezing temperatures of Europe, to century (38°C) plus heat at the Alice, in just a few days. Another surprise appeared in the form of a shapely young female geologist sent out from head office to participate in outback fieldwork.

At the time, females were never seen in bush survey camps as no separate facilities existed for them - feminism and affirmative action were yet to arrive. It was decided that Josie would only participate in day trips from the Alice, complete with the luxury of hotel provided lunch boxes.

We spent a few days fiddling around the Aileron area with Josie and others before she was dispatched back to her desk at Head Office. Serious work east of the Alice could now begin.

Our base was Ross River Station. Every morning I dropped off geologists at particular locations in the hot, shimmering, dry desert. They spent the day searching for possible sources of nickel mineralisation before I collected them at different, predetermined spots in the evening. This was common practice on geological explorations. I needed a good memory not to lose people as most maps of desert areas were totally inadequate references in those days. Nowadays it's so easy - punching the GPS receiver stores exact locations.

Surveys in desert areas were not normally conducted in summer due to the increased danger of working outdoors in extreme temperatures.

There were no service stations or mobile phones to ring for help. I remember reading of several tourists vehicle becoming stuck in the sand on the road to Ayers Rock and being found dead soon after. The isolation and heat seemingly drove them mad. But this summer, nickel ruled the markets and nothing would stop the frenzied search.

The heat seemed to affect the battery on my machine. To get started in the morning, two Land Rovers were parked close to the choppers nose and connected in series to provide twenty-four volts. This procedure was dicey, but worked. It meant I was not game to shut down my machine away from base.

All was progressing well when a new geologist arrived, direct from an English winter. Mike was a young chap who sweated profusely while sitting still. We had no such luxury as air-conditioning. Notwithstanding, he elected to be dropped off in the morning to do an easy walk down a dry creek bed. That evening, he was not immediately visible at his pick up point, so I collected the other geologists and we returned to search for Mike. Combing his survey route showed no sign of any life. Even the crows were resting, hidden in shade.

The shadows were lengthening, soon a decision was necessary. I would not fly after dark again without adequate equipment and navigation aids being available.

'It's almost time to head home,' I said to the anxious geologists on board, 'You have to decide whether to stay and search or come back with me.'

'Right, understood. We'll have to come back with you, we don't have enough water left to spend a night out.' It was not sensible to put more lives at risk.

I had five litres of emergency water on board but I would not risk using that with the temperature likely to persist above the century well into the night.

While circling the designated pick-up area, and just as I was about to head home somebody said, 'I think I see Mike sitting by that heap of rocks on the left.'

I turned and saw him sitting in shadows, motionless, almost completely camouflaged by the background. We landed, grabbed Mike and dashed for Ross River, arriving just on dark. He was limp and exhausted, having finished his water hours before we found him.

Next day, sufficiently recovered, Mike was bundled onto a southbound plane to head office. His taste of the outback was short but it almost killed him. Had we not seen him at the last moment, a full search would

200

have found his shriveled body next day. Mike had no idea how close to death he came by not trying to attract our attention. Some people think that because they can see a search aircraft, the searchers will automatically see them, and remain motionless. Having been involved in many searches, I know this false assumption has cost lives.

After several weeks another pilot relieved me.

Before being wed, the news that I had been accepted for a permanent posting to Fiji was like the gift of a ticket to heaven. I would be home almost every night, instead of spending months away in an outback camp, somewhere in Australia, without even a phone to call my wife. I was accustomed to being separated from loved ones but it stressed Mary and this affected me. In those days, few helicopter jobs provided the opportunity to be home based. The situation is quite different now, although these positions are still prized.

Fiji was a new area of operations for the company. Rumor had it that the boss went there for a holiday with his ever-present 'secretary.' It seems that at some point she remarked that there were no helicopters and why didn't he do something about it. This tale was fanciful enough to be true.

Our posting was envied by many but I was the only pilot/engineer who wanted the job. To my knowledge there were only three of us in Australia at that time who were licenced to fly and maintain helicopters and fixed wing aircraft. One was my cousin in Adelaide who was with an airline, the other worked for our company but didn't wish to leave his established home. My years of sweat, study and deprivation were paying off. I had proved that when it came to keeping an aircraft flying safely I could think laterally, keep the customer happy and save money. Working as a motor mechanic had taught me to fix components rather than just ordering a replacement, waiting until it arrived and grounding the aircraft in the meantime.

Two aircraft were allocated and shipped to Fiji's capital, Suva. Both were Bell's, one a two passenger 'bubble' type G4. The other, a J2 model where the pilot sat in the middle front of the cockpit, with three passenger seats on a bench behind him.

The late Don Hutton, a mature, senior helicopter pilot, was appointed manager. He had the operation set up when Mary and I arrived in mid March 1970.

In May, Don persuaded his wife Betty to leave their home in New Zealand and visit him. Soon after she arrived Mary and I accompanied them to dinner at a tourist hotel built in the shape of a giant turtle. The large dining room featured a high ceiling and during the first course a gecko fell off and dropped into Betty's soup with a splash. Either the temperature or the taste of the soup was not to the lizard's liking, so it swam out, jumped onto Betty's breast and then ran into her hair. She was unimpressed with this display by the local creatures, left Fiji and never returned.

Perhaps this and our lack of work resulted in Don leaving soon after, with me becoming the boss. Minor events can certainly change people's lives and sometimes the course of history. Don's departure gave me the opportunity to expand my experience and to manage an overseas outpost. I'm still thankful for that small lizard falling off the roof. I was wholly responsible for the success of the operation. If it didn't make money, we would lose our posting. A challenge I was eager to take up.

Initially, another licensed engineer was also based in Fiji. A single American man, Kirk Samsell, was jovial, conscientious, and liked by almost everyone. He loved a drink but never seemed to suffer a hangover. He took to boring holes in the eyes of coconuts, adding strong liquor, then resealing the fruit. These he buried in the communal front garden facing our private beach in the suburb of Lami. If Kirk felt like a nightcap after a night out, he had to dig. Some mornings, our front lawn looked like the beginnings of a construction site.

Kirk was recalled due to lack of work leaving Mary and I on our own. We became a family operation. Marketing, sales, maintenance, spare parts storage; record keeping and flight operations were up to me. Mary was my unpaid personal assistant, answered the company phone, typed and helped me clean the aircraft. If my machine or I had a problem while out in the jungle, I didn't have a local saviour. A rescue pilot would have to travel from Australia unless I was able to walk out and fit to pilot our second chopper. This situation certainly made me careful when flying or maintaining my machines.

The rules imposed by the local aviation authority prevented us from accepting many charters. They were duplications of the British system and completely oriented towards airline type operations. No consideration was made for aircraft that could slow to a stop in the sky, or making flights of less than a minute. We were required to report every landing and takeoff, utterly ridiculous, especially when moving many parts of a mineral drilling rig a few hundred metres. At first I ignored this edict to save time, but soon came to realize I would have to induce a rules change and the sooner the better. On the next rig move over a short distance, I was on the radio almost continuously for an hour and jammed the system completely. The local airline and other operators complained bitterly about disruption to their schedules, so the rule was modified for helicopters.

Having won that round I decided to push for further changes. No allowance was made for us to fly slowly and safely in weather conditions that grounded aeroplanes. Grasping the wasp by its feelers, I asked the aviation authority's number two man to fly with me while the south east monsoon blew low clouds and rain all over the Suva area.

Roger and his wife were social friends, he accepted my invitation to come for a weekend, unofficial flight. The weather at Nausori Airport, our base, was marginal but the tower turned a blind eye and allowed us to takeoff. I had to go for broke if I was to show Roger what helicopters could do. Gradually, I safely broke all the British rules regarding permitted visual flight in bad weather.

Flying toward a solid cloudbank sitting on top of a jungle-covered ridgeline, I saw Roger's knuckles grow whiter as he gripped a metal stay. Coming to a hover just below the cloud and above the trees on top of the ridge, we were able to see that it was safe to slide down the far side. This, and other manoeuvres I demonstrated, were a revelation to Roger. He was a good fellow, but a fair weather, private licensed aeroplane pilot and predominantly office bound. He realized that enforcement of airline procedures in our case was ridiculous. My gamble paid off. I didn't lose my licence for breaking the rules and thereafter we were allowed greater flexibility.

I faced a similar problem on the maintenance side where calendar inspections were required at very short intervals, regardless of the hours flown. Again, slanted to busy airline aircraft but ridiculous for my average flying of twenty-five hours a month. So I kept two sets of books, a mythical, but legal one on local paperwork and another detailing actual inspections to a schedule as approved by the Australian authorities.

The Fijian economy was small and few companies or individuals could afford the high cost of helicopters. We did support an exploration program looking for gold that provided bread and butter income, but I had to be prepared to fly at a moment's notice or alternative transport would be utilized.

One day my task was to fly a businessman to a tourist development construction site. We flew along the coast, west of Suva. While traversing a rare barren heap of rocks and boulders amid the steamy rainforest, my passenger asked me to land.

On the ground, he examined the rocks, took samples and we departed. I wondered why he was so interested in this heap of rubble. Some months later I heard this businessman had won a multi-million dollar contract to construct a new highway to connect the capital, Suva, with the town of Nadi. His lease on the only readily accessible pile of stones suitable for road building meant he had an unbeatable commercial advantage. It was another example of great opportunities arising from seemingly worthless material, for those who have eyes to see.

The gold exploration company I serviced weekly in the rough, jungle covered mountains behind Suva gradually spread its area of operation. Some days I visited numerous helipads on their lease. The camp dog, a friendly imported creature, often followed the workers.

One day I dropped in to an outstation helipad to collect a geologist and both he and the dog got in.

'Don't worry, I'll hold Taffy's collar.'

After takeoff I turned my head and saw Taffy sitting quietly on the floor, unrestrained. I'm sure he attempted a smile to reassure me that he would behave. After that flight Taffy often traveled with me, sometimes the only passenger, using the helicopter as his personal transport. He often waited for me at outstation pads and when I opened the door, jumped in and behaved like a perfect mute passenger. Sometimes he politely declined to get off for several stops before leaving me to pursue his doggy interests. He never put a paw wrong, unlike some humans I have known.

One day I collected a sling load of roofing leaves and flew them to a new camp. The load of dry leaves hanging on the cargo hook was not heavy but completely filled a large net. During the flight it began raining and the leaves collected moisture like a sponge. This load had to be delivered some distance up into the hills. I struggled to climb as it became heavier and heavier. It was touch and go as to whether I'd make it or be forced to dump the carefully gathered building materials into the jungle. Just clearing the last ridge, I thumped the soggy leaves into the prescribed clearing. It was the first and only time I carried a load that doubled its weight in flight.

Other loads could be extremely troublesome. Those with a large surface area catch the wind and throw the chopper around. Others can unpredictably go berserk when a certain speed is reached, flying up into the aircraft. I know of one case where a load suddenly snatched a five tonne machine upside down. The pilot could not release until the load flew down and began to turn him right side up.

It only takes a second to push the electric release button on the control stick but that can be too late to prevent damage. Sometimes the load fails to release electrically and the additional delay before the manual release can be activated results in disaster. A manual can not tell how an underslung load will behave – caution, experience and good judgement are required. I have had metal pipes behave differently when wet or dry – (moisture changes the Reynolds number of any object moving through the air). The possibilities are endless. I constantly reminded myself that in aviation, wittingly or otherwise, everyone and everything was waiting to kill me in an unguarded moment.

I flew for a Japanese exploration venture in the Savu Savu area. After a contractor completed geological work, the mine, port, township, connecting roads and bridges were planned using three-dimensional aerial photographs. This engineering design was meticulously done back at headquarters in Japan. They used the average height of thick jungle treetops in the photos to determine the contours of the rugged terrain below.

After all this careful planning, someone at headquarters decided to muddy their boots and examine the proposed mine area on the ground. Intense embarrassment and much excited jabbering resulted. It was discovered that the trees in the valleys grew to almost double the height of those on top of the ridges. Their perfect design was destroyed. The Japanese went home, never returned, and the mine did not happen. I was most disappointed at this failure, having hoped to gain considerable revenue from the venture.

Monsoon weather with its attendant low clouds and rain covered much of Fiji when a call came in from the police. Three Indian schoolboys, on a walking expedition through the mountains of central Viti Levu, the main island, were six days overdue. The policeman asked if I could assist.

I had conducted search and rescues before, but the weather would make the task difficult. The boys started their trek from the northwestern part of the island in sunshine and headed south, walking into the monsoon affected mountains. Indians were not known to venture far inland, being predominantly shopkeepers and sugar cane growers in the northern coastal areas. Only Fijians lived in the inland jungle covered mountains. Perhaps these lads wished to prove something.

On the first day we easily found two of the boys. One was in fair condition and made it to a Fijian village, the other, we found in a hut some distance away. He was severely exhausted and I flew him to the hospital in Suva. Next day we attempted to find the third lad. During their walk he had become ill and was unable to continue, so the others left him on the bank of a stream and went for help. The first boy we found elected to guide me to where they last saw their friend.

The weather was atrocious in the highlands. Rain and low clouds churned the treetops. I made two attempts in the morning to penetrate this soup but had to turn back both times.

In mid afternoon the weather improved slightly and I knew this was likely to be our last rescue attempt for the day. There was some speculation as to whether the sick boy was still alive, after almost a week in the rain and cool mountain nights, but we had to try and find him.

Once airborne, I could see forward perhaps fifteen metres and gained the plateau where the lad had been left. The cloud was still down amongst the jungle treetops but we found the stream the boys had walked. There was just enough space for my rotor blades in a natural tunnel formed by trees on the sides, cloud above, and the rock-strewn stream below. It was an eerie world of misty, ghostly shapes that raised my hackles. Extreme concentration on the controls resulted in my knuckles matching the pale colour of clouds in the trees. We slowly twisted and turned, following the stream. I hoped there would be enough room to swing my tail around and turn for the return trip as the tunnel was narrowing.

'I think we are close now,' my guide said.

Thank heavens; my nerves couldn't stand much more.

We crept around yet another corner when he said, 'I think this is the place. Can you land here?'

There was a rock above water close to the right bank so I said, 'I can put one skid on that rock. You can get out but do it slowly, don't jump.'

While balancing delicately on part of one skid I nodded to my passenger. A sudden shift in weight could cause the chopper to roll sideways into the trees before I could stop the movement.

'OK. I will see if he is here.'

'Don't be long or I'll leave without you. I have to keep flying the helicopter and can't relax.'

'Sure, sure' and he was gone.

Less than a minute later he returned carrying what looked like a bundle of rags. Inside the wet garments, emaciated and sick but still alive was the boy. It only took a moment for both to be strapped in. Very carefully, I turned around; chopping down small branches with the main rotor to ensure that the delicate tail rotor would not foul the trees.

The trip out of the devil's lair seemed shorter. First aid was administered to the casualty before I took him to Suva hospital. The sick lad was found to be suffering from bronchial pneumonia. They doubted if he would have survived another night but I believe he made a complete recovery.

These tasks are nerve-wracking but satisfying when a good result ensues. On this occasion the boys' headmaster wrote a letter to the editor stating that 'he would like to thank me for my personal concern and bravery'.

The Minister for Communications, Works and Tourism, having read the official police report, wrote me a personal letter. Among other things he stated, 'the youth Rajendra owes his life to your skill and determination in operating your helicopter in most difficult and hazardous conditions'.

Very flattering but sometimes one has to ignore the rules when life is at stake, even if personal comfort and safety is at risk. When conducting a 'Mercy Flight', decisions to fly at night or in bad weather when not normally permitted are left to the pilot's discretion. The rush to be a hero must be quashed and replaced by hard nosed calculations regarding the odds of a successful outcome, in the light of personal experience. Difficult, life saving flight requests occur during many pilots' careers. Often it requires more courage to say no than to go, as anyone hates to be suspected of lacking in moral fibre or necessary skills.

Late one evening I received a call from the Chief Minister's Department.

'Phil, we've got a problem. Can you fly vegetables to the Principal Chief's island, down in the southeastern end of the Fiji Islands?

'Vegetables?' I queried.

'Yes, the chief is entertaining Prince Charles who will be arriving tomorrow on the royal yacht Britannia. It seems they need European vegetables for the official luncheon ashore. The boat that was to have taken these has broken down, so we need your help.'

'I'll have to call you back after I work out if I can get to that isolated island. It's a long way. And I will have to defer another job I had booked.'

After numerous phone calls asking to borrow fuel in isolated locations, I called the Minister's office.

'What's the verdict?'

'I can make it with a hundred kilograms of vegetables providing the royal yacht supplies me with forty-five litres of petrol.'

'I'm sure that can be arranged.'

Plans were finalised at 1 am and it seemed only minutes before the alarm woke me at five. I had to fit floats to our machine before departing as most of the flight was over water. A runner called me to the phone at the airport tower halfway through this task. My modest workshop in a shipping crate lacked such conveniences.

'Sorry Phil,' a voice on the phone said, 'the Chief has decided he can manage without the vegetables. We are cancelling the trip.'

Bloody marvellous, I was up half the night for nothing.

As I toiled at returning the chopper to its original skid configuration a greengrocer's vehicle appeared and the driver asked me, 'What would you like done with these veggies for the Chief?'

I felt like saying, you can stick them up his backside, but did not. The Chief was a nice guy and it was probably some bureaucrat that had caused this nonsense.

'The jobs off, so please yourself.'

When the Britannia arrived in Suva's harbour in 1970, preparations for celebrating the colony's independence began. We saw Prince Charles hand the country over to its original inhabitants. Among the many gifts to Prince Charles from Fiji I can still remember the dozens of hapless, upside down turtles, flippers fruitlessly beating the air for hours. These, along with pigs and garden produce, were spread out on the oval below the official raised dais. That evening Mary and I watched fireworks over the harbour from the private beach in front of our small rented house.

During the country's first election campaign I flew many of the political aspirants, all Fijians or long term white settlers. I asked one Chief what would happen when the numerically greater Indian population, originally imported as cheap labour for the cane fields, gained control of the Parliament. We'll just chop them up and throw them into the sea was his answer. Fijians were known to be fierce warriors if necessary.

Many years later I recalled that remark when the Indians did achieve majority but were too afraid to form a government for fear of retribution. The race issue has had its ups and downs in Fiji ever since.

One electioneering trip with the Cambridge educated Chief who would become Fiji's first Prime Minister posed a dilemma. To begin the day's tour of villages we needed to cross a few kilometres of calm, warm water. By law, an emergency dinghy was required to be carried for that flight. But its weight, added to that of my two hefty passengers, meant the aircraft would be overweight. I could not leave one passenger behind and I could not carry less fuel and make the trip. I weighed the odds and went ahead

208

with the flight. Life is rarely perfect.

Most of the isolated villages we visited had never seen a helicopter before, so I was treated as a VIP and sat in front of the mob with my passengers. It was fortunate that the traditional drink, yanqona or kava is non-alcoholic. Participating in the welcome ceremonies meant I didn't appear churlish by declining to drink a toast. Much later I learnt that Kava can be an hallucinogen if too much is drunk. Though astringent, I liked the drink that many whites described as tasting like dishwater.

Occasionally, to escape the phone and seven-day a week duty, Mary and I packed a picnic lunch and took off in the chopper. We flew to a small island just five minutes from the airport. It was completely encircled by coral reefs, making access by boat impossible.

At our private hideaway, we sunned on the beach and swam in unpolluted clear water. The island was also a home for thousands of birds and coral sea snakes. The latter were brightly coloured, venomous serpents, which constantly wriggled up and down the beach to and from the sea, ignoring us as we did them. They swam all around us when we cooled off in the sea. One day Mary inadvertently stepped on a two metre long specimen while getting out of the chopper. It just lay there and waited for her to get off its back before wriggling away to the sea.

On one trip to our private island haven we were caught while dozing after lunch. Hearing a discrete cough, on opening our eyes we were amazed to see a white couple on our beach, politely trying to avoid embarrassing us. We hastily rummaged for towels to cover ourselves.

'Sorry, didn't mean to intrude. Thought you might have some trouble with the helicopter?'

'No, no, we are just having a day off. You must have had a hell of a job walking over the reef?'

'It wasn't easy but we thought you might need help.'

We offered them a cup of tea for their efforts but they declined. They had to get back to their speedboat because of the tide. No doubt it would make a good story for them to tell at the yacht club.

Mary was keen on animals so a cat and dog joined the family. The dog came from the condemned cage at the RSPCA pound, was part Doberman and an ex police dog. He protected our cat from marauding ferals, never barked, and guarded our house very cunningly.

If we were both away any stranger entering our grounds was arrested in mid stride by the firm pressure of teeth just above one ankle, gripped from behind. This was the first indication of a dog on the premises. If the person made any attempt to move, tooth pressure on the ankle increased. We often found hefty Fijian men, entering the premises to read our electricity or water meters, stopped in their tracks and sometimes held for hours. Mary frequently rescued our Indian gardener from his perch up a tree in the yard. Our dog was well trained by the police and we could not imagine why he lost his job.

Mary grew up with servants in England but Fiji was the first time she had employed one. Housemaids certainly eliminate much drudgery but can cause a clash of cultures. One day Mary noticed a favourite pantsuit was missing and asked our housegirl about this.

'Missus mi Kerri Kerri im.'

'Well I don't know what Kerri Kerri means but if you have taken them, bring them back please.'

'Yes Missus I bring them tomorrow.'

Mary asked friends about this custom and was told that if a Fijian expresses admiration for some item it is necessary to offer it to them. These items can of course be 'Kerri Kerried' back by the original owner after a reasonable period. But if items are not offered due to ignorance they are sometimes taken regardless. It's all part of learning other people's cultures.

My employing a local helper demonstrated another aspect of this. I pointed out the usual working conditions and mentioned that after a year of service the worker would be eligible for three weeks holiday. Several prospective employees shook their heads and said they weren't interested. I could understand their reasons. Why work for a year to enjoy a holiday, when in Fiji the coastal tribes go fishing and swimming whenever they feel like it. Europeans were supposed to be smart. Why did we behave so strangely and expect them to do it as well.

Mary, being a horse lover, joined the Pony Club where we purchased one for her to ride. I sometimes assisted at gymkhanas and one competition day while monitoring a jump was amazed to hear Americans talking on my cheap hand held walky-talky radio. Unbelievably, I was receiving the Los Angeles Police Dept. Headquarters radio station. It was a freak accident of nature that enabled the low powered, normally only line-of-sight transmissions to reach me.

At one Fiji Show held in the town's main arena, Mary took her horse over high jumps and I later did various tricks with the chopper while maneuvering at much less height than the horses achieved.

After a year we flew to England for three weeks leave. The company agreed for us to stop over in Honolulu at their expense on the return journey so I could visit local helicopter operators. It was to gain insight into providing joy flights to tourists. Unfortunately, Mary developed an upset stomach after we arrived. She spent the next day with its sweeping view of Waikiki beach, confined to our hotel room on the 21st floor.

Meanwhile, I ventured forth to eat breakfast as room service had to be ordered twenty-four hours in advance, much to my amazement. The queue to get into the hotel's dining room was staggering; it must have numbered almost a hundred. I gave up and walked out, thinking that there must be another restaurant nearby. All I found at 7.30 am were touts on the footpath inviting me to view strippers in action. Defeated, I returned to the hotel and eventually obtained breakfast before beginning the day's business.

My meetings with local operators produced little I didn't know. An abundance of well-heeled tourists and nearby spectacular scenery were needed to prosper at providing joy flights. However, my visit provided an independent view to report to head office.

Next day we flew across the Pacific and back to our work routine.

I am fortunate to have viewed most of the major Fijian islands and spectacular coral reefs from a low level. On occasion, in amazingly clear water, I saw large whales close inshore. Taviuni was an interesting, twenty kilometre long island. Its southern aspect rose thousands of meters from the sea floor to hundreds of meters above the surface in an almost vertical slice. I was told that pirate ships and legitimate sailing schooners replenished their water barrels off its coast without having to send sailors ashore. The vessels simply drifted up to an overhang and fresh water from above poured onto their decks.

Tombarua Island, just ten minutes by chopper from the airport was a resort frequented by affluent tourists. The architect who designed the World Trade Centre in Toronto was a frequent visitor. He always booked me to fly him there and back instead of utilising the cheap but tedious boat transfer. As a result Mary and I were invited to spend a free overnight. The accommodation was tasteful, luxurious and rather unique in that each of the dozen separate bures, or apartments, faced a private beach in front of each patio and the central pool sat behind our back door. It's the only place I have ever stayed where the waiters and barmen knew all the guests' by name and discretely recorded the cost of drinks, the only extras.

Our social calendar included a diverse spread of engagements. One weekend, I landed on and floated in sheltered water inside the reef so several fishermen passengers could easily catch dozens of fish. These helped to feed visitors at a school fete. Other friends took us boating and water-skiing. Our original small flat on the waters edge in the suburb of Lami seemed to suffer constant rainfall so we moved to a three bedroom house closer to the city centre and airport. Us expatriates were well catered for by numerous clubs. We only belonged to the Pony Club but enjoyed others as visitors.

I flew Robert Trent Jones Jnr., the American golf course designer, to Wakaya Island when a consortium considered developing it as a millionaire's playground. He was most enthused about the island and said it would be the only course he designed with one hole on a different island. I advised the group regarding an airstrip location on this 2,200 acre, (890 ha) exotic, tropical retreat. After a long sumptuous lunch of fish, clams, venison and pork, all harvested locally, we flew back to Suva. The flight entailed twenty minutes over water and half way across my stomach urgently wanted to dispose of the clam I had eaten. It was touch and go but I flung the chopper at the nearest beach and just made it behind a bush before dropping my shorts and erupting. I have not knowingly eaten clam since; it's been the only kind of meat to give me a problem. Perhaps that mollusc was not fresh; none of the unusual aboriginal foods affected my stomach.

Some years after leaving Fiji I discovered a full page ad in the British Airways in-flight magazine, promoting Wakaya to potential part owners.

An American phoned and said he and his wife couldn't face a taxi trip from their five star Fijian Hotel to Suva. They wished to use my helicopter instead.

I happened to have another job in their area the day before they wished to travel, so to minimise the cost we agreed that I'd stay in the hotel overnight and then fly them next morning. They were a friendly Texan couple and the three of us spent a pleasant evening together. After flying to Suva, Mary and I took them out on the town that evening, ending up at our house for drinks and coffee.

'Why haven't you got any modern helicopters here?' asked the husband.

'It's the old chicken and egg story. Until you get the business they can't be justified and the business is slow until you do. I think the company is hardly making any money here as it is. Seems it's not prepared to take the risk, so we do what we can with old machinery.'

'What if I gave you a few million to set up shop with new turbine choppers?'

'Well, the Fiji Government has given us an exclusive seven year

License to Operate. It can only be voided if we fail to provide satisfactory service.'

'You could arrange to nullify that licence couldn't you?'

'I suppose I could but would have to study the implications first.'

'Why don't you do that and let me know.'

After further chat, we drove them to their hotel.

Here was another opportunity to set myself up in business. I knew doing so would mean burning my bridges with Asia's largest helicopter company, one that held a virtual monopoly in Australasia. It would also mean spending a long period in Fiji to consolidate the business.

I checked the credentials of our Texans and found the man was one of three brothers who owned an oil company so I'm sure his cheque would not have bounced. Ultimately, Mary and I decided it was too much of a risk and did not take up the offer. In retrospect, I think my angel was guiding me. Later, another pilot left the company to set up shop in Fiji and is still flying there. Airfast spawned many pilots who became significant operators in Australia and overseas. One is still the principal of PNG's largest helicopter companies and John, (Flame-out), is known for owning the original largest heli mustering company in Australia.

In May 1971 my sister was married in Adelaide. I flew over for the event. It was great to catch up with family and I stayed with my parents. They quizzed me about our life in Fiji and mother wondered if another Latz was on the way. I said it was not planned just yet, the medical facilities being rather basic. That visit broke a drought, we had only been visiting England and ignoring my folks in Australia for the last few years.

Months later, while away on local leave, the pilot relieving me ran out of fuel a few minutes from the airport. He managed to land in a flooded rice paddy, partially severing the tail boom. The company decided to ship the helicopter back to Sydney for repairs, but first I had to remove it from the muddy field. I soon underslung most of the machine out. But the weight of the main cabin section proved a problem and it could not easily be stripped any further. I enlisted several people to help me lift this section out of the soggy ground and instructed them to throw it up and away as I lifted. Standing in mud up to their knees they did assist me get the cabin section airborne and then threw, while I tried to fly it away. Alas, it was too heavy and I only gained a few forward metres before it fell back into the mud, as did all my friends, their feet stuck. With difficulty I persuaded the slime-covered workers to try again. Next time, a gust of wind helped me lift and I managed to fly away and land the last piece at the airport. After repairs in Sydney that machine flew again but did not return to Fiji so I was down to one helicopter, the three passenger Bell J2.

The summer monsoon was well established when several high priced experts, Doctors of Geology, arrived from Canada to inspect and evaluate a client company's mineral lease.

'Can we fly out in this weather?' they asked as I briefed my two VIP passengers on safety procedures. As usual, early solid cloud cover hovered just above the treetops.

'We could wait for weeks to get a better day. Let's go and look. If it's too bad, I'll come back and try again later.'

The control tower gave me special clearance and we departed into a hot damp gray world. Nothing else was moving at the airport; the weather was too bad for fixed wing aircraft to operate. For the next half-hour I flew from memory, just below the cloud and perhaps twenty metres above muddy river waters below. It was dangerous to consult a map, I had to keep my focus outside and the aircraft in the centre of a tunnel bounded by high, vertical rock faces or steeply sloping valleys.

'You seem to have done this trip before,' commented a passenger as we turned sharply into yet another river gorge.

'Yes. Luckily in good weather, or else we'd be flying up a lot of dead ends.'

'I'm surprised they let you takeoff.'

'They know me in the tower. I took some of the guys up for a trip and showed them what we can do in a chopper. Now, they just let me come and go but it sure annoys the airline guys who are waiting to fly.'

'I can see why you weren't too fazed about heading off this morning.'

'Technically we shouldn't be flying, but during the south east monsoon some exploration camps would have to shut down unless I was able to safely supply them.'

'This is the home stretch,' I said while turning sharp right to follow a stream up another steep sided valley. 'The camp should be just a few miles up here on the left.'

It was, and soon I was enjoying a coffee while my VIP passengers and the resident geologists studied survey maps and assay results from the area. Then they all disappeared into steamy jungle paths to look at the neighboring mud and rocks.

'We'll be back for lunch,' someone said, leaving me to continue reading my book.

Later, people drifted back, deep in technical discussions until someone

214

asked, 'Where's Frank? Was he with you Ralph?'

'He was, then said he was going to join your party.'

A search was quickly organised. I flew over the area but found no sign of Frank in the few clearings. It was almost impossible to see the ground through the dense jungle, so I returned to base after a thorough search. I hoped if Frank was lost, the sound of the helicopter should at least give him some direction.

While eating my lunch, bad news arrived. Frank was found on a jungle trail lying face down, his head in a puddle about three centimetres deep. It appeared he had suffered a stroke or heart attack and happened to fall in a small pool of water and drowned.

In hindsight, it was thought that the stress of transitioning from the minus 40° C winter in Canada to plus 30° C steamy heat plus a long Pacific flight and physical exertion probably overtaxed his heart.

The mood on board was certainly subdued as we flew back. Frank lay in a plastic bag under the bench seat instead of sitting on it and chatting. It was the first time I had taken out a live passenger and brought back the same one, dead, on the same day. Our radio calls require us to give the number of persons on board, dead or alive. Sometimes I might have wished a difficult passenger would drop dead, but that had not been the case on this trip.

I've found most pilots soon learn not to be affected by sudden deaths. We just ignore any surrounding mayhem or heavy emotion in the air, remain detached, and concentrate on flying. This apparent unconcern often spills over at home and appears to be a problem shared by some other occupations. Some people find refuge in religion or drugs. I've found it rare to find a teetotal professional aviator in commercial operations.

My task on another day appeared to be a simple assignment. It was to collect a coffin from an island about ninety kilometres south of Suva. The deceased was a chief of some importance, warranting this considerable expense. The coffin would be securely tied to the litter on the outside of the helicopter; similar to the casualties choppered to hospital in the M.A.S.H. television series.

I flew out, found the village and landed on the nearby beach. A moving farewell ceremony began. After an hour or so the coffin was eventually placed on the litter and amid further wailing I fastened it securely and started the engine.

On attempting to lift off, the weight of the load on one side tried to tip my machine over. I stopped the engine and explained my dilemma. The coffin would have to remain behind. After much discussion I was told that this was not possible, the chief could not travel in his underwear, so to speak.

'There is another possibility,' I said. 'We'll put some stones on the opposing litter to balance the chief's weight and hope it's not too heavy for me to take off.'

I knew Fijians of importance were often of generous stature and could easily weigh 150 kilograms. Stones were found, loaded, and after another farewell ceremony I tried again. This time I was too heavy to become airborne.

'I'm sorry, but the chief will have to go without his coffin.'

Another long discussion followed, and amid more wailing, the chief was removed from his enclosure and reverently placed on the litter, wrapped in tapa, a traditional cloth like material.

Third time lucky I thought. It was. Arriving back at Nausori airport, I found police waiting for me.

'What took you so long?'

'It's a long story. Why are you here? I was expecting an ambulance.'

'It's coming. We are investigating a suspected murder and are taking charge of the body.'

'Nothing to do with me, he was in a coffin when I arrived to pick him up,' I grinned.

'His family says he was poisoned by rivals so an autopsy is required,' said a policeman before leaving.

In mid 1971 Mary became pregnant. Expectant mothers at the Suva hospital had to bring their own newspaper and rags for use during the delivery. We heard other horror stories such as unwanted human parts being fed to dogs, so a move back to Australia was most desirable. Career wise, I needed experience flying larger, turbine engined helicopters. As a relatively senior member of the company I was able to obtain a posting flying to offshore oil rigs in Bass Strait. Mary was happy as it meant I would be home every night. Allan, currently working on the offshore job would replace me in Fiji. I had met him some years ago in New Guinea. He was an ex British Army officer pilot and struck me as a gentleman.

When they arrived, we found his wife to be another matter. She had become a 'Manager's' wife and seemed determined to throw her weight around. She told us to get out of the manager's house and into a hotel so they could take up residence. Big deal, manager of one helicopter, but

216

the title of Country Manager's wife had seemingly gone to her head. Mary was most upset; packing our shipment was incomplete. We'd been told by friends that use of an agent would result in many items being broken in transit, however insurance would replace them. But if we packed our belongings, insurance was not available. We chose the latter option and trusted our ability to pack well. It proved to be an exhausting but wise decision as nothing was broken or damaged.

It was a relief to leave Fiji as any responsible position involving constant duty is wearing. Our stay had been interesting but soured by the manner in which we were treated before departure. It was time for a new beginning even though I was moving to the bottom of the heap again. At least my career prospects would be greatly improved in the long term. Few pilots, outside of the military, flew the 'Huey' type helicopters I would soon be operating.

After flying to Sydney, I completed a technical course on the engine fitted to the thirteen passenger Bell 204/5 helicopter which I was to fly offshore. With that test passed, I bought a second-hand car and we drove south to begin my new job in Sale, Victoria. Hundreds of kilometres from our destination, Mary began to have stomach pain. This was a bad omen, she was only several months pregnant. I began to feel the full weight of responsibilities, duties and care needed to be a good husband. The honeymoon was definitely over but at least we were back in Australia.

Above: *Our car, helicopter and I at Nausori airport in Fiji.*
Right: *The 'mercury sniffer' goes flying from Nandi.*

217

CHAPTER 11

Remember, gravity is not just a good idea - it's the law
and can't be repealed. ~ The Aviators Guide Book

On arrival in Sale we moved into a company transit flat. Soon after, Mary was admitted to hospital with abdominal pain. We were fortunate in that a very experienced and competent gynaecologist, Dr Hercules, had relocated to Sale before our arrival. A slim, harried-looking doctor, he left his lucrative Melbourne practice after driving through a red light at a busy intersection when badly fatigued. Thankfully he escaped injury. Without him it's unlikely Mary's pregnancy would have resulted in a successful outcome.

The good doctor and I had many discussions in the hospital car park. Several times he said our unborn child had only a 50% chance of survival. I constantly visited the hospital, coping by myself at home and initially, learning a new demanding task. It was a worrying and wearisome time with non-stop activity and uncertainty hanging over me.

Eventually, our son was born three months prematurely, considered a very early successful delivery at that time.

My training on the large thirteen passenger helicopters took almost a week. I failed my first flight out to the rigs under supervision by John (J.C.). He had praised my flying years earlier, when conducting my helicopter license test, but this was a different matter. I was expected to fly like an airline pilot, not a bush one. I could hold my height and heading to a precise degree but it required constant concentration, something I thought better reserved for landings and takeoffs at the offshore platforms. To emphasize my failings, another flight under supervision was required before being let loose on my own. J.C. was an ex military pilot and ran his civil outfit in a similar manner, which sometimes grated on me but I began to metaphorically salute officers again.

Out of ten pilots, eight were ex military. The other two were senior members of our operation, so I was the real exception. It was a new type of flying, one where I re-learnt to be part of a team. The contrast to my previous post was enormous. In Fiji, I was totally in control of the whole operation - from phone enquiries, to flying the task, maintaining the aircraft and all the records. My flying had been 'seat of the pants'. I only fleetingly checked the aircraft instruments to ensure all were showing normal readings. The flying was largely by reference to rivers, valleys and mountains, even my map being rarely used.

Now, I just turned up as per the roster, checked my allotted aircraft, was handed a manifest and flight plan before boarding passengers, briefing them and departing. A few minutes after leaving the shoreline, called coasting out, often the sea and sky merged so constant scrutiny of the instruments was necessary.

I found a project home for sale in a new development. It came with carpets, curtains, light fittings and emerging lawns. We could just afford the deposit and essential furnishings were acquired on lay-by.

After some weeks, Mary and our son Gavin were released from hospital. He required feeding every four hours, so the sleepless nights began. I'm sure I was an inept father, having had no training or found any books on parenting. But changing nappies and bottle feeding are tasks soon learnt.

A first child is always demanding but fortunately my flying tasks had become largely routine. Getting to work for an early start on cold mornings remained a challenge, especially after years in warm climates. The Bass Strait weather was often fickle, having disabled many a yatch during the Sydney to Hobart race. I was told it could be as bad as the North Sea off the coast of Scotland but our aircraft were not as well equipped as theirs. And our machines only had one engine - if that failed offshore our chances of staying dry were very slim. Naturally, we practiced for emergency landings with the engine off, but in a calm lake adjacent to the helipad complex at Longford. It was an inkling of the real thing but I sure hoped I would never have to drop into the open sea. An emergency dinghy was no match for the cold winter water and frequent ten metre waves I saw below me in Bass Straight.

Our son, Gavin, grew normally and soon was crawling everywhere. He sometimes went missing and could be found visiting his redheaded girlfriend next door as our properties had no front fences. It seemed he was beginning his walkabouts early in life. I hoped I would be around later in his childhood to help guide his explorations.

We were becoming a suburban couple and when not flying I occupied myself with building a pergola, enclosing the carport and drinking with the boys on Friday nights. Mary came home with a Dalmatian one day. At that time, a rare breed in Australia. The dog was probably inbred, seemed quite stupid and dug holes all over my garden. It probably didn't get enough exercise.

Mary befriended a young English couple who visited our house occasionally. Liz and Kim could not afford to heat their home whereas we had a large built in gas heater. Gas was cheap, so having arrived from a hot climate we ran our house at 26° C during winter. This temperature was too much for Liz who stripped down to a bra and slip as the evening progressed, revealing her shapely figure. A strip, even without the tease, is always interesting.

Before Christmas 1972, Mary's parents flew from the UK to visit their new grandson. I always got on well with my in-laws and we were happy to welcome them to our new home. After leaving us they even rode the Ghan to my birthplace.

As my first winter flying offshore approached we faced different weather patterns and icing. Snow covered the mountains to our north and cold fronts swept through from the Antarctic. Strong winds didn't normally affect our operations but we stayed home when they exceeded 35 knots (50 km/hr) as personnel were likely to be blown off the exposed helipads into the sea while trying to board.

I learnt to read the waves and white caps; the wind could be howling from one direction and a few minutes later swing through 180 degrees as a front passed. Unless I made a correct change of heading I would be blown way off course. It was a matter of pride that we didn't request rig beacons to be turned on unless the weather was very bad, such as when sea fog covered the platforms.

This fog usually sat about thirty metres above the sea. We flew out just above the waves and below the fog while homing on the beacon. Before our ETA we slowed until sighting the platform legs rising out of the sea and disappearing into the mist. Then it was a matter of stopping beside the legs, climbing vertically and sliding onto the helipad. Knowing each platform, we avoided flying into a mast or antenna.

Landing on the Glomar Conception, a floating drillship, in wild weather was also an interesting exercise. I don't think our passengers were aware of the danger and skill involved in achieving a successful landing. Everything moved. Low clouds tore across the sky, rain slanted over the windshield, waves roared past the ship while the helideck lunged up and down four metres in a corkscrew motion while rolling five degrees. The approach and landing was an interesting three-dimensional exercise in judgment much like throwing a stone at a flying bird. We had no electronic guidance such as that available at airports. No clever electronics in the aircraft to help us land, just the eyes in our head and the feeling in the seat of our pants.

220

After achieving a hover over the helipad we had to read the heave of the ship so as not to descend as the deck pitched up. It had to be caught going down, and after contact the rolling motion had to be immediately countered, otherwise sideways movement could rip our flimsy floats off. While on the gyrating helideck it's necessary to 'fly' the machine so it doesn't slide off. A rogue wave could have thrown us over the side and possibly a passenger getting on or off, so we always kept one eye on the oncoming seas as well.

Aircraft carriers have a batman waving paddles to help guide pilots to a landing - we had a plume of smoke from the engine room funnel. This plume indicated turbulence behind the bridge structure and above the helipad, another complication to the landing. To make it even worse, the smoke contained warm carbon dioxide from the ship's engine room. This often upset our engine due to the sudden change in air temperature and oxygen levels, causing power fluctuations. It was character building work! My knuckles gleamed white on the controls until after departure.

Our company set limits on the ship's heave, pitch and roll allowed for an attempt at landing but around Christmas, New Year, football Grand Finals or other auspicious events the radio operator seemed to interpret the inclinometer readings on the bridge loosely.

Most of our passengers were regular workers commuting to the platforms. Before leaving Longford we were required to give a safety briefing, similar to the airlines. One morning I spoke in German to see if anyone noticed. If they did, it was never mentioned.

Eventually I scored a job away from the daily offshore routine. It was to fly a technician to inspect lighthouses around the Tasmanian coast. Our four passenger Jet Ranger had plenty of room for Dave and his equipment. It was a pleasant jolly, sightseeing along Tasmania's varied coastline, interspersed with landings to service the automatically operating signposts for ships. We reached Strahan on Tasmania's rugged West Coast, at the end of day one and I landed on a vacant allotment close to town, not far from our hotel.

After dinner Dave and I decided to have a nightcap. Being a Saturday night a live band was playing in the room adjacent to the long bar at which we stood. Next door, the dance floor was vacant and young ladies sat on chairs lining the wall. It seemed their men were drinking at the bar some distance from us. A typical country pub scene until the males moved to surround Dave and I, pushing between us to order drinks. Dave began to bristle and I tried to placate him, we were badly outnumbered. The dozen

221

young men raised their voices and made threatening gestures at us. A fight seemed imminent.

The door to the bar opened and a man entered.

'G'day John,' shouted Dave.

'Hello mate, fancy seeing you in town,' said John after catching a glimpse of us amid the throng. As John approached, our tormentors quietly melted away.

I gathered our savior was a local boy. He and Dave had worked together before. I asked him why we had been threatened.

'Well, they're a bit inbred out here. On Saturday nights, for a bit of sport, they beat up any strangers in town. If there aren't any they fight each other.'

As we left I noticed the men were still at the bar while next door the girls were dancing with each other.

The remainder of our trip was uneventful but I visited some interesting lighthouses. One, over a hundred years old, was built in England and arrived in small pieces on sailing ships. The tall, circular, tapering tower, was constructed from thousands of individual foot sized rectangular hollow blocks of cast-iron. Each bolted together on the inside and fitting together like bricks in a wall. The slightly circular 'bricks' had been hand filed to mate perfectly with their four neighbours, all being marked to ensure correct assembly. I was told this structure had been completely erected in England before being dismantled for shipment. Its construction must have provided employment for hundreds of skilled craftsmen.

I wondered if the different stages of my life fitted together as well as the tower's parts or were there gaping holes? Would I stand strong for a century? Was my steel sufficiently tempered or would it bend and break in a storm? Would a chance lightning strike hit me? I hoped my angel would help with answers and protection.

We 'did' all the lights, including the one on Matsyker Island, Australia's southernmost light. The wind was so strong on the first day I flew there, it was not safe to land. The helipad was affected by strong eddying up and down draughts. Just like unseen, bottomless potholes in the sky, the type that injure unsecured passengers on airline flights.

Having several days off in Hobart, I made my first visit to Australia's only legal casino at that time, the Wrest Point. Knowing how to play blackjack, or 21, I decided to have a go. There was only one table offering fifty cent minimum bets, surrounded by women. Intrigued, I stood behind the bevy of ladies, discovering them to be working-class housewives. Upon noting their winning rate phenomenal, I simply placed my money next to theirs. Soon, the dealer changed, and the ladies stopped betting. Cards were dealt to uninterested women gossiping, until another dealer appeared. Betting began again and the slow accumulation of profits continued. I have never seen so many blackjacks appear in the bettor's favour. These ladies had the table psyched. There was no other explanation I could see. Returning next day to make more beer money I found the same players and same results – it was not a fluke and still intrigues me.

In September 1973 Mary flew to the UK with eleven month old Gavin to visit her parents. I was rostered to be away in Tasmania for three weeks supporting Esso's offshore oil exploration program off the north coast. Two of our helicopters were to be based in Wynyard. It was a welcome break from our scheduled Bass Straight flights.

On arrival at Wynyard I was amazed to discover a railway line across the airport and main runway. At this aerodrome, aircraft gave way to trains. It did not affect us so we didn't carry a rail timetable, but a train on the runway could have surprised some visiting pilots. I am not aware of any other airport in the world where this occured.

My first Saturday night arrived and I joined our crew to have a few beers in Burnie. We drove to a dance hall in the large, by Tasmanian standards, semi-industrial town.

On arrival we found dozens of girls sitting in groups, drinking and chatting without a male at their tables. The men were leaning on the bar, showing no interest in the ladies.

I struck up a conversation with a local man.

'Why are all these young girls sitting around and not dancing?' I asked.

'You must be a visitor to Tassie.'

'Yes, I am.'

'Well, you should know that here the girls fall pregnant at sixteen, are married at seventeen and are divorced by their early twenties.'

'So why won't they dance if they are divorced?'

'They might a little later but now all the ex husbands are watching. If they appear to be having fun with another man the ex's might beat them up. Sometimes the guy they are with as well.'

Sure enough, later in the evening we danced with a few of the girls and our crew left without being hassled.

After returning to Sale, a letter from Mary said she was not coming home unless I accompanied her to assist with childminding. My passport had expired and Mary's approval, by way of a signature, was required to renew it. I got around that detail, collected a new passport and flew to England for two weeks. Our return trip was a horrid, twenty six hour ordeal. In those days British Airways cabin service was shocking. Some hostesses didn't even know how to warm a baby's bottle. None of us had any sleep and it was a great relief to get home.

In February 1974 the company decided we should obtain our helicopter night flying qualifications. My instructor, one of our crew, had me flying completely on instruments. This is much more difficult as a chopper is inherently unstable in flight, whereas all civil aeroplanes are not. The finale was another check flight with a Government Examiner who 'failed' all the cockpit lighting so I ended up holding a torch in my mouth, both hands being occupied on the controls to ensure a safe landing at Sale airport. Naturally, I made no mention of my other flight without lights.

Our duty roster was a cushy number with two or three days off a week, but the frigid winter climate reminded me of my time in Mount Gambier. With a family to support, going walkabout was more difficult. During good weather the scheduled flying became so routine that I switched to autopilot when arriving at work. At times, when flying alone in the empty skies over featureless grey ocean I shut out the world and practised flying on instruments. One day, I looked outside after doing this for five minutes and found myself in the company of several fighter planes. The R.A.A.F. always notified us if active in our offshore area. Looking around, I spotted Australia's only aircraft carrier, the Melbourne, ahead of me. It was sailing below my flight path and their pilots were practising landings. The carrier radar would have spotted me so the fighter jocks knew I was there. The Navy chose not to tell us of their intrusion into 'our' airspace and none of the airborne pilots called me on the radio.

A chance came for us to move as the company won a contract with Esso to fly offshore in Kota Kinabalu, in the Malaysian State of Sabah, North Borneo. Only two of us were required for this plum tropical posting. The positions were highly contested, as had been the case for Fiji. I won selection as the number two man, probably due to my valid engineering license. It would again save the company money.

Mary welcomed the prospect of moving to an exotic location closer to England. Our eighteen month old son was growing normally, after the rigours of his early days. He didn't need any special care or medical attention and suitable schooling was not an issue.

The third pilot hired was a Malay National. Mike, an ex military officer had been well trained in England. He and his young Malay wife, Pat, spent

224

an indoctrination period with the company in Sale and the four of us clicked socially. The colour of their skin meant nothing to us, although others were less accepting. I believe we were the only company people, apart from the boss, who invited them into their homes. We tried to make their stay enjoyable, knowing what it was like to be strangers working in a foreign society.

In April 1974 we packed up house, our third international move in four years. My new boss Kevin and I flew to Kuala Lumpur to obtain Malaysian licences before flying to Borneo.

Arriving in Kota Kinabalu, Kevin and I checked into the Borneo hotel. Reasonably priced rental housing would take time to find. Our hotel was twenty five metres from a sandy beach, which was protected by an outlying coral reef. The yacht and golf club were within walking distance. Our office, next to the airport runway, was a three minute drive. I thought our work and social situation could hardly be bettered as I settled into a hotel room facing the sea. It was so far removed from my childhood at the Mission.

Before Mary and Gavin arrived I spent a month, without success, trying to secure a rental house. With three of us inside, the hotel room seemed very small. Little did we know, almost three months would be spent in that room before moving into our newly renovated home.

In mid May, Mike, our Malaysian pilot and I traveled to Darwin to collect our Australian registered, ten passenger Bell 204 aircraft, and fly it to Kota Kinabalu. We were already weeks late in beginning our contract so a speedy trip back was expected. Our machine was fitted with large fixed float bags, which reduced the cruising speed to 95 kts (176 km/hr). Unfortunately at that time, the Indonesians were having a confrontation with the Western world and would not allow any non-airline, foreign registered aircraft to refuel at their airports. Many transiting aircraft had been stranded at Jakarta or other locations for months, unable to obtain fuel except by theft or bribery. For our five day ferry flight, I was told that our Singapore based DC 3 had positioned drums of jet fuel for us in strategic locations. We found this only partially true, which almost resulted in us being jailed and having our aircraft impounded.

Our travels began inauspiciously. Mike had problems with immigration on our arrival at Darwin, but I managed to convince the officials to let him in without a visa or onward ticket and saved the Company an $8,000 fine. Then I discovered our aircraft was due for an inspection. We flew it to Wyndham where company engineers and pilots were servicing an offshore contract with a large Sikorsky. They found a worn flying control cable that needed replacement. This meant another delay. Breaking down in Indonesia was unthinkable. Our aircraft had to be in very good condition. Also, we had over 1,400 kilometres of ocean to cross on our one engine, with the total distance to Kota Kinabalu being 3,520 kilometres. This meant over twenty hours flying if all went to plan.

We expected problems with officialdom enroute as we only carried a précis Telex confirmation of our flight authorisation. Normally, many typewritten copies on official letterheads were required. As 'grease' we carried Playboy magazines (banned in Indonesia), bottles of Scotch and U. S. dollars. Dark-skinned Mike also spoke Malay/Indonesian, which was invaluable.

Eventually we left Wyndham and refuelled at Kalumbaru Mission. Our first over-water leg was to the drilling rig *Margie*, which happened to be positioned in the Timor Sea, off the West Australian coast. The rig was supported by our company from Wyndham. *Margie* was easy to find and filled us up without fuss.

We carried 44-gallon (200 lit) drums of fuel in the passenger cabin but had no way of pumping this into our main tank during flight. Landing was necessary to refuel, not having a long range tank in the cabin. To reach our landfall at Kupang, another refuel was required, this time on *Big John*, a rig serviced by Bristow helicopters. Halfway across the Timor Sea I began to call them but received no reply. I continued to call, without success. We had sent a message to the rig so they should have been expecting us. The sea below with its known shark population began to look very unfriendly. Our stomachs tightened with tension. *What if the rig had sunk – we would probably do the same.*

The weather was clear so it was a huge relief when a dot appeared on the ocean directly ahead. When we saw the tall drilling superstructure our joy increased, but our radio calls went unanswered. After circling several times a breathless clearance to land was given. The radio operator apologised, it seems the Captain had forgotten our arrival so the beacon and all radios were off. After fuelling, we were soon on our way again and arrived at Kupang well before dark. Our relief at achieving an uneventful crossing soon turned to dismay when finding no fuel at the airport.

Kupang was the most dismal place either of us had ever seen. The surrounding countryside was barren, stony and with barely a plant in sight. The only communication with the outside world was a telex located in the Governor's residence. The Telex operator was missing, a large bribe no doubt being required to get a message out. Either way we could be days in this bleak dump. The only accommodation was a very primitive guesthouse with no running water and empty spaces in the walls awaiting some form of window. Even Mike, an Asian, would not eat the unknown food offered so we resorted to our contingency supplies of tinned food.

Mike and I were so depressed we bought a large case of full size bottles of Bintang, the Indonesian beer. It was so old the glycerol preservative had separated and lay in the bottom. Locals gathered around the holes in the walls and watched in amazement as we demolished the case. They might just be able to afford one bottle in a good year. Our misery was such that intoxication seemed the only solution to our woes, but the beer had little effect and we went to bed sober.

Next morning we were at the airport early, gauging the wind and carefully checking our fuel state. We had no way of obtaining a weather forecast so had to make our own assessment of meteorological conditions. It seemed a tailwind was blowing. If the gods were kind and the tailwind strong enough we could just make Waingapu, our next stop on Sumba Island, and hope fuel was available there. Having discussed the alternatives we decided to fly to a more fertile and hopefully civilised area.

The wind was kind and added forty clicks to our ground speed. We found several drums of old fuel marked Bristow Helicopters after making Waingapu. Technically the fuel was out of date and should not have been used before being re-tested. Also, it did not belong to us but Mike told curious locals we had a joint venture with Bristow and were yet to paint their name on our helicopter. We got away with the swindle and quickly filled our tank after checking the fuel for water. I'm sure the bottle of Scotch we gave away helped our cause.

My calculations predicted we would not reach Bali, our next fuel stop, unless the tail wind held. Again we set off, prepared for an unscheduled landing, probable impounding of the aircraft and possible imprisonment for us. We could legally only land at the few ports nominated on our flight authorisation. Indonesia's rulers were paranoid about the possibility of helicopters secretly landing insurgents to challenge their dictatorial rule.

I suspect my angel was as busy as my prayer wheel – a pilot's circular slide rule, used to check our progress. The tail wind held and we reached Denpasar Airport with ten minutes fuel to spare. We were almost surprised to find drums of fuel waiting, labeled for us. A great meal and night spent in a four star hotel in Bali at company expense helped compensate for the previous depressing evening. We had gone from hell to heaven in twelve hours, what was next?

A challenge appeared as we faced another ocean crossing the following day. Black thunderstorms formed ahead of us as we flew towards the small island of Masalembo. To refuel, we had to find that dot in the sea. The island had a radio beacon but we were told it rarely worked. Failing to find the island would mean a rescue from the water. This was not to be considered in view of the Indonesians attitude to foreign registered aircraft. We could not return to Bali, having used our fuel there. Our asses were in a sling again.

My angel and our navigation saw us reach the island even though the beacon was off. From there we felt it was a downhill run. Just 160 kilometres of water to cross before reaching the coast of Borneo, an island we could not miss. Also, now we'd be able to obtain fuel at airports where Western companies, or our own company helicopters, were based. For a consideration we hoped the airport fuel tanker drivers would fill our aircraft and then write the other, locally registered helicopters callsign on their paperwork to make the transaction legal.

Our first stop on Borneo was at Banjarmasin where a tanker promptly refueled us, after being bribed with cash and a Playboy. This was a lucky break, we didn't have to transfer fuel from the companies locally based helicopter to ours at night, after the airport closed.

No sooner had the tanker left us when a large helicopter belonging to Pertamina - the state oil company - flew in and officials covered in brass disembarked. Had they landed a few minutes earlier and seen our aircraft being fuelled, we could all have landed in jail and had our aircraft impounded. It was another lucky break so we lost no time in leaving for Balikpapan, where we spent the night in an American owned helicopter company staff mess. Obtaining fuel there was not a problem as National Utility Helicopters operated over a dozen large machines and our uptake was not questioned.

Next day we were on the home stretch, after a morning spent flying to Tarakan, we only needed clearance out of Indonesia. But the officials would not accept the validity of our flight authorisation. They said we could not leave until Jakarta had confirmed its authenticity. It seemed their radio was not working very well so this could take two or three days.

It was obvious; a sizable 'gift' was required to speed our departure but we could not bribe the half dozen people involved. We had given away all our Playboy magazines, bottles of Scotch and only a few US dollars remained. We could only shrug our shoulders, use flattery and hope for the best. The officials left but didn't take our passports so we considered our options. The Malaysian border was only thirty minutes flight time away. Our companies locally based American pilot agreed that making a run for it was the best course of action. He suggested we do it after the airport closed at 3 pm.

We gave the impression of accepting the delay by tying down the helicopter and leaving the airport. Returning after 3, we saw an aeroplane landing so not wanting to be spotted, hid in a deserted hanger. Peering through nail holes in the corrugated iron wall we saw passengers being dropped. The aircraft departed at 3.40 pm. Soon after, shutters were closed in the tower and the last parked car left the airport.

'We'll wait five minutes and then go,' Mike said.

'Are you going to fly?' I asked. Being Asian, I hoped he would.

He agreed to, but at the last moment said it would be better if he worked the radio and let me fly. *This made me the guilty party.*

I started up and left in a hurry. There was little chance that military aircraft would be scrambled to intercept us as the nearest was based an hour away, even if our departure was noticed. Besides, we were only being held on a technicality. No doubt the officials were peeved at not receiving a bribe and could make trouble. We sighed with relief on making the border, landed at Tawau and were checked into Malaysia. Despite the long shadows, Mike said we should continue to Kota Kinabalu. Both of us could legally fly after dark, but technically only in an emergency.

'I know the guys in the tower. It won't be any problem,' he said.

Fortunately the weather held as we passed close to 4,100 metre high Mt Kinabalu. I didn't want to face one of its wild storms. The lights of KK came into view as we cleared the last jungle ridge in darkness, at an elevation of 2,000 metres. The city never looked better. Our trials were behind us, a cold beer and warm bed awaited. Much better than being stuck in limbo in the third rate squalor we had experienced in Indonesia.

Next day, our joy at completing the ferry in good time against all odds was tempered by an irate blast from John Simler, the Company's manager in Singapore. He had been dragged out of bed at midnight by angry officials in Jakarta and threatened with all sorts of repercussions to his aircraft operating in Indonesia. The officials in Tarakan had got through to Jakarta earlier that evening – so much for the two to three days quoted.

It was some time before this 'incident' settled down, but it did not affect our operations. At the time the two countries often 'spat' at each other, particularly over border incursions into Malaysia by Indonesian patrols.

Little love was lost between them and I heard that gurkhas employed by the Malaysians were known to deal with foreign troops found in their territory by slitting every second soldier's throat as they slept. Next morning, the live half of the patrol fled in terror and never returned.

Within a few weeks our helicopter was placed on the Malaysian aircraft register which removed the stigma of belonging to a 'whitey 'company. I was also granted a Malaysian engineering license on the strength of my Fijian one as both countries used the same British system of regulations. This allowed me to sign for duplicate inspections, which are required by law when critical components are disturbed. My many qualifications had again enabled me to obtain a prime posting within the company. Another string to my bow. I was pleased to be gaining more experience in overseas operations in pleasant locations. These jobs also meant we received allowances for airfares to fly home for leave so regular trips to England were affordable. I felt my career was progressing, not stuck in a hole in some unpleasant backwater.

One day, while our company's expat families were still living in the hotel awaiting rental housing, Mike visited us and began to play with one of our staff's children. Unfortunately, the child's mother saw this and said loudly, 'Don't play with that black man.'

I winced as I saw how this racial slur hurt Mike. It was especially galling as all Asians love children - their own and other peoples. I somehow felt that stupid racist remark would have significant consequences, which it did. We could only work in Malaysia at the pleasure of the authorities. Mike, being highly qualified and well connected, had considerable influence in his sphere of aviation.

After almost three months in our small hotel room, our newly renovated, large wooden stilt house in the suburb of Likas, ten minutes drive from the airport, was ready. We employed a maid, as was expected, to wash, clean and perform babysitting duties. She spoke little English so we began to learn Malay and even attended night classes. Gavin also learned to speak the language of his sometimes keeper. It was not normal for white expatriates to use public transport so I bought Mary a small Daihatsu two stroke powered car, allowing her to shop and have a social life. At the market, lobsters could be bought for almost nothing; the locals would not eat them, supposedly due to long-held fears of spoiling. Mary soon found she had to leave Gavin at home when mingling with locals, as dozens lovingly stroked his blonde hair, quickly making him irritable.

One evening Andy and I went to a kedai, or small Chinese owned 'corner shop,' to buy beer. These places stocked everything from ikan billis, or small dried fish, groceries to laundry powder, cigars and alcohol, all mixed in a big jumble. Andy was from Adelaide, did geology at uni with my cousin, and was a wine lover like myself.

'Look what I've found Phil,' he said while extracting a bottle from under Chinese herbs.

He showed me the label - 1947 Penfolds Liqueur Port. We took it to the counter and asked the price.

'Seven Ringitt la.'

'Cannot la. So old, no good.'

Most Chinese knew nothing about table wine and goodness knows how long it had been in his shop.

'OK, I give you half price.'

Under two dollars for this aged iconic port, what a find. Having established the price, Andy asked if he had any more. We took home half a dozen each. One of my bottles eventually made its way home to Australia. I still have that memento, although I fear the Genie escaped.

Our normal once daily flights to Tembungo rig only took thirty minutes each way. We three pilots were not overworked, most of the day our two aircraft just sat on the ground. Our backup aircraft, a Jetranger, was obtained locally. The weather was usually good in the morning, but afternoon storms often spawned large waterspouts which made an interesting obstacle course to negotiate.

Mary and I joined the golf club, purely to use their swimming pool, just a short walk from the adjacent yacht club where we were also members. The latter had comfortable chairs outdoors under tall coconut palms overlooking the beach and magnificent sunsets over the South China Sea. It was natural to join our families there for a beer after work and almost impossible to leave before sunset. In this idillic tropical setting, Gavin developed a taste for beer. At almost four years of age he managed to lift other people's pint mugs and steal a sip while they weren't watching. When people guarded their beer he tried ordering his own from the bar. The unseen squeaky voiced request was politely declined.

We shared ownership of a three-metre runabout boat with our expatriate engineer. Using the boat was easy as we had differing days off. Few hotel rooms were available in Kota Kinabalu and tourists were rare. Consequently, we found uninhabited, unspoiled islands within twenty minutes boating distance. Oysters could be chipped off the rocks, and barbecues enjoyed on the white sandy beaches. Often we swam nude with a few select friends. A wonderful life in a tropical paradise.

Some Australian women we met socially didn't have it so good. They were married to local professional men whom they met while both were studying at universities in Australia. After graduating, these women found their husbands low local pay prevented them from fully socializing with other white expatriates. Many could not afford to visit their parents in Australia and none would accept dinner invitations. They could not afford to reciprocate and were possibly ashamed of their low standard of housing. They were trapped in the country. Leaving meant surrendering their children, as most were married to Muslims. These practical matters were not dealt with during their university education. Over the years I watched many cross-cultural marriages fail.

Our house didn't have a telephone and I learned it would take several years to connect. To cater for emergencies, Esso provided us with a pager. One night it woke me after midnight. Hurriedly dressing, I drove to the nearest public phone, a kilometre away and rang Esso's operations room.

'There's been an accident at the rig and we need a medivac right away,' the person explained.

'Have you looked outside?'

'No.'

'The sky is full of sparks and there are bloody great thunderstorms between us and the rig. To say nothing about possible water spouts. I dodged half a dozen this afternoon while the storms were brewing. I can't see them in the dark. I'm not going out there now; our chopper is not designed to fly in water.'

'I see, so I'll tell them you're not flying?'

'Not till first thing in the morning. What's the problem?'

'I don't know, they didn't tell me. I'll buzz you if we need an early flight.'

I hung up and drove home.

My pager didn't sound again and I departed for the rig as scheduled at 8 am next morning. Soon after takeoff into a clear blue sky and just after crossing the coast, the artificial horizon - my primary night flying instrument - slowly began to lean to one side. I would have relied heavily on its indication had I flown the previous night. It would have led me to fly into the sea unless I was sufficiently awake to cross reference other instruments. The artificial horizon normally displays a red flag when not functioning correctly, but this one did not. When flying by visual reference, these failures don't matter, but on an overcast, overwater night flight, can be fatal. Especially if occurring just after departure when transitioning

232

from airport lighting into a black void while still at low altitude. Murphy had tested me again, but I resisted the temptation to be a 'hero' and it probably saved my life. Luckily my guardian angel was well awake and prodding me.

Returning from the rig, I noticed a passenger with a bandaged little finger. I had been dragged out of bed and asked to risk my life for that!

During our stay, an oil well blew out on a production platform off the coast of Brunei. It eventually undermined the platform, which fell into the sea, releasing over 10,000 barrels of oil daily to the surface. A wide oil slick drifted hundreds of kilometres up the west coast of Borneo. By the time it reached us the remaining crude had solidified to form small floating lumps. This oily goo created the most incredible sunsets as the sea appeared to be on fire and when seen from the air flashed with all the colours of the rainbow. I haven't seen anything like it since and don't particularly wish to as the pollution it created must have been massive.

During our stay, Sabah was in effect a dictatorship, although regular elections were held throughout Malaysia. We soon learned not to talk politics. Some expats we knew were deported with only twenty four hours notice when they spoke critically of the State government and the ruling, all-powerful Chief Minister. At the time, he was reputedly the world's third richest man and had three wives including one Australian. We heard she was guarded and lived in luxury on the Gold Coast.

The 'Boss' kept two luxurious Grumman G2 executive jets in a hanger adjacent to our office. We heard his were the most exclusive and expensively outfitted of these top of the line executive jets in the world. I managed to bum a ride on a 'test' flight once and their performance was also amazing.

Apart from flying the 'Boss', they were often sent to Los Angeles to bring back fruit and vegetables for the Chief Minister's parties. Sometimes we received a few of these 'goodies' from an Australian friend who worked in the hangar. For some of the 'Bosses' parties, shapely blonde white expatriate females were invited to hand out drinks and hors d'oeuvres. For this simple duty they received a gold Rolex at the end of the evening.

We were told the Boss also owned a large hotel in London and a golf course in a fashionable county south of the city, in addition to the several palaces he maintained in his home state.

Sabah was being extensively logged at the time and all timber concessions were reputedly in the hands of a few people. Occasionally we benefited in a small way when visiting the town's nightclub where patrons sat in almost total darkness, often watching a central spotlit dance floor. We usually went with Terry and his wife, a blonde with curves in the right places. The drinks were horrendously expensive, but we didn't buy any as Terry and his wife took to the dance floor immediately following our arrival. Soon after returning to our table, invariably a well-dressed local male arrived and asked to dance with Terry's wife. She always accepted. As a result of her short performance under lights, a complimentary unopened bottle of Black Label Scotch arrived at our table, a gift from her dancing partner. Presumably a timber tycoon who gained great prestige among his friends by dancing with a white skinned blonde. Blondes could certainly have lots of fun in Asia.

We had no reason to criticize Sabah's benign dictator, if he turned on us we could always go home. Some years after we left, the central government in Kuala Lumpur became embarrassed by the 'dictatorship' and sent in troops to ensure a scheduled election was democratic. I was told that previously, elections were rigged by stopping any opposition candidates from nominating by the simple measure of placing police around their houses. This was to 'protect' them and prevent them from leaving home. Being unable to nominate, only the Chief Minister's cronies were rightfully elected to Parliament without cheating or bloodshed. Prior to the Chief Minister's departure after the 'clean' election, Boeing were building him a very special 747 aircraft with every conceivable gold plated luxury aboard, including a sauna, but the latter was eventually scrapped as being too difficult to incorporate. I know that my old friend Mike had the enviable job of travelling the world and wining and dining prospective purchasers for this VIP aircraft. It was felt to be far too ostentatious for Malaysia to flaunt.

One evening over a drink at the yatch club after work someone said 'Why don't you come and run the hash with us on Monday Phil?'
'What's the Hash?'
'Well, a bunch of us run around the jungle getting covered in mud and leeches. Then we drink beer and sing bawdy songs.'
'You must be crazy, running in this humid heat.'
'Well, it's not serious running. When the paper trail markers stop we mill about while the keen chaps rush around looking for bits of paper to begin again.'
'How far do you run?'
'Not far, perhaps six to ten kilometres. Usually takes about an hour.'

234

I decided to give it a try. The following Monday, driving out of town to the designated starting point on the fringes of primary jungle. I was introduced to a few of the other starters before a bugle sounded and cries of 'On, On' filled the air.

'Just stay with me, you'll see what happens,' said Andy as we jogged off along a rough bush track in company with a few dozen other men.

After about five minutes the pack re-grouped around a now stationary Hash Horn as the front runners spread out shouting 'Checking.' The paper trail had ended and scouts were searching for a new lead. Then someone shouted 'On, On' from off to one side, the 'Hash Horn' blew his bugle and the pack left the track and took off into the jungle. Pounding feet splattered mud everywhere. Some runners slipped and fell, their appearance now resembling aboriginal dancers. Several streams were crossed, filling shoes with water. Then the cries of 'On, On' from the front runners and blasts from the Hash Horn were again replaced by 'Checking.' The trail was found again and we skirted a village while the inhabitants watched in amazement as mud covered expats pounded past them amid cries of 'On, On.'

Sometimes, the trail came to a dead end and began again behind the pack, reversing the running order.

My instinct for location and direction indicated that after about thirty minutes we were heading for home. More diversions and checks followed until we hit the road leading to our starting point. The tail straggled back to the parked vehicles. Front runners were already into cold beers from a large icebox.

'Better check your feet,' said Andy, 'we often get leeches.'

I found none on me but some people did have bloody socks.

A group formed around the esky and I was introduced to more of the hashmen.

'What do you think Phil' asked a bank manager. 'Enjoy your first run?'

'Sure, good way to get some exercise.'

'Well come again next week. Cranky is laying the trail, he usually does a good one.'

'Same area again?'

'No, could be anywhere.'

Then the Hash Master called the group to order and made announcements. I was surprised when he said 'Come over here would you Phil."

He welcomed me to the K2 H3 – Kota Kinabalu Hash House Harriers and produced a pewter pint pot of beer.

' Phil, a Hash tradition is that you have to drink all this without stopping, if you can. The pot is known as the Hash Vomitorium, and if you can't drink it down in one go you have to pour the remainder over your head.'

The group began singing 'Drink it down, drink it down down down' as I struggled to empty the pot. I had to stop, took a breath and dumped the remainder over my head.

Then the mob began singing 'He's a hash man, he's true blue, He's a bastard through and through.'

I had been initiated into the Hash.

Some other runners were then cited for penalties such as short-cutting the run, singing in tune or similar heinous crimes. Their penalty was also to empty the Vomitorium into or over themselves.

I learnt of the 'Down Down' after the beer in the chest was exhausted. It entailed moving to continue drinking at a restaurant in town somewhere, but eating was entirely optional. I didn't go after my first run, being expected at home for dinner.

On subsequent occasions I joined the 'Down Down' gang in town, leaving my car safely at home. The group booked a small, none too posh, eating establishment and sounds of bawdy rugby and other licentious songs filled the air as sweaty mud covered hash men swigged copious amounts of beer interspersed with chillie crab, chicken and beef.

As the night progressed, raconteurs stood on a table to tell the latest filthy jokes. One night Andy, an Esso geologist, was on the table telling a good story when hot chillie sauce was poured inside the back of his shorts. Engrossed, he didn't notice until his backside and testicles seemed to be on fire. We found a hose at the rear of the restaurant where he dropped his shorts, stuck his bum in the air and I hosed him down. He found some butter, applied it liberally to his privates and we carried on with the drinking. I don't know what Andy told Heather when he got home that night.

'Why are some guys leaving and then coming back after a while?' I asked Andy.

'Didn't you know Phil, there's a brothel next door. Cheap too, I'm told.'

I stayed with the booze and bawdy songs.

Around 11 pm I'd catch a bus to our home stop, stumble the block or so to our metre and a half high front gate, climb over it and fall in a heap on the other side. Unlatching the gate was too difficult. Then discarding my muddy clothes, I left a trail to the front door where I stepped out of dirty runners and walked naked to the shower. Our house girl lived elsewhere and her first job on Tuesdays was to collect my discards as she walked in, then wash them.

My wife spent Monday evenings with other Hash widows somewhere. I don't know what they did but I'm sure their outing was more dignified than ours.

The Hash House Harriers began in 1938 as a result of two expatriates in Kuala Lumpur feeling the need for exercise. Gymnasiums were rare so the pair ran around a field on Monday after work to sweat out some of the weekend's alcohol intake. Adjacent to the field, a restaurant called The Hash House plied its trade. Tired and sweaty after running in the tropical heat, the friends fell upon a beer or two at The Hash House.

The two runners became three and as the numbers swelled people became bored with the same turf and began to run further afield. Then, a paper trail was laid to add interest to running in the sweltering heat and a hash culture began to form. A hare was nominated to lay the trail, complete with false leads, gaps in the shredded paper clues and suchlike. The trails moved to jungle territory, along bush tracks, up and down hills, across muddy streams and then back to the starting point. The larger hash runs such as Kuala Lumpur, Singapore, Jakarta, and Hong Kong managed to have a 'Promotional' brewery truck at the end of the run so free beer was available to quench the runners' thirst. In those days, only males participated. The Hash House Harriers, also known as H3, grew and spread all over the world as expats took this experience home with them.

When I was Singapore based, the opportunity arose to run the Hash in Kuching, Jakarta and also the Mother Hash in Kuala Lumpur. I found the runs a good place to meet very helpful, no nonsense people with numerous useful contacts in many areas.

The K.L. 'Mother Hash' were serious runners. I did manage to short cut on this strenuous outing without being caught due to my good sense of direction and bushcraft.

Job frustration in third world countries can be daunting but the Hash was one way to sweat it out of the system. Heavy drinking or other activities are entirely optional and some people enjoy the Hash as an interesting way to stay fit.

Our tropical paradise in Borneo also had a cold side, to be found at the Kinabalu National Park, located 1,600 metres above sea level. It featured well designed A-frame houses with spectacular views of Mount Kinabalu while enjoying sitting in front of a log fire during the cold evenings. The starting point for the trail to the summit of Mount Kinabalu, Asia's second highest mountain, began nearby.

An expatriate oil worker and I did the climb, hiring a guide who carried our sleeping bags and food for the overnight stop in a hut at 3,030 metres. Bungkili, our slim guide, wearing a thin shirt, shorts and thongs, seemed unfazed by the load he carried, or the cold.

At 4 am next morning, we required little urging to hit the trail as our sleeping bags proved inadequate for the temperature at this altitude. The thin air had us gasping during the latter stages, but we made it to the summit in time to witness a spectacular sunrise as Borneo unfolded below us under clear skies. After such a view, the stroll down was anti climatic but my muscles were sore for days afterwards.

We were well settled when Mary's parents flew out to visit. The day after arriving my mother-in-law collapsed with exhaustion. Her husband, though a medical doctor and eye specialist, didn't know what to do. Seeing her symptoms I mixed a teaspoonful of salt in a glass of water and told her to drink it. She did and recovered within an hour. Her husband was amazed at my simple fix – which I remembered from my time in Darwin. A similar but tragic case occurred when a young couple arrived from an English winter to K.K.'s heat and high humidity. They kept their small baby fully clothed and covered by a blanket. It became sick and died from dehydration in a few days. Unfortunately ignorance was not bliss.

My misgivings about Mike being insulted by the 'black man' comment were confirmed when he resigned after less than six months. It did not bode well for our operation. I felt that, on principle, he would work to have us replaced.

Mary and Gavin flew to England to be with her parents for Christmas. I joined them in January and we took off to ski in Austria. Though not yet four, we put Gavin onto children's skis. He cried during his first forays on snow but before long we had to chase and redirect him to prevent an excursion into dangerous areas. In later years, he became a very competent skier.

Soon after returning to our tropical paradise, we learned our company had lost the contract after only a year's work. It was awarded to a local company based in Kuala Lumpur whose boss played polo with influential people. We were offered the opportunity to switch companies, but the pay was so low, none of us accepted. Just as well, that company later folded with many employees being unpaid for months. One of these jobless expats, Robin, flew for me in Hong Kong and P.N.G.

We found ourselves packing up house and living in the Borneo Hotel again. Before leaving, the Hash chartered the steam train that ran from Kota Kinabalu to Beaufort. It was a unique finale to our stay, as most of the expats and their families we knew joined us for this social, boozy day out. Over the next few years many of these new friends visited us as they passed through, or were based in Singapore.

I had been offered employment with our sister company, Airfast Indonesia at a reasonable salary and accepted. It meant being Singapore based and working in Indonesia on an awful tour schedule of six weeks away, then three weeks at home. Mary decided to return to England while the dust settled so she and Gavin flew off, leaving me to ferry our helicopter back to Singapore.

It was not a happy time for either of us. We were unsure how to resolve our current situation, my tour schedule again being a concern. I just had to hope another, better job offer would arise. Returning to Australia was not an answer, pilots worked similar tours there, without the provision of airfares. Our enviable, home based jobs had gone. I worried that I had led my family down a difficult road.

For now, I had to concentrate on flying my machine to Singapore, through new territory, then across the South China Sea, a six hundred kilometre water crossing, without landing on hostile Indonesian soil. I definitely did not want a repeat of the trouble we had flying up from Darwin.

Our 'Island Paradise' near KK, forever gone!

CHAPTER 12

Helicopters can't fly; they're just so ugly the earth repels them.
~ The Aviators Guide Book

Terry, the engineer, and I departed Kota Kinabalu with sad hearts and flew south down the coast, reaching Kuching without any problems.

Next morning at the airport, I filled out the required eight copies of our General Declaration, using the only available sheet of carbon paper. It seemed to take forever. We then staggered into the sky, our machine heavily laden with cans of fuel which Terry planned to pour into our cabin tank as we flew over the South China Sea. It was not to be. After an hour and a half I turned around and flew back to Kuching. The continuous cloud, almost to water level, combined with driving monsoon rain defeated us.

The immigration and customs officers were pragmatic and decided not to check us back into Malaysia and out again, just for an overnight stopover. Our original set of paperwork would suffice. What a difference compared to Indonesia, where in the worst case we would have had to wait days for a new flight clearance. The following day we successfully made the crossing. At four and a half hours it was the longest flight I had ever done in a helicopter without landing to refuel. Terry refueled us manually as we flew over the white capped sea. Not having landing permission, we weren't game to sit on an Indonesian island for a few minutes.

In Singapore I found John Simler, previously the company manager in New Guinea and an old friend, still working in the office. The trouble I caused John on leaving Tarrakan was forgotten. I was sent to Jakarta to complete an aviation medical, required twice a year. Much of their equipment was antiquated, but I was amazed to find an anachoidal, or soundproof chamber to test hearing. Many theory exams were required to obtain an Indonesian licence, for which I dutifully studied. I found the various exam questions ambiguous and written in 'pigeon english.' Later, learning that a pass mark was determined by the size of my Companies bribe. It didn't matter which box I ticked or what I wrote.

After giving the authorities finger and palm prints, my travel and work permits were obtained after a few weeks. I required a local pilot's license and valid medical. Also a visa and work permit plus a Surat Jalan, or permit to travel around Indonesia from one province to another and a Kim Card. I don't know what the latter was for? These six documents all had different expiry dates but theoretically any one being invalid meant I could not travel or work. A bureaucratic nightmare for our Singapore office to keep track of dozens of employees paperwork.

When our crate of household goods arrived from Kinabalu it was placed in storage as Mary decided to remain in England and place Gavin into kindergarten. We still felt very unsettled and uncertain of where our future lay. This temporary arrangement caused stress in the family but the bills had to be paid. I resigned myself to bachelorhood and continuous months working in Indonesia. Letters were written searching for a better job but my resumes were one of many. I learned another disturbing fact – my employers pay cheques had been known to bounce. That happened to me as well.

A rival company's chief pilot in Kuching was grounded for causing a minor accident. Having a valid Malaysian licence, I was rented out to do his job for several weeks. I found myself flying the Governor and senior government ministers around the State. They used helicopters extensively and had helipads everywhere, even next to major government buildings in the middle of town. Before returning to Singapore I ran the local hash and met more interesting people.

At the end of July 1975, having received my Indonesian paperwork, and now possessing three valid flying licences, I flew to Palembang in Sumatra. A driver took me to the Shell Company coal exploration camp at Tanjong Enam. After arriving, I noticed a plume of smoke rising from a hole in the ground close to town. It seems the smoke came from an underground coal seam that caught fire many years earlier, during mining.

Shell were drilling a large area to determine the extent of coal seams and we moved their drills. Our Bell 204 helicopters were aerial cranes, first dismantling, then slinging out parts of the specially designed equipment to a new location and placing our load precisely in position, reassembling the rig again. This work had to be done in the correct sequence, requiring precision flying guided by a loadmaster's radio patter and our underneath mirror.

Our task could not be learned verbally so I spent a whole day visiting several rig sites watching the process. I had to learn the names and position of rig parts to know where to hover when the load was hooked on, and where to aim to place it at a new location. Time could not be wasted shuffling about with a load. Even worse, indecision could cause accidents with people being blown over by rotor downwash, or hit by a load. After my day on the rigs, I knew what to expect and what to do when in the cockpit.

Then 'Bomber' Wile, an ex navy pilot, had a fully opened cabin door come off in flight. It flew up and mangled his main rotor blades. He quickly landed in a grassy field to inspect the damage. The blades sported large holes, but Grant, an ex Vietnam pilot said he'd seen much worse get home. Grant flew the damaged machine back to our workshop so new blades could be fitted. The blades cost more than our annual salary.

After that incident, I never flew, or let my pilots fly, with the door fully open unless specially approved restraining devices were fitted. Though not approved by the flight manual, it was much safer to operate with the doors partly opened and firmly tied to the seats or other strong structures inside the cabin. The reason for flying fast with open doors is so long objects can be placed inside, protruding from the cabin like miniature wings. I have never known a door to come off when the doors were tightly roped. With one helicopter awaiting parts we were kept very busy. On one hectic day I spent almost six hours in the cockpit without leaving it.

Getting spare parts into Indonesia was incredibly difficult so we had a special 'facilitation man' to overcome this problem. An ex-government intelligence officer, he knew the right people, was paid US$1000 a month in expenses, no questions asked. It was an enormous amount by Indonesian standards but his job was to ensure our parts got through customs quickly. Potential delays for time sensitive imports seemed universal in Indonesia as government officials were paid very poorly. They could not survive on their salary, so topped it up with bribes. Everyone knew the system and acted accordingly. The size of the bribe depended on who or what was required, its urgency and financial ramifications.

Having spent months in the field I was due four weeks leave and an airfare to England. On the way I stopped in Kuala Lumpur to do my Malaysian medical. Afterwards, I had a beer or two with my ex Kota Kinabalu friends Heather and Andy, now K.L. based. While driving to the airport, we saw my flight taking off for London. This meant I had to fly back to Singapore as British Airways only visited KL once a week. Mary was not happy after driving to Heathrow to collect me and I wasn't there. I didn't arrive until the following morning, twenty four hours late. It's the only flight I have ever missed. Mary had rented a flat in Cheltenham and Gavin

242

was attending kindergarten there. His third in three different countries, perhaps setting the travel pattern he would follow prior to marriage. In those days it was almost impossible to make a phone call out of Sumatra, but amazingly letters arrived from England to our camp within a week. Mail was the only reliable communication though telegrams were used for vital information.

On my return journey, I happened to arrive at Heathrow hours ahead of time. I had my British Airways ticket endorsed so I could leave on an earlier Qantas flight. It also gave me a better chance of being allocated a seat as I was travelling low priority, subject to load, on a cheap ticket. My strategy backfired. The Qantas jumbo developed an engine problem so we were all dumped in Frankfurt while the aircraft flew back to London to be fixed. We were accommodated in a hotel adjacent to the airport, but I was so annoyed I went to the only bar open at that late hour and drank beer at exorbitant prices, which I charged to my room. The bar was deserted except for the resident whore, and practicing my German, I was amazed at the prices she charged.

Next morning I threw my key in at reception without pausing as I walked out of the hotel. I've no idea how much my drink bill was. The airport terminal was in a shambles with three hundred extra people trying to get on any flight to Singapore. With my low priority ticket, only my elbows and ability to speak German got me on a flight that day. My angel sure helped me again. All the different languages in use reminded me of my childhood, growing up multilingual.

While away, one of my Indonesian travel documents expired, but I was needed back at work immediately. I was to fly to Jakarta to renew it, even though not supposed to travel there.

'Nukulu will meet you the airport and fix immigration,' I was told.

Due to being given a cheap low priority ticket I only managed to get on the last flight, arriving in Jakarta around midnight. By then my 'facilitator' had given up and gone home so I was escorted to the Chief of Immigrations office. He was tired and irritable. In broken English he made no bones about my transgression of the law. Amid table thumping he said I would be deported on the morning's first flight. I was to get my paperwork in order before returning.

'I'm sorry, your travel documents are so complicated. Perhaps I can pay a fine?'

I hoped it might be possible to bribe my way in. He would have none of it. I wasn't going to push my luck and possibly be charged with bribery, so apologized profusely as best I could in Indonesian.

Luckily, my passport was not stamped 'DEPORTED', which would have had serious implications. I was allowed to spend the night in the company hotel instead of being forced to sleep at the airport. The company 'fixing, grease man' must have had words with someone while waiting for me, I was not badly treated. It took another week in Singapore before I could return to work in Sumatra.

When I flew to Jakarta for a medical in 1975 the Australian national elections were approaching. Many Australian expats worked on the Shell contract, they asked me to bring back postal vote papers from the Australian Embassy. I went to some trouble to obtain these plus candidates names and political affiliations. We dutifully filled out voting forms and sent them off. Months later I was annoyed to find that having been out of Australia for more than two years, my, and probably many others votes, would not be counted. Didn't the government think we listened to radio Australia.

I was prepared to work over Christmas 1975, having just returned from leave. With the drilling shut down and most people away I decided to amuse myself by making a large shanghai, or slingshot, to keep the hordes of dogs away from our almost deserted camp site. I never got to use it. At the last moment, being allowed to leave and spend Christmas in Singapore. By dint of knowing enough of the culture, language, bribes, having a white skin, sharp elbows and being tall, I got to the front of jammed airport queues and made it home just in time for Christmas dinner with friends. Mary and Gavin remained in England.

New Year saw our work busy as ever. 'Bomber' Wile got himself lost and short on fuel. I eventually found him and just had time to drop a fuel drum before dark. He had no pump but used a household bucket and a banana leaf as a funnel to pour the fuel into his tank. Part of his penance was shouting the bar that night. Many years later, on another Shell contract in Papua New Gunea, I would again come to his rescue with more fuel.

Our loadmasters spent many months being sand blasted by us every day, without relief. One, a cultured gent who rarely got to see his family in England, amused us by completely disrobing, then climbing up four metres into the open structural beams of our large 'house wind,' to drink his beer. 'House winds' were open huts made of local undressed timber and leaves, pergola like in structure and built to any required size. It made no difference to him if ladies happened to be present, though they were rare. At times he even howled like a monkey. He did this when the British Ambassador came to visit our bar. That evening he eventually came down,

244

pulled on a pair of shorts, then spoke to his consular representative in his normal 'proper,' upper class, accent. I believe he was making the point that he needed a break at home but his rosters were inflexible.

This gentleman had good reason to shout at me one day. We were flying the usual underslung loads from a tricky pad with a tailwind on takeoff. I elected to try and get the job done but one load proved too difficult and didn't clear the trees. I dragged the 1,300 kilogram lump of steel through the topmost branches trying to gain speed so I could climb away. This frightened the hell out of the loadmaster who screamed 'release, release.' He thought I might follow the load into the trees. I did have to release the load; it was not coming out of the foliage. We gave up then and finished that job the next day. I fished the undamaged load out with a long line.

George (Nature Boy) arrived to fly on this contract. Unlike our time together in P.N.G., this time I was a pilot on the same job. Our working area was largely populated so George was clothed while flying and our client also had safety regulations concerning attire. When possible, George found a quiet corner of the campsite to sunbathe his whole body. I believe it was then that he confessed his formidable weapon could be disadvantageous in sexual congress. It was simply too long for many. So much for penis envy.

A power generation expert from Scotland stayed with us at one camp. He was to renovate a dilapidated coal-fired, steam turbine plant the Dutch built fifty years ago. It was moth balled when the Japanese provided a new power station. One evening, the Indonesians managed to crash the new plant completely and it could not be restarted without electricity. Consequently, a large part of Sumatra was without power including our freezers full of precious imported goodies.

After a short discussion, the Scottish expert left the bar with a box of matches and drove to the old, deserted, plant. He poured oil on a rag, found wood chips and coal and lit a fire in the boiler room. Several hours later he had enough steam to run a turbine and produce electricity. Then came the tricky job of starting up the new power station and feeding consumers without again overloading. By midnight the lights were back on. We rejoiced knowing our beer would stay cold. It just goes to show what can be done with a box of matches and some resourcefulness.

Due to lack of interest by others I was made the senior pilot while on site. This meant extra duties, scheduling the flying and maintenance requirements. It also meant I flew Shell's senior aviation safety inspector,

Jamie Rees, the famous World War II fighter ace, on his visits.

Mary and Gavin returned to Singapore in January 1976 and we took over a reverted properties detached house in Changi. It was the beginning of a long association with this type of accommodation. The rental cost was very cheap by Singapore standards but the government did virtually no maintenance on these houses. Any improvements were entirely at the tenants' expense and could not be recouped. The British built hundreds of these detached dwellings for their military personnel after World War II and on independence, sold them to the Singapore government for a dollar. The houses were grouped on estates throughout the Country, without dividing fences. Some were next to parks, others golf courses or tennis courts. Our backyard joined a large park that housed Changi prison, the high walls facing us several hundred metres away.

In March we departed for Sydney on holidays. Our next stop was Gavin's birthplace, Sale, before flying to Adelaide for my father's eightieth birthday. My parents had moved to there for health reasons, also to join my mother's sisters at a Lutheran nursing home in the suburb of Glynde. That move ended a forty two year stint working for the Mission in the Territory.

Once celebrations ended, we flew to Perth, again staying with friends. I was amazed at the low cost of riverfront properties, in comparison to other cities. We managed to find a townhouse in Maylands, right on the river. We purchased, carpeted and curtained the property in three days before heading back to Singapore. The townhouse was mostly an investment property that could perhaps be a useful residence in the future. Singapore was also closer to Perth than any other major Australian city. We had earlier sold our first house in Sale for a good profit. That town was prospering due to more oilfields being opened up in Bass Strait.

The holiday time we spent together caused Mary even more grief when I disappeared to work. She said it was difficult changing roles from being 'the man of the house', then dropping that role when I reappeared. She didn't have any close friends in Singapore, just wives in a similar situation to commiserate with. We found being separated for long periods causes more strain when living in foreign cultures. It can so easily cause couples to drift apart, or find new partners. Almost all the married crew I worked with were unhappy with the lengthy time spent away but the bills had to be paid. Mary felt I was never home when problems arose and had to be dealt with.

It was not a happy time for either, but at least I didn't visit the numerous cheap whorehouses in Sumatra. Others of our crew did and I sometimes went with them, just to have a beer and chat with the girls. It made a change from the monotony of working every day and living with the same people.

I constantly searched for alternative employment; Airfast seemed to be heading downhill in Indonesia. The Australian company, reputedly once the third largest helicopter operator in the world, was now in financial difficulties. My old friend John Simler offered me a lifeline. He had joined the local subsidiary of a large American company, Evergreen, and offered me three months contract work, hopefully to be extended to full-time employment. I jumped at the chance and resigned from Airfast. My separation became effective on the 6th of June 1976 after over eleven years employment in four different countries.

During the break between jobs we decided to move to a reverted properties house at Seletar airport. Our existing house was now on the fringe of the new Changi airport and a long way from any of Singapore's International Schools, which Gavin would soon attend.

The houses at Seletar had only just become available; many had been empty for years and needed renovations so we decided to select the best possible. Though locked, with my climbing and lock picking skills, I found my way into almost half a dozen without breaking anything. We selected No 13, in a street called Hyde Park Gate. The Department approved our choice and we had the house painted before moving in on the 21st June. It was a rambling three-bedroom home with Amah's, (housemaids') quarters at the rear. Later, we obtained permission and paid to have a cement floored patio added to the front, directly accessible from our lounge room.

We felt that our situation was improving immeasurably as Heli Services, my new employer, had their office, hanger and several aircraft based at Seletar. The aircraft being locally registered, I again had to complete a very complicated licensing procedure. This included filling my ears with oil while lying down and then standing up quickly to see if I fell over. It was the first and only time I had done that particular test. Eventually I jumped through all their hoops and was issued with Singapore license number 17 H on the 31st of June 1976, twenty five days after leaving Airfast.

While waiting for the paperwork to go through I trained on my first twin engined helicopter. It's always a major step transitioning from one to two engines, whether flying aeroplanes or helicopters, having to learn the procedures for continuing flight in case of an engine failure. I had eagerly awaited this promised opportunity and spent many hours familiarising myself with the complexities of the multi-million dollar Bell 212 model. My training was completed over a period of twenty-six hours in which I flew less than six hours under instruction. Years later when I transitioned pilots to this machine, a minimum of ten hours was flown with my student. Then he had to complete another ten hours flight time under supervision before going solo in command. Again, my engineering knowledge of the machine's systems greatly speeded my endorsement.

At one stage in my training, while hovering a few metres above the ground, I thought we were going to crash. Darby, my instructor, while fiddling with throttles, allowed the main rotor revolutions to slow to 75%. This is well below the point where the tail rotor is effective, so our machine began spinning uncontrollably. An interesting demonstration of what not to do. The only way he could regain control was to add power to speed up the main and tail rotors, but this made us spin even faster. People rushed out of maintenance hangers on hearing the strange sounds our machine was making. *There goes my job I thought, while bracing myself for the crash. The chopper that ploughed into Goldfields House in Sydney was spinning like us, but our problem had not begun with a mechanical failure.*

Gradually, Darby regained control, the spinning slowed and eventually stopped. I don't know how many revolutions we did, perhaps ten or twenty. I will never forget that exercise and did not try to replicate it with my students. My angel worked hard protecting us that day.

The rest of my training was uneventful and I flew out to Manila on 1st of August to start work in the Philippines, flying a Bell twin. It was not a hardship posting. Us four chopper crew we were based on the Island of Mindanao, over 700 kilometres south of Manila and living in a first class hotel in the coastal city of Cagayan De Oro. The flying involved moving materials and men engaged in constructing a power-line through difficult trackless terrain. Our machine was required to be available every day during daylight hours so two pilots and two engineers were assigned to the task. One pilot flew the afternoon shift, then next morning's stint, followed by twenty-four hours off while the other did the same. This routine ensured we didn't exceed our daily duty hours.

Mindanao had its fair share of beautiful young women, some being found in the numerous bars or dance halls. The other pilot on site told me he had a leave pass from his wife and seemed to pick up a different girl every other night. He was a Frenchman and it seemed they all went for him. The two engineers and I just enjoyed the good food, cheap beer and scenery. Besides, I was still feeling my way with a new employer and aircraft. My work schedule was geared to four weeks on and two off, also a better deal.

The French pilot told us the girls frequenting the better dance halls were not obliged to go with any male and didn't accept money for their favours. If offered cash other than a fare home we heard the answer was – 'No thank you, I am not a whore.'

Late one evening I was woken by a loud rumbling sound, followed by the hotel shaking. It was a moderately strong earthquake. Soon all four crew were out on our third floor adjoining balconies, beers in hand, watching the action in the town and port from our vantage point high on the hill.

'Look at that power line going down,' said someone as sparks danced hundreds of metres along a main thoroughfare and set fire to a broken gas main.

'Look at our pool' I said as our building rocked and swayed. Large waves were flying over the side, flooding the surrounding area.

Destructive fireworks continued in the city, accompanied by many sirens.

I looked at the structure around me, noticing a two centimetre wide crack through one wall. By now our building had stopped moving. No one seemed concerned so we continued viewing the chaos. None of the hotel staff suggested we evacuate the building so when the sirens diminished we returned to our beds.

Next morning I flew as rostered but while returning to the airport for the midday pilot change, could not contact the control tower for permission to approach and land. Doing so without clearance can incur heavy penalties. I knew of one pilot in Singapore who was deported for flying into a prohibited area. After unsuccessfully trying all means of contact, I flew a normal circuit around the airport but didn't receive any light signals either. *Something really unusual must be going on.* I couldn't circle indefinitely so landed at our usual pad. It was a huge relief to be told that the thirty metre high control tower had been evacuated not long before my arrival when a large crack was discovered, threatening the structure.

Later that day I discovered the quake caused a tsunami which came ashore during the night, drowning an estimated two thousand people. I believe the quake epicenter was a few hundred kilometres to our east in the Sulu Sea. Luckily our town was protected by an intervening landmass.

A week after the earthquake, I was asked to fly a visiting United Nations delegation. After arriving at the designated pick-up point I was shown a map of the proposed route.

'That's way inside the rebels stronghold,' I said.

'Don't worry, you will be escorted by an armed Air Force Huey gunship.'

'You must be joking. The gunship is camouflaged and our white helicopter will be a sitting duck. Besides, a gunship will really get the rebels excited. Sorry, our insurance does not cover flying in war zones.'

'But it's not a declared war area.'

'For insurance purposes it is.'

'Well, how do we get in there if you won't take us?'

'Your problem, try the military.'

I couldn't help them, so climbed into my machine and flew away. There was no way I could risk our expensive leased helicopter on such a mission. Even in many of the established power line clearings, theoretically outside the rebel territory, I had seen civilians carrying powerful weapons.

On another day I was asked to collect the remains of a wreck. A Philippine Air Force Huey experienced an engine failure about fifteen kilometres from the airport. I was told the pilot made a heavy landing, after which the machine caught fire. They said one cargo net would do to collect the remains, the faulty engine already having been removed.

They weren't wrong. Of the original fourteen metre long aircraft, just a few burnt oddments remained in the open field where the Huey had force landed. I suspect stored munitions left by the troops when evacuating ensured that the fire was hot enough to burn metal. By contrast, I have seen many other helicopters force landed without sustaining further damage after failure of their engine.

Unfortunately after a little over three weeks working on this contract I was told to ferry the aircraft back to Singapore. The power-line was incomplete but it seems further payment for our service was in doubt so we had to go home. I'd hoped to gain more hours and experience operating my first twin engined machine.

Our engineers fitted the large, essential, ferry fuel tank that occupied much of the thirteen passenger cabin space. However, there was still room for cases of the excellent San Miguel beer that cost about the same as Coca-Cola, also numerous bottles of the local rum and gin that cost virtually nothing and dozens of prime mangoes and avocados. Due to oversupply, the latter were being fed to pigs. Bartering secured the fruit for a few beers, as opposed to paying three dollars for each in Singapore.

A cynical point of view might suggest that perhaps President Marcos stayed in power for so long because cigarettes, booze and females were

250

all very cheap and readily available. Also the predominantly Catholic population could readily expunge overindulgences on Sunday. I was still very cynical about most faiths. I trusted in a 'divine' truly catholic force, or being, in the universe that responded to independent, un-programmed spirituality. Many other pilots I spoke to expressed similar sentiments and when saying '*Thank God*', did not necessarily think of God belonging to a particular faith.

In the Philippines, with nicotine, alcohol and sex so cheaply available to the population, little else apart from food was necessary for a happy life. Certainly, my time there was akin to a part time holiday. Most of the crews preceding me had to be dragged out, figuratively kicking and screaming.

As I didn't fly the aircraft over from Singapore and without any other information, I had no idea how much the ferry fuel tank held when full. It was obviously sufficient to cover the long over water sectors of the trip. Our first stop after leaving Cagayan was Zamboanga, in southwestern Mindanao. This hop only took several hours but it happened to be a Saturday morning and the customs officer had gone to the market to buy food. John, the engineer, filled all our fuel tanks and then we searched for the official to clear us out of the country. We eventually found him at a fruit stall. He stamped our paperwork without asking for a tax clearance or other awkward questions. We rushed our departure from the Phillipines, the aircraft being leased by the day from another Company and not earning us any revenue now. Normally on ferry flights I carried up to US $5000 in cash to cover costs and contingencies but there was no time to arrange this either. I was financing this trip on my credit cards and chequebooks.

Arriving back at the airport to depart for Kota Kinabalu in Malaysia, we found our aircraft sitting in a large pool of jet fuel. The fully filled ferry tank had overflowed via a vent. Fuel was still running out onto the tarmac. John and I had a quick discussion; then he crouched in the puddle under the aircraft and put his thumb over the end of the pipe venting fuel. I got in and started the first engine. It was unlikely a spark or our engine exhaust would ignite the fuel vapour rising from the hot tarmac but I didn't fasten my seat belt until the rotor downwash blew away the fumes.

John climbed into the co-pilot's seat and we took off, still streaming fuel. Several gutted airliners, full of bullet holes, were stacked to one side of the parking area and bore testimony to earlier rebel action at the airport. We left in a hurry, not having the thousands of dollars needed to strip and renew the curling asphalt in the parking area caused by our fuel overflow.

It was fortunate this international airport was deserted on a Saturday afternoon.

With a sigh of relief I climbed to a safe altitude and activated our international flight plan. Our path took us over various coral reefs and tropical islands including Jolo, which I later discovered was a rebel stronghold. We were not aware of being shot at and the flight progressed uneventfully until approaching the Malaysian coastline in the state of Sabah.

I had planned to track over low lying ground north of the 4,100 metre Mount Kinabalu, but that area was now host to violent towering, black, tropical thunderstorms rent by lightning flashes. We had hoped to reach Kinabalu sooner, but the delay in Zamboanga scotched that prospect. I pointed the aircraft to fly south of the mountain instead, where the weather appeared much better. All went well until abeam Mt. Kinabalu when the cloud tops began to rise from their base in the steamy jungle-covered valleys below. Neither the aircraft or myself were licensed to fly inside clouds so we had to go above them. I obtained clearance to climb to 10,000 feet (3,030 m). Technically this was as high as we could go without breathing supplemental oxygen, which we did not have. Soon I requested 12,000 feet (3,636 m) to clear cloud, all the while casting glances at the weather behind to ensure an escape route remained open. I could see that the airstrip at Ranau was still clear, so continued.

From previous experience I knew that breaks in the solid cloud cover would appear when we reached the coastline near Kota Kinabalu, only fifteen minutes distant. However, the white wall ahead was still rising and I was forced up to 14,000 feet (4,242 m). Airliners on our route were now flying below us, through the clouds. Poor John, sitting in the co-pilot's seat, became distinctly uneasy. I reassured him that soon I'd be able to descend to the low-lying coastal plains ahead. I checked my fingernails; they were still pink and not turning blue, a sign of oxygen deficiency and addling of the brain. Just off to our right, Mt. Kinabalu was being lashed by a black boiling storm, laced with flashes of fire.

We still couldn't top the next cloudbank and I had to climb above 16,000 feet (4,848 m). John became even more agitated. He probably thought I was losing my marbles due to lack of oxygen. He began to shiver as the air temperature was now 3° C.

Only a few minutes later (which seemed like hours) the cloud sloped downward and breaks appeared. Then I saw the jungle briefly, through a hole.

A few minutes later, we flew over a large gap, with green visible below. I reduced the speed to zero and power to idle and we descended vertically in the break. Like an elevator, falling at 2,000 feet per minute (610 m), we watched the cloud beyond our nose sliding rapidly upward. This vertical ride down took over four minutes before I resumed normal horizontal flight below the clouds. John's face resumed its normal colour as the temperature became tropical again and more oxygen was available.

We soon landed at the airport, completed customs and immigration formalities and were enjoying a beer at the yacht club, my previous haunt, happy at having overcome the day's challenges. Not having closed my bank account in Kinabalu I was able to use my cheque book to pay for our overnight expenses.

Next morning, we didn't fill the ferry tank completely, so our departure was normal. After flying past the rich oilfields in the Sultanate of Brunei in good weather we stopped at Sibu to refuel before continuing to our overnight destination, Kuching. In the Malay language kuching means cat and we were about to become the mouse as the weather turned foul. I had to creep along just above the jungle in limited visibility and heavy rain. As the weather worsened and I could hardly see the trees twenty metres ahead, paddy fields appeared below.

'John, we should try and land here until the rain eases.'

'I think that's an excellent idea.'

By now, he was probably wishing he had never volunteered for this trip. There is nothing worse than being a frightened passenger when you can't see where the driver is going.

My idea was good, but finding a firm footing for our skids in the flooded paddy fields proved difficult. I tried putting the rear of our skids on the bank between fields but our two tonnes of weight demolished them.

'John, see those dead tree branches to the right? If I hover over them can you get out and place them on the paddy bank. I'll try landing and see if they help support the weight.'

He was happy to get onto terra muddy firma rather than hover when barely able to see outside. John jumped, sank almost to his knees and within seconds was drenched from head to toe but managed to position the branches. I moved over, sat the skids on them and slowly settled. The skids were not visible in the mud but with the weight spread wider the machine became secure. After waiting a few minutes to ensure our tail didn't tip down, I shut off the engines. The only sound now was the avalanche pounding on the cabin roof.

Then I heard voices. The owners of the paddy field were shouting at us in Malay.

'Silakan datang dan beristirahat di rumah kami.' ('Please come and rest in our house.')

My Malay was sufficient to understand the gist of the suggestion and it would be most impolite to refuse. We left the chopper and squelched through the mud to their home. I didn't expect much in this isolated jungle area. Their dwelling consisted of one room, perched on stilts above the mud, with not a chair or table in sight. We sat on a mat on the slatted wooden floor. In one corner, a smoking fire perched on river stones struggled to stay alight. While being ogled by numerous offspring I tried to remember conversational Malay. John knew none at all and was a silent spectator while I haltingly explained our problem. I hoped we wouldn't be held to ransom for the demolished paddy banks. The horsepower I had at my disposal had created damage that would take many sweaty hours to repair.

My fears were groundless, our hosts were overawed and treated us as VIPs. They offered us some strange home-grown greens and berrys. We politely declined these, also fire-warmed brownish liquid out of a black pot. It could have been anything, certainly not tea or coffee. We were offered beds for the night – dirty mats on the muddy floor.

'Terima Kasi. Tetapi waktu hujan berhenti kita harus pergi atau bos kita akan menjadi sangat marah.' ('Thank you very much,' I said. 'When the rain stops we have to go or our boss will be very angry.')

The prospect of fighting off malarial mosquitoes was horrific, no nets were evident.

'Orang penting seperti kamu mempunyai seorang bos?' ('Such important people as yourselves have a boss?') was the query.

'Ya, kita pekerja miskin seperti kamu. Kita tidak mampu mempunyai mesing terbang.' ('Yes, we are just poor workers like you - we can not afford expensive flying machines.')

'Ah, kita mengerti.' ('Ah, we understand.')

Fortuitously, as our conversation languished, the heavy rain eased and the visibility improved. Amid protests and promises that a feast would be organised for us if we stayed, we squelched back to our waiting steed and took off. After an uneventful overnight in Kuching we made it to Singapore the following day. Crossing the big pond (South China Sea) was becoming routine for me.

My joy at having accomplished another tricky ferry quickly turned to dismay when I checked my mail and found I had been terminated. John said he was sorry but there was insufficient work and being last on meant

254

I was first off. I had only been promised three months work but now was in trouble again. We had just established ourselves in the house at Seletar, I'd bought a second-hand car, and Gavin had begun school. I was offered a job in Sydney with my previous employer but they seemed to be going bust so that was the last resort. What were we to do now? I don't know if my angel or the devil intervened on my behalf.

Top: *Memories of happy single days.*
Above: *Were we to leave our tropical retreats?*

CHAPTER 13

Flying isn't dangerous. Crashing is what's dangerous.
~ The Aviators Guide Book

The week following my termination, Mary and I debated our future. While doing the rounds looking for employment, a tragedy occurred. A pilot flying on Bristow Helicopters heli-rig operation in central Sumatra was killed in a freak accident. Bristow's were one of the world's safest helicopter operators but in this case a primary flying control servo snapped and the chopper speared into the ground. Intensive investigation in the U.K. found a virtually undetectable small flaw, deep inside a metal rod, which suddenly spread and caused the failure. Unfortunately it's inherent in the design and construction of helicopters that some primary controls and structures cannot be reasonably duplicated or 'fail safely'. One simply cannot have a spare rotor blade waiting to spring into action if another should fail. Also, because choppers 'pick themselves up by their whiskers' so to speak, the construction must be as light as possible otherwise little payload can be carried. There is a constant compromise between safety, performance and other factors, bearing in mind that most commercially operated aircraft have to earn their keep or would not exist.

After hearing this sad news I went to see Bristow's Area Manager when he returned from Indonesia. I had the heli-rig and aircraft type experience necessary for the job, held a current Indonesian licence and was ready to go to work immediately so felt I had an outstanding chance of being employed. It almost seemed too good to be true but found there was a snag.

'There are many senior North Sea pilots waiting for a Singapore posting,' Chuck said. 'After temporarily filling the vacant slot in Sumatra, I'm afraid you will be sent to work in Iran when a replacement pilot arrives from the UK.'

It was a great chance to join one of the world's top helicopter companies. We had heard that young children, particularly with blonde hair like our son, were known to disappear in Iran and never be heard of again. The risk was too great. We decided we could not accept an Iranian posting.

I explained our decision to Chuck the following day.

'That's commendable of you to mention your apprehension about Iran. In the meantime we've got you booked to fly to Pakenbaru next Monday on our regular crew change. Our managing pilot will flight check you at our base in Duri when you arrive.'

How lucky could I be, I had fallen on my feet this time. I was going to a super new job prior to my official termination from Heli Services. The terms and conditions were wonderful; we worked for a week, had a week off, followed by two weeks on and two off. My salary was also better than any I had previously received.

On arrival at our base in Duri, positioned in the centre of an oilfield spreading over a hundred kilometres in almost every direction, I found our crew were accommodated in porta-cabins. Each having two bedrooms, with a shared bathroom and toilet between them. Normally your room was not occupied while you were away.

Bristow's had the best pilot checking system I'd come across. First I had to demonstrate my competence in performing all the emergency procedures on the two aircraft types operated, called a base check. Then came training and testing on the specialised tasks performed while moving the rig. Finally, I was signed off as competent in our area of operations or 'line flying.' Nothing was left to chance; the flying was very intensive. Our four Bell Hueys each flew an average of two hundred hours a month, continuously lifting maximum weight underslung loads. Two pilots were assigned to each aircraft, alternating duty, flying one shift in the morning and one in the afternoon. We supported a specially designed Parker rig, which I was told had found more oil than any other heli-rig in existence.

Drilling locations were in holes cut out of the jungle. All were laid out in exactly the same manner so we knew what to expect at each site. For example, the Geronimo line was always strung in the same place. This line was a steel cable strung from the top of the derrick, stretching to ground level at a forty five degree angle. It enabled anyone working on the upper platform to quickly reach ground level via a flying fox if the rig caught fire or blew out. Though decked with flags, it was a constant danger as we worked all around it picking up or dropping loads while the rig was working.

It became a virtually precision operation as the rig was torn down, flown by us, and re-assembled many times. Each move entailed around 250 loads and other operators were amazed to discover our record time from rig release (lowering the tall derrick and beginning dismantling) in one place, to spud (or beginning drilling) in a new location was two and a half days. Deeper drilling, heavier rigs in difficult country, like Papua New Guinea, can take a month to move but we were super efficient in every regard and rarely delayed by weather.

Some of us also flew the little four passenger Bell Jet Ranger. As these accumulated only half as many flying hours, one pilot was sufficient, although we often had a trainee Indonesian pilot on board. This greatly restricted the payload but the Indonesian government had decreed that we must train local pilots.

Another aspect of heli-rig operations I had not seen before was that Bristow insisted on safety clearings being cut into the jungle every six kilometres along all regular routes. It meant we could safely land within a minute or so, should a problem occur. These clearings were made by a local crew, who initially deployed into scrubby jungle by rope ladder from a hovering chopper. We were trained in flying that technique and also winching, the latter only being used in emergencies.

Our own locally produced area map was another new feature I had not found before. It showed drilling locations and safety clearings, in addition to towns and villages. The master map was a transparency a meter and a half long by a metre high. I only discovered this when a volunteer was requested to update it, which I agreed to do. The master was accurately amended by reference to satellite photographs, obtained from NASA. Dozens of our large keyhole shaped rigsites and the smaller safety clearings could easily be seen in clear weather, when flying high above by airline.

Given that we had probably the best pay and working conditions in Asia, I was amazed to find a lot of discontent and bitching among the pilots at Duri. We usually had four or five different nationalities on the job, including American ex Vietnam pilots who loved to stir up the Brits. Our chief pilot was an American with questionable leadership skills. The other Australian pilot and I kept clear of the discontented backbiting. We quietly did our jobs and enjoyed our time off in Singapore.

Mary was much happier. We had a settled routine, I didn't go away for months on end and she made many friends. An Amah (housemaid) was employed to wash, clean and help with minding Gavin. We joined a club for relaxation with friends while Gavin cavorted in the Olympic sized pool.

The Singapore government sponsored the arts so the Bolshoi Ballet entranced us for only a $1.50 entrance fee. Singaporeans felt that there was no money in artistic endeavour, these needed heavy subsidies to attract any interest. For the same reason it cost peanuts to attend the Singapore Symphony Orchestra's performances. The Sunday Tiffin curry lunches at

258

the famed Raffles Hotel were another matter – we helped celebrate their hundredth anniversary.

With a stable lifestyle, we were able to fully appreciating the multi-cultural benefits Singapore had to offer. My posting to Iran had not been mentioned again. I worked hard to be a model pilot while keeping my head down.

We enjoyed trying lip smacking food at restaurants featuring specialties from dozens of different countries. Servants looked after the chores and I was only away for short periods. Mary seemed happy and in Singapore children could run anywhere safely. Soon, many friends and workmates moved into houses on our estate and all night parties abounded. My career path was on an upward curve again with a company that promised employment somewhere, virtually for life. This bush boy was on track for more adventures and ready to take on the world.

To celebrate our good fortune we invited more than fifty friends to a party at our place. The Big Marquee man arrived with tables, chairs, and constructed a roof over half our front lawn to keep guests out of the house. Dirty Dan's, an excellent restaurant in nearby Jalan Kayu, provided huge tubs of delicious curried beef, mutton and fish plus a mountain of rice. The whole exercise cost around one hundred dollars as guests largely brought their own booze.

Mary purchased four dozen coloured condoms at a chemist's shop. The quantity obtained caused much giggling and curious glances by shop assistants. They were bought so we could hold our enclave's famous platypus races. Our group in Seletar has been the only place in the world where I have come across this sport. It entailed pouring a few litres of water into a condom, tying a knot in the end, leaving a quivering flattened sphere of latex with a tail.

The races were conducted on a wet concrete or tile floor, usually on a patio adjoining the garden. The contestants pushed their platypus from start to finish line with their noses. Each platypus needed careful transport to the starting line on a large plate to prevent it escaping and bursting if dropped.

Collisions between platypuses and people usually occurred, with tipsy males crawling over similarly carefree female contestants, sometimes knocking both to the floor, bursting a platypus and inadvertently creating a wet T-shirt 'contest.' Slippery, round platypus are very difficult to nose drive in straight lines, so many races become an interesting tangle of wet arms and legs. This mattered little, contestants being lightly dressed for tropical weather. Well-endowed females seemed to be particularly prone to 'accidental' collisions with men, much to the delight of other males.

Much later, one of our guests bid us farewell and staggered away. We assumed he was walking to his home, perhaps fifty paces away, but instead he weaved toward his beat up Volkswagen. I intercepted Eric and suggested he walk home and will always remember his reply.

'Thon't be thilly Pil, I'm far too piththed to walk!'

With that, he got into his vehicle and drove home straight across the park, rather than use the road, just managing to avoid a metre deep storm drain.

Late next morning, loud banging on the front door woke me. It was the Big Marquee man, wanting to be paid. He was grinning from ear to ear.

'Was a good party la.'

'Yes, why you say so.' *Had he been hiding in the bushes?*

He pointed at the lawn next to our patio's platypus racing course. It was covered in dead condoms, which had burst on hitting sharp edged grass. He was not to know they had only been filled with water.

Removal of the marquee revealed several males sleeping soundly in chairs, and one lying under a hedge. No doubt our Chinaman left with a good story about decadent white expatriates.

It was voted a great party and Greg, one of the attendees, was a good cartoonist. He made up a satirical, humorous book about the nights events and people, which circulated around Singapore. At that time Greg was a lowly Australian loadmaster who I transported and worked with in Sumatra. Fifteen years later, as Captain of a Swiss registered Twin Otter, Greg took great pleasure in flying me from Yangon (Rangoon) to our work-site in northern Myanmar (Burma).

Our first Christmas party with Bristow, a sit down dinner at the Hilton Hotel, was a dull, boring British affair until I began eating the orchids decorating our dining table. This simple act broke the formal, black tie mentality prevailing and became one of my party tricks.

Crew changing to Sumatra frequently meant we often spent hours waiting at airports for our notoriously unreliable and often dangerous Garuda flight to arrive. One morning, at the now closed Paya Lebar airport in Singapore, I watched a Concord depart with its usual accompanying thunderous roar. During the take-off, one engine spat out some of its innards and I saw a spinning, red hot turbine wheel, career down the runway at speed behind the aircraft. This occurred after the 'stop' decision speed was reached, so the pilots took off on three engines, as required by the manual. They'll be back after dumping fuel I thought, and that's what occurred. I had witnessed a million dollar plus cost event, perfectly handled by the crew.

Once I looked up the exhaust pipes of a Concord taking off from Heathrow. I was close to the supersonic flyer, a passenger in a 747 next to depart. Talk about the fires of hell, Concord sure shattered the peace and burnt a small lake of kerosine escaping earth. Mentally crossing myself, I hoped my angel would prevent me being roasted in this or any other world. Apart from Gavin's christening, or when visiting my parents, I had not entered a church. But adherence to high standards of ethics at work proved a winning formula. With a great duty schedule I felt I was being a better father, able to spend more time with my son.

At work, due to Government requirements to train Indonesian pilots to replace us, it was necessary to monitor and instruct them. Theoretically they were already qualified to fly in command. Unfortunately their training was done locally, on the cheap, and of such a low standard that much work was needed before being allowed to fly on their own. Some took over eighteen months to qualify on both our aircraft types. We heard their flight training was done three at a time, one flying, the other two observing from the rear cabin seats. All being in the aircraft, they were required to log, for example, one hour, though each received only twenty minutes instruction while at the controls. Some said the instructor inflicted cigarette burns on their arms when he was unhappy with their performance. It's hardly surprising their standard was so low.

Heli-rig work continuously pushed our helicopters to their limits, so a high level of skill was required to avoid an incident or accident. For example, our Bell 205A choppers were one of the very few made that can legally fly away with an underslung load we could not first hold in a hover. This negated one of the basic principles taught to students - if you don't have enough power to hover, how can you be sure the balance is right and there is enough additional power to fly away. We were breaking all the conventional rules but in our case could do so safely because the loadmaster told us our load weights. These were all measured initially by a large scale hooked to the load, then raised by a crane to obtain a reading. Because our cargo was lifted on the aircraft's belly hook, its effect on the aircraft centre of gravity would not cause a crash. We used the inertia in slowing (overpitching) our heavy metal blades to snatch us into the air and gain forward speed. This could be done because our engines, in tropical temperatures, were governed to their maximum power limit, regardless of the demands we made of them.

It's probably not generally known that a heavily loaded helicopter is like an aeroplane in that some forward speed is required before it can climb away. This is known as gaining translational lift. When snatching our nominal maximum 1,820 kilogram loads off the ground, the rotor revolutions slowed and we had to jump forward with precise timing to attain translational lift (at about 28 km/hr) before the rotors reached a critical decrease, or the load would have to be dropped. When translational, with more lift generated, the pitch and drag of the main rotor can be reduced which allows its speed to become normal, allowing a gentle climb to commence.

When the rotors slowed, red and amber lights flashed on the instrument panel and a loud siren pounded our ears reminding us to act quickly and correctly to prevent a crash. Pilots new to underslung load lifting with this machine had to be restrained from panicking and jettisoning the load. Many admitted being badly frightened at first. The Slumberger down-hole tool testing rack we flew was worth millions of dollars and some tools were practically irreplaceable in reasonable time so dropping and wrecking that load was not an option.

This lifting procedure entails a very delicate balance, as slowing the main rotor does the same to the tail rotor, the two being geared together. The slowing tail rotor loses 'lift', so the chopper tends to spin and usually maximum rudder pedal movement is required to prevent this. The reverse procedure naturally applies on landing heavy loads and practise is required to land it in the correct spot, when lift is lost after slowing. There was little room for error, the timing and amount of control movements by both hands and feet having to be all correctly synchronized over a few seconds during liftoff and landing or the helicopter or load could be damaged. In comparison, I found that while flying landings or takeoffs in an aeroplane I had all the time in the world to react.

Loads we hated flying were the drilling crews portacabins. These rectangular boxes had a large surface area, and always rotated slowly in flight. As they turned, the ends caused less drag than the sides so they constantly swung to and fro in a semi circular motion. All loads dragged under a chopper influence it in some degree, and in the worst cases, can take control of the helicopter. Some have even suddenly flown up and hit the machine before being dumped. The portacabins, even when flown slowly, gave a horrible roller coaster ride that could not be smoothed out except by slowing almost to a stop. Movement of the controls was pointless, we suffered slow torture as the nose pitched up and down while jerking and swinging from side to side, often for the thirty minutes it took to reach our destination. They were not a load to be flown if suffering a headache.

On one occasion we did a short rig move across the equator. I believe I crossed the imaginary line more than twenty times that day.

Many expat pilots didn't want the responsibility of constantly monitoring, advising, cajoling and at times quickly snatching the controls from a trainee Indonesian aviator. It also meant flying with extra weight or less fuel. I volunteered for this thankless task, seeing it as a means to advance my position within the company. It did; the results coming much quicker than expected. At home, I used this training situation as a joke, saying the Indonesians tried to kill me every day at work. In fact, they only got me into a tricky situation about six times when I had to quickly take over to prevent a crash.

Due to the continuing dissension and low morale, head office was aware that a shakeup was required at Duri. Before leaving, the American managing pilot told me he was recommending that I replace the incumbent chief pilot who was being transferred. I was amazed at this news; being an Australian and a new boy in a traditional British company. My volunteering for extra duties and lack of complaining seemed to have paid off. Then my friend Ian, whom I first met in Western Australia, arrived to occupy the managing pilot's house in Duri. He was originally British Navy trained, flew with Alan Bristow in the early whale spotting days, and was about to marry an Australian girl.

I was appointed chief pilot, ten months after joining, which ruffled a lot of feathers, especially those Brits who had been with the company for many years. With the boss being 'half Australian' and Stewy, another Australian as my deputy, we certainly had a change of guard and soon the stirrers gave up and a happy, cooperative atmosphere resulted. Aussie pilots seemed more prepared go the extra mile, unlike some others churned out by large military training machines.

During my life and job changes, I managed to meet many people. Some of these, like Ian and John, kept reappearing in my life. I was slowly becoming part of an old boy's network, which would prove advantageous in the future.

When Ian married Di in the Australian Embassy in Singapore I was his best man. The ceremony was conducted by a young man of typical Asian appearance who spoke with a broad Australian accent. He tried to talk

263

Ian out of proceeding, before eventually pronouncing the couple man and wife. It was the most unusual wedding I have attended, followed by the longest reception as well. It was held in a bar at the Shangri-La Hotel until we were thrown out at four am.

With Ian away on his honeymoon, I became the top company man in Duri and on occasion had to 'entertain' visitors from head office in England. Hoping to further enhance company staff camaraderie, I decided to try and start a hash run. It would provide some exercise before the inevitable sedentary pastime of thirst quenching after a hot day's work. Especially as the oil company had negotiated a special deal whereby alcohol from Singapore came into our camp duty free so it was almost as cheap to drink beer as Coca-Cola. I managed to start a hash and memorable evenings followed. One run was laid over a log across a bathing pool used by girls from an adjacent brothel. A lot of runners somehow lost their footing and fell off the log, amongst the shapely, naked girls who had been persuaded to bathe at that time.

We also held many 'Down Down's' in the bar at this brothel, just a few kilometres from our quarters. The camp's portable barbecue was set up with steak and veg obtained from the mess hall. Madame took some persuading to allow us to bring our duty free beer to the bar but when these were passed around to everyone the problem was solved, with a few steaks for the staff as well. Business was never better for her.

One night I decided to indulge in a massage after a tiring run. Suspecting mischief, I kept my shorts on and was lying innocently on my stomach when the door flew open and the boys doused me in beer.

On another evening the hat was passed around and a deal struck with one of the working girls. She prostrated herself on the bar, naked.

'OK you randy studs, lets see who can get it up,' shouted the Hash Master. 'She's free for the first taker.'

That sorted out the men from the boys. Quite a few got their gear off but ribald encouragement from bystanders was not enough to prevent brewer's droop. In our other life, back home in Singapore, I knew the wives of some who wanted to climb onto the bar top. Eventually a young single oil worker proved he could stay up to the test, joined the woman and cheers rang out when their brief 'marriage' was consummated.

Thirty years later I was approached by the hash historian in Kuala Lumpur who found my contact through the hash fraternity. He confirmed various details, then told me I was going down in history as the father of the Duri hash, which still runs. Another claim to fame that is not the most salubrious.

264

Then a new pilot, an ex-officer just out of the British navy, arrived. His attitude was that of a superior person gracing the colonies by his presence. Years later, when responsible for hiring, I never employed ex military pilots until they'd been out of service for at least two years, having learned the realities of commercial operations. In the military, the focus being to complete missions at any cost, whereas we only flew if overall this resulted in a profit, otherwise our jobs could go. Correctly dealing with the civil authorities and bill paying customers was another matter.

Soon after the new pilot arrived I was woken around midnight by our chief engineer banging on my portacabin door. The British boy had created a huge problem by insulting a local who happened to be a senior government aviation maintenance inspector from Jakarta. The government man said he was going to shut down our operation immediately, which he had the power to do. Unknown to me, as the only hotel in town was full, our chief engineer had put this inspector into the empty room adjoining that of our new pilot. When the new boy came home from the bar, he wanted to use the bathroom and found the Indonesian there.

'What the hell are you doing,' he shouted. 'Get out, black men aren't allowed in here.'

It took much groveling and diplomacy to placate the inspector and persuade him not to ground our operation. Obviously I found him another room to sleep in. I had a few words to say to the new boy. He realised he was in big trouble and needed to change his attitude. Becoming the laughing stock of our camp kept him very quiet instead of pontificating about the superiority of the British. I had no more trouble from him and we eventually became friends.

My flying skills were seriously tested once when a complete hydraulics failure occurred while flying with a load under my Bell 205 helicopter. We train for emergencies but it's white knuckles when it's for real. I had to drop the load while flying it a metre off the ground, at slow speed. It's not possible to hover, the force required on the controls is too great. The electric hook release didn't operate so I had to resort to the backup manual system, which requires taking one foot off the pedals. Murphy was testing me; one failure often leads to another. Having eventually shed the load, I had passed the grassy landing patch adjacent to our hangar so had to fly away and come in again. These maneuvers took a lot of strength as the controls are very heavy to move without hydraulic boost. I managed to set the machine down on the grass at slow speed and slide to a halt without rolling it over. Of course it was expected of me – I was the chief pilot. My audience dispersed, the event concluding without a spectacle or any bent metal.

Back in Singapore, Mary became involved in helping with riding for the disabled at the pony club, which was attached to the polo club. We became members; the fees being modest compared to the thousands of dollars required to join other clubs. One of the most expensive we heard of during our time in Singapore, cost over US $50,000 to join, having its own golf course. We heard the waiting list for the exclusive Tanglin Club was estimated to be fifteen years. For some people, cost was not an issue; it was all about social prestige.

Though prestigious, our club's main thrust revolved around the welfare of their horses. The clubhouse was a wooden shed, but it did sport a bar and a barman who rarely had a spare moment after six on weekends. As a spare man, not interested in horses, on Sunday afternoons I found myself timekeeping polo chukkas and then organizing the outdoor evening barbecue. Very few expats ate at home on Sunday evenings because traditionally it was the Amah's day off so help was unavailable. Always an extremely busy night for restaurants in Singapore.

Gavin attended the Tanglin International School close to the C.B.D. Luckily one of the teachers lived a few houses down from us so he travelled with her. The school maintained very good discipline and I believe achieved commendable results. The syllabus and term dates were geared to the British system.

During one of my off periods, to escape the sometimes claustrophobic atmosphere in Singapore, we drove to Malaysia and visited the Genting Highlands. This is where the original tea, coffee or rubber plantation owners sited their holiday houses. Most were grand mansions. We stayed in one where striking mosaics on the floors depicted country scenes and animals. It was rejuvenating to get away to a cool climate for a week and be able to play golf.

This trip had an interesting beginning. The used Mercedes 280SLR I purchased, with a view to exporting to Australia, broke down on the causeway linking Singapore and Malaysia. Being stuck between two countries, neither wanted to come to our aid but eventually the matter was resolved and we continued on our holiday.

In May 1978 our high time helicopter reached 10,000 hours flight time. The machine was only ten years old and I believe this was a world record for daytime-only flying in such a short period. Plus being done while lifting maximum weight loads for virtually all its life so it had been no easy run.

266

Our maintenance department did a fantastic job, often working all night to ensure all our four large machines were available every day. The only exception being the machines major overhaul, done every thousand hours. It was completed in a few weeks, very quickly by industry standards.

Our record was celebrated at an official function on site, attended by our Asia and U.K. managers. A large, specially painted feature board stated: *'Caltex and Bristow, a 10 year partnership that moved more damn iron, in less time, to find more oil than any helirig operation in the world. Over 334,199,516 pounds of iron, for 156 wildcat locations - May 1978.'*

Those numbers equate to over 151 million kilograms lifted, to drill 156 oil wells in new areas. I estimate the figures represent around 100,000 heavy loads carried under the helicopter. All this with only one fatality. It was an enviable achievement and I was proud to be involved. The bush boy was still proving himself, making important contacts in Europe, and now involved in this world record.

My local knowledge was demonstrated during Asia's large forest fires when smog was so bad we couldn't fly. Even Singapore's Changi airport was closed for lengthy periods. Before long, our rig was short of diesel and had to shut down to ensure electricity was available for the fridges and freezers. At times food is more important than oil. The situation became desperate as the rig personnel could not safely walk out through tiger infested jungle.

Caltex and Parker drilling managers begged us to attempt to fly fuel in, save the situation, and them a lot of money. I elected to try, though technically the visibility was so bad I should not have become airborne. It was only possible to see the ground when looking straight down, while flying very low. To complete the flight I had to memorize left and right turns while first following forty kilometres of roads. It was a bit crazy, flying the aircraft on instruments while navigating visually. A bit like driving and staying on the road by reference to overhead power lines. Even if I found the rig, I still had to get home again. I felt awfully lonely. The radio, normally so busy, was silent with no one else flying. If my engine was to stop, I prayed it would happen while over a road, otherwise I would not be rescued until the weather cleared.

At a predetermined point, I left the dirt track and maintained a compass heading above solid jungle for ten minutes. I'd have to fly right over the rig to see it. My angel led me there. While tightly turning around to land, the rig disappeared. But I knew where it was and soon headed home after dropping off my load.

Today it's so easy, just program the GPS and it will lead you there. Aviation authorities now constantly warn pilots to maintain 'situational awareness' so that equipment failure will not leave them stranded. I believe technology is again leading to a drop in some skills, while providing benefits and potential dangers.

Another testing time occurred when a new rigsite flooded after many loads had been dropped there. No one knew how long the equipment would remain underwater so we were requested to fly it out if possible. This was an uncharted procedure, I selected our best pilots to help me with the task. For some lifts it was necessary to strip the aircraft, gaining extra payload to compensate for the weight of water inside loads. Our loadmasters worked in metre deep water, finding and identifying parts of the rig by feeling for them with bare feet in the muddy liquid. Slings had to be shackled on at the correct spot, which meant swimming underwater. At least the loadmasters didn't have to fight off crocodiles.

Our task was made more difficult as the location was uncharacteristically sparsely wooded; the only fixed objects above this large lake were hundreds of metres away. It made hovering over a point virtually impossible as the waves created by rotor downwash moved in every direction. The only static near reference was our loadmaster holding up a sling, but he disappeared under the helicopter's nose on approach. To compensate, we fixed on him while trickling slowly above and then watched in our rear facing mirrors to see if he could hook the load on as we drifted past. If he was unsuccessful, we flew away and repeated the process. The loadmasters were unable to give us details of loads; their radios were not waterproof. It was a mystery to see what appeared in our mirrors as we lifted up. An unusual and potentially dangerous job. Some of our loads had to be skied across the surface while water drained out, enabling us to fly away.

One load I lifted snagged on an underwater object, causing my rotors to slow rapidly and my machine started to spin. Any helicopter pilot will recognize this as a classic rollover situation, spinning while attached to the ground with no real visual reference. Rolling over into the water would not only destroy the machine but could kill the loadmaster underneath me. I managed to stop the spin by reducing pitch, regained my rotor revs, and then tried lifting the load again. This time it broke free and I flew away. We were sure glad when that tricky task was completed.

Later, in P.N.G., I knew an operator who lost three helicopters in several days while collecting water in a suspended drum. The difficulty and danger associated with hovering over open water is recognized. Virtually all machines now used for planned open water rescues have expensive, sophisticated autopilots fitted to minimise the risk.

During my time off in Singapore I had been working on several patents. I wrote a provisional application for one and sent it to America. The other was done by an attorney in Hong Kong and I was eventually awarded a UK patent. It was for a lockable, multiple toilet roll dispenser, which I hoped to have manufactured in Hong Kong. While at a hotel in Austria, I had been told an estimated million toilet rolls disappeared from tourist facilities in Europe every day during the summer holidays. People took them, instead of buying paper tissues. My dispenser only allowed use of the spare roll when the first was unravelled. I travelled to H.K. on various occasions to develop my patent.

On one flight with Cathay Pacific a typhoon lashed Hong Kong as we approached. All other airlines had been diverted to Taipei. Cathay were allowed to attempt a landing as Kai Tak was their home port and they knew this notoriously difficult airport intimately. I knew it didn't meet international standards due to the proximity of obstacles, so special procedures were required. Quite a few aircraft had come to grief there because of its challenges. Runway over-runs resulted in the aircraft falling into the ocean, which lapped close to one end of the tarmac.

Thoughts of these previous disasters crossed my mind as I wondered how we would fare today. The turbulence from hills to the north became extreme as we began our long approach to land. The gale force winds blowing over the mountain range hammered the aircraft while ragged storm clouds boiled just above us.

The cabin was only half full so I carefully made my way to the empty rear section and chose a window seat on the right. The rear is statistically the safest place; first class passengers pay much more to arrive at the scene of an accident half a second before cattle class. Our severe, jolting ride continued, it was the roughest turbulence I ever hope to experience. The engines, no doubt on auto-throttle, alternated between a quiet sigh and a full-throated scream, trying to hold our speed constant. The wings flapped up and down many metres, as though trying to help us remain airborne on this wild ride.

Eventually, the famed checkerboard was reached (this being a large display of red and white painted squares perched near the top of a hill) which indicated that pilots must now turn right to line up with the runway. On reaching the airport boundary, we flew into a wall of water and lost all visibility. The engines roared and we soared upward to repeat the physical and mental torture for another fifteen minutes during our second attempt to land. Some hostesses began crying with fear, troubled by the pounding the aircraft was taking. I consoled them, saying that everything would be fine, becoming a councilor and 'expert' on aviation matters.

After another horrendously rough ride, we arrived at the checkerboard again and banked to the right. I saw the ailerons on the wing go to full deflection and hit the stop but the aircraft did not respond by rolling out of the turn. This was interesting. The wind velocity had exceeded the capability of the aircraft to respond to the pilot's demand. Eventually we lurched out of the turn and lined up with the runway. I saw the Aero Club building go past just below me and thought that a landing would be made.

It was not to be. At perhaps twenty metres above the runway the aircraft was rapidly blown sideways beyond the airport boundary fence toward the nearby high-rise in Kowloon. The engines roared, the nose went up, and we missed the buildings by a few hundred metres. The pilots set course for Taipei, much to everyone's relief.

We landed in Taiwan without incident but while being marshaled into an overcrowded parking area in wind and rain, I watched with horror as our right wingtip approached that of another aircraft. Fortunately the marshaller saw the problem and we stopped with our wing just a few centimetres under that of a 747. Another close shave. We were told to sit quietly and waited another ten minutes before pushback and deplaning occurred.

Due to the ill will between China and Taiwan, Cathay were not normally allowed to land in Taipei. We were unwelcome guests. It took the best part of four hours to clear the airport and be transported to a hotel.

Eventually ensconced in my room I checked the service directory and discovered a standard contract form among maps and the multi-lingual welcome literature. The blank contract, I was amused to discover, was for the supply of a woman, which I recall, cost US $20 for the night. My single friends told me that in Indonesia the price ranged from a low of US$5, Singapore, around US$60 and US $80 to 150 in Hong Kong. In Asia the freewheeling attitude to sex was carried to extremes by some businesses. I was told of hairdressers who draped their male clients with a cloth reaching to the floor around the barber's chair. For a small extra charge the client enjoyed a blowjob, given by a young girl kneeling between his legs and opening his trousers while having a haircut.

Next afternoon, the typhoon having abated, we flew to Hong Kong without incident. While waiting to board in Taipei, I spoke to several other passengers about our previous adventure. One Hong Kong businessman travelling first class and wearing a solid gold Rolex embossed with diamonds told me that he was so upset and frightened by the previous flight that he would never fly Cathay again. For myself, I had somewhat enjoyed the experience of watching a professional crew take the aircraft to the edge of its limits. Having done so many times myself when dealing with bad weather or unexpected circumstances.

Knowing a few Cathay pilots, on the return trip to Singapore I was invited to the flight deck. I mentioned the interesting ride into Hong Kong.

'Yes, we have been talking about that,' said the Captain. 'On the second approach we reckon the aircraft was hit by an 80 Knot (150km/hr) crosswind gust. If this had happened after touchdown you would probably have been blown into the high-rise.' I just hoped my angel was not getting tired of protecting me. Never the less, Cathay is a favourite airline which had some of the best pilots and maintenance standards in the business. Good cabin service is not the most significant consideration in my book. Like buying a used car, what's below the polished exterior is more important.

On one occasion, while Mary and Gavin were away, I was invited out for dinner. It was a calm, balmy night with a soft, full moon hanging in the sky above. Six of us had wined and dined copiously earlier in the evening and were relaxing in easy chairs on a private lawn. Our host produced a joint, which he passed around. I had never tried marijuana before and soon found myself seemingly bathed in a rosy glow of light and feeling as though the world was at my fingertips. I would never have dreamed of trying to find grass in Singapore, I knew of expat families who had been instantly deported for this offence. Their passports were also stamped, denying re-entry to the Republic. Alcohol was legal and enough of a trip for me.

Because I worked off shore tours with Bristow it meant we didn't have to consider where we lived in Singapore. Prior to Gavin's lift across the Island to school ending, finding housing closer to town where he could be collected by the school bus became a priority.

We looked at houses in other ex-military estates and found a lovely place in a good location. Immediately available, we became suspicious after finding the previous tenants only lasted several months. The house was the last in a cul-de-sac surrounded by jungle, seemingly an idyllic location to escape Singapore's busy, noisy, high-rise. Further investigation revealed that the prior occupants had lost pet rabbits, cats, and finally, a medium-sized dog. The surrounding jungle must have held large pythons to account

271

for such losses. We didn't want to risk losing our only child to a snake so turned down the house.

Through the aviation grapevine we heard a house was becoming available on a reverted properties estate much closer to the C.B.D. and Gavin's school. The incumbents were moving to Saudi Arabia. We took over their place with six months left on the lease and counted on working a deal with the government to retain the house. It was a spacious, airy, brick, two-story ex Colonels' residence at the end of a cul-de-sac having a separate two-bedroom servants' quarters, bathroom and toilet. I immediately put us on the waiting list for this dwelling, even though we were living in it. A risky ploy as we might be allocated another house, but one we were prepared to take. Sub-leasing was explicitly banned on the lease document.

Our first relocation, from Changi to Seletar, had required a small pickup truck. For this move, it took three loads on a five-ton machine to shift our belongings to Rochester Park, close to Holland Village. I was obliged to remove my small backyard workshop at the old house, it being our original wooden shipping crate. The easiest method was to burn it to the ground. As the flames took hold, I heard loud hissing and spitting sounds, soon followed by the sight of an angry two metre long cobra, its hood extended, sliding out from under the raised floor. We were leaving Seletar so I did not attempt to kill it and the upset snake disappeared into the surrounding parkland.

Singaporean incomes were rising and the demand for detached houses such as those on ex military estates was growing fast, causing long waiting lists. We were greatly envied by others in having a house close to town, in a fashionable area, at quarter the price of that available in the private sector. Our place was also far superior in room size and the unfenced garden space available. Normally, short-term, two-year contract expatriates had little hope of obtaining such houses.

After a few nervous months, the government agreed we could be allocated a house in Rochester Park, which contained about forty detached dwellings. I made an appointment with the department head to see if we could be allocated No 30, the house we occupied. I carried a bag containing a plainly wrapped bottle of good Scotch whiskey with me. After sizing up my man during the interview I realised it would be inadvisable even to offer to buy him a cup of coffee, let alone any form of 'gift'. Singapore was so different from Indonesia; here I could have wrecked any chance of success by offering an inducement. I think the official respected my deference and politeness and eventually agreed we could move into 'our house' when the lease expired.

'How soon afterward?' I asked.

'Probably twenty-four hours. We have to check the house first.'

My heart sank. Fancy having to pack and move three truckloads before moving in again a day later. I thanked the boss, and left. One win for the day was enough; I'd try and negotiate further after signing the new lease.

Months later I returned and saw a lesser official. I was ever so humble and after completing the documentation, began to carefully flatter my man in Singalese (Singapore english).

Eventually he agreed that the house keys could be handed to him, whereupon he would hand them to me and we could move in. A technical requirement had been satisfied but what a huge relief it was to hear those words from the normally unbending bureaucrats. They say fortune favours the brave but diplomacy certainly has its place.

Mary sourced a new Amah, our previous one didn't wish to leave the Seletar area. Her name was Chey, she was of Malay/Chinese descent and lived in one of the two servant's rooms. Chey was a marvel. Slim, middle-aged and apparently tireless, she had been well trained by the old school of British colonial masters. She became a second mother to Gavin and tended to spoil him. On occasions it became necessary to chastise our seven-year-old son for bossing her about.

I believe the school bus arrived at our house around 7.30 am. By now, Chey had woken, bathed, dressed and breakfasted Gavin who appeared at our bedside to bid us good morning before the bus arrived. He made it to school without us raising a finger. Chey would later prepare our breakfast, hot or cold, as directed, before we began our day.

If Mary was entertaining friends for morning coffee or afternoon tea, biscuits and cake would appear at the appointed time while she sat and chatted to her friends. We left any mess for Chey to clear away.

She cooked, washed clothes, ironed, made beds and cleaned the house during the day. After serving our evening meal, clearing it away and washing up, she was free to retire. Due to business and social commitments, we were usually out late several nights each week and Chey would baby sit Gavin for us. Undoubtedly the best servant we ever had.

On one occasion I was unexpectedly obliged to entertain visiting VIPs from head office. Unable to contact Mary, I phoned Chey, asking her to do one of her curries, highly regarded by our friends. When Mary arrived home, Gavin had been fed, the dining table was immaculately set and pots were bubbling on the stove.

'Missus, Master telephone. He say cook curry five people la.'

'I see, do you have everything you need?'

'Yes Missus, is all OK.'

'Good, I'll go change and then sort the pre-dinner nibbles.'

When I arrived home, after bathing, only the wine and bar needed sorting.

Chey made impromptu entertaining very easy and enjoyable, even if my wife was sometimes unaware of the impending event. Visiting bosses always felt privileged to enjoy a home cooked meal, spending so much time in hotels.

Our guests were invariably impressed with the competent and timely manner in which Chey served a two course meal, followed by cheese, coffee and liqueurs on our garden patio. It was a huge contrast to the awful meals served at the mess hall in Duri, which catered primarily for local staff. Expatriate oil company and other senior people were allocated housing, lived with their families, and imported most of their food from Singapore as its transport was provided free. They didn't care about the standard of food in the mess hall. Bristow's staff were among the few whites who ate there, only our managing pilot being provided with a house.

When working in Duri, I eventually brought most of my food in from Singapore. I cooked on a small two element electric appliance, which just fitted next to the hand basin in our bathroom. The oil company housing complex also contained a nine hole golf course, tennis courts and swimming pool. These facilities being free for our use, somewhat compensating for the poor food. With us pilots rarely having time off during the day, it was mainly our engineers who made use of the recreational facilities.

On one occasion, I escaped from our base and flew the small five seat helicopter supporting seismic surveys. Rod, an Australian and the Coordinator in charge and I were the only whites on this job. We lived on a houseboat moored to a riverbank on which a raised helipad had been constructed. It was a twenty metre walk from my flying 'office' to the bar and my bed. It was a relaxed, almost holiday-like atmosphere. Peaceful water views, good food and servants, but Rod was the only company. The downside was having little to do apart from work. Even this was slack, the large seismic project had not begun. Head office were yet to release details so the cutting crews could begin work. Consequently, about three hundred local labourers were tented twenty kilometres away in the jungle, restless, with time on their hands.

University staff were on holiday so students from northern Sumatra joined the labour gang, earning money to pay for their education.

Caltex invariably used local contractors to carry out specific projects, Indonesian labour laws being subject to local interpretation. Contractors were only paid on results and the methods used to obtain these could be draconian by western standards. One morning, after completing my scheduled flying, I returned to the houseboat to find Rod throwing down a large Scotch whisky.

'You got a problem?' I asked. This was far from his normal behaviour.

'Jesus Phil, the bloody work hasn't even started and I've got a murder and serious injuries on my hands.'

'What's happened?'

'Well it seems those smart assed uni students got the mob all stirred up over working conditions and wages and made all sorts of demands. To quell the revolt, I'm told the boss contractor got his hoons to grab the student ringleaders and drag them out in front of the workers. The boss then laid down the law regarding their employment. To illustrate that dissent would not be tolerated, he hacked off a troublemaker's arm. For emphasis, he then chopped off the other arm.'

'Blood thirsty bugger.'

'Yeah, well, when he realised the student was going to die from loss of blood, he hacked off his head for good measure and asked volunteers to beat up the other stirrers. I'm waiting for a radio call from the police and when it's safe you can pick up two injured people and take them to hospital.'

'Where was the union rep. while all this was going on?' I said, doing a bit of stirring myself.

'Ha bloody ha, the students were probably trying to organise one. You know the only employers that allow a union are the expat multinational companies. No local bosses would tolerate them; they'd make big trouble for anyone trying that trick or simply disappear them. It's a jungle out here. You can find tigers and elephants but certainly no sign of a union.'

The radio crackled with the message that I could pick up the injured.

Arriving at the labour camp, two young males were unceremoniously bundled into the back seats and I flew them to hospital. They received no attention by their minder during the flight and appeared to be unconscious. I have no idea if they survived. The labour contractor probably gave the police a bottle of whisky and told them his actions were self-defense. Many such issues were solved with a sufficient level of bribery.

Once back in Duri, my morale was dented when the only crash during my tenure occurred. One of our experienced pilots presumably had a mental lapse. He didn't intervene when the Indonesian he was supervising reduced power to idle after landing in a safety clearing. They carried a crew to renovate the metre high helipad on which they sat. Timber rot and white ants will render a raised pad made from softwood jungle trees unsafe after six months. We kept records listing construction dates. After landing on old pads, the aircraft should always be kept light on the skids. If the surface or supports begin to break, it's possible to become airborne immediately. This time the helipad did collapse and as the aircraft had no power to take-off it fell on its side into old tree stumps. We salvaged our poor bird. It was rebuilt and soon went back to work.

Our helirig continued to find new oilfields but inevitably these moved further and further from our base. Rig moves were being flown over longer distances and planning became more difficult as round trip fuel could not be carried, so more fuel was required at the rig site. Naturally we used fuel to position the fuel we needed. Computers were not available then, but I developed a formula to calculate the days and flying hours required, related to rig distance from our base, which affected the time working on site, and the length of the actual move. After fine tuning, my formula worked very well and amazed a lot of people as it had never been attempted before.

One of the first tasks, after clearing the jungle at a new rigsite, was to fly in Sam and his mini rig to drill a water well. The irony was that on several occasions Sam found oil instead of water.

At one drilling location a bear cub wandered into the camp looking for food. He stayed and grew alarmingly. For safety, a steel cage was made for him to live in. When the rig moved he flew with it, slung under the chopper. Eventually someone decided to let him go after almost a year of captivity.

On another occasion a fully grown tiger decided to visit the rig site. This sent all the workers running to the safety of their portacabins as the tiger prowled, presumably looking for a meal. The driller happened to be an Indonesian; the only local qualified to run the rig. Tommy was a good company man and hated to see drilling stop. He said he came from a family of tiger killers and would chase the big cat away so everyone could get back to work. When Tommy ventured outside, the tiger had different ideas and attacked him. He managed to roll under a raised walkway, but before the feline was chased away by the sound of a dozen advancing people banging pots and pans, Tommy was bitten on one shoulder and arm. We flew him to hospital and he was back at work in a few weeks.

276

In December 1978 we were booked to fly to England for an eight-week holiday over Christmas. Late in the afternoon, several hours prior to leaving for the airport, Mary drove into town. The heavens opened and torrential rain engulfed Singapore. A little later Mary phoned to say our Mercedes was stuck on Orchard Road with the engine seized, having ingested water. After collecting her in our other car, I frantically phoned a garage to collect and fix our Mercedes while we were away. Of course, it was also stuck in a no parking area. Meanwhile, rain pelted down and radio stations reported widespread flooding.

Our taxi failed to arrive and the rush hour having begun, it was most unlikely to come. I didn't believe the operator who said it was on its way, being over half an hour late. Desperately I walked to the nearest main road in the bucketing rain and tried to flag down a cab. We were now over an hour late leaving for Changi airport. Fifteen minutes passed without an empty taxi in sight. I eventually flung myself into one stopped at a red light. Apologizing to the occupants, I explaining my dilemma, saying I was there until able to take over the hire.

The other passengers expressed their sympathy, but it was another twenty minutes before I returned to my worried family. Eventually arriving at Changi two hours late, we expected to have missed our flight. The airport was in chaos. Most airline crews, due to take over arriving aircraft, had also been delayed by the flooding. Luckily we had no problem joining our flight.

During my time in England, Bristow's paid for me to complete my chief pilot course, even though I had been doing the job for months. This entailed a trip to Aberdeen, where snow fell during our attempt to land in darkness. We went around on the first attempt and I saw no lights below so knew the visibility was bad. On the second approach I remember the engines roaring as we descended to the runway, reverse thrust occurring while in-flight, hastening our descent. I believe our BAC 111 aircraft was one of the very few passenger craft certified allowing this procedure. It was certainly a strange experience for me. Several days at Aberdeen, with horizontally blowing snow and bitterly cold weather, left me distinctly averse to ever working at that company base.

After my course it was time to ski in Austria and visit our old friends in St Anton. Mary and I went there for a week, leaving Gavin in England before I returned to collect him. We then skied at Lech for three weeks before returning to England and Singapore. By now, Gavin, at the age of six followed us down the steepest runs. For many years our ski gear was left with Mary's parents in Cheltenham, which was very convenient.

In April 1979, my good friend and our managing pilot, Ian and his wife Di, were replaced by a laid back American couple. Soon after, Halim arrived from Egypt, having worked on the companies offshore operation there. He was supposedly Egypt's best civil helicopter pilot and was selected to come to Indonesia to broaden his experience. Our other base had given up trying to teach him to fly underslung loads. I was asked to take him in hand. It was his last chance to make good before being sent home in disgrace.

Next day I took Halim out and flew the machine while chatting, getting him to relax and observe procedures.

He certainly had his tail between his legs, having lost all confidence and fearing an enormous loss of face. Quite apart from the dramatic drop in lifestyle if he and his family had to leave Singapore.

It took a week of coaching and coaxing before I could relax while Halim flew. He mastered the new skill and was able to fly easy loads by himself. I had saved the pride and honour of Egypt. Halim was so grateful he fawned over me like a young puppy and did almost everything to please, except offer me his wife.

Once I accidentaly caused one of our young trainee Indonesian pilots to lose face among his contemporaries. While cruising, I asked him to show me his actions in case of a particular system failure. The correct procedure required pulling a circuit breaker. He attempted to do so but could not as his left hand fingernail was too long.

'Zueldi,' I said, 'You have to decide whether you want to be a professional pilot and if so that long nail will have to go.'

We talked about safety issues for a minute or so until I realised my microphone was switched to the company frequency instead of just intercom. My sermon had been broadcast to four other company aircraft and the local radio operators manning ground stations. I apologised to Zueldi but next day none of our Indonesian pilots sported long fingernails. They were worn because in Indonesian custom it showed they weren't manual workers.

One downside to our short working periods was the three trips a month we averaged with Garuda, the Indonesian state airline. One particularly frightening flight occurred when returning to Singapore on a Fokker F28. These jets were relatively simple, strong, and built to handle rough conditions. Being the smallest aircraft Garuda operated, newly graduated local pilots who barely looked old enough to shave flew them. We heard that these highly prized airline jobs were not always obtained on merit, but by political or financial intrigue on someone's part.

It was not a happy feeling to entrust one's life to these young, inexperienced neophytes, especially when the weather turned nasty as it did on this trip. Approaching Singapore on the short thirty minute flight from Pekanbaru, a large thunderstorm loomed ahead. I saw this through the forward cockpit windows from my passenger seat as the crew door to the cockpit was secured open. It was a relaxed scene up front as the young captain read a paper and the co-pilot sat back smoking while resting one foot on the instrument panel. Instinctively I tightened my seatbelt as the black clouds drew nearer, eventually enveloping us.

I looked out of the window as we began to descend into Paya Lebar airport, (since closed and replaced by Changi International), seeing only black clouds. We continued descending as confirmed by the engine sounds and increasing cabin pressure until suddenly popping out of cloud over Kalang Basin. Shocked, I saw high rise buildings towering directly ahead and to our right. We were descending into the housing blocks lining the south coast of Singapore. The engines roared; we just cleared the real estate but were in no position to land on the runway passing us on the left, so climbed into the bowels of the storm. We had only just avoided plowing intro someone's living room and being cooked in a high rise fire.

I recalled a story I heard that the Singapore aviation authorities had banned all Garuda F28's from attempting an approach to land on instruments, or during bad weather conditions, except in emergency, for the very reason just demonstrated. The authorities did not want aircraft crashing into their housing and ruining the tourist trade.

I watched the other twenty passengers who continued to read or doze, unconcerned and unaware that we had almost died. My brain churned as the aircraft shuddered and shook in severe turbulence with lightning flashing around us. I suffered, rigid, for twenty minutes before we broke out of cloud again. It seemed like a lifetime and I half expected to die as I knew that thunderstorms had destroyed many aircraft.

The second time the pilot managed a rough landing and I eventually walked into the terminal, still shaking and on jelly legs as though I had drunk the bar dry during a long flight. My Guardian Angel was still with me and I told him how much I appreciated his help. After these challenging flights one certainly appreciates being alive.

I kept my Garuda ticket stubs and years later found that I survived over a hundred and twenty flights with them.

Soon after that harrowing trip, I and many of my Duri pilots went down with dengue fever, carried by mosquitoes from a pet monkey. Mysteriously, the monkey dissapeared from its cage soon after the disease was discovered. The fever laid us out for several weeks. I felt fine, until attempting to get out of bed and moving about. The symptoms appear similar to chronic fatigue syndrome and though dengue supposedly does not re-occur, I experienced the same lassitude many times over the coming years. One of the pitfalls of our interesting and sometimes exotic overseas lifestyle is collecting tropical diseases.

With me away half the time, Mary joined Singapore's top mixed choir. In time this opened avenues into aspects of Singapore society we didn't know existed. Many world class performers stopped off in Singapore and often stayed at private houses of well-to-do expatriate arts supporters. These top classical pianists or vocal performers allowed people who were friends of the household to attend their practice sessions. We enjoyed free intimate convivial evening performances, interspersed with food and wine, allowing us to meet some famous names.

On one occasion the *Straits Times* noted that an internationally known singer was to perform with the Singapore Symphony. The artist was James, who I boarded with at Tilly's in Adelaide in 1953, while he completed a scholarship at the Conservatorium. He was travelling with his wife, an opera singer, and I met them both backstage after the performance. This meeting resulted in them, and half the Singapore Symphony returning for extended drinks at our house which severely dented my cellar.

In September 1979, my parents and sister flew in to visit. Dad was eighty three years old and it was his first overseas trip. He was amazed at the way Chey waited on him hand and foot and anticipated his needs, never having received this sort of attention before. We explained that Asians revere children and the aged, treating them almost like mini gods. It was a huge contrast to Western society and he certainly deserved this pandering after the harsh life he had endured.

During the family visit, Henry and Jillian Scully took us out to swim at a five star hotel swimming pool. This type of life and activity was also new to my father and I imagine he thought we lived a privileged existence.

We first met the Scullys a year earlier, through mutual friends. Henry was a slightly built Singaporean entrepreneur with a somewhat checkered history. He willingly confessed having done time in Changi prison for forging the Prime Minister's signature. This incarceration, he said, taught him a hard lesson and he would never spend time inside again. His bloodline was Indian, Chinese and Malay. He was married to the daughter of Singapore's past president. Jillian, a motherly lady, served as the principal at a high school and was the epitome of respectability. Their two well-behaved young boys completed the picture perfect family.

Over the following months Henry persuaded me, along with other professional expatriates, to invest money with him. In retrospect, it seems crazy but Henry was a mad genius in the way he persuaded people to part with their savings. He even convinced various of us to give up highly paid jobs to pursue his supposed business enterprises. We also met one of Henry's prison supervisors who invested money with him, which helped allay our doubts.

Henry suggested I leave Bristow's to pursue my inventions. He said he would set up a company in Hong Kong for me. His connections would manufacture and assist with worldwide marketing. It seemed a very attractive proposition as one entrepreneur in Hong Kong had told me he would order thirty thousand of my toilet roll dispensers when available.

Remaining with Bristow's would inevitably mean having to leave Asia and serve time in Aberdeen, flying on North Sea operations. That eventuality was most unappealing so I foolishly borrowed money from Mary's parents, in addition to our own savings. Henry received over sixty thousand dollars from me before I resigned from Bristow's to begin working with him. Many of my friends were amazed that I left a top job with one of the world's best helicopter companies. And to think I did all this without a written contract or receipts for monies given to Henry.

During the good times our group of 'investors' were treated to exclusive, expensive dinners in the Hyatt Hotel boardroom, located adjacent to the kitchen. A private room, seating up to a dozen, it came to be known as the 'staff canteen' Waiters only intruded when summoned by a bell controlled by the 'chairman' at the head of the table, quickly attending to our needs before leaving.

Henry paid for us to enjoy an expensive three week ski holiday in Austria in March 1980, just after I left Bristows. We returned to Singapore in April, Gavin and Mary's visas being good until the end of the school year in June. In the meantime, my Hong Kong company was to be set up by Henry, it would enable me to remain in Singapore as an employed offshoot of that entity. For weeks, I remained in limbo, meeting Henry and others involved in his schemes. Nothing much seemed to be happening, Henry always saying he was getting things 'organised'. He suggested I occupy myself by purchasing expensive university textbooks on contract law and studying them, which I did. This knowledge was to prove useful years later.

In July, when school holidays began, Mary and Gavin returned to England while I remained, waiting, worrying, and hoping for action.

To pay the bills I relied on Henry for money. I never knew how much, if, or when this would occur. It was a fraught, worrisome and depressing time without employment, my family absent and a visa limited to a three week stay in Singapore. I knew trips across the causeway into Malaysia to obtain a new visitor's visa would eventually be questioned and refused. Jobless expatriates were not allowed to remain in Singapore unless they were family members of a breadwinner. This rule caused marriages, or name changes to occur among some ladies we knew, de-facto partners being treated as visitors. We knew our personal details were recorded on the Government's central computer so it was not possible to 'disappear.' Also, Gavin would not be allowed to attend school when he returned as I was not working. I would be failing my duty as a husband and father.

Night after night my stomach churned as I hoped for good news the following day. My privileged, cosy world was shattered. Disgrace and financial ruin stared me full in the face. Afterward, I realised it was Henry's intent to force us out of the country after stripping all the money he could get. He also encouraged us to borrow funds to make matters worse. *How would I pay back Mary's parents?*

Ulcers or suicide, which was it to be for me? It was the lowest point in my life. I was alone in Singapore with ultimately only myself to blame for this predicament. I spent many hours in our pool, hugging a beer and trying to find a solution, without success. I wondered if Henry's promises would ever materialize. Several other friends were in a similar situation and we all tried to remain positive. By August, having been unemployed for five months, my financial situation was critical and I didn't know when I would be refused another visitor's visa for Singapore.

The school year was about to begin. Mary and Gavin held return tickets, but I wondered if we would be thrown out of Singapore penniless after

they arrived. I was desperate to resolve this crisis – the alternative would mean returning to Australia on our knees, heavily in debt.

Left: *The Duri Hash H.Q., our hanger shown behind.*

CHAPTER 14

Try to make the number of landings equal to the
number of take-offs. ~ *The Aviators Guide Book*

Salvation arrived with a job offer from Pat Lloyd, asking me to rejoin Heli Services as their operations manager. This meant going back to aviation when I had my heart set on a career in the business world. It would mean admitting failure. In a confused and desperate state I was torn between Henry's rosy picture of the future and returning to plough old fields.

Pat said I had to decide quickly as he was on the verge of bringing out a man from England. I rationalized that at least his offer kept me in Singapore where I could see what happened with Henry's schemes and my money, so I accepted.

I rapidly became immersed in a new job. As my mind returned to a normal logical state I realized how depression and anxiety had so scrambled my brain I stupidly hesitated over accepting Pat's offer. Soon I recognized how lucky I was that my angel had provided another escape from a hole I had dug myself into.

Heli Services was the local subsidiary of a large American aviation company, Evergreen Inc. and the only local helicopter operator. I renewed my Singapore flying license, and was granted a work permit. It allowed me to enter the country as a local, as opposed to joining the long visitor queue at the airport immigration desk. My world completely turned around and my family rejoined me. What a relief it was to have clawed my way out of that deep, dark pit of despair.

Now that I could see a tangible future and had a responsible job to address, I saw Henry in a different light. We attempted to recover our money from him, knowing it would not be easy. I had no receipts for cash cheques written but an official summons from a legal firm did recover $27,000 as Henry had not registered a Hong Kong Company as promised. I was still owed much more. Malaysian friends suggested having Henry kidnapped by the Kuala Lumpur Mafia. During our investigations we discovered that termination only cost $300. Bizzarely, knee-capping was double, it left the victim alive. Many different measures were considered, but being guests in the country we had to keep our noses clean. Buzz on the grapevine said Henry owed money all over town. How would we achieve what others could not?

Mary found a solution, with me frequently travelling to other countries and often only home at weekends. She harassed Jillian, the principal, at her school to the extent that Henry's respectable cover was threatened. Loss of face is a powerful force in Asia, and Mary used that to full effect. Blackmail, perhaps, but normal methods rarely work when dealing with crooks. We didn't care, just wanting to be repaid.

Henry sent Jillian to do his dirty work. We met in the front bar of the Goodwood Park Hotel and sat at a corner table furthest from the lone barman reading a paper. Jillian handed me several large brown paper bags stuffed with used $10 and $20 notes.

'Henry said it's all there but you should count it.'

To avoid scrutiny I began furtively counting the hundreds of creased notes under the table. I felt I was acting out a scene in a B-grade movie but certainly didn't want the police to arrive and ask if we were handling drug or other ill-gotten cash.

As a waiter approached I hastily hid my booty and waited until our coffee had been served, before continuing the count.

With the tally completed, I thanked Jillian and walked around the corner to a bank in Orchard Road, only relaxing after handing my money to a teller. Now I could pay back my debtors.

The sad sequel to this saga occurred several months later. Local papers reported the Scully family's death, classified as murder/suicide. The press mentioned Henry bought gas bottles but he discovered at the last minute that a regulator was required to achieve a controlled gas release, so the death plan was delayed till the following evening. Their neighbour mentioned hearing hymn singing from the household before the gas overtook them.

We heard unofficially that Henry had been threatened with violence and knew he was terrified of suffering physical pain, so took the easy way out. Rumours also circulated that he persuaded Jillian to take money from the school safe, promising to repay it, but never did. This ensured the end of her career, so she was 'forced' to join him in death rather than dishonour the family name.

It was a bad ending, especially for their two innocent boys but many others suffered. Collectively, the hotels used by Henry admitted to being owed over a million dollars for lavish meals and the use of suites. Several locals we knew who borrowed heavily to 'finance' Henry committed suicide as well. One of our married friends was forced to conduct a fire sale of their belongings to enable the purchase of tickets back to England to build a new life from scratch.

We were among the few from several dozen in Henry's clutches that came out of this saga relatively unscathed, somewhat scarred and sadder but wiser. It seems my angel knew about money matters.

My first overseas assignment after joining Heli Services took me to Brunei. I was to check the cost and availability of facilities to base two helicopters and half a dozen crewmembers to fulfill a new contract. I had never visited the country before.

'How do I get to this place called Seria after landing at Bandar Seri Bagawan?' I asked Pat, my new boss.

'Hire a car at the airport, turn right and drive to the end of the road.'

I found his instructions, though lacking detail, got me to my destination after driving ninety kilometres, almost the length of the country. At the time, this oil rich nation had not built modern hotels or roads even though a new palace for the Sultan was being constructed.

Due to the country's wealth, no personal or company taxes were levied, with health care and schooling free to Brunei's indigenous population. In company with Kuwait, the country enjoyed the highest per capita wealth of any other nation. Distribution of this largess was at the royal family's discretion and I heard an example of how this could be utilised. It seems one of the Prince's wives didn't disclose her preferred birthday present until about a week before the day. She desired a pink Porsche! That colour could only come from the factory in Germany so a jumbo was chartered to deliver her present. This charter probably cost more than the exclusive car.

A local driving licence cost less than a dollar per year, so I got one. Foreign licences saved me from many speeding fines as I could plead ignorance and an imminent departure 'home'. The Brunei licence came with twenty pages of rules and diagrams on road behavior, written in three languages. I quote several, *Do not be inconsiderate of slower traffic ,always remember it has its rights on the road as well as the car.'* Another, *'Car owners should remember that they can more or less control the drivers actions when they are in the car, and can help considerably to improve the traffic problem by helping to see these instructions carried out by their drivers.'* I wondered who was required to hold the licence, the driver or the owner?

Obtaining a licence to drive there was the least of my problems. The oil company we were to fly for demanded exacting pilot qualifications including:

1. A high number of total flying hours
2. At least two hundred hours on the twin engined contract helicopters
3. An instrument rating on helicopters – not common then
4. An accident free record
5. Preferably be below fifty five years of age
6. Be happily married but have no children of school age
7. Be of good character and preferably of European or Australian background
8. Be available and willing to relocate to Brunei.

I scoured the world to find such pilots and ended up with very capable people from England, Holland, Australia and one American who was acceptable. He had worked in Norway and his wife was European. The crew caused no problems but our client expected me to visit every few months. Once, while discussing personnel with the very British, ex Fleet Air Arm aviation boss, he mentioned that one pilot was a good aviator but a 'lower decks' person. Knowing the English class system, I knew those two words meant the subject male was not considered 'officer' or management material.

Trips to Brunei were no hardship as the country was yet to ban alcohol and the hospitality provided usually meant very social, late nights. I remember one overnight visit when I traveled purely to represent the company at our crew's Christmas party. From the time the Boeing's wheels hit the runway at Bandar Seri Begawan, until I left the airport having cleared customs and immigration, only three minutes elapsed. It's a hard record to beat and shattered all my previous best times for clearing an international airport. At Heathrow, on a bad day, I can recall a thirty minute wait before even disembarking the aircraft, followed by a ten minute walk to terminal three before joining a lengthy immigration queue.

Brunei, being a Muslim country, meant prostitution was officially unthinkable. Yet, a few miles across the border, in Sarawak, young girls were provided to single males overnighting in a village longhouse as a sign of hospitality. Sarawak was also technically Muslim but in isolated villages old customs prevailed.

It seems male transvestites were allowed in Brunei. Perhaps they provided some relief against the strict sexual mores. I was surprised to discover them working on offshore oilrigs. They flew out in our choppers as male 'unskilled' hands and returned to shore dressed in mini skirts, fishnet stockings and high heels, showing off their slim legs while sporting lavish makeup and hair styles. Such a change to find these foxy 'women' seated in our helicopters. An interesting contrast, compared to the burly redneck rig crews usually found travelling with us.

It was a taste of the original Bugis Street in Singapore, where tourists flocked to rub shoulders with scantily dressed 'ladies' of the night, most sporting large bulges between their legs while mincing about on high heels and promising prospects a good time. We took many visitors there; it provided a total contrast to Singapore's soulless, scrubbed image.

We won the Singapore government's first contract to move harbour pilots around Singapore's many ports by helicopter. The company bought a small twin engined Bolkow 105 helicopter to enhance safety when flying offshore. A pilot from England was hired to help with this expansion. Unfortunately, John's attitude once again reflected that of a master helping out ignorant natives in the colonies. This resulted in him ignoring another pilot's warning and flying into the prohibited area over the Sultan of Johor's palace to avoid bad weather. The Sultan, himself a helicopter pilot who reputedly hated most white-skinned people, immediately phoned the tower, ordering the offending helicopter to land at nearby Johor Baru Airport. After doing so, the police grabbed John and drove him to the palace with sirens blaring. John was taken to see the Sultan with a gun in his back. He was told if he made any sudden movements, he would be shot.

John was reluctant to describe his dressing down by the Sultan but said he had been called a white pig, among other things. Claiming immunity due to weather just brought on another stream of invective. When the Sultan finished venting his anger at John he was returned to the airport but forbidden to fly his machine back to Singapore. Mike and I flew over to bring him and his aircraft home. John's attitude changed after that incident, similar to the other arrogant Brit I had suffered in Sumatra.

That Sultan was notorious for many reasons, but what I can say is that he kept a retinue of very good polo ponies and was no mean player himself. When competing at our club his team swept into town in half a dozen expensive Mercedes Benz. The Sultan's number plate was embellished with just a crown. In some Asian states, winning at polo was the ultimate in social prestige; many Brunei Princes also took the game very seriously. To avoid having to rely on other countries' aircraft, Royal Brunei Airlines was founded to fly their polo ponies around Asia – passengers came later.

Our membership of the polo club proved to be a financial and political winner. When we first joined, the membership consisted of a small group of polo and horse lovers. Often, wild nights occurred in our small tin-roofed clubhouse as the riders played and partied hard. One evening, after a few drinks, a European female polo player dragged a visiting white professional player out onto the grass and wrestled with him, ripping off all his clothing apart from underpants. It was not a sexual attack; she was proving her strength. Another day, two lasses fought a duel in the carpark, using their cars as weapons. Two other members' wives just changed husbands, instead of fighting.

In later years a large, modern clubhouse with swimming pool and squash courts was constructed. Membership numbers and joining cost soared, and I sold our investment for a very tidy profit after leaving Singapore.

Meanwhile, our company won a helirig contract in Bangladesh. I flew there every few months to argue with the locals about payments and tried to sort other problems in that difficult operating environment. We had two helicopters based at Syhlet airport in the northeastern part of the country. At times we operated within sight of armed guards manning towers on the Indian border. Bureaucracy in Bangladesh was incredible; for example the customs regulations were those promulgated by the British to prevent strategic materials being exported during the Second World War. Many other regulations had never been updated. It was probably too difficult for ever changing governments to reach any agreement as a coup seemed to occur almost every year.

Bangladesh had been given a large grant by European countries to develop its oil and gas reserves and so earn export income. Part of the plan was to teach the Bengali's petroleum exploration techniques. Sun Oil were contracted to advise PetroBangla, the state oil enterprise, on how to run a drilling program. In theory, PetroBangla officials made the decisions, after advice from Grady, the managing consultant, and the Drilling Manager. In practise, much aid money was wasted due to the reluctance of senior Bengali officials to authorize urgent unanticipated expenditure. It was probably especially galling for them as many specialised expat oil workers earned more in a week than their top public servants received per annum.

For example, the Bengalis were so reluctant to spend thirty thousand dollars chartering a freighter aircraft to bring in emergency equipment that a quarter of a million was wasted on drilling rig downtime. Of course, our helicopters also sat on the ground until the charter eventuated and drilling was able to re-commence.

The senior pilot organizing our crew manning the two Bell Huey helicopters used for rig moves and logistics support needed to be a resourceful person, accustomed to dealing with Third World challenges. Scheduling the flying and maintenance was the easy part. Electricity and water were often only supplied to our rented crew house for several hours a day. We sank a well, power coming from own two large imported diesel generators. Kitchen staff, food purchases and menus needed supervision. I had trouble finding and keeping two managing pilots, working back to back, to organize essential services and maintain morale. Virtually no entertainment or sport existed for westerners, just wall to wall people, many with outstretched hands. Avoiding boredom during slack periods or days off seemed to be a problem. Of course, the Internet or satellite TV was not available.

Despite our best efforts I once received a telex advising me that a pilot, after drinking locally made alcohol all night, had jumped into a helicopter next morning. He flew it to the rig site even though it was his rostered day off. Naturally, he was terminated immediately. I had little option but to employ a number of American Vietnam vets. They had the required licences and qualifications to operate our U.S.A. registered machines. Most were OK, but some had rather freewheeling attitudes, which caused me headaches.

Every week one of our aircraft met an International flight bringing in frozen food for the drillers who had to have their steaks. On one occasion, early in the contract, customs refused to clear the pallets of perishables. They stood on the black asphalt airport apron in the searing summer sun. It was obvious that a bribe was required to prevent thousands of dollars worth of food spoiling. The Parker drilling manager refused to pay and began sending telexes overseas instead. The airport officials refused to back down and watched the shipment putrefy. It became a health hazard and had to be destroyed. The drilling manager had made his point; he was not giving kickbacks as these tended to escalate. We heard this form of corruption was so entrenched that customs officers didn't receive any salary, instead had to pay to get their jobs. After that one occasion when nobody gained and telexes scorched wires at a high level, frozen food shipments were not delayed.

Cheap labour and massive unemployment in Bangladesh resulted in many inexpensive handcrafted artifacts being available. I carried some of these back to Singapore where they found a ready market. The locally produced jute carpets were also very cheap so I imported them, after forming a Singapore company. Mary was good at selling these to schools and the retailer, Courts. They sold them as the Managing Director was a polo playing member of the club.

In July 1981, we flew to Australia for my annual holidays and packed various goodies from Bangladesh in our luggage. Mary easily sold these items for up to ten times their cost. Beginning in Brisbane, we visited friends, then flew to Sydney and Adelaide before making it to Alice Springs. I showed Mary and Gavin our house in Hermannsburg. We drove to Palm Valley in a rented four-wheel-drive and camped 'illegally' in the bed of the Finke River, my 'tribal' country. Eight year old Gavin was not impressed with sleeping under the stars. Our next stop was in Perth for three days, before returning home to Singapore having 'done' Australia again.

The following year, during Gavin's school holidays, we tried summer skiing at the famous mountain resort of Zermatt, reached by rack railway. Our hotel sported a view of the Matterhorn plus an indoor heated swimming pool. In the mornings it took us an hour and three different cable cars to arrive at the Klein Matterhorn summit, at an altitude of 3,820 metres. Exiting the car, we walked through a short tunnel to the other side of the mountaintop, emerging to see a large sign in four different languages. The words told us not to move quickly and if feeling faint, to immediately report to a first-aid station. We just sped away in bright sunshine. Sadly, the sun gradually turned the snow to mush so skiing was banned after 1 pm. During the afternoon we swam, walked and played tennis.

Quite frequently, helicopters flew up and down the valley until the light faded at around 9.30 pm. I was told they searched for missing tourists, lost while climbing the Matterhorn. It seems up to several dozen climbers perished every summer, notwithstanding the requirement to pay for a registered guide. Perhaps having no age limit or necessity to show a medical certificate before starting the arduous climb to 4,478 metres was a factor.

It was a wonderful holiday in a car-less enchanting village and we happened to be there for the Swiss National Day celebrations which featured a spectacular light show in the surrounding valley.

Our return journey entailed changing from a local train to the Zurich Express The fast train was scheduled to depart two-minutes after we arrived. Four English lads on a package tour befriended us and relied on our German language skill to find the correct platform for the express.

Having seven items of baggage comprising skis, boots and suitcases, it took us a minute to disembark and rush down the platform to view the notice board. The Englishmen trotted along behind but when we discovered that the express left from the same platform but on the opposite side, we rushed back. The Poms' stayed behind, perhaps thinking we had forgotten something. It was too late to inform the boys, the express arrived. We barely had time to throw all our gear on before the doors hissed shut, the second hand on the platform clock flicked over twelve and the train left the station with Swiss accuracy. The Englishmen's despairing faces were left standing there. They mentioned having spent all their money, had no credit cards, did not speak the language and would now miss their package tour charter flight home. We felt sorry for them, and had no idea how they might get back to England.

We financed our skiing holidays by taking on extra-money making activities in Singapore. One year I completely refurbished a sports car before selling it. Another year we bred and raised a dozen pedigree pups from our pet Dalmatian. One of these became the Champion of all classes dog in Malaysia. Mary's carpet sales were another source of income.

When the new Changi airport was fully operational the authorities decided to make a photographic record for promotional and historical reasons. Much of the area was on land reclaimed from the sea. They came to our company, being the only local helicopter operator, for the airborne shots.

The switch from Paya Lebar to Changi was a marvel of organization and happened overnight with no disruption to flights. By chance I flew into Paya Lebar the evening of its closure and out of Changi the following morning and experienced no delays or inconvenience.

Some days prior to the photo shoot, I attended a briefing at the airport. I was escorted to a conference room and introduced to four heads of department. *This must be serious stuff.*

'For how long will we have to close the airport while you do the photography?' asked a bureaucrat.

Close the airport – I was amazed, don't these people know anything about helicopters?

'That will not be necessary. 'I'll just keep out of the way during airline movements. You have hundreds of metres between the two parallel runways. I only need about ten metres anywhere from the ground on up, wherever the tower wishes me to park, in the sky, or on the grass.

'That's wonderful, the airlines won't have to reschedule their flights?'

'Certainly not.'

'Very good. No further discussion is required but you should visit the tower and brief the controllers.'

'Sure, I'll tell them what to expect.'

The control tower, poised like a large eyeball on a thin tall stick, stood between the airport runways. My escort punched a code into numerous security doors before we gained the lift that whisked us up to the state of the art, eye in the sky. The view was impressive and the radar screens displayed many arriving and departing aircraft not yet in sight. After briefing the controllers we left.

The photo shoot was a fun trip. The experienced photographer knew where he wanted to be so we flitted around like a dragonfly between airline arrivals and departures. I kept out of their way and during a busy period, a controller asked me where I was.

'Look outside, I'm parked ten metres away from your windows on the north side of the tower.'

I saw a controller swivel his head and seeing us hovering just outside his air-conditioned console, he smiled and waved. No one was going to hit us without demolishing the control tower in the process.

Shortly after, a Cathay Pacific jumbo began its approach to land. I'd heard that Cathay pilots were among the highest paid in the world.

'Can we get some close-ups of him landing?'

'Standby, I'll ask the tower for permission.'

Clearance was given; the Singaporeans wanted the best photos possible, although it agitated the captain of the airliner. That skipper did not want a pesky little helicopter anywhere near him during the serious business of gently achieving one of his six or eight landings for that month. He voiced his displeasure in a very superior tone - the controller took no notice. Unless their safety was compromised, which it wasn't, the captain could not overrule the controller's clearance and tell me to go away.

As the Jumbo descended I curved in toward it on a parallel flight path, on his left side so the captain could easily see us. Just before touchdown I couldn't resist broadcasting 'Smile, you're on candid camera.'

The Jumbo landed heavily and bounced – it was a rough arrival in Singapore for those visitors. When the pilot called to notify switching to the ground control frequency, his voice was laced with tension. We had not made his day but ours was terrific, the film was in the can and it was great fun exposing it.

Another photographic job we did several times a year was for a major

292

container shipping line. This company photographed their loaded vessels passing each other in opposite directions in the vicinity of Singapore. As the two ships were only in close proximity for a minute or so a specialist ship photographer always arrived from London, just to do these photo shoots. He did these alone, first rigorously briefing us. The routine was dependent on the position of the sun and any surrounding landscape. It was a frantically busy few minutes changing to pre-arranged positions while the specialist shot off hundreds of exposures on the myriad loaded cameras he had to hand. I could speak to the vessels during this exercise but they did not slow, soon being widely separated.

In those days, aerial photography of Singapore by foreigners was not permitted unless a government official was carried on board. This generally took a week to arrange and any films exposed were surrendered to the official for processing and possibly censoring in the government laboratories. This was to prevent other powers gaining intimate knowledge of Singapore's defence sites. Many overseas film companies, not knowing of this regulation left without any airborne film of the city, unable to wait for permission. The authorities chose to ignore the fact that detailed photographs of the island taken from space could be purchased from NASA.

On another memorable trip I flew into the very rigidly controlled prohibited area above the residences of the Governor and head of Singapore's government. This flight was cleared at the highest level and allowed the government photographer to record whatever he wanted in the normally sacrosanct precinct. As I approached the red line on the controllers' radar screens they warned me several times that I was flying into danger, even though I kept repeating my flight plan special clearance number. Eventually they gave up, probably after checking with the military who told them it was not necessary to launch a fighter to shoot me down. All pilots knew that anyone inadvertently flying over the boss' houses would be deported and barred from entering Singapore again, unless a very special clearance had been obtained. I knew of one who had been kicked out.

Another interesting flight involved a vessel that became stuck in the middle of the Malacca Strait with a propeller problem. It was an American Navy charter supply ship and when I landed on board with the propeller expert, men in civilian clothing rushed up and saluted me like crazy. As usual, I was wearing a uniform and captain's epaulettes with four bars. I was taken to offer my compliments to the skipper. He was fishing on the stern of his hundred metre long command, wearing only a dirty wide

293

brimmed hat and a pair of shorts.

'Grab a coffee and relax on the bridge,' he said. 'It's air-conditioned.'

With that greeting he returned to his fishing seemingly unconcerned about supertankers charging past close by on both sides. These huge vessels had to chart a precise course down the straight when fully loaded, their hulls almost scraping the sea floor in some areas. Often, their propellers left a visible trail of mud stirred up from the bottom.

Hours and many coffees later, with the complicated variable pitch propeller fixed, we left. It was too late to make Singapore so I flew to Kuala Lumpur instead. Neither of us had any overnight kit, but that was no problem − good hotels accepted cash cheques from pilots wearing a company uniform.

My American host said his office would pay for dinner in our four-star hotel's best restaurant and I didn't argue with him.

'Gravlax!' he exclaimed on sighting the menu. 'I wonder if it's the real thing?'

It was Scandinavian gravlax and he ate six courses and insisted I try some as well, despite the extravagant price. After tasting this fish, I agreed with my host that the real thing is a sensuous delight, enhanced when someone else pays. I preferred it to genuine Russian caviar which I sampled years later, supplied by our Russian crew in Papua New Guinea.

These odd jobs flying out of Singapore kept my skills and licence current but I was still responsible for our pilots operating in up to seven different countries. On one occasion I did four countries in four days, working in all of them between airline flights. In 1981, I noted we had thirty pilots on the payroll, flying in many different parts of Asia. Most worked tours, rosters and airline ticketing for crews to the world's continents being scheduled by me, in addition to my other duties. We had no fancy computer programs to help then. Our Singapore Company's monthly balance sheet disclosed revenues of over a million US dollars per month, which pleased head office.

I usually managed to get home for the weekend but never knew which country I'd be visiting the following week. This was usually decided when the boss, the engineering manager and I had lunch together on Mondays. It was inadvisable for me to book any social functions for more than a few days in advance, but most of our friends were in a similar situation so impromptu dining out and parties were the norm. Eating at our local under a housing estate high-rise was cheaper than dining at home so we were good customers. The odd rat seen running down a drain next to this open-air Chinese eatery didn't deter us. Gavin often joined Chinese and

Malay children from the estate in ball games in the adjacent open space, after he had finished eating. He was not racist and often caught busses to visit a good friend living several kilometres away. We had no qualms about his safety or getting lost. In contrast, during ten years in Singapore I never once caught a bus, always driving myself or using the cheap taxis.

Mary and her close friend, also a riding instructor, decided their husbands should learn to ride properly, so Basil and I turned up for an early Monday morning session. All the other beginners were Chinese. A few Mondays later Mary persuaded me to leave my bed for another lesson. I was not enthusiastic, it had been a heavy weekend. Basil was not keen to repeat the exercise so he jumped into a jumbo and flew it to London. The class began and our mounts dutifully walked around in circles. I fell asleep and woke up heading for the ground, headfirst. Instinctively stretching out my right arm I broke the fall. I allowed a helpful Chinese lady to massage my aching wrist. It hurt like hell but I managed to grit my teeth, smile and thank her. After completing the lesson I went to a specialist orthopedic surgery where an x-ray confirmed a bad collis fracture. One of Singapore's top bone doctors, a tutor at the University, put a cast on my arm and wrist. No x-rays were taken after immobilizing my broken bones to confirm they were set properly.

I am accustomed to driving a manual car using one arm if necessary. By 9:30 am the same day I was in my office at Seletar Airport. The local staff were amazed to see me, they thought I might be away for days. That evening, my right arm began to throb badly so I went to a hospital. They found the cast restricting my blood circulation, so it was cut off and a modified splint applied. This trouble was the first in an unhappy episode with my specialist. It culminated in me asking the doctor's receptionist to show me the only x-rays taken of my wrist. I had previously been told these prints could not leave the doctor's surgery, but when the receptionists back was turned I crept out the door with them. On my next visit to Australia, when my father was hospitalised, I took these x-rays to a specialist. He said I had perfect grounds to sue for negligence. My wrist had not been set correctly or properly checked afterwards.

Suing was a practical impossibility in Singapore at that time. The doctors had virtually all the lawyers tied up and the only junior I could find who wasn't, told me it was pointless to proceed. He said big name lawyers and experts from the medical profession would shoot us down in flames and judges always favoured 'the establishment'. Being an expat made matters even worse. So I gave up and have my bent wrist as a constant reminder of a horse in Singapore. In general, the local medical facilities were very good but I suppose anyone can have a bad day.

In the 1980s the Australian Embassy in Singapore was not renowned for speedily processing paperwork. After hours, the staff's officious, condescending attitude disappeared. They knew how to throw a party. At least the ones my wife and I attended.

As members of the Australian and New Zealand Association of Singapore we met diplomatic corps personnel socially. This resulted in an evening invitation to the small patch of Australian territory in the middle of Singapore. There, we stood on hallowed ground, not subject to the rules outside. It meant we could gamble without a special licence.

We attended the 'Almost Melbourne Cup Night' in 1984. Special T-shirts were produced to mark the occasion. The food was provided by Qantas, in cardboard airline boxes, to reinforce the Australian emphasis.

Obviously horses were not allowed in the embassy, instead, frogs were raced with a commentator giving a jump by jump rundown on the action or lack thereof. To control the unfortunate frogs a special racetrack had been constructed. It was a wooden box about a metre long, half a metre wide and ten centimetres high. Inside, six partitioned lanes ran the length of the track, these covered by a Perspex top to ensure the racers couldn't jump out or change lanes. A classic example of necessary invention. It seems that for Australians, it's absolutely vital to bet on some sort of sport on Melbourne Cup Day.

A book was operating. The frogs could not be interfered with, except by vocal encouragement which became rather raucous when a frog refused to move. I would like to say I won some money on this esoteric form of sport but cannot remember.

In February 1983, my father was hospitalized in Adelaide. The prognosis was not encouraging, so I flew down and stayed for a week, visiting him daily. During that time South Australia was suffering from drought, bushfires and a recession. Land prices were at rock bottom. Seeing an opportunity, I bought five acres in one of Adelaide's best suburbs with a view to retiring there. After Father was discharged into my mother's care at home, I flew to Singapore and soon after returning, visited Bangladesh.

Arriving in Dhaka, I found it necessary to visit Parker Drilling to co-ordinate operations so prepared to see the manager early next day.

'Good morning Sir,' said the taxi driver, opening the door for me. I carefully inspected the battered vehicle's interior before stepping in. These taxi's were so old that in some, parts of the metal floor had rusted away to reveal the pavement below. No effort was made to cover the dangerous holes. Bangladesh was not a rich country and new cars were rare.

My conveyance this morning seemed reasonably sound.

'Do you know where the Parker Drilling office in Gulshan is?' I asked.

'Yes, I am knowing that esteemed establishment Sir, we shall be there very directly.'

'Good, and don't hurry, we don't want to hit anyone.'

Some drivers were so keen to impress an expatriate they bulldozed their way through the thousands of tri-shaws on the road.

'No Sir, I am being a very safe driver for twenty years now.'

They all say that I thought while winding up both rear windows and locking the doors. The security guard opened the hotel parking area gate.

While waiting to enter the road, dozens of hands were thrust against the taxi windows, deformed beggars asking for a handout. I was told that some parents deliberately deformed these unfortunate people soon after birth. This was done to provide a beggar's income in the usually large families, paid employment being almost impossible to find.

We soon entered the suburb of Gulshan, an elite area that housed embassies, ambassadors and the wealthy. Here, high walls and security fences insulated the upper crust from the poor and starving population. Few pedestrians were to be seen and beggars knew that loitering in these precincts was pointless.

On arriving at the Parker Drilling office compound we found the security gate locked and unattended – we were too early.

'Just park and wait,' I told the driver.

'Yes, I am your servant Sir.'

It was only 8.30 am and I was beginning to perspire. It would be another scorching day. Sadly, air-conditioning was unheard of in ordinary taxis.

The dusty streets were empty until a woman appeared, walking with a steady dignified gait towards us. She was tall and slim, had chocolate-coloured skin, a narrow waist and large firm breasts. Her classically chiseled face and generous lips were topped by long dark hair. A voluptuous, hourglass, centerfold figure. Passing within a metre of the vehicle, she continued to her destination without hesitation. I saw every detail of her proud, youthful beauty – she was devoid of any clothing.

'Why is this woman walking around Dhakka's best suburb naked?' I asked the driver.

'Sir, I have to tell you, I think she is being a very naughty girl because she probably entertains men who are not her husband. We are not recognising that these people exist and so we do not see them. If they are not seen, does it matter if they are wearing clothes or not I am asking you?'

How can you beat that logic, and this in a country where the population is meant to be Muslim.

'I see, but do you suspect, even though she can't be seen, she might be advertising?'

'Sir, you will need to be asking her this question.'

Communications into and out of Bangladesh were almost impossible except by telex. I recall one occasion when I needed to make an important call to the office in Singapore. After bribing reception with a few US dollars and waiting in my hotel room for almost twenty four hours I eventually made voice contact with the outside world. This, in the only accommodation of a reasonable standard in a city of millions.

After that trip I arrived home to find my father had died. It was pointless trying to pass on this news while I was in Bangladesh - I could not have made it back to Australia in time for the funeral. Besides I had seen him just a few weeks earlier. We had never been close as he spent much time away when I was a child and I left home at age twelve. His passing did not cause me much grief. I been told many times that I had no feelings – life events and aviation erased them. My brothers and mother had organised his burial so I went to work in our Singapore office as usual.

During another of my visits to Bangladesh, the hotel water supply failed and took three days to fix. A bucket of water, collected from the swimming pool and carried to my sixth floor room was used to flush the toilet and wash. The hotel had three wells and pumps, all being left to fail before any were repaired. Without water, the air-conditioning was inoperative - at a time when eggs could be fried on the footpath in the noonday sun. This inconvenience was nothing compared to life for most of the city's population. I remember passing one stagnant, muddy pond, perhaps ten metres across, in which a number of locals were busy. One was soaping himself, another brushing his teeth and about three metres away a squatting person was gritting his teeth and obviously defecating. It would be months before monsoon floods flushed this and hundreds of similar 'bathrooms' around Dhaka.

The hotel had some redeeming features. Two excellent asphalt tennis courts and a professional coach, whom I usually played against, were bonuses. On one occasion I found partners to make up a doubles game but had to purchase tennis shoes locally. It was a hot day and during one point I found myself stationary at the net for a minute or so before jumping quickly to intercept the ball. My landing was hard and hot, I had literally jumped out of my shoes. I only wore the uppers – the soles had melted and were stuck to the court.

Another benefit was room 503, the British Airways crew hospitality room. It was furnished with a bar, refrigerator, chairs and tables. Being a pilot, I was allowed to visit and was especially welcome if I brought along some alcohol to share. Although the B.A. pilots considered themselves far too grand to drink with their cabin crew, I had no such illusions. It was beneficial to all, having different industry compatible persons to socialise with. Especially for the girls, they were not game to walk anywhere outside the hotel during their stopover due to a constant male crush touching and pestering them.

When the company employed a specialist salesman, I showed him the ropes in Bangladesh. Bob and his wife were old friends. We had been neighbours on Seletar Airport and Bob was also involved in the Scully scam and Henry's extravagant socializing.

One objective of this trip was to visit and familiarise ourselves with Shell Oil's proposed helirig operation in the hilly country north of Chittagong. After overnighting in Dhaka, we caught a taxi. Halfway to the airport, our transport ground to a halt. We hopped out to see what the driver was doing under the open bonnet. It was obvious that the wire connected to the ignition coil had broken off. Our driver picked up the wire, stuck the loose end into his mouth and stripped off the insulation with his teeth. The wire had to be reattached to the coil, after bending he managed to grasp the nut between his teeth, turned his head and undid it. The wire was reattached and we drove off and caught our flight. Bob had his first sample of life in Bangladesh.

After deplaning at Chittagong airport, we had three choices of transport: a man powered-rickshaw, motor powered trishaw or the one solitary four-wheeled taxi in the parking lot. Thinking of doing Bob proud, I chose four wheels. Our transport had to be pushed to start, but eventually enough volunteers were found to get us away. When the engine stopped halfway to town, Bob burst out laughing.

'Does anything in Bangladesh work properly?' he asked.

'The tax collectors,' I replied. 'They are there at every turn.'

We again got out to see what the driver would do. He raised the bonnet, pulled a plastic fuel line off the carburetor, stuck it into his mouth and sucked. After getting a mouthful of petrol, it was spat into the open carburetor, sans air filter. With the help of a bystander we pushed our taxi and managed to get the engine started and progressed another few hundred metres before the engine stopped again. This time the driver admitted we were out of petrol and after producing a gallon can from the boot said he would go to town and get some.

'But there is being another small problem,' he admitted. 'I am not having any money.'

Bob again burst out laughing and gave him a five hundred Taka note. The driver grabbed it and after flagging down a passing trishaw, was gone.

'I see what you mean about Bangladesh,' said Bob. 'I notice you haven't raised an eyebrow.'

'No. Did you see the heaps of rusting machinery, trucks and earth moving equipment we passed earlier on.'

'Yes, what happened there?'

'All that millions of dollars worth of gear is in a customs bonded compound, waiting for payment of duty. It was all new when given to Bangladesh years ago by foreign governments as aid, but the Bengalis said duty had to be paid before it could be imported. The donors refused, and now after years of sitting in the rain it's worthless. I heard that a shipload of free aid grain from Australia was sold to the Indians by the Bengali generals to avoid being wasted, for the same reason. That sale money probably ended up in a Swiss bank.'

'No wonder the country's a basket case.'

Our driver proudly returned bearing a can of petrol as though he had performed magic. We eventually got to our zero star hotel. After lunch it was time to visit Shell. Braving the beggars, we walked the few blocks to their office, finding it in total disarray. Almost all the staff had been sent home. A major cleanup was taking place inside the premises, where broken glass lay everywhere.

A security guard told us what happened.

'I am telling you the trouble is that many Bengalis are cricketers and can throw things very well. For some reason they are taking a dislike to Shell's operations. They smashed all the windows on the second floor with stones, as well as these bottom ones.'

We left the guard muttering to himself and returned to our hotel. Next day we flew back to Dhaka. It was not a good time to visit Shell as we learned that hill tribe rebels had kidnapped one of their Dutch employees. A ransom demand arrived, accompanied by one of his ears. His release was negotiated and he left the country, never to return.

Bob sampled the bureaucrats' final clutch of formalities prior to leaving

Bangladesh. A valid ticket for the day and flight had to be presented just to enter the new air-conditioned terminal building. Then we queued to check in with the airline and obtain a boarding pass. With this in hand we stood in another line to present a completed currency declaration form to officials. It was meant to show our cash on arrival and our spending in local and foreign currencies while in Bangladesh. The only place that accepted one particular credit card was our hotel, and then for only ten percent of the bill. Cash was needed for all other purchases, which were only officially allowed in local currency. The exchange rate between official and black market rates for US dollars was markedly different so our currency declaration forms usually required considerable fiddling to hide the dollars which had gone into the black economy. I always exchanged a minimum amount at government rates and received an official receipt, which satisfied the airport officials.

Then another queue was joined behind the immigration desk and finally we presented ourselves at the baggage claim where all our outgoing bags were opened and inspected. I have no idea why, having packed many kinds of local goods, nothing was ever queried. Were they still checking for exports prohibited during WW II? After this nonsense, we were finally allowed into the spartan departure lounge where Bob went to the toilet.

Returning, he said, 'There's nothing in there except a few taps and holes in the ground. I thought this was a new terminal that the Australians built as a gift.'

'That's right, the Americans did the runway and Strines the terminal building. I flew out of here three days after it opened and by then all the plumbing had been stolen out of the men's toilets - just bare concrete and a few taps remained. A bit of copper pipe is worth a lot here. It's still palatial compared to the old terminal at the Air Force Base. That building was covered in bullet wounds from various internal struggles. I've seen several coups since coming up here but so far foreigners have been left alone.'

'I know it's tough in Indonesia but this lot take the cake,' he muttered.

It was always a great relief to board the Thai Airways flight to Bangkok.

Needing more pilots, I hired Rick, an American, after checking his resume and speaking to previous employers. He seemed well qualified to fly for us in Bangladesh but the situation had changed and we now needed him to go to the Seychelles. That job was a very cushy number, flying once a week while on full pay with all expenses paid. I explained this and mentioned that any of our regular pilots would have gone there on half pay but could not as a F.A.A. (American) License was required to fly the aircraft.

It was rumoured that this job was funded by the C.I.A. A drill-ship was supposedly looking for oil in what seemed a most unlikely location. A coup did occur in the Seychelles about a year later but I have no idea if the drilling was a cover for other activities. The exploration vessel could be seen from the shoreline and was just a ten minute flight away. This weekly scheduled flight hardly overtaxed our two on site-pilots and support engineer.

The drill-ship had already been on location for six months, double the time normally taken to complete a well. Nobody complained as all were well paid, living in a sub-tropical dream location with beaches covered in topless bathers from the Northern Hemisphere. At some point a film company shooting in the Seychelles tried to charter our machine. Bo Derek was starring but due to technicalities that job did not eventuate. What a change from working in an isolated, malaria-ridden swamp

After many more months the drill-ship pulled anchor and went away. Our Seychelles contract was terminated. After a break, Rick was happy to carry on with the aircraft – it was being shipped to an offshore job based in Mombassa, another holiday resort on the beach in Kenya. Here, Swedish and German blondes exposed their bodies to the sun.

For this contract, we required two twin-engined helicopters to be manned so I hired additional crews. One new employee, Nigel, and his wife moved out from England. I didn't meet either of them but was told that she was extremely attractive. I noted this as beautiful wives often seem to attract trouble. Meanwhile, other problems had my attention. Contrary to instructions, one of our Thai maintenance engineers arrived in Nairobi without U.S. or local currency required to buy a visa on arrival. This resulted in him being imprisoned on Christmas Eve. I couldn't achieve his release so he spent Christmas in jail.

Some time later, reports came through to head office that Nigel's wife was disrupting operations in Mombassa. We were told, because she was a dipsomaniac, nymphomaniac. The sort of woman some men dream about but never find. However, not the best wife for a pilot who may be required to give an optimum performance in an iron bird, early in the day, after leaving bed. Another problem to solve to ensure the operation ran smoothly.

Rick came out of that assignment smiling and by chance his next posting was another easy offshore job, based in Bangkok. Three dream holiday postings in succession for lucky Ricky but we got him on the next one – Ras Al Khafji in Saudi Arabia. There, the only parts of female anatomy he'd see were perhaps dark eyes and fingers.

When we won the offshore job in Saudi in 1983, bets were taken on our ability to perform this five year contract. We knew the odds were stacked against us. The sole existing operator had been working in the country for years and had forged strong political connections. The lack of one official stamp on a document meant we couldn't even begin the process of submitting reams of necessary paperwork. Without that stamp, permission to import the twin engined, thirteen-passenger contract helicopter and spares was impossible. With deadlines approaching, it seemed we faced failure, huge loss of face and censure from our head office in America.

I can't say how our multi million dollar contract was saved by obtaining a small piece of correctly shaped rubber, but doors began to open. I found myself on a flight to Saudi to obtain an operating permit and specific flight approvals, now being able to import our aircraft.

The Thai Airways flight from Bangkok to Dhahran was a pleasant prelude to the harsh realities awaiting me.

After landing and completing immigration formalities I found the customs area to be a vast hall, devoid of any furnishings except for a few scattered tables on which papers were spread.

'Good afternoon,' I said on finding a uniformed officer.

His stern scrutiny didn't change as he pointed at my suitcase and rotated his index finger. I opened my bag and stepped back. It was not enough. He kicked my bag and rotated the palm of his hand 180 degrees. Now I understood, I was to empty the contents onto the floor. I did, and watched in dismay as the official kicked his way through my carefully folded clean clothes, searching for prohibited items such as alcohol or Playboy magazines. Being a good Muslim he was not going to defile himself by touching an infidel's possessions. Eventually, after scattering my gear over a large area, he slapped a green sticker on my suitcase and walked away. I was left to retrieve my crumpled clothes and jumbled toiletries. After a struggle I closed my bag and left the building to face the searing heat outside. Next time, I thought, I'll bring a clean garbage bag to simplify re-packing. I did, and received a green sticker on my plastic bag.

A taxi took me to the airport hotel where we received a discounted airline rate, thanks to our American head office I.D. cards. After checking in I found an armed guard sitting in the elevator. He watched me press the button for the second floor and then returned to his newspaper. I discovered the third floor was entirely reserved for female airline hostesses. The guard ensured no males visited them.

The entry of single females into Saudi Arabia was strictly controlled. Foreign workers such as doctors, nurses and domestic servants from Bangladesh and the Philippines were confined to female only quarters. This policy was sometimes carried to extremes. For example, the secretary and board member of our American parent company, a grey-haired sixty year old lady of impeccable repute was not allowed entry for a board meeting because she was single.

In contrast, it was interesting to see the airline hostesses from the third floor being collected and leaving in the latest model Cadillacs and Rolls Royces. I doubt their destination was a public place such as a tea or coffee shop. I heard that many of the girls working on Saudi flights owned dwellings in Chelsea and other expensive London suburbs. It also seemed that blonde was the preferred hair colour among these girls, who had perhaps graduated to 'interesting companions,' in contrast to the solitary boredom of a hotel room in Dhaka.

They reminded me of a statuesque Australian blonde we knew in Singapore who confided that she made large amounts of money by partnering highly-placed Indonesian officials in Jakarta. Likewise, I was told that in Saudi, white, western, single women were rare and sought after by rich locals, to be flaunted as a form of one-upmanship. In general it appeared Arabian females had little intrinsic value except to produce offspring, preferably male. For example, I heard that if a male was killed by accident, compensation of 5000 Riyals was paid to the family. A female victim was valued at 2000 Riyals, however if married, she was always assumed to be pregnant with a son in the womb and he was valued at 3000 Riyals.

Being my first visit to Saudi it was important to quickly learn the local customs. In other countries, a bar was usually the best place for information, but here the hotel coffee shop had to suffice. Being lowly infidels our value was akin to that of a pig and it was important to remember this, particularly when dealing with officialdom. Protocol meant my first visit was to the Airport Manager. He'd approve our helicopter operations to prevent us from being shot down. As in other dictatorial regimes, privately operated helicopters were regarded with great suspicion and strictly controlled. Especially ours, operating in a new area.

I arrived at the manager's office well before the scheduled meeting. At ten o'clock I was offered a cup of tea and told that he was busy. At twelve thirty I asked politely if I should have lunch and then return.

'Yes, you can do that, he is still busy.'

After lunch I continued my vigil. On various occasions, as tea and refreshments went in and out I saw the boss sitting back and reading newspapers. He didn't seem pressured but I made no mention of this. Later, I was advised that the office would be closing. This routine reminded me of stalking game as a child; quiet waiting was often essential to ensure a kill. I'd learnt patience again while doing business in Asia.

'Perhaps the manager will not be so busy tomorrow?' I ventured.

'You could come again tomorrow if you wish.'

'Thank you, I will.'

I had been quietly put in my place. Had I raised my voice or thumped the table, weeks could have elapsed before achieving an interview. In my case this occurred after several hours wait next morning. The Saudi boss spoke perfect English and was very friendly but made no mention of the delay in seeing me. Honour and protocol were satisfied and the manager's minions were instructed to deal with our vital flight clearances.

I heard that many gung-ho westerners failed the waiting test, resulting in long delays to their projects.

It was also necessary for me to visit aviation officials at Jeddah. While being driven around the city, we passed a vast, deserted, multi-story housing estate. All the large flat roofs were even equipped with helipads.

'Why are those hundreds of apartments empty?' I asked the driver.

'Simple. The foreign architect forgot to include separate lifts for males and females in each block, so none can be used. He fled, and was lucky to escape with his life.'

Much media comment and books have been written documenting the excesses and harshness of local life in the Kingdom. Much remains unsaid, for fear of retribution. The book 'Princess,' written by an exile, is an exception. Everyday petty crime, so common in the West, was largely unheard of due to the cruel penalties imposed on criminals. But I knew 'gifts' were expected at the highest level to ensure an enterprise's commercial success. Others in the company dealt with that matter.

Certain aspects of religious fervor and security concerns required much care to circumvent. One example, as any possible form of swine products were banned, a grease gun became a 'synthetic lubricant pump.' Grease could conceivably contain pig fat and only the military were allowed to import guns. A good local agent was more than a commercial necessity to conduct business; he could keep us infidels out of jail. Obviously, much has changed since Iraq invaded Saudi and the American military flooded in.

The Kingdom constructed long motorways to link major towns. I was staggered to see, parked beside the road in the desert and stretching for many kilometres, what must have been thousands of the largest earthmoving equipment made, all standing idle. In contrast, many of the immaculate six lane motorways were not fenced so camels walking across were a constant hazard.

On the road journey from Dhahran to our base almost three hundred kilometres north, the four-lane motorway suddenly became two. Many wrecked cars lay beside the latter road, especially adjacent to a hilltop. It seemed that locals relied on Allah when passing blind, so head-on collisions occurred. When viewed from the rear, stationary vehicles appeared to be in perfect condition. After driving past, the front was seen to be a mangled mess, a metre shorter than it should be. Not a hub cap or wheel was missing from any of the vehicles, it was not worth losing a hand.

I was told Saudi was the best place in the world to break a bone. The Kingdom paid the highest salaries and so had the best orthopedic surgeons.

On another visit I flew to Kuwait and was amazed at the number of abandoned high-rise apartment blocks in the city. My local mentor told me these were empty because they were more than ten years old.

'Why do people move out after such a short time?' I asked.

'It seems none of our desert sand is good for mixing with concrete to make lasting structures. To avoid the possibility of a building collapse, people are forced to relocate to another Government provided apartment. Naturally, important structures like the Royal palace are built with imported sand.'

This situation seemed similar to selling refrigerators to Eskimos.

I was driven to our base at Ras Al Khafji in an oil company car in convoy with a high ranking official from Japan. Our documents were scrutinized at the seemingly makeshift Saudi border. Unfortunately the oil company VIPs Thai Airways First Class return ticket featured an ad for cognac, with a picture of the bottle on the rear page. This depiction of the demon drink so enraged the gaudily uniformed Saudi official that he tore the ticket to shreds and threw the pieces onto the ground. He stomped it into the dirt before turning on his heel while shouting and gesticulating for us to get out of his sight.

The VIPs minder frantically gathered up bits of ticket and dirt before we drove away with screeching tires. Another reminder of the lowly status of us infidels.

An aspect of some Muslims' behaviour became apparent on my first Thai Airways flight from Dhahran to Bangkok in cattle class. On departure, it was apparent that most passengers were of the faith as they wore traditional robes and most ladies were veiled. Twenty minutes after takeoff, a queue began to form at the toilets. The economy section of the aircraft was transformed. Men had removed their headgear and now wore shorts and flashy, colourful beach shirts. The women re-appeared in tight low cut blouses, mini skirts, fishnet stockings and all of them seemed to be downing the free alcoholic drinks.

After our meal was served, and more drink consumed, the cabin fell into total disarray with people being sick over seats, each other and into the aisles. Some males tried to reach the toilets but fell down in the aisle and couldn't get up. Their friends were too inebriated to be of any assistance and the slim hostesses wisely didn't attempt to touch the males and retreated to their galley. The women passengers formed into a group, some giggling furiously while others fell asleep and began snoring. I managed to find a seat at the front of the cabin, the mayhem largely behind me.

Gradually the retching subsided as people fell into an alcoholic stupor. Sprawling among food from overturned meal trays, their own and others vomit. The sight and smell was revolting. Approaching Bangkok I was one of the very few in economy awake and with a seat belt fastened. The hostesses had long ago given up trying to enforce the safety requirements. I was never in danger unless we had a sudden stop and all the bodies piled on top of me.

It was another memorable journey which I related to my boss. After he had a similar experience we always travelled business class on that flight.

I carried on to Athens after my next business trip to Saudi as our holidays were due. Mary and Gavin were scheduled to fly in at seven the next morning.

Arriving, it was lovely to see Annie again, unfortunately her partner John was away on business. We first met when skiing at St Anton, Austria, they were part of our gang that invariably flew in from all over the world every January. Annie, a Kiwi, met her American partner there, as I did my wife.

Annie asked me about the flight as I had been forced to travel via war torn Beirut.

'I was not impressed with the M. E.A. aircraft. The wings were dirty and covered with oil stains, can't have been washed in months. One wonders what else they haven't done.'

'Yes, it's been hard for them with the war in Lebanon. It's a wonder they have any planes left.'

'It's the only way I could get here without a detour to London and

307

losing a day. I had my fingers crossed that Beirut airport would be open, I had to change planes there. As you know it's been closed for years.'

'What's it like there now?'

'Pretty awful. All the airport buildings are covered in bullet holes, a shambles inside, with burnt out vehicles and equipment lying around the apron. I was sure glad to get out of there.'

At Annie's, the contrast to Saudi was huge; here I could enjoy good food, wine and female companionship.

Later we discussed the matter of collecting my family.

'Don't get a taxi, they'll rip you off,' said Annie. 'Last week our old Volkswagen was declared un-roadworthy. We were forced to leave it at the airport. It's only a worn tire but quite safe to drive. If I took you to the airport in our other car now, you could drive the Volks home. Then you'll have a vehicle to collect Mary and Gavin tomorrow as I have to go to work early. You won't be checked tonight or early tomorrow and it means we'll have the Volks back here.'

Being in a mellow mood after the excellent food and wine, it seemed a great idea so Annie drove me to the airport.

The Volksi started OK and I followed her home, frantically trying to remember the one way system and distinguishing landmarks in the darkness.

Once back, port and coffee followed and I eventually got to bed at 2am only to find my alarm clock had stopped. I set my mental alarm to full volume and desperately hoped it would wake me after a few hours sleep. I was certainly raising the odds against a happy reunion. Mary would not be amused if I failed to meet them after their fourteen hour flight from Singapore.

My Guardian angel woke me and helped me to the airport. The timing was perfect; I arrived just as my family walked out of the door.

Mary was naturally happy to see me but aghast at the thought of me driving an old, battered, technically unfit vehicle on the 'wrong' side of the road in a totally unfamiliar city.

'Are you sure you can remember how to get to Annie's? You look rather hung over as well. Bet you got to bed late.'

I nodded sheepishly.

'Well, if you get lost or this old heap breaks down I suppose we can get a taxi.'

Fortunately I remembered the one way system and was relieved to get us back to the suburb of Glyfada.

John returned later that day. In the evening our hosts took us out for a meal. We enjoyed genuine Greek food on the terrace of a restaurant with the moon filtering through trellised grapevines above.

While driving home, John blew the car horn four times as we approached a lone female walking on the footpath. The pedestrian faced the oncoming vehicle with a dazzling smile on her face and opened her coat. The headlights shone on her statuesque figure, dressed only in skimpy pants and a bra. When realising our vehicle was not slowing, she slammed her coat shut and spat at us as we passed.

Her profession was obvious but I said to John, 'Why did you beep four times?'

'Well, four means I am offering the maximum price, one beep is minimum. Four beeps got us the display.'

It's always interesting to learn local customs in a new country.

John and Annie showed us Athens and then we caught a ferry to the island of Myconos where nude bathing was permitted at Super Paradise Beach. This country boy was enjoying his jet set lifestyle. The dazzling sandy beach and aqua sea, where some of Europe's beautiful people displayed their nude bodies was about as far removed from the dust and flies of Central Australia as one could get. After a relaxing week we flew to Heathrow and skied in Europe before returning to Singapore.

At ten am on Christmas Day, 1983, our presents had been opened and Mary was preparing the turkey when the phone rang. It was not a social call. A million dollar theft had occurred and our helicopter was required immediately to conduct a search.

Many times our social events had been ruined by other people's problems but responding to emergencies and disasters were part of my job.

After arriving at our hanger I found a policeman and construction company representative waiting. They briefed me on the purpose of the flight. One of the world's largest earthmoving scrapers had been stolen in the early hours of the morning. To transport the seventy tonne machine from the development site, a massive low loader had also been taken. The thieves assaulted the night guard and tied him up. The day watchman raised the alarm. Unfortunately, robberies of this nature were not unusual. Stolen equipment was invariably loaded onto a barge and quickly towed the sixteen kilometres south of Singapore to Indonesian waters in the Riau Islands group. Those islands were a haunt for pirates who preyed on passing vessels, even boarding super tankers. Expensive Singaporean pleasure craft were taken and the owners held to ransom. An Indonesian construction company had probably commissioned the scraper theft.

In 1990, it was said that Singapore's large earthmoving projects had increased the size of the country by one-fifth (now 25%) by reclaiming land from the sea, so the thieves had a range of equipment to choose from.

It's going to be one of those days I thought. Mary won't know when to start cooking the turkey, and will have to entertain the several stray bachelor friends we had invited to share our Christmas fare.

I was about to submit an international flight plan when the policeman walked in, still chatting on his radio.

'Stand by,' he said and then addressed me. 'The flight is cancelled, the stolen equipment has been found.'

'Where was it, on a barge?'

'No, jammed under an overhead walkway. Being a high, wide load without police escort the driver left a trail of broken tree branches. These were followed and led to the stolen equipment. We are now hoping to catch the crew of the barge. They may still be waiting for their illicit cargo.'

'Well it'll be a happy Christmas for some,' I said as we left the office.

Later, we heard the theft had been well planned. It failed because a section of road including that under the overpass was resurfaced a few days previously, raising it by seven centimetres. Just enough to trap the stolen goods. The driver didn't hang around and try to release the machine by deflating tires.

Another task we flew on various occasions entailed flying buyers to a large crude oil tanker anchored offshore in international waters, in the South China Sea. It was a good navigational exercise as we couldn't rely on the ship's beacon working. It seems the reason for these flights was obtaining samples of oil on offer and discussing its price. We heard the oil at this floating 'service station,' was actually 'wastage' offloaded from Indonesian tankers, pausing on their way to Singapore's refineries. The poorly paid skippers were no doubt given cash for the state-owned oil they traded, which must have been a good little earner for all involved in that corrupt trade. After some months the trading tanker departed, so the cash cow ceased for us as well.

In February 1984 Mary took Gavin to Perth to begin boarding school at Scotch College. He was only eleven at the time. To ensure he gained a place for his first year of secondary school, he had to attend year seven first. We chose Perth, being the nearest city with 'proper' schools, also, several of my cousins lived there.

Some months after Gavin left, my world fell apart. Mary found a letter from a lass declaring her love for me after our cat was accidentally locked in the spare room and peed on my files. She opened the contents to dry them out. Our relationship was already far from perfect but this was too much. She suggested we seek counselling but I saw that as postponing the inevitable and besides, I was away most of the time. My absences resulted in us living different lives and I drifted away from the relationship, finding fleeting solace elsewhere.

Many years later I read an article discussing a seminar presented to aviation professionals by a noted American aviation psychologist, Jerry Berlin. He said 'We tend to choose pilots for their emotional deprivation. This is a healthy reaction for pilots but big trouble at home. Normal people talk about variations of feelings – most pilots don't even know what that means.'

I still have difficulty in that regard and note that later in my career when hiring pilots it was instinctive to choose people with a certain attitude. That is, calm, cool, unemotional men most likely to be untroubled by disasters and trauma around them. They'd remain detached, just getting on with the job.

I fully accepted responsibility for our marriage problems. Little more needs to be said, I had been unfaithful and felt a separation was inevitable.

Mary returned to England for their summer. She flew back to Singapore when Gavin arrived from Perth to spend his school holidays at home. We continued to live a life together for our son's sake and did all the usual family things before he returned to school.

At the office, our work dried up and I found myself hired out and back in PNG on a helirig job. This took me away from my awkward home situation. We flew for BHP, their setup was totally disorganized in comparison to the slick professional operation I oversaw in Sumatra. The Parker Manager in charge of drilling - an Australian possibly trying to impress - had cut costs to such an extent I threatened to ground the helicopters if proper food hygiene and essential safety concerns were not met. A book could be written on the problems and near accidents associated with that job. It was a great relief to get out after flying every day for over three weeks. My old friend 'Bomber' Wile, who I worked with in Sumatra, and John, who suffered the ferry flight across Borneo with me, were also on that PNG job. And several of the Philippine engineers from the Bristow team in Sumatra maintained our Bell 205 helicopter. In the Asian helicopter scene, it seemed many of the same players kept reappearing in different countries, working for different employers. It was

311

a relatively small, incestuous industry at the time.

After my return to Singapore, the company decided that I should obtain an American flying licence. This would allow me to fill in on our important long-term contract in Saudi. The company utilised a school in Fort Worth, Texas and Thai Airways flew me there from Singapore. To help with beer money I took along a dozen fake Rolex, Cartier and other name watches, which cost almost nothing in Singapore. US customs carefully inspected my baggage but didn't find the hidden goodies or they would have been destroyed. I sold them for a tidy profit after arriving, which paid for my beer.

I checked into a motel close to the school and after several days study sat for the theory exam, an easy multiple choice test. Then waited for the result to allow a flight check with an official examiner.

After passing the medical examination, I rented a cheap car and became a tourist. Other students decided to obtain Texan driving licences and I joined them. The computerised multiple choice theory exam proved easy but my car, though quite safe to drive, was lacking some sort of paperwork and could not be used for a driving test. Instead, the rental yard owner gave me his personal Ford L.T.D., a monster of a vehicle. Prior to setting off, my Government examiner seemed unfazed at having to show me where the light and other switches were on this 'tank.' The test concluded successfully and this licence was to prove very useful after leaving the USA. I find it amusing to think that of the ten different jurisdictions that have issued me with driving licences, the only road test I've ever taken in over sixty years of driving was in Texas. This contrasted sharply with holding up to four different countries valid aviation licences which made it necessary to complete half a dozen medical examinations every year by different authorised doctors.

In the meantime I waited for my exam results. It seems the company that supplied paper to the Federal Aviation Authority's computers in Oklahoma had gone on strike so results could not be printed out. It didn't bother me; I was enjoying an unofficial paid holiday. I found great places to visit such as Billy Bob's, an acre of drinking cum entertainment complexes under one roof, where beer was free until seven pm. Though I thought American beer insipid, it was better than having to pay for the stuff and I always left without having done so. Other patrons stayed, and perhaps being slightly intoxicated, spent freely on overpriced drinks and live shows, including indoor bull riding.

I found other bars where soup and salads were free, provided one purchased a drink. It was an interesting learning curve and many people bought me drinks just to hear my accent and traveler's tales.

By chance, friends from the Singapore Polo Club owned a property not far from Fort Worth and happened to be visiting their permanent home. I was invited to lunch and saw how the American upper crust lived. After driving onto their ranch, I noted many 'noddy' pumps lifting oil out of the ground. Several immaculate private polo fields were also in evidence before I reached the large, imposing family residence with adjacent garages and horse stables. My friends said the oil belonged to them and to top it off, I learned that 'Daddy' owned a bank in town. My cheap rental car hardly impressed them, but it was an educational interlude.

After several weeks wait, I was allowed to do my Check Flight, although the theory exam results had still not arrived. My examiner said it was great for him to fly with an experienced pilot. I found his tests easy and routine. We were flying home when he asked me to slow and come to hover while at a thousand feet (300 m) above the ground.

While coming to a stop, in our peripheral vision, we saw something approaching us at high speed. We both involuntarily ducked, even though a fatal mid air collision seemed only milli-seconds away. The speeding object stopped, centimetres away from my side of the cockpit. With my heart pounding and shot full of adrenaline, I saw it was our own rear cabin door which had sprung open, broken its restraining strap and slammed forwards under the influence of the rotor airflow. I moved the stick forward to regain speed and the door closed as the airflow pushed it shut. With our pulses returning to normal we realised the door catch must be defective, having vibrated to 'open.' I had been tested again in a frightening incident.

It was time to go home, my license could follow in due course. It would be from the sixth country allowing me to fly their aircraft.

In Singapore, I flew locally before Mary and Gavin jetted in from opposite directions to spend Christmas with me. Mary and I accepted that separating was inevitable but would not divorce until Gavin was older. We maintained the appearance of a normal marriage, but one where my work forced us to live apart. She decided to live in England and Gavin would complete his education there, after his year in Perth.

Early in January 1985 I joined them in the UK and we skied at Verbier in Switzerland for several weeks, Austria having little snow. A slalom race was held for visitors and I upset Gavin by winning a gold medal for the seniors' event. He tried too hard and crashed out during the juniors' medal run.

Before this holiday, a high-ranking Japanese tourist was lost while swimming at Desaru, a beach resort just north of Singapore, in Malaysia.

We were asked to search for his body. I was the only pilot available but my passport was in the Saudi Embassy awaiting a visa. It was necessary for me to clear customs and immigration in Malaysia and Singapore twice a day to fly this task. One of our engineers was a private pilot and his passport photo showed him wearing a white pilot's shirt. Mike said I could borrow it, so for four days I went in and out of Singapore and Malaysia using a false passport. Singapore immigration did not require me to attend as we were 'locals,' but at Johore I gazed out of the window and talked about the weather and missing tourists, all the while averting my face, while Mike's passport was stamped. I hate to think what might have occurred had I been sprung, especially after John's earlier brush with the Sultan of Johore.

During the four day body search, I flew almost twenty four hours. Mostly adjacent to pandanus trees lining the shore, at a height of five metres. The Japanese even enlisted a Bomoh, or 'medicine man' to predict where and when the body might appear, to no avail. When we gave up, I flew the widow and a company official who both spread flowers on the water where the man disappeared. It was such a relief to return Mike's passport.

Another noteworthy episode occurred soon after when I flew two visiting American VIPs, General Electric Vice-presidents, to their factory in Malaysia. They required a chopper with two engines and two pilots. The engines part was easy, but we didn't have another chopper pilot immediately available, so Mike filled the breach again and flew as my co-pilot. Just before landing at the factory, one of our six fuel pumps failed, not a serious problem. Never-the-less, we should have stayed on the ground with this failure, but getting it fixed quickly was a major dilemma, so we departed with our passengers none the wiser.

Our return flight was normal until I reduced power and lowered the nose to begin our descent into Singapore's Seletar Airport. Almost immediately, an engine flamed out. The warning console lit up with red lights. Not being heavily loaded, I could easily continue our approach but the single engine's power was insufficient to hover and taxi in to our parking area. I would have to slide the aircraft onto the grass next to the airport runway.

Mike, who maintained the aircraft, and I, immediately deduced that the failure was due to lowering the nose, which uncovered a port in the fuel tank and resulted in air being pumped to the engine, stopping it. This possibility should never have been allowed in a fuel system as we still had almost an hour's fuel left in other fuel tanks, but we were stuck with the design.

314

I raised the nose and continued my approach to Seletar, just a few minutes away. Mike immediately tried to re-start the failed engine while I concentrated on making an uneventful landing. The machine had overhead throttles, which makes them difficult to manipulate precisely for engine starting, while maneuvering the aircraft and speaking to the control tower.

I was cleared to land and on short final approach when Mike got both engines back on line so I landed and hovered in normally without having to mention our problem to the VIPs.

The company's service included collecting and returning customers to their hotel. Our Malay driver said he overheard our passengers speculating on what happened when all the red lights appeared, but ignorance can be bliss.

It was the first engine failure I suffered in over 7,000 hours in the air. Luckily it happened when I had another engine to keep me airborne. My second failure occurred over jungle, again with the spare engine enabling a normal landing. My engineering background was a great asset but thankfully my angel guarded against 'just bad luck' bringing me down.

In February 1985, my recently obtained American licence was put to use in Saudi Arabia. A new English pilot was having difficulty obtaining his work permit so I filled in for him. I shouldn't have been flying in command on a business visa but got away with it for three weeks. The Japanese and Saudis ran a tight ship and security was strict, even in those pre 9/11 terrorist threat days. Just getting to the heliport required signatures from heads of military, police and security on the pass required to clear checkpoints. All passengers' bags were searched before being loaded and we took off exactly at 7.30 am so any late arrivals missed the flight and needed a lot of explaining to keep their job.

This rigid adherence to timetables was partly necessary due to the tension between the Saudis and Iran, located just two hundred kilometres across the Persian Gulf. That may seem a good distance, but an Iranian fighter could leave its airspace halfway across the gulf and hit Saudi oil tanks or cities only a few minutes later. One of our flights took us to within ten kilometres of the war zone boundary with Iran so Saudi radar could easily think we were a hostile aircraft when returning. I was told that on several occasions Saudi fighters were within minutes of shooting down our helicopter before being told we were friendly - notwithstanding our flight schedules always being submitted a month ahead. The possibility of a mistake was illustrated when a missile downed an airliner crossing the gulf close to our area and all on board perished.

With poor visibility over the gulf, and having to rely only on my dead reckoning, I was very careful not to stray into hostile Iranian airspace. It was rarely enjoyable flying. Man made pollution from numerous refineries and sudden dust storms made life difficult for pilots and the aircraft. If I had created an incident, my lack of a work permit would have had me jailed, an unthinkable consequence. The dust, salt and chemicals in the air also increased the workload for our maintenance crew as engines breathe a lot of air and suffer from pollutants, just like humans.

We lived within a large oil company compound and it was safe for us to drive inside the fence. If venturing into town, special care was necessary because as foreigners and infidels we were automatically in the wrong if involved in any sort of incident. An accident did not bear thinking about. When travelling to our base from Dhahran a local always drove.

Occasional visits to a coffee shop in the bleak, dusty commercial area were the extent of our entertainment. Local television was rarely worth trying to fathom, and I couldn't remember when I had last gone without an alcoholic drink for over three weeks. I heard that smuggled scotch was available at hugely inflated prices even though the newspaper showed pictures of bulldozers crushing confiscated bottles.

Expats working regular tours brought in kits to make their own booze as people's private premises were sacrosanct unless causing a nuisance or selling alcohol made at home. Our crew didn't bother; we lived in several portacabins close to local workers who might complain about smelling alcohol.

Communications within and to other countries was excellent but we were careful not to criticise or discuss politics over the phone as our line could be tapped at any time. We often heard strange clicks and background noise when calling overseas. Falling foul of the law was unthinkable as we heard that infidels were sodomised so badly that hospital treatment was sometimes required.

Eventually I was able to escape and return to Singapore, where another misfortune awaited me. Head office had decided to close down the Singapore operation. My marriage had collapsed and now my job was gone too. Pat Lloyd was the best boss I ever had, but our American superiors were upset because the Singapore crew sidestepped some of their edicts. Those 'good ole boys' simply did not understand Asian sensibilities and ways of doing business. Also, that year our operation made a profit when they did not, which further rubbed salt into the perceived wound. To drive home their irritation, the last person hired, our friend Bob the salesman, was persuaded to join the 'enemy' and throw us out of our offices.

316

Fortunately, I was offered the chief pilot's job with Rotorwork in New Guinea. They were expanding and needed someone with mid-sized helicopter experience. Moving to Mt Hagen, a provincial capital in the western highlands situated 1,629 metres above sea level, was not an exciting prospect. I was told there was no desk and barely a chair for me in the small, tin roofed wooden shack my new company called home. After thirteen years, I would again have to shop for my food, cook and fend for myself.

I had two weeks to pack up after ten years in Singapore. It was pointless trying to find another locally based job as companies were firing, not hiring. At least I would continue to work as an expatriate, with air fares, housing and schooling assistance as part of my package.

I was flying out with just a suitcase so personal items went into storage until deciding on my longer term future. Mary had a shipment sent to England, which included our eight-place rosewood dining table and chairs. She left with enough furnishings to fill a house, which we planned to buy in Cheltenham.

It was a gut wrenching time for me as I burnt my past in the form of old paper records and tried to sell our television and other household items. I received little reward for my goods, the market was flooded as many other expats were forced to leave due to the general economic downturn in Asia. Thousands of dollars worth of kit was virtually given away which did nothing to boost my flagging spirits.

My parting with Mary was anticlimactic; I would visit England when I could. We were both setting off to unknown futures. She was naturally bitter about my infidelity while I would suffer an increased financial burden and was moving to a town with three single white women. Was this payback for my past sins? My emotional turmoil was a mixture of painful regrets, humiliation at failing my partner badly and some relief that the break had occurred. We could both regroup and begin a new chapter, hopefully without badly affecting our son.

Free alcohol on the flight to Port Moresby temporarily dulled the pain of despair and uncertainty. My recent trip to PNG had illustrated how awful life there could be, compared to the pleasures of Asia. People speak of turning points in their lives; this was one in spades for me!

I couldn't anymore blame or say it was God's will – fate and my own free will had brought me to this unhappy state.

Before falling asleep on the overnight flight I wondered why I had to keep suffering these reversals of fortune? A dull, boring, predictable job almost seemed attractive.

CHAPTER 15

Learn from the mistakes of others. You won't get too
many chances yourself. ~ The aviators Guide Book

In 1985 the Port Moresby airport and its surrounds were a stark introduction to the country – sweaty crowds, dust and disorganised traffic congestion. I wearily checked into the Gateway Hotel after my overnight flight and began the process of obtaining my local licence. It meant another involved medical examination and passing their Air Law exam. During my earlier visit, I had flown on a validation of my Australian licence but this was only good for a month.

Within a few days I completed the statuary requirements and flew Air New Guinea to Mount Hagen where I had been allocated a cosy two-bedroom house in a compound containing several similar dwellings. The house was perfect for my needs but the office facilities at the airport were a different matter. Tony, the boss, his girl Friday, Betty, and I were accommodated in a dismal tin shed that was divided into a few rooms containing two offices and a spare parts storage area. In Singapore I had my own spacious office, now I had to borrow desk space or write on my knees. There was no photocopier. I had to walk next door to the Mission Aviation Fellowship (MAF, or Mexican Air Force as they were jokingly referred to) and sign for each reproduction made. Tony kept a close eye on each page copied, being very cost conscious.

Betty was a happy, easygoing co-worker and was married to our senior pilot Dick Anderson. They lived next door to me in the same compound, not far from the centre of town. We all got on well and years later Dick would become the operations manager and eventually, general manager of the company.

Although my accommodation in Mount Hagen was perfectly adequate, I now had to shop and cook for myself. I employed a houseboy, six days a week, to clean my premises. He also washed and ironed my clothes. It made my austere existence a little easier. There being no social life to speak of, I threw myself into work. This diverted my mind from the depressing situation I was in – no friends, no money, no family and no company after a long days work. Satellite television was a savior, when I had time to watch.

The Company had won a Shell exploration contract working in the Sepic River area, conducting a seismic survey from a Mission airstrip called Hauna. All workers were accommodated on a houseboat in the middle of the river. Shell stipulated that all personnel traveled in twin-engine helicopters, so recruitment, training and rostering kept me busy. The company manual was obsolete so I spent many nights at home, working until midnight, writing a completely new manual. I also had to change my boss's mindset. He was a seasoned bush pilot, now he needed convincing that multinational companies expected professional pilots to wear smart uniforms to match their top-notch qualifications.

Meanwhile, I flew odd tasks around the highlands and was getting to know the country better, in between training newcomers. During my time at the helm, I employed dozens of pilots from all over the world. All were flight checked and those new to PNG, regardless of their experience, underwent an extensive training program before being allowed to fly by themselves. PNG is known as having some of the most demanding flight conditions anywhere in the world due to it's combination of high temperatures, humidity, violent storms and ever changing weather amid the wild, high mountains.

Some new boys had never flown in the jungle before, so I showed them how to land safely, while heavily loaded, in small clearings surrounded by sixty metre tall trees. Others had never seen high mountains or tropical storms. Specialised tasks were also taught.

Local knowledge was most important, particularly in the highlands, as dozens of different gaps through the mountains needed memorising. Clouds usually prevented us from flying in a straight line over the continuous east-west mountain chain in the highlands. This rose to 14,800 feet (4,367m) at the highest peak, Mt Wilhelm, in PNG and even greater heights just across the border in Irian Jaya.

The eventual installation of reliable GPS receivers in our aircraft did not negate the initial area training program. We often had to fly miles in the 'wrong' direction, twisting and turning while following the only safe route home in bad weather, in a 'tunnel' between steep mountain ridges and low clouds. The lack of navigation aids also meant that instrument or night flight was rarely a safe option, even if our helicopters had been equipped to do so.

To summarise, pilots new to PNG first had to obtain a local licence and then pass our in house aircraft type, role, area, and in some cases, route checks. Initially they were restricted to fly only in designated areas until their local knowledge grew. After more experience they were also checked and/or trained to land on high altitude mountain top telephone repeater stations. These sites were located at altitudes of over 12,000 feet (3,660m) and those locations in the tropical 'thin' air, combined with turbulent strong winds, up and downdrafts, clouds and rain, presented the ultimate challenge in achieving a safe arrival. Especially when heavily loaded as the high temperatures we experienced equated to landing at altitudes of up to 17,000ft (5,180m) in a standard atmosphere or temperate climate. Unsuccessful attempts resulted in bits of chopper being left, scattered around peaks. The dozen or more high mountaintop repeater stations probably saw at least one chopper crash occur over the years.

When training new boys, this wreckage was a grim reminder of the skill and judgement required when stretching the aircraft and pilot's performance to the limit. One mountaintop wreck I retrieved was entirely due to another company's new pilot not being trained or even told to carefully check the aircraft's performance graphs for landings at altitude. The flight was doomed when he took off; he was just too heavy to arrive safely at his destination. Fortunately no one was hurt when the aircraft spun and crashed short of the helipad.

Some tasks we performed were outside the altitude/weight performance graphs given in the flight manuals, they did not cover our operating heights in the 'thin' tropical air. We did our own testing, creeping carefully into the unknown.

The Bell 205 Huey, for example, was optimized to operate at low level in Vietnam, so I tiptoed into new territory when lifting loads up to mountaintops. These underslung loads could always be jettisoned if things went wrong. Lifting maximum loads up the hill invariably resulted in reaching an engine or transmission limit while landing, depending on the aircraft type flown and current air temperature. The gauges needed very carefully watching to avoid damage.

I remember one lad, primarily a maintenance worker who wished to begin a flying career. He was sent off to do an easy job close to town to gain experience. Away for an hour, twice the length of time the task should have taken, he returned with the job uncompleted. He was unsure where he had been during the flight. After that he remained in the workshop.

Another mature, highly experienced pilot arrived with a clutch of newspaper cuttings detailing some of his exploits in Australia. I flew with Cedric for many hours but his performance and decision-making did not equate to his age and claimed experience. I felt uneasy about letting him loose on his own so had another of our experienced pilots fly with Cedric. He felt the same. To save face we offered Cedric a job as a radio operator. As the pay and prestige were much lower than expected, he soon resigned. I was glad to see him go.

Months later, on a day of exceptionally foul weather when not even helicopters were flying out of Hagen, we were amazed to hear a low flying chopper pass the airport and heard Cecric's voice on the radio. All our experienced pilots were sitting on the ground. Was he thumbing his nose at us?

Later that day Cedric and his two geologist passengers were missing. It was pointless trying to mount a search until the weather improved. Finding them would be difficult; no emergency beacon signal had been reported. Fortunately, villagers heard an abrupt cessation of sound, then found the crash site, only ten kilometres from Hagen. All on board perished when the helicopter hit the jungle at high speed and a steep angle. We think he lost control when becoming disoriented in very poor visibility.

Cedric's new employers had not bothered to phone me about his history. I was astounded; it was always the first thing I did when hiring. That simple communication could have prevented the tragedy. It was little comfort to think that my decision to scrub Cedric was proved correct. Events such as these remind the accounts department that airfares, accommodation and training costs, up to ten thousand dollars per pilot, are more than justified if such occurrences are prevented. The old saying - 'if you think training is expensive, try having an accident', is certainly correct.

One of my early jobs in PNG was flying prefabricated huts from the nearest road to the shores of the then isolated Lake Kutubu, with a Bell 205 'Huey'. Once, while re-fuelling, a vehicle raced up to the helicopter. The driver hurriedly told me a patient in the vehicle was hemorrhaging severely after childbirth. Could I fly her immediately to Mendi hospital? Of course, was the answer.

To minimise blood loss, the Australian nurse was clamping an artery inside the woman's uterus with her hand. In a moment, both lay on the flat metal floor of the Huey, totally unrestrained, and we took off. There was no time to fit the large cabin doors so an uncoordinated turn could have resulted in both sliding out and dropping hundreds of metres to the ground. The patient's husband sat on the only seat in the cabin as all the others had been removed to save weight. He, unsurprisingly, appeared rather frightened during his first helicopter ride.

The ten-minute flight with our unconscious patient seemed to take forever. She would not have survived hours of road transport on the rough, winding roads around the mountains. On arrival at the hospital helipad the woman was whisked away and we heard that she recovered completely. This was the first of many lives I helped save in PNG.

The Shell seismic job at Hauna expanded to require two large Bell twin-engined and two smaller single powered machines flying daily. This contract meant training and checking over twenty pilots on rotating duty so I happily spent half my time there, not having to shop or cook. Two of my old friends arrived to work on this job. One was Alan, a whiz engineer, who I first met in Kota Kinabalu. He and his wife subsequently followed us to Singapore, where they were neighbours at Seleta, before returning to live in Australia. The second was 'Bomber' Wile, to whom I had flown fuel after he got lost in Sumatra. He managed to stray again and I rescued him for the second time.

The PNG Department of Civil Aviation had given me approval to train and convert pilots to our single-engine helicopters, but I wished to obtain approval for the Bell twin as well. Some backscratching was done and I gave a sample conversion to the DCA examiner, after which he authorised me to do the same to other pilots.

Shell looked after the welfare of their contract people very well. Once I dropped in to a jungle pad on our evening milk run, just to deliver frozen chips for the solitary expatriate's evening meal.

One day, an aircraft disappeared not far from where we were flying. I particularly remember this event among the dozens of aircraft accidents I attended over the years. This one happened when a relatively new pilot tore the wings off his BN Islander twin, it's surmised, while trying to fly through a line of thunderstorms. The wings, minus engines, were found kilometres from where the fuselage of the plane had speared dart like into the jungle. It was a nasty prang as the cabin section's height was reduced to less than a metre, from which numerous bodies had to be extracted. Over a week after the accident I was asked to lift the bodies out using a fifty metre long line. A landing area had not been cut due to very difficult terrain at the site. After placing the net load of cadavers on a nearby dry riverbed, the net was reattached to my belly hook on a short line to be underslung to Vanimo, the nearest town. Unfortunately, the heat and humidity had rendered the bodies to such a state that even while flying fast the stench reached me in the cockpit. I believe people who say the stink of rotting humans is one of the worst smells imaginable.

In August 1985 I flew to Singapore, collected Gavin, and we both jetted to England. He had flown in from Perth after we terminated his schooling there. Meanwhile, Mary found a two-story town house in Cheltenham, which we purchased for £40,000. It seemed a lot at the time but was close to town and Gavin's new school. I occupied the third bedroom, which had just enough space to fit a single bed, small wardrobe and still allow the door to be closed. I could barely turn around without falling onto the bed. I guess having small rooms minimized the cost of building and heating. Mary and Gavin, being permanent residents, occupied the larger bedrooms. The contact with civilization and family lifted my spirits. Briefly I could be a father again.

The local hardware shop's profits must have surged as I installed double glazing, ran power wires to our garage behind the small enclosed back garden and generally fixed things up.

My teeth were also fixed. Problems had occurred after losing a filling while out bush. This minor inconvenience resulted in my having great difficulty in speaking, eating or drinking when my tongue was rubbed raw. Such events reinforce the important of maintaining good health when constantly in isolated areas.

Soon after returning to PNG, I found myself on the Shell contract. Additional accommodation had arrived on a barge called Marella, whose deck was covered in portacabins. Marella became my choice of accommodation as raucous parties often continued till late on the Petaj, originally a luxury vessel cruising the Great Barrier Reef. It contained about a dozen small cabins below decks.

Many of the seismic contractors personnel were hired straight out of university in England and spend weeks in the steamy jungle before having a few days off in comfort on the air-conditioned Petaj. All our meals were eaten on this vessel and sometimes, after a wild night, we found eggs unavailable for breakfast. Partygoers had thrown them at each other and demolished the lot. At times a total lack of potatoes occurred for the same reason.

I remember one young graduate, fresh from the UK, who I collected from Wewak. Later that day I dropped him off at a jungle camp. The unfortunate lad stepped out of his tent during the night to relieve himself, tripped and fell into a nipa palm. These palms are the stuff of nightmares, covered in thousands of long, sharp, infectious needles. I believe hundreds of barbs pierced his body, 'nailing' him to the enfolding branches. After his rescue, I medivac'd him out in the morning. He returned to England after attending the hospital in Wewak. We never saw him again.

In some areas, nipa palms stretched solidly for kilometres. When flying a single engine chopper, I always went around those lethal patches of needles, not wanting to chance falling into them if the engine failed. Rescue would only be realistically possible by helicopter winch.

A bar was constructed on the raised bow of the Marella, in front of the bridge. We now enjoyed a civilized drink 'at home' without having to catch the dinghy transport to the Petaj. I happened to be there on opening night, had a beer, and then left, returning to my cabin. Rain had fallen, and while descending the only makeshift walk way to the deck, I slipped on steeply sloping, wet, shiny steel. Falling awkwardly, the left side of my chest landed on a bollard. I knew there was a problem when pain shot across my torso. It was several days before I could move sufficiently to crawl into the dinghy and be flown to the hospital in Wewak where my ninth rib was found to be broken. Thereafter, a large sign proclaimed the bar to be 'Ye Olde Busted Rib Cage'. *First a hash run, now a bar, what else would I be responsible for naming?*

An aviation disaster befell me on that contract, while conducting training on a Belll 212. After a long, hot day, during our last flight to base with an empty aircraft, I asked my trainee to simulate an engine governor failure. He was an experienced fixed wing twin turbine pilot, so I didn't expect him to perform the required action on the wrong engine. That one incorrect switch movement resulted in extensive damage to the turbine - metal was melted. We landed on one engine.

Many incidents occur and aircraft and lives have been lost in training. It's often a fine line to simulate the real thing in flight, before it becomes a disaster. Unfortunately, simulators are not universally available. That mistake resulted in pay deductions for my trainee and me, and cost the company dearly in repairs and lost revenue. I had to accept part of the blame as I was in command. It was a severe lesson on how one moment can undo years of working very long hours to help a company succeed. It was another blow to my already austere existence.

PNG featured four isolated road systems serving local areas, all cut off from the outside world. Most were on highland plateaus protected by mountains, large rivers or both. All vehicles using these roads had been stripped and flown in. Usually inside DH Twin Otter freighter cabins, the largest aircraft able to use the short landing strips.

We had helicopters capable of lifting over 1,800 kilograms so I had a special cradle made. It enabled us to pick up different types of vehicles from under their wheels without so much as scratching the paint. The cradle was light and could be quickly dismantled for transportation in the chopper cabin.

In July 1985, the first complete vehicle I transported was a Toyota utility. We were the only company with this capability. To gain access to the Simbai plateau I had to fly over a steep mountain ridge rising from the Jimmy Valley. The lowest part of the ridge had a house perched on its crest with just enough room between the leafy roof eaves, and the nearby jungle for my flying vehicle to pass through. Fuel was critical so I timed my climb to fly the vehicle through this gap.

As the Toyota sailed past the house, a few metres above the ground, I saw the astonished occupants looking out from a raised veranda, their eyes bulging on proverbial stalks, pondering the miracle of a vehicle flying past their lofty home.

The Toyota was delivered safely and I believe it was a first for PNG. As word spread we flew many complete vehicles.

Another sling job was to fly bulldozers into an inaccessible road system high in the mountains. These dozers naturally had to be stripped down. After dropping off one such maximum weight load a cry came over the radio.

'Phil, that dozer body is not quite in the right spot, it should be another five metres closer to me.'

'Sorry, too late, I can't move it now, it's your baby.'

After lifting the maximum weight at sea level, dropping them at high altitude was always a controlled descent into the ground, with maximum power applied, once our speed fell below 18 knots (36 km/hr).

Another regular task was assisting authorities to maintain law and order in isolated areas. The Wahagi and Tari valleys were renowned for virtually continous tribal fights of varying intensity and numbers involved. Flying police to one such affray, we found dozens of warriors facing each other in two opposing ragged lines, formed on hilly ground. As in medieval times, the weapons were spears, bows and arrows. The fighters advanced, released their missiles, then ran for cover. The ready availability of guns was yet to come.

We joined the battle. My Bell 212, loaded with passengers, created sufficient downdraft in slow flight to blow hurled spears and arrows harmlessly into the ground before reaching a target. It became an amusing game for me to intercept missiles, often launched from patches of long grass.

The warriors soon gave up; they were wasting their weaponry. I chased them, sending many tumbling head over heels down steep mounds.

One weekend the boss paid for a dozen company employees to go white water rafting through the Wahgi river canyons. We set off in several rubber dinghies. It was a different, exciting way of seeing the country, looking up at wild mountains, instead of down. The rapids were a challenge and required furious paddling to prevent capsizing.

Our office cleaner was the only person thrown out while negotiating one bucking passage. A PNG national, he couldn't swim but we weren't worried, all of us wore lifejackets. When he failed to re-appear we became concerned, frantically scanning the muddy water. After almost a minute, curly hair appeared beside the dinghy, we grabbed it, hauling him aboard.

'Mi cumup undenise dispella lik lik bot,' he explained.

He surfaced under the dinghy and it took him a while to move to the side.

Several months later a group of American tourists began the same tour. They were waylaid by 'rascal' tribesmen while floating down the shallow, populated, slow-moving early section of the trip. These locals pushed the dinghy to the bank and surrounded it. All were armed with machetes or guns. They told the captives their possessions would be stolen and the women raped. Then they said they'd kill everyone and throw their bodies in the river to remove the evidence.

I was told that the expatriate tour guide pleaded, bargained and used every method he could think of to save their lives, but the tribesmen were adamant, none would survive. With nothing to lose, after creating a diversion, the group got the dinghy away from shore and furiously paddled down river. The tribesmen ran along the bank, throwing stones while chasing the dinghy, but eventually the terrain beat them and the party escaped. I heard those lucky tourists left the country on the first available flight.

To my knowledge, the river has not been rafted in that area since. This was one of the many examples I saw where a few lawless individuals ruined a potential business venture that could have provided local employment if nurtured.

In December, I finished my evening task of writing the company's new operations manual. That monkey was off my back. The task was done longhand, before I bought a typewriter sized Olivetti M15 portable computer. It could operate on its battery but didn't have a hard drive so all operating systems and files had to be loaded by floppy disc before beginning work. Tediously, again at night, I wrote several helicopter costing and other programs on the old 'Symphony' spreadsheet, saving much number crunching.

On December 25th I flew to Port Moresby, enjoying a sumptuous Christmas lunch at company expense. Then caught the evening flight to Cairns, arriving in Townsville the next day. I was there to collect a used Bell 212 the company had just purchased. The aircraft was fitted with a Sperry autopilot, new to me. Kevin, who I had previously worked with in Asia, arrived to show me how to press 'George's' million dollar, sophisticated buttons. He accompanied me to Thursday Island, demonstrating. Ignorance or improper operation of 'George' could crash the aircraft in seconds. Unlike most fixed wing autopilots, in this helicopter, the operating servos are fitted to primary flying controls in series and not in parallel. For the technically minded, this means that pilot operation of the controls does not necessarily override the autopilot – the effect being like disconnecting the steering on a car. I'd have to train our pilots so it was important I knew how to drive George.

We reached Coen before darkness fell, only to discover the hotel closed. The townspeople were away for a race meeting. One couple who remained saved us, kindly provided beds and dinner. After Kevin left me in T.I., I made it to Moresby the following day to complete the aircraft import documentation. Before flying to Hagen, I was photographed, interviewed and written up in the national newspaper.

In January 1986, a mob rampaged through the main street in Hagen, smashed every window they could find and looted many premises. We were stuck at the airport until early evening, when the police regained control. Fortunately, our shiny new offices had been completed, so we passed the time in comfortable surroundings. At last, I had a desk and filing cabinets at the airport, instead of having to keep paperwork at home. The rampage and destruction in town was repeated several times over the years. At times, we became accustomed to hearing frequent gunfire. Fortunately the phones mostly worked so worried wives or mothers were reassured after hearing the news.

Soon after this event, I was invited to a garden party in Hagen attended by many local expat managers. I don't know why the hostess took an interest in me as hundreds of single men lived in the area. Jo said I looked harried, hunted and beset by misfortune. This meeting led to dinner at their home and a mutual regard for her and her husband, Nigel. Their friendship, outside of the incestuous, closed aviation shop, provided a relief valve and Nigel's ever present humour helped me remain sane. Was my angel at work here again?

I chose not to risk getting close to any of the only three white single teachers. They had many suitors, two of the girls finding husbands. One of our pilots' wives living in Hagen, made a play for me when her husband was out of town. Just as in Singapore, I was not going to fall into her web.

I escaped from PNG in March and flew to England. We had booked to ski with friends in the south of France, at Puy St Vincent. This entailed flying to Turin and catching a bus to our destination. I was amazed to see that some villages we passed through in northern Italy reminded me of PNG, they appeared so starkly poor. Unpainted buildings and unpaved footpaths illuminated by one feeble light in the main street were evident. Returning in daylight, we saw massive fortified gun emplacements, remnants from WW II, strategically placed to guard roads through mountain passes.

Our skiing routine worked out well – Barry, his son, plus Gavin and I took off up the mountains together in the mornings and had a great time attacking all the steep slopes and powder snow. The two wives gently slid down easy runs before meeting us for lunch, after which we all skied together.

One day, Barry's crazy, fearless son fell out of a chairlift. He hung below the chair, suspended by his parka, which caught on a footrest. Ten metres below, an icy rock-strewn stream flowed down the mountain. Barry and I were seated in the following chair and saw the drama unfold. The lift had to be stopped and slowly wound back, while we waited and hoped the garment held. It did, a stern lecture following. I believe Barry's son was eventually chosen to train with England's Olympic ski team.

At school in Cheltenham, it seems Gavin's 'Singapore Chinese' business sense was active. Being a dayboy, he bought and carried loaves of bread to school and sold slices to hungry boarders at a good profit. He also backed Australian sports teams visiting England and invariably collected more money, which he said infuriated his classmates. Perhaps that is why he is now a financial planner.

New Guinea soon claimed me again and in April I made an interesting survey flight in a Bell Jetranger. This aircraft's fuel is normally exhausted after 2.75 hours in flight but on this trip I spent hours above 10,000 feet (3,030m) at low power. After landing a few times and carefully dipping the fuel tank, we headed home where I landed with twenty minutes fuel remaining after being airborne for 3.15 hours.

In June, my old friend John Simler phoned from Hong Kong and offered me a job there. It would entail much cockpit time flying loads to build power lines, so I declined. Hong Kong is an interesting place to visit but I didn't wish to live and work there.

Also in June, Shell completed their seismic work and our contract was scaled down to one twin-engined machine. It meant laying off many of our pilots, fortunately plenty of notice was given. It had been a lengthy contract; we flew over eight thousand hours with no accidents and few incidents. I believe it was the largest ever single seismic contract flown in the country at the time. To complete the job, we lifted most of the equipment onto several moored cargo vessels by helicopter.

During subsequent survey flights I flew Shell geologists around the remote areas of their lease. One day, while sitting alone on the ground at Hayfield inside my thirteen passenger machine, it began to shake. Kids swinging on the tail stinger, I thought while getting out to admonish them. It wasn't children, it was the ground moving. Our work area was not affected, but on returning to Hagen I found the 6.9 magnitude shake had caused considerable damage. One large building in the main street was condemned. In my flat, not even a herb or spice jar had fallen from their narrow shelf. My angel must have done a quick trip to hold them in place.

In August, 1986, my mother arrived in Hagen. She was with a church group from Adelaide visiting Lutheran missions. They were billeted with church people but their schedule allowed me to show her where I lived and cook dinner for us. We skirted around the subject of my attendance at any religious establishments although I was well aware that my mother's brother headed up the Lutheran church in PNG. He was based outside Lae, which we rarely visited as our opposition had a base there.

Apart from the golf club, much expatriate social life centered around the Pioneer Club, situated above shops in the middle of town. A business club, it provided a civilised atmosphere, good food and housed several full size billiard tables. Very few nationals were members. My friend Nigel, produced several comedies presented by the Hagen Players, on a makeshift stage in the Pioneer Club. His wife, Jo, an accomplished amateur thespian, usually played a leading role.

Theatre nights were a hoot with a great deal of audience participation, almost all knowing each other. I attended many rehearsals and became the general dogsbody, not game to take a part, possibly being away for the performances. Once, I did have to stand in, playing a small part with only twenty four hours notice. It was not possible to learn all my lines, so a newspaper was used to hide the script. I waved it around, stopping the movement briefly to read my lines.

One of our company directors, Mick McDonald and his delightful wife Robyn, lived in a coffee plantation manager's house ten kilometres out of town, complete with in-ground pool and grass tennis court. Occasionally, Tony and I were invited for a Saturday afternoon's social tennis, swim and tea. It was gracious living, a far cry from the dirt and squalor to be found in most of Hagen's streets. Little did I dream that some years later I would be the master and only inhabitant of that house. The longtime national housekeeper, Cora, an excellent cook and custodian of the 'castle,' was like a personal servant who even did the vegetable shopping for me. Years later again, I saw the house trashed and burnt as retribution against 'privileged' white expats.

The company's only fatal helicopter crash occurred in October 1986. A quiet, popular, very experienced PNG pilot, Mike was conducting a mineral stream sampling survey with two geologists and a local field assistant on board. They were operating in a sparsely populated area of steep terrain, a hundred kilometres south east of Hagen when reported missing. Early next morning we sent two aircraft out searching. No crash beacon signal was heard to pinpoint the missing aircraft. Dick landed in villages nearest Mike's previous known survey locations, and quizzed the locals. He soon struck it lucky. At 8.30 am finding a national who had survived the crash. The man was badly injured but able to tell Dick that one geologist was not in the aircraft when it crashed. After a quick flight he found the stranded man and a broken steel wire across the river. It seemed the aircraft had struck a Water Resources stream gauging cable crossing the river being sampled. The wire must have caught the landing skid upright tubes, swinging the chopper straight down into the water. The survivor managed to scramble out of the submerged cabin and was washed down the swiftly flowing river. Though badly injured, he probably felt his only hope was to float down the river to where he had seen a village.

Now we knew what had occurred, and that a previously unknown (to us) cable existed in a country where suspended wires in virgin jungle were very rare.

Remains of the broken cable showed Dick where to search for the wreckage. He found one skid protruding just above water level. An almost impossible task to find that clue without knowing the exact location as the river was littered with dead trees, some appearing almost identical to the skid tube.

I flew into the site with a large machine, then lifted the cabin out of the river. Two bodies were found inside, the other passenger's remains were

330

eventually found in the river. It seems the surviving national was not strapped in, which is why he lived. A rare case of this omission proving beneficial. The autopsy found the deceased had all had died from broken necks.

This accident prompted a countrywide search for known wires across isolated rivers and other jungle areas. All statutory authorities and other likely parties were quizzed. A master map was compiled showing all known wire hazards outside of urban areas and then distributed to interested parties. Our machine had been caught, but hopefully others would be saved in future. Hindsight is easy and critics can always find something that could have been done, but the important thing is to learn and benefit from a tragedy.

One important aspect of my job when indoctrinating new pilots, was to cover safety aspects of flying in PNG. For example, one question I asked was 'What killed more soldiers here during WW II than bullets?' It was very rare to receive the correct answer – mosquitoes, which brought on malaria. It's a strange conundrum that both desert and jungle survival revolve around water – one too little, the other too much. I didn't have the time to spend days briefing lads new to tropical jungle operations on all possibilities. The important thing was to teach them to properly assess the environment, ask questions and act accordingly.

It was also important for them to learn some New Guinea Pidgin as soon as possible even though English is the official language. Communication with national staff and servants was done in Pidgin – a mixture of European languages, Police Motu and 'place talk,' or words from the over seven hundred different tribal languages. I had first learned Pidgin during my earlier visits and was amused by the method of expressing previously unknown common nouns. For example, a bath plug becomes 'hat bilong eye bilong was-was'. A bra was a 'calaboose bilong su-su,' – i.e. the milk was jailed.

More people from my past arrived in PNG, this time a Bristow helicopter manager, Chuck and his wife, Linda. He had been my manager in Singapore for a period, and Mary got on very well with Linda, Alan Bristow's daughter. They arrived to assess the situation as Shell decided to drill an exploratory well in their extensively surveyed area. By chance I met them, and a senior accompanying pilot I knew, in the hotel in Wewak. Our company would miss out on the major contract to fly the rig in; it was too heavy for our aircraft to lift.

In the aviation industry 'chance' meetings are not unusual. One day, when flying the small Jetranger, I was diverted to rescue a visiting computer expert from inside a coffee factory compound outside the town of Kundiawa, an often troubled area. Spears and arrows were flying over the high perimeter fence and it was feared the place would be torched, a favorite trick to force an issue.

I was able to land safely and my passenger leapt into the cabin, sitting behind me. On reaching Hagen, he thanked me before disappearing.

Perhaps a year later I found myself queuing for scarce taxis outside the terminal in Sydney, having just arrived from Port Moresby. A cab eventually appeared and as the man ahead of me turned to approach it, he saw me and said, 'I know you, you landed and saved me on my first visit to PNG, from inside the coffee factory. It's my turn to help now, hop in to the cab and I'll take you home.'

He refused to let me contribute to the fare.

In 1986, I spent Christmas in Australia, first visiting Brisbane where I had been able to organize some time with an old girlfriend. After flying to Sydney, the same applied. Of necessity, it seems I was reverting to my early bachelor days, with lady friends in every port. My lifestyle was such that a regular compatible 'friend' was again a difficult proposition.

Adelaide was my next stop, staying with my mother in her compact two bedroom flat at a church run old folks home. Gavin arrived soon after me, and I became part of a family again. We played tennis, golf, visited friends and relatives before spending a jolly Christmas with all mother's offspring except her son Peter.

Gavin was becoming an expert UM, or unaccompanied minor, airline traveller. He flew back to the UK in January 1987, with hundreds of thousands of miles in his logbook.

He returned to school as a boarder, so Mary would not be tied to the house and could work. She visited me in PNG after getting him settled in. I showed her the sights and other friends amused her while I was working. She saw what my life was like and how I earned the money to support her and Gavin. I had little surplus, though fortunately the company paid most of Gavin's school fees and I was allowed several airline tickets to England every year.

On one Friday morning, Mary, a visiting surgeon friend, his wife and I assembled at the airstrip before sunrise. I was to position a helicopter in Madang and providing the others with a lift. We would all spend the weekend at a holiday resort on the coast.

The weather was good and after departure I climbed to clear the mountains on our route. As we left the Hagen Valley, the sun began to rise and an incredible vista emerged from the shadows below. The towering bulk of Mount Wilhelm was dotted with puffy clouds and filled the sky to our right. All around lay varying heights of rugged jungle covered terrain descending to the Jimmy Valley thousands of metres below.

As the sun rose, the surrounding colours changed through the spectrum – rose, green, brown and then white when full sunshine reached them. It was a magical morning with nature displaying its full splendour for our enjoyment.

My personal cassette sounded in our headphones, the heralding trumpets in the Hallelujah Chorus adding to the glory and majesty of the moment, drowning out the noise of the helicopter.

We were hanging high in the sky with a panoramic view, enjoying some of the best sights and sounds man and nature had to offer. It will always remain in my mind as one of the most perfect journeys I have ever flown. My passengers seemed similarly awed.

This trip reminded me of one of my many commuting flights from England, when sunrise illuminated Mount Everest, hundreds of kilometres away on the horizon. But that trip to Madang was much more intimate, real, and touched my jaded senses.

A month after Mary returned to England, Shell needed a helicopter immediately. They were pre-stocking supplies for their drilling program and had parked several barges in the wide mouth of the Sepic River. One dragged its anchors in the muddy bottom. As it headed out to sea the watchman wisely jumped overboard. Five days passed before the barge, loaded with millions of dollars worth of casing, was missed. I went out with several observers to try and find it. Local fixed wing pilots flying the coastline were asked to report a sighting.

The Sepik is a mighty river, which dumps hundreds of large trees and so much fresh water into the Bismarck Sea that islands forty kilometres off the coast are reported to drink surface 'sea water.' The fresh water being lighter, floats above the salty stuff and is palatable.

The first day's search along the coastline proved fruitless. Being loaded with steel, the barge presented a low profile. Next day, equipped with lifejackets, we flew much further out to sea and found our quarry had been pushed fifty kilometres offshore. I reported its position, a tug could now fetch it.

That evening I phoned Tony and he said, 'Phil, you should have claimed salvage on that barge.'

I was surprised at his remark but found he had good reason to make it.

Shell had reneged on promised work, for which the company specifically purchased another multi-million dollar aircraft. Their cavalier attitude had significant financial consequences for us. Of course, it was now too late to negotiate compensation over a salvage claim. Shell took more care of their barges after that. If it had sunk or was lost at sea their drilling program would have been delayed by months and cost many times the barges value.

Soon after, we lost an early model leased Bell 206B helicopter we operated. While working on a seismic survey, after landing on an incomplete pad surrounded by jungle, the machine tipped rearwards and damaged its rotating tailrotor. The site now had to be enlarged to enable a rescue chopper to land there with an engineer and parts. During that process, a tree fell across the unserviceable chopper's cabin. With the machine now badly damaged, it had to be lifted out for a workshop repair. I flew there in our Bell 205 to sling out the cabin section. It was to be taken to the nearest airstrip, Wabo, on the banks of the wide Purari River. After picking it up I was unhappy about the way my bulky load was hanging and swinging to and fro. Returning and trying to re-sling it might have resulted in more damage so I reluctantly continued. During the twenty-minute flight to Wabo, the load rotated, in addition to swinging.

My approach to land at the airstrip entailed flying over the river. At a height of about thirty metres, while slowing, the sling holding my load untwisted with a roar, spinning the cargo hook rapidly, then everything fell off the hook. Quickly banking, I watched my load hit the water, narrowly missing several people in a canoe and almost swamping them. They came ashore and complained bitterly, but I managed to fob them off with a few cigarettes, which probably avoided a claim for compensation against a 'rich' white man and our company.

My load floated down the deep river for a minute then disappeared forever into the mud.

The final irony to this sad tale was that when receivers moved in to take over the ailing company from which we leased that helicopter, it was found to be still on the books as an asset years after it became a home for fish.

The reason for the load falling off was probably caused by the manual release cable being flung outwards by the rapidly spinning hook mechanism and becoming caught between the hook rim and restraining bodywork. This could result in the manual (as opposed to the electric) hook release operating and jettisoning the load. Someone had made the manual release wire too long, making it easier for a loadmaster to find and pull if the electric hook release failed. The person overhauling the complex hook mechanism wouldn't be aware of the possible consequences of his action. It's another lesson in the importance of exactly following specifications when working on aircraft. Murphy is just waiting for a chance to strike. I certainly did not release the load.

My job was rarely boring. During the next few weeks I flew six different helicopter types and used the company Cessna 182 as personal transport. Not having flown many hours over the past twenty years in stiff wings, I was rather concerned about having to land at the, by PNG standards, easy one-way strip at Ambunti. Practising a few landings in Hagen to ensure I could get it right, left me feeling a little better.

My stomach was tight as I turned onto a long final approach at Ambunti. I tried to ignore the steep hill at the end of the short, upsloping grass landing strip and the vertical drop into the wide Sepik River just before the touchdown area. Pilots who flew into here every week could do this with one eye and one arm, I reminded myself while lowering the flaps.

Relief flooded through me as my touchdown occurred just inside the markers, using less than a third of the strip before taxying to the parking area.

In May, pre-election campaigning began in earnest. I flew politicians to many villages where they and their cronies handed out hundreds of brown paper envelopes. I don't know what was in them but they sure looked very similar to ones in which our local staff received their pay. Of course we never became involved in local politics, that could be disastrous. I flew various Prime Ministers and Opposition Leaders over the years and Mr Somari (now Sir Michael) was the only one of those I respected. I'm told he has changed since those days

The elections were always a chaotic time for the aviation industry. The ballots went on for weeks due to the difficulty of reaching people living in isolated, rugged terrain. Every helicopter not on a permanent contract was utilised to fly polling teams, politicians and other officials from provincial centres to remote areas. As a result of the frenetic activity, I believe pilots often exceeded the legal flying and duty time limits. Logbooks invariably had the excess flying hours entered later, during quieter times.

Great pressure was put on all of us to continue flying in those pre-GPS days as it could be very difficult for a relief pilot to find polling teams in remote villages. Due to the steep mountainous terrain and associated bad weather, a mark placed on a map did not ensure a replacement pilot found the team without wasting a lot of time or running low on fuel. He might visit half a dozen hamlets located next to the dot on his map, before finding the correct one.

I was required to spend most of my time in the office but helped with flying at times so others could have a day off. On one such occasion I was tasked by the Mendi electoral officials to collect tribal leaders and drop them off at the polling station in Pangia. This took some time and I had to land my five tonne Bell 212 in many unprepared tricky sites as we searched for particular persons among the numerous villages. Eventually all thirteen seats in the back were filled and while en-route to the drop-off point I was contacted by ATC and asked to radio the office. The message was terse, I was to cease operations and fly home as the electoral commission had deemed it unsafe for me to continue operating. I dropped off my passengers at Pangia and told the electoral official in charge that I was ceasing operations.

'You can't do that' he said. 'The first load of ballot boxes will soon be ready.'

'Sorry, my Company has told me it's not safe to continue. If anything happens I will be held accountable.'

'You can't go, the situation is desperate. I'm told some of those guys you brought in are planning to disrupt the whole election process to get their man elected. We must move these ballot boxes safely to Mendi. Why don't we go and see the Provincial Governor and get him to summon the riot squad.'

I reluctantly agreed. After flying to Mendi we eventually found the local Governor and soon after, the riot squad arrived. I told the Company what had occurred and was left to use my own judgment.

We returned to Pangia with the specially armed police. Soon the cabin filled with locked metal ballot boxes and I departed without incident. The crowd of thousands were kept at a safe distance by pointed guns. Returning for the final load the mob seemed restless with the boxes slow in coming from the nearby polling station. The encircling crowd pressed nearer and I sensed the police were about to lose control. I shouted to my loadmaster, a PNG citizen, 'Tell them to hurry with the boxes, I may have to leave at any moment. And get ready to close the door quickly, I don't like the way this situation is going.'

More boxes arrived and during loading some men rushed the helicopter. Perhaps half a dozen flung themselves into the cabin and as the loadmaster tried to remove them, more got in.

'Close the door,' I shouted.

He did and began to run around the nose to get into the co-pilot's seat beside me. I couldn't wait for him to get in; the situation was deteriorating too rapidly. The police could do nothing except shoot people, resulting in the mob hacking them to death on the spot. I lifted straight up and as I did so men grabbed the skids and were pulled clear of the ground. At about five metres I dropped the machine down and then jerked up quickly again. This reversal of forces shook off the stuntmen and I departed without my loadmaster. En-route to Mendi I radioed the office and asked them to arrange for police to detain my unauthorized passengers when I landed. I had no idea how many were aboard; one was sprawled in a narrow space between boxes and the cabin roof while other heads, arms and legs were visible amid the jumble of ballot boxes.

I was not overly concerned as experience had shown that the people in the back would not pose any danger during the twenty-minute flight. They just wanted a free ride to town and would say they were guarding the boxes. In these circumstances, normal rules such as noting passenger numbers, safety briefings and the wearing of seat belts are meaningless!

It would have been easy for me to refuse to fly; however, when possible I tried to assist authorities and prevent crimes being committed.

At Mendi I was pleased to see police on hand to deal with my stowaways. No doubt they would be beaten up and released - the imposed Westminster justice system was often useless in this society. I was told police were badly under resourced and virtually any smart lawyer could get a criminal off on technicalities.

Having done my bit to help ensure the integrity of this ballot, it was time to go home. On the way I diverted to Pangia to collect my loadmaster. Things had quietened since the voting sheets departed, however I landed well away from the polling station and my crewman quickly got in. Flying home, he told me gossip confirmed that none of the ballot boxes would have survived the journey to town by road. The opposition was positioned to capture and destroy them as occurred elsewhere. No native police would risk their lives to defend those bits of paper.

That electoral scenario was typical of what occurred in many PNG locations. Some places required extra precautions, other sites were boycotted as unsafe for aviators and at some others, sticks and stones were thrown at my helicopter.

After the madness of the elections, I was booked to fly to England. My passport sat at immigration in Moresby for a work permit renewal and when I arrived there, could not be found. Being due to fly out the following evening, I decided to try and get a new one from the embassy. Sadly, as required, no-one of the required status in Moresby had known me for two years. I decided to play the Aussie expat card and visited the local branch of my bank and asked to see the manager. Being white skinned, I was taken to his office immediately. He introduced himself and his accent confirmed he was Australian.

After explaining my problem I said 'Your bank's manager in Hagen, knows me. I'll pay for you to phone George to confirm my identity and then perhaps you could sign this passport application on his behalf?'

Terry knew about immigration problems. He was happy to go along with my suggestion after chatting to George, a mutual friend.

Soon I was back at the embassy and they promised to have a new passport ready for me the following day.

My problems weren't over yet as my shiny new document didn't show an entry into the country.

I checked in early for my Singapore flight and the moment the immigration desk opened I was first in line.

'Where is your entry permit or visa?' I was asked.

'I delivered an aircraft and flight crew don't need visas in transit.'

'Where's the aircraft?'

'Mt Hagen.' Not untrue, I didn't say when the delivery was done.

'Why aren't any other stamps in here?' he asked, flicking through the blank pages.

'You can see that passport has just been issued. I had to get a new one as my papers and money were stolen in Hagen. All I want to do is just get the hell out of this country,' I said raising my voice and waving my arms. Again, not untrue, but the timing had moved. 'I don't ever want to come near this place again.' I was laying it on, but didn't want to go too far so lapsed into silence, my point made.

By now a queue of varying skin colours had formed behind me, many listening intently.

The uniformed officer facing me gazed at the ceiling, no doubt considering his response, then looked at me. 'I don't know whether to believe you but you can leave this time.' He stamped my passport violently, his desk shuddering, then waved me through.

I stopped off in Singapore where a friend was the assistant manager at the famed Raffles Hotel. He gave me a very good rate to stay in one of their old, but spacious rooms. After dinner with a lady friend, we decided to swim in the deserted pool. It was a romantic setting, with palms and flowering plants softening the hard lines of the surrounding two-story accommodation. My lady companion and I began to feel amorous. After finding the correct depth of pool, I leaned back against the edge and she climbed on top of my opened swimming trunks and impaled herself. A spare arm kept the pool surface agitated, so people in overlooking rooms could not properly see into the water. Then a bus disgorged dozens of tourists who filed past a poolside table dispensing Singapore slings. They had no idea we were making love right in front of them. It was a great turn on for us. These occasional highs somewhat compensated for the bad times and privation of living in what many people referred to as a 'Stone Age' country.

After arriving in England in July, Gavin and I spent a week being summer tourists in London. We visited the Tower and joined the throng filing past the crown jewels. I also found the publishers who printed diploma and degree certificates for various British universities. After some smooth talking, they gave me blank original documents. These, when photocopied and filled out, enabled friends in PNG to obtain jobs, for which they were admirably qualified, but lacked a piece of paper to enable the issue of a work permit. I only provided blank diploma sheets to a few people where public safety was not involved.

Our town house in Cheltenham sat in the middle of a row of eight joined together under a 'flat' roof. The walls were sufficiently thick to prevent neighbours' activities intruding. One evening, on arriving home, Mary found water dripping onto her bed from the light bulb in the middle of the bedroom. God, I hate flat roofs. It cost plenty to have, it seemed, half a ton of pitch poured on our roof to stop all the water pooling there and causing a leak. The extra weight caused the wooden roof supports to sink lower, catching more water. Many pounds weight and pounds sterling were poured into roof repairs to keep the house dry.

A month of enjoying civilised living soon passed and I headed for Heathrow again and the long commute to keep up the mortgage payments.

Soon after returning, one afternoon I was patrolling PNG's border with Irian Jaya, in the area south of Vanimo, a rebel hot spot at the time. My passenger in the co-pilot's seat, an Indian colonel, scouted the countryside with a view to deploying his troops.

I was flying fairly low and slow, with the border on the left when my passenger said, 'Phil, I tink we should be turning right straight away. I see someone down there pointing a rifle at us.'

Half a second later our belly was exposed to the gunman, quickly followed by our vanishing tail. Back at camp I landed and checked for bullet holes but didn't find any. If we had been shot at, no obvious damage ensued.

Late that day I flew back to Wewak by myself, having provisioned the troops. Earlier, large storms had crossed the Sepik Plains, leaving myriad pools of water dotted amongst the black, recently burnt grassland. Flying down the coast, I had the plains on my right and continuous towering, spark-ridden storm clouds out to sea on my left. It was not a time to venture offshore.

Gradually, the sun began to set, transforming the harsh countryside and forbidding weather over the sea. The pools of inland water became rubies set in black satin. Rainbows appeared, including a circular one just outside my windscreen. Storm clouds dressed themselves in ever changing red, pink, purple and violet hues for my pleasure. I was alone in a spectacular light show of huge dimensions. To my mind, these magical ever-changing sights cannot be truly captured by machines, fully described or reproduced in art; the scale is too grand. Human sentiment, 'soul' or 'spirit' is necessary to absorb and appreciate the spectacle.

I reluctantly returned to earth, thinking how fortunate I was to experience such wonders and beauty. The contrast between nature and man was hugely emphasized in that primitive, often cruel country where life could be so cheap.

Mary and Gavin arrived in Mt Hagen in December 1987 to spend Christmas with me, my spare room accommodating them. I took time off work to be a family again. In that month I also sold my ten acres of land in Adelaide for a good profit, we would not be settling there. Mary and I were seeing each other for our son's benefit and our relationship remained amicable.

Gavin left to return to school in England and Mary visited our mutual friends, Heather and Andy, in Sydney. We owe them a huge debt of gratitude for nursing Mary during a bout of illness she suffered while there.

A few months later I had the nearest available helicopter to attend an early morning aeroplane crash site so I quickly prepared to take off. My first stop was at the hospital to collect a doctor, then headed for Bomai. It appeared that the twin engine Islander had crashed into the jungle while trying to overshoot at the one way strip. The low upward sloping cloud covering the area may have given the pilot a false impression and disguised the rising ground ahead, which exceeded the loaded aircraft's climb performance.

On arrival, we found the villagers had located the nearby crash site and carried the badly injured pilot, luckily the only occupant, to the airstrip. Another aircraft was on its way to stretcher the casualty to the Goroka hospital as he was in no state to have to sit up in my small Hughes 500 cabin. The doctor treated the pilot's obvious injuries and I assisted, while we waited for his transport to arrive. The patient was conscious but in a bad way, frothing blood while moaning horribly.

When the Twin Otter arrived the patient was quickly loaded but relief turned to despair when the aircraft's engines could not be started due to a failed battery. Frantic radio calls resulted in another aircraft and battery being promised forthwith. All we could do was wait helplessly as a life poised on the edge.

It's a gut wrenching feeling, seeing a person tortured by injury, slip away by degree and being unable to help. We watched the minutes crawl by, listening for the sound of approaching engines.

I remained, as insurance, until the unconscious patient was eventually flown out. Sadly the golden hour had been lost and we heard that the pilot died on the operating table. He may have made it but for the failed battery. My guardian angel has served me better.

Sometime in mid 1987 I flew a team of CRA exploration geologists to scout an unexplored lease acquired by their Company. It was just a few kilometres from the known gold bearing Porgera valley where Placer were conducting evaluation drilling to determine the size of a commercial orebody.

CRA's area featured several steep escarpments, deep valleys and even contained several active volcanic vents. We also found an uninhabited plateau at an altitude of over 9,000 feet (2,740 m) with much higher peaks nearby. This treeless area was devoid of population or gardens, as viable crops could not generally be grown above 8,000 feet (2,440 m). Though close to the equator the nights were bitterly cold at such altitudes. Most days had a narrow window of sunshine before cloud and rain set in.

On the morning of our visit the sun shone and while surveying a passenger complained of having something in his eye causing him discomfort so I landed next to a clear mountain stream. I was told there was no record of expats ever having visited this grassy, remote mountain plateau.

While the geologist washed out his eye I will forever regret not kicking over some of the stunted tussocks to see what lay beneath them. This valley would soon become the site of what was later described in the Bulletin magazine as a '*Stone Age Goldrush that made the Yukon seem mild by comparison.*' Numerous nuggets were later found among the roots of the grass over which we walked.

Some months later an exploration camp was set up at the western end of the plateau which came to be known as the Mount Kare gold deposit. CRA chartered our helicopters to support the exploration and soon stories began to emerge. We heard that large nuggets by the dozen could easily be dug up with an ordinary shovel. CRA tried to keep their find secret but tribesmen from the adjacent Porgera, Tari and Paiela valleys arrived to begin prospecting. By law, in PNG, alluvial gold belongs to traditional landowners and the Mt Kare plateau happened to be in an unclaimed boundary area. Ownership was hotly disputed by all the adjoining clans but in the meantime feverish digging continued along the main stream which washed away upturned mud.

CRA began to build a permanent camp and considerable helicopter activity followed. I helped out with flying on various occasions. Due to the altitude, 4° C was normal most mornings and once I noted a frost. While sitting around a fire after the evening meal, local men wandered in with large coffee jars full of nuggets. We negotiated a purchase by weighing a chosen nugget in our hands and then making an offer. In the early days these lumps of 85% pure gold were bought for a small percentage of their actual value. Later, gold buyers arrived by helicopter with scales, large amounts of cash, and departed with kilos of gold.

We heard that twenty million dollars worth of gold was found in the first few weeks. Banks in town were full of the yellow stuff and a friend told me that he sold a new truck to a local who paid in cash. Fellow tribesmen jumped in the back, and the new owner drove off. Unfortunately, the man had never driven before and after leaving town, lost control on a steep downhill grade. He rolled the vehicle into a valley, killing himself, others, and maiming many passengers.

During the period when gold was easily won, up to a dozen or so choppers from various companies ferried people and supplies in and out of the small valley. It was not safe to walk out to the nearest town carrying gold, so large queues waiting for helicopter transport snaked away from three different helipads. Sometimes even the helicopters had to queue before a landing pad became available. Flights were usually paid for in nuggets and it was rumoured that many pilots did very well out of this. I was told that the owner of one company accumulated over a hundred kilograms of gold.

Our company, being contracted to CRA, were not involved in this flight for gold trade as CRA tried to prevent the stripping of their potential assets. To add insult to injury, there was no definition for alluvial mining and CRA gratuitously flew out persons injured when deeply dug pits collapsed.

We flew in mineral drilling rigs to identify the source of the alluvial gold scattered down the valley. One enterprising shopkeeper set up premises to house generators, freezers, videos and a satellite television set-up, all of which our large helicopters flew in at huge expense. This entrepreneur said he would recoup his investment in a week as live chickens sold for sixty dollars and the cost of staple foodstuffs like rice and soft drinks were marked up tenfold. Conversely, it was reported that the brief favours of a woman cost less than a can of Coke. Gambling helped the men pass the time between mining.

One day, while walking among the miners, I saw a woman pan what I estimated to be about four hundred dollars worth of gold in fifteen minutes. A book should be written about the fortunes made and lost and lives affected and lost as a result of Mt Kare gold.

We lost a pilot at Mt Kare. Early one morning while walking into our office, I heard Ben calling us on the radio. He said Robin, our pilot, was unwell and needed a medevac as soon as possible. While arranging this, Ben called again to say what was needed now was a flight to collect the body. This news was shocking. I knew Robin had passed his aviation medical a few months ago, had not complained of even minor ailments and flown the previous day. Robin first worked for me in Singapore, then flew for our company in Hong Kong, before moving home to be New Zealand based. Now he was dead and I had to inform his wife, whom I knew personally.

'Hello, is that Cheryl?' I asked.

'Yes, hello Phil. I suppose you are going to tell me Robin is coming home late again.'

'Afraid it's worse than that.'

'Has he crashed?'

'Sort of, I'm very sorry to tell you he died earlier this morning.

She laughed and wouldn't believe me at first, hung up, then called back almost immediatly. The autopsy found his heart had given up. It was riddled with highly toxic chemicals, accumulated during his early crop spraying days in Egypt when dangerous substances were treated in a cavalier way.

We were extremely busy and the loss of a pilot made matters worse. On the last Sunday in February 1988, I hoped to have a rare day off when

343

the phone rang at 8 am. I was to pack my bag and fly a large helicopter to BHP's loading facility at Kiunga immediately. The national workers at the massive OK Tedi mine had rampaged, parked vehicles on the Tabubil airport runway and went on strike. Contact with the mining town had been lost as strikers cut the phone lines, radio links and barricaded the only road in. It was not known if people had been injured or killed in revenge attacks, as grudges were known to exist against expatriate bosses who enforced safety or other 'inconvenient' work rules. The mining company also made many enemies because of dumping overburden into the Fly River, causing problems downstream. We were needed to fly in riot police to restore order, communications and break the strike.

Three other choppers were already parked in the ship loading yard at Kiunga, downstream from the mine when I arrived. At the afternoon briefing we learned the plan was to conduct a dawn raid. Riot police were to be inserted into the town where native and expat families lived.

Flying in close formation, we were to come in low, hidden in the river canyon bordering one side of the town. Then the plan was to jump out of the canyon at the last moment before landing on the oval. We should only be exposed to potential gunfire, while airborne, for less than half a minute. It was known that the nationals possessed many firearms.

We departed at first light next morning. Having the largest and slowest aircraft, I led the formation, observing radio silence. We had no idea what to expect on arrival. As the leader, I hoped I could remember where to jump out of our deep riverbank cover to give us the shortest run in before landing.

The counter-attack caught any opposition napping. Police soon regained control while we flew in reinforcements. Fortunately, only minor injuries were reported. Soon the airstrip was cleared for normal operations and the mine brought back into production.

In May 1988 we were contracted to fly offshore in support of a drillship, the Chancellorsville. As the only company pilot with offshore experience I had to head up this job. Before it began, a small jet had to be chartered to bring in a vital part from Cairns, so our aircraft could commence operations on time. The engineers worked through the night fitting a new transmission case so I could depart next morning. My fuel gauge indication also needed calibrating after fitting long range tanks so I began plotting this while flying to Thursday Island. A survey crew were waiting there to position the rig in the middle of the Gulf of Papua. My task was to fly them and their special equipment to the rig as it passed T.I.

After my harried and hurried departure, the rig was late and we waited in T.I. for almost a week. During this time we drank the island's entire supply of the best available, aged red wine as my hosts had a very generous expense account.

Late in the day I was given the message to launch for the rig, moving toward us, still some distance to the west. It was not at the position given me. I couldn't raise them on the radio, which meant they were more than forty-five kilometres away. I had another difficult decision to make – whether to abort the mission or press on and hope we saw the rig before dark. Going back would delay positioning the vessel and cost the oil company thousands of dollars. Also, I had a raging headwind to fight if we turned around and wouldn't make it back before dark. The paperwork involved with the late arrival could delay my departure next day. While considering my options, I called the rig again and received a faint answer. They were out there, so my decision was made. We just had to find them in the gathering gloom. Why did fate or 'the Gods' have to do this to me again?

I landed on the drillship just before dark and spent the night being towed toward PNG. Next day, I flew provisions onto the vessel from Daru before leaving for Moresby. Not having a base there, I had to set up a check in and departure lounge to accommodate regular crew changes to the rig. Also, formulate and write standing orders for our first offshore operation and train other pilots to take over from me.

On my first trip out I carried a radio technician to fix the inoperative rig beacon. Technically, I couldn't go unless the beacon operated, but only a few people knew it didn't work. If I missed the vessel after the planned one-hour flight, I could carry on to Daru, or return to Moresby.

The weather was kind, allowing me to easily find my destination. Their refueling system, located under the helipad on the ship's stern, needed inspecting. While checking it, a hideous roaring sound of head splitting dimensions, hammered me from behind. *Had the ship broken in half?* Spinning around, I saw a massive anchor chain unravelling into the sea, barely a metre from me. Leaping away in horror, I saw the last links flail towards me before disappearing over the side. When the last of the metre and a half long links disappeared, a hush fell over the ship. With my pulse racing, I ran up stairs to the helipad area and sought the reason for this frightening occurrence that could have killed me.

'You were very lucky,' Hank told me. 'We lost three of the ships positioning anchor chains overboard on the port side but fortunately one did not release. If it had, the four chains, each tensioned to 150 tons on the starboard side, would have caused the ship to heel over by up to twenty degrees as we were pulled from our previous location.'

'God, with that deck angle my chopper would have slid off the helipad into the water. I didn't secure it because of the dead calm sea. What a lucky escape. Why did it happen without warning?'

'Our Jesus Switch was playing up so the skipper asked the radio tech you brought out to look at it. The Jesus Switch is meant to save us by pulling the ship off the well if a gas blowout occurred, otherwise the ship would sink instantly. I reckon you'd better get the radioman out of here before the skipper kills him. We'll lose another few days while the workboats find the anchor chains on the sea bottom, grapple them up, then feed them into our winches again. And those poor buggers have been working for forty-eight hours already. We had a hell of a job getting the anchors properly tensioned, they kept slipping on the Gulf's unstable seafloor.'

My angel had been busy again, I thought while flying back to Moresby. It stands to reason he knew about 'Jesus Switches'. It seems the unfortunate radio tech had fixed the beacon and the ship's radar but was not paid for any of that as a result of his last effort. Another irony was that the beacon receiver (ADF) in our aircraft then failed. Again, it was off to the rig illegally; I would have to claim my ADF failed after departure if an incident occurred. Meanwhile, I relied on my eyeballs to find it amid the storms and rain showers.

For three months I barely had a day off. I was flying almost the maximum allowable hours, including considerable intensive training. I also wrote the offshore and specific instruction manuals applicable to Moresby operations. Eventually I escaped to Cairns in mid-July and rewarded myself by checking into a fancy resort to recover.

346

CHAPTER 16

The probability of survival is inversely proportional to the angle of arrival. ~ The aviators guide book

Exhausted, it was late in the day when I checked in. After hanging a 'do not disturb' sign outside my room I climbed into bed and almost instantly fell asleep.

A loud banging sound roused me. Then the door opened as I struggled to wake and two men entered the room.

I groggily raised my head as the men walked in.

'Are you okay?' one asked as I managed to sit upright.

'Of course. What's the problem?'

'The DO NOT DISTURB sign has been on your door for two days. You hadn't appeared, so we wondered if you were alright.'

'Have I been here so long?'

'You checked in the day before yesterday.'

'Good heavens, I've slept that long. Right now I could eat a horse. Thanks for waking me.'

They left.

After resting in Cairns for another day, I flew to Brisbane to meet Gavin who jetted in from England for his school holidays.

In July 1988 the south bank of the Brisbane River, opposite the city's skyscrapers, had been transformed for Expo. It seemed the locals had also matured, being less deserving of the 'country hick' image I had noticed previously.

We were fortunate to have a VIP pass, so didn't have to queue for any of the popular exhibits, but a good standard of dress was expected. The Swiss chalet featured a short ski slope with real snow. It was amusing to ski down this three second run in a suit and tie. And all this in the middle of a sub-tropical city. After Expo, we visited the Gold and Sunshine Coast's before both returning home.

I was no sooner back in PNG when the national workers at the OK Tedi mine-site rioted, disabling the airstrip and communications yet again.

347

This time they did a proper job, looting and burning many premises and stealing much alcohol. Buildings were still smoking when I flew the riot squad in a day later. They easily gained control as the troublemakers were either inebriated or sleeping off hangovers.

Afterwards, when flying officials over the town to survey the damage, at first sight the golf clubhouse seemed in good condition. Then we noticed the intact roof was a meter above the ground. The building had been torched, along with numerous others.

Some residents had frightening experiences. Drunken revellers took over the hotel and vented their spleen on strangers. One visiting businessman, hearing screams, hid in a cupboard for hours until the looters moved on. We evacuated over a hundred people who felt themselves endangered. The businessman was so traumatised he chartered a jet from Cairns to fly him out immediately, saying he would never come back. Others evacuated on special airline flights at a fraction of the cost.

After control of the mine was regained, I remained on standby for a few days in nearby Tabubil. The only hotel in town had satellite television. Coincidentally the Olympics were on and shown live. It was a luxurious change, watching TV all day instead of working from sunrise to sunset. The OK Tedi mine lost around one million dollars daily when not producing so they thought nothing of our modest thirteen thousand dollars per day charge for two helicopters.

For many years we delivered fortnightly payrolls to Hagen's many nearby coffee and tea plantations. Cash was dropped in canvass bags next to a waiting manager while we slowly flew past at a low height. Another company decided they could perform this task much cheaper using an armoured car so we lost the job.

Via the grapevine I heard that numerous attempts were made to steal the payrolls. At first the 'rascals' tried shooting out the vehicles tires and windscreen but this did not stop it. Their next move was to drop a tree in front of it on a narrow backwoods road and quickly block the rear so the vehicle was trapped. Being armoured, the 'rascals' still couldn't get in. The occupants immediately called the police on their radio, but they could take hours to arrive. Next a favourite weapon, fire, was quickly set under the hapless vehicle. Now the occupants had to get out or be cooked and to hell with the cash.

That was the end of the armoured car and the payroll run was ours again. Always an interesting trip, most flown while cruising at treetop height, the safest place to be. We even flew the payroll in shocking weather

348

when nothing else was airborne, knowing the route so well. I often did that fun trip; it took me out of the office for an hour. Only once did I have a problem that went unnoticed until preflighting the aircraft after the first pay run. One rotorblade had been struck by a hard object, causing a dent consistent with contacting a smooth slingshot stone. Neither my passenger or I noticed anything suspicious during the flight but the damage cost the company upward of twenty thousand dollars for a new blade.

On another task I came across an old friend, Stu Rawlinson who had been my deputy chief pilot in Sumatra. Stu was flying a large machine and temporarily on loan to an opposition company. They had an arrangement with Bristows, for whom he still worked. He asked why I was still living in PNG. I told him I had little choice, because when Hevilift was sold in 1988 the management team were part of the deal, agreeing to stay on for several years to safeguard existing contracts and profitability. The sale of the company was organised by Mick McDonald, now our General Manager, a wily entrepreneur and long time PNG resident.

It was a legal requirement and necessity to spend much of my time in the office ensuring the revenue earners; my pilots, were out happily working. Also preparing bids for new work and suffering audits by many visiting oil and mining company specialists. Often I was the only pilot available to immediately respond to urgent radio or phone requests for a helicopter. One such call for a doctor and police involved a company pilot.

We soon took off to a location seventy kilometres south of Mount Hagen. Hopefully the casualty would be found before our arrival.

After landing close to the accident site, we heard an amazing story. Ned, an experienced PNG supervisor, had been checking local labour cutting seismic lines and helipads in virgin jungle. Our pilot, Dave, was asked to take Ned to an unfinished site. On arrival, Dave found he could only rest part of one skid on a tree stump. Ned said he would hop out for a moment and if staying, wave Dave off. After disembarking and exchanging a few words with his boss boy, Ned signaled the chopper to leave. Standard procedure was to take off and circle until receiving a radio call with further instructions.

Later, Dave told me he felt the helicopter lurch after takeoff and checked his underside rear view mirror. Horrified, he saw what appeared to be a body falling to the ground. Banking sharply, Dave watched Ned crash into the trees.

Witnesses at the site said that Ned leapt at the helicopter as it lifted above the stump. He grasped a skid but didn't let go as the chopper took off. Why he fell before alerting Dave, or simply hung on until someone shouted over the radio, will never be known. Ned's remains were found but he had not survived.

It was a somber crew who flew back with the body. Much speculation followed. Why would a man with years of experience using helicopters in the field do what Ned had done? Later, rumours surfaced that he was facing a messy divorce.

My friend Dick, after many years flying in country, had a similar experience while transporting two Government officials. Old hands develop a sixth sense, as I did, about village visits and on this occasion he felt uneasy. Visitors can spend hours talking, but this time Dick didn't shut down the engine after landing or even reduce the throttle to idle, but remained ready to fly immediately.

In minutes, the officials reappeared, running for their transport, pursued by angry villagers. Just before the mob's stones and spears hit the helicopter, Dick took off. Only one passenger made it into the cabin. Soon after takeoff a banging sound was sheard. The underfloor mirror showed a passenger grimly hanging onto a skid and pounding the cabin skin.

The shaken official was quickly lowered to the ground. As he got in, Dick said that man was the whitest national he had ever seen in PNG.

A bizarre sequel to this event occurred some months later when the company received a lawyers letter. 'Tarzan,' said he had broken a finger during his rescue and was now seeking compensation for the injury. His life had been saved but that was not enough, 'Tarzan' wanted money as well. Dick said he threw the letter in the bin and nothing more was heard.

PNG locals had a saying, 'Mi tryim tasol,' - I might as well try it on. Some nerve, to sue your saviour.

A different problem trapped a visiting pilot. He delivered a leased Hughes 500 helicopter to us from Sydney. The visitor found Hagen OK but when an engineer needed a test flight the ferry pilot jumped in and took off without my knowledge. I would not have allowed a new boy to do testing in strange territory, unless fully briefed and checked first. Not knowing the local rules he became distracted watching for other traffic while following the control tower's instructions. He massively over-sped the main rotor when making a hurried steep approach. The horrified engineer on board said he expected the rotor blades to fly off and was preparing to die. Luckily they didn't. The machine was grounded for weeks waiting for five new blades. The visitor went home in disgrace, having cost his company dearly. This incident occurred because the pilot didn't realise that completely reducing power in Hagen's thin tropical mountain air would cause such a massive over-speed so quickly.

A few months later I was the only pilot available to search for a missing chopper in the Adelbert Range, some distance from Madang. Flying toward Mike's last reported position I heard the beacon's signal but had no search meter to guide me to its location. The signal could be coming from anywhere. Finding its source would have to be done by ear, triangulation and memory of surroundings. With dismay I noted the rugged jungle-covered terrain below was split by dozens of steep hills and valleys. Without the beacon's signal, a visual search of these could take days. Mike was reportedly collecting sacks of coffee beans so hopefully he was in or near a village in the green maze below.

To triangulate his position I dropped behind scattered ridgelines to check where and when the beacon signal was lost. A simple time honored method but it's necessary to memorise much terrain to work toward the signal source.

While narrowing down Mike's probable location, a flare shot up ahead. Flying towards its origin, a clearing appeared, then a small village, and finally I saw a helicopter on its side.

Mike waved as I flew overhead and appeared uninjured. He was sure glad to see me and we landed back at Hagen only hours after he had departed there that morning. On the way home he said he had snagged his skid in a cargo net full of coffee which rolled the machine over as he lifted off. Fortunately, the resulting flying debris didn't kill or injure any bystanders or he would have been in big trouble. Mike worked for another company so I was not responsible for the aftermath of this accident. It was one of the few crashes I attended with such a happy ending.

Due to a shortage of pilots I elected to fly during the Christmas and New Year holiday period as it meant another pilot could be at home with his young family. Over the years I had become accustomed to missing family birthdays, anniversaries and other celebrations. My feelings had long been dulled and emotion repressed so they didn't interfere with making a life saving decision at any time. I simply switched personal matters off so a feeling of loss didn't occur. This form of martyrdom even gave me pleasure – as I'm told some people get from depravation or self-harm. Was this a form of atonement for my past sins, or my inbuilt work ethic? Probably both.

It sure was a routine and boring existence, that December, living on an accommodation barge moored to the bank of the muddy Kikori River at a place called Middletown. All that remained of the deserted 'town' amid

351

the encroaching jungle was the rusting skeleton of a hanger built during a period of oil exploration decades before. At least our location was upstream from the malarial mosquito-infested delta mudflats and islands leading to the Gulf of Papua.

The Christmas day flying schedule had been arranged so we could all enjoy an extended lunch before returning to duty. I finished the morning's flying and was relaxing when the dispatcher found me.

'Phil, we've just had a radio call from the police.'

'What's happened?'

'It seems the workers got on the booze at a logging camp. Someone was stabbed. They want you to fly a medivac to Daru hospital.'

'Well there goes my hot ham and turkey.'

'We'll keep some for you.'

I found the logging camp and landed. Various people including a policeman appeared. One male wore bandages around his middle but surprisingly climbed into the helicopter without assistance. The policeman told me he and the victim's assailant were also travelling to Daru, the latter man to face attempted manslaughter charges.

'Your rifle unloaded?' I asked.

He nodded.

'OK, give me the magazine.'

After settling my three passengers in the rear cabin seats and briefing them in Pidgin they began chatting amicably. The accused was not handcuffed but was the policeman's responsibility. Their conversation suggested that none posed any in-flight danger.

After landing behind the police station in Daru I let my passengers out. As the three of them casually strolled away I shouted 'Corporal.'

'Yes boss?'

'Do you want this?' I threw the rifle magazine full of bullets to him – he had quite forgotten it.

On the flight home I wondered if the incident had been set up so the trio could hitch a ride to Daru, the provincial capital, for Christmas. This trip would cost some organisation over four thousand dollars. Cold ham and turkey eaten in solitude was not the best or worst Christmas dinner I've had, but as they say, something is better than nothing.

Some weeks later, attempting to have a Sunday off in Hagen, the phone disturbed me again. One of our pilots was in trouble and had to be rescued. A Swiss national, Herman was meticulous in everything he did. It seemed inconceivable that he had caused a problem. Trevor dropped me in the

352

Jimmi valley to complete our client's flying program and then flew Herman to hospital. While exploring, it seemed he slipped, hit his head on a rock, felt dizzy and decided not to fly. Just as well as x-rays revealed a cracked skull.

Herman said his lack of balance was probably due to dehydration. Though parked next to a river, it was unwise to drink from it.

Conversely, disposing of used personal liquid could also be an issue for some people. Especially when needing a toilet while surrounded by thousands of people listening to a politician's promises. Rarely could a public convenience be found, and any pilot walking into the bushes would be followed by dozens of curious locals.

Usually we parked in the middle of a playing field and stayed with our machine. With a full bladder in this situation, I just turned my back on the spectators and let fly on the ground while facing my machine. Of course, most could see what I was doing and so I've been cheered by thousands for the simple act of urinating.

I don't know how modest pilots coped but it must have been a problem for the female pilot flying for another company. It's on record that she had several accidents. I suspect they were purely a result of dehydration as I was told she had excellent piloting skills and was an experienced aviator. It was suggested she obtain employment in another country if she wished to continue flying otherwise her PNG licence could be in jeopardy. She did depart, but in sad circumstances and in a box. A trusting lady, her death occurred while selling her chattels prior to leaving the country.

Another constant concern was the health risk posed by malaria. Highland areas were generally considered safe but exposure to a sudden cold night at altitude could trigger an attack. Most of us regularly working in tropical areas didn't take anti-malarial pills continuously, necessary for full protection. We heard that long term use had been known to adversely affect the liver and eyesight. I also knew people who caught malaria even while taking the recommended dosage constantly. Already having the disease, I felt it better to hit my system with pills when an attack occurred, always at around six pm. Invariably, after spending a feverish night, I could safely fly next day if necessary. New pilots were presented with our practical knowledge of malaria control, but I urged them to make further enquiry and their own decision on drug use. The best defence was to avoid being bitten by mosquitoes but that was almost impossible in some areas.

After my last tour to PNG, I took the recommended malarial 'purging' drugs and have not suffered an attack since. With global warming occurring,

I wonder if the disease will become endemic in northern Australia?

In March 1989, my break took me to Brisbane, then Adelaide and Singapore before arriving in England. Gavin and I departed to ski at Les Arcs in France where good spring snow was reported. Mary decided she didn't want to ski anymore and stayed home. This decision suited Gavin and I, we could ski all the most difficult runs without feeling bad about Mary being left to ski with strangers.

One warm, sunny day, I took to the slopes in shorts as I rarely ever fell over. Some Scotsmen saw me and appeared on the piste in kilts the following day. One run we skied stretched for over ten kilometres. It was the longest in Europe and began as a black run, for expert skiers only. Including the return to our village, it took us almost half a day to complete that challenge. Another, we didn't try, was the almost vertical slope where most world speed records for skiing are achieved.

Once back in PNG, we won another offshore contract. This job meant flying out of Kerema, a place where no proper accommodation existed. The company bought a houseboat and we managed to park it adjacent to the shoreline, within walking distance of the airport. Pilots now captained two quite different ships. Fortunately we had resourceful people within the company.

My close friends in Hagen, Jo and Nigel, moved to Australia permanently. I would visit them there but it certainly left a large gap in my social life. Having been treated as part of their family meant I had accessed a much larger social circle, unavailable to most single males. I was asked out to 'civilised' dinner parties where conversation other than sport or possibly finding a woman took place. Breathalisers were unheard of so the only hazard to getting home safely meant avoiding pigs or people in the middle of the road. Even this problem was avoided when I was offered a bed for the night. That was history now and left a large gap in my life.

Then I had a frightening experience while slinging a heavy load into a mountain village. On short final approach, my Bell 212 developed a sickening vibration that shook the entire aircraft. I had no idea why and the instruments were no help, being a blur. After immediately turning right down a steep valley, I reduced power to a minimum and descended. While considering where to crash land my machine into the trees the shaking stopped. Cautiously applying power, I returned to the loading point. The shaking episode probably took ten seconds but was one of the worst frights I have ever experienced. It felt like the aircraft was about to fly apart in the air.

354

The engineers thought it might have been an engine compressor stalling but I knew otherwise, having experienced one of those rumbling occasions previously.

Subsequent ground testing could not reproduce the incident, but the main transmission was changed and it did not reoccur.

In August, Gavin flew out to Australia during my next leave. He was interested in zoology so I arranged for him to spend several weeks in the bush with my brother on a field trip out of Alice Springs. He arrived there direct from England. I heard it took him a week to acclimatize to rough desert living though he did shoot some photos that won him a school prize. After the Alice trip, he visited me in Brisbane before returning to the UK. Having turned sixteen, Gavin travelled without the 'humiliation' of having a UM (unaccompanied minor) label tied to his wrist and arrived home without a hitch. I was glad his school reports improved, earlier ones mentioning that he appeared unsettled. Was that due to an absent father missing most school 'events' that other parents attended?

Eventually Chevron asked us to assist their large exploration and heli-rigging operations based at Poroma, with one Bell 212. It was a long line load lifting operation and none of us were experienced in this type of flying. I had no time to hire qualified American pilots. Instead, Roger and I taught ourselves to pick up and drop off cargo from the left-hand (co-pilot's) side of the aircraft. We looked straight down at a load suspended a hundred and fifty or two hundred feet (45 to 66 metres) below us.

This is when I found that after many years, I had developed a gyroscope in my head which didn't like flying when turned 90° from its normal upright position. Younger pilots find long line work much easier, they probably haven't developed this sense. I found longlining one of the most difficult tasks to learn, more so than flying on instruments. It was made worst by having to lean out sideways, my body being bent in an unnatural position while handling the controlls to precisely place a load hanging far below. I found myself mentally sitting on the load and moving the aircraft correctly from there.

Flying with Roger, we began our contract after only a few hours practice. Fortunately we were mostly carrying wooden boards used as a base for the drilling rig. We changed seats, while being refueled, to share the load and relieved each other on the controls but the left seat pilot had to fly the load hookups and drop off's. It was monotonous, tiring work flying from dawn till dusk, weather permitting. I particularly hated the stressful landings, but was a necessary skill to learn. Our loads were meant to arrive in a stable state, at the correct spot, a metre above the ground, not swinging wildly and threatening the ground crew. It took a lot of practise to achieve this without a ground-based loadmaster's help over the radio.

Our base was a campsite on the Iagifu oilfield, located on top of a thousand metre high ridge. At day's end, the camp was often covered in cloud. Getting home meant either dropping our longline or stowing it in the cabin, then creeping in over the jungle, while only able to see a few metres forwards. We entered the cloud at a specific location and slowly hovered in for half a kilometre on a compass heading, skimming the trees. When the foliage stopped we were over our cleared home-site and helipad.

After six stressful weeks, the job finished. Now I had to set about hiring pilots with long line experience. Obviously it saved cutting large holes in the jungle to make landing areas.

In the middle of this intensive flying, a lady friend arrived to stay and I hardly saw her. She had her handbag snatched, so don't think she had a wonderful visit.

My friend Dick, now the manager, became interested in using large Russian helicopters to compete with the American machinery on heli-rig contracts. He flew to Russia, evaluated the available choppers and we began to investigate their use in PNG. It was fraught with potential traps but possibly great rewards as well.

In November, I flew after dark for the first and only time in PNG. I had been practicing my instrument flying when it was safe, but not in the mountains. Late in the day, a shooting victim needed collecting from a village south west of Hagen, in the foothills of Mt Giluwe. It was just possible for me to fly there and back before dark, but I spent over ten nail-biting minutes on the ground before my casualty was loaded. On departure, I barely saw the tall trees on either side of my flight path out of the clearing. Soon after takeoff all went dark under a solid overcast sky and I was onto basic instruments. An eight thousand foot (2,440 m) ridge reared between us and Hagen. Fortunately I was able to gain sufficient height under the cloud base to see the town lights. Keeping them in sight ensured that I cleared my main obstacle, even if I didn't see it. My Jetranger had instrument lights but no navigation aids. If the lights stayed on, I'd certainly find the unlit airport. Thankfully my angel kept the clouds and rain away so we soon landed safely.

On 4th of December 1989 our Bell 'Huey' with ten passengers on board, crashed at Porgera. No fatalities occurred but one person suffered head injuries. The accident was due to a mechanical failure causing the engine to lose power, just prior to landing in a congested, hilly area. The aircraft was written off and the wreckage bought by an old friend from our Singapore days.

Also that month, our main opposition wrote off two helicopters in a single week. A Civil Aviation report stated that, on average, slightly more than two aircraft crashes occurred every month during the years 1983 to 1988, the total being a hundred and twenty five. Considering the size and small population of PNG it's not an enviable record but speaks volumes about the difficulty of operating in one of the worlds most challenging environments.

One morning we were requested to evacuate two unmarried expatriate female teachers from a Government school near Lake Sirunka. This lake was situated in an old volcanic crater at over two thousand metres above sea level. Prior to PNG's independence a yacht club run by expats from nearby Wabag town, a provincial centre, flourished on its shore. However, when independence from Australia took effect, the nationals burnt down the club and destroyed all the sailing boats. It was their way of striking at the symbols of colonialism and previous masters without fear of retribution. The indigenous people in the area were well known for their war-like tendencies and frequently burn down each other's houses over age-old grievances. Once I timed a 'cooking' as it was known – in just two minutes a pile of ashes marked the remains of a dwelling.

I asked if any police were being sent with me and was told they were already at the school. I certainly hoped so, but loaded extra fuel in case that information was incorrect, as often occurred.

The landing and pick-up proved uneventful and I headed back to Mount Hagen.

'Had a rough night last night?' I asked, not knowing if they had been threatened, mistreated or even gang raped.

'Oh my God it was terrible,' said one.

'It will haunt me forever,' said the other.

Not wishing to distress them further I shut up. They were so relieved, atbeing rescued, the words just tumbled out.

'We woke up to screams sometime after midnight and rushed out to investigate. We found a mob of local men waving flaming branches, axes and machetes were chopping up our headmaster. We were so terrified and didn't know what to do so we ran into the bush and hid. Then we heard more screams and children crying but we couldn't see what was going on.'

357

'You must have feared for your lives as well?'

'God yes, after a while the shouting and screaming stopped and we just heard our hearts pounding. We waited for ages, then crept back to our quarters and found the mob had gone. It was very cold so we quickly grabbed warm clothes and blankets and went back into the jungle and managed to get a bit of sleep. Luckily it didn't rain.'

'It was.'

'After the sun came up we waited in the bush close to the school until some of our pupils arrived, then ran out and sent some of the older students to get the police. We told the kids not to touch anything and tried to keep them distracted. There was lots of dried blood, torn clothing and bits of human flesh next to the headmaster's house. Soon some of the parents came and they looked after us until the police arrived. They used their radio to call for you to come and get us as we don't have one. The other dreadful thing is that they chopped up the headmaster's wife and three young kids as well, the police said while we were waiting.'

'Any idea why they were all killed?'

'The police were told the headmaster failed some students from one clan and not another and this was payback for his actions. Boy are we glad we only teach juniors.'

After landing at Hagen I wished the girls well. I later heard they were so traumatised they returned to Australia, feeling they couldn't teach in PNG anymore.

No national teachers could be found to man that school and over the next few months, I saw the headmaster's house, teachers quarters and school building gradually walk away as everything was dismantled and stolen. The concrete slabs were visible for a while and then the jungle swallowed those as well. Sadly the children had no school to attend, but unfortunately this situation was not uncommon as infrastructure previously set up crumbled after independence. Age-old tribal rivalry and customs would take generations to change. Unfortunately, the lack of education would not help to speed the process.

In mid December I met Mary in Sydney. She wished to begin divorce proceedings to enable her to remarry. We settled the important issues over an amicable lunch at Doyles fish restaurant. She would have the house in Cheltenham to use or sell. We agreed to delay finalizing the divorce until Gavin gained his majority to avoid any custody issues arising. Neither of us wanted to waste money on lawyer's fees. I was very happy for her, and hoped her new man would prove to be a better husband than I had been.

During this leave I did a Cook's tour, driving the secondhand Holden I bought. Friends in Cootamundra, Sale, and Melbourne were visited before arriving at my mother's place in Adelaide. I felt my choice of marque justified when the generator stopped working. The sole garage in the only country village for many kilometres, replaced it with a unit off the shelf and had me on my way in twenty minutes.

After spending Christmas with family, I departed for Brisbane from my sister's place in the Adelaide Hills. On a narrow tree lined backwoods road, a pheasant flew into my windscreen. Its head became jammed under the sun visor and the body dangled grotesquely in front of my eyes. I removed the bird and threw it into a ditch, but its smell remained on my hands for most of the day. Ironic, as people owning shotguns always seem to say the protected, awful smelling creature just happened to fly into their vehicles and die on the road.

Back in Hagen, my social life had dwindled. Still, always having been a food and wine buff, I sometimes spent Saturday afternoon cooking batches of food for freezing. I entertained a few friends at home, one extravagance presented being Crepes Suzette. My curries were also much appreciated as I had purchased large quantities of spices in England, most being unavailable locally. Fortunately, the local market provided me with fresh, organic fruit and vegetables in season and wine was still available in a few outlets.

My working time seemed largely to be taken up with paperwork or training new pilots. In addition to the 'locals' – Australian and New Zealanders, I was employing aviators from America, Canada, Switzerland, England and Norway. One young pilot phoned me regularly from California. I told him he needed more experience before being considered. Greg called every few months for several years, reporting his progress and repeating his determination to get a job in PNG. His persistence won me over; he was eventually employed and proved a very competent and loyal pilot. Our national travel lady, Sally, was flat out organising monthly tickets worldwide for almost thirty pilots and a few less engineering staff.

Then the Russians came into the picture. A group of three administration heads arrived in March 1990. I flew them around some of our typical work areas, one being above three thousand metres. They were astounded to discover our contract aircraft flew five to eight hours every day for weeks, until due for routine servicing. We told them the same would be expected of their aircraft on a helirig job. They left, shaking their heads, astounded at commercial realities in the West.

In April 1990, the Hon. Gareth Evans, the then Australian Foreign Minister, arrived for an official visit. Various staff and media accompanied him. It being my duty, I endured the humbug of flying him and his entourage of more than a half dozen to several highland locations. The Minister sat in the co-pilot's seat and we chatted. He struck me as an intelligent, friendly man but the nonsense and waiting that accompanies flying such VIPs is wearing. Later that year, the Australian Prime Minister, Bob Hawke, was scheduled to fly with us. I gladly palmed that trip off to a senior pilot.

On another VIP trip with heads of multinational companies from London and Australia we arrived at the 'exotic' Ambua Lodge late in the day where I found both helipads already occupied. I was obliged to land in a native garden adjacent. My rotor down-wash overturned about a metre of creeper like plant. The garden's owner immediately arrived and demanded $1,060 for the damage and parking.

I left the liaison officer to deal with that matter and adjourned to the bar with the rest of the party. The 'fix it' man soon joined us and said a deal had been settled for less than $100. The locals often plucked a number from thin air.

After leave in England, I returned to PNG in July to greet our 'Russian Contingent.' They arrived in an Antonov An-124, one of the world's largest jet freighters. It held three Kamov Ka-32 helicopters plus a multitude of spares. The Ka-32's are somewhat unusual machines sporting two sets of three main rotor blades. One set is mounted above the other, turning in opposite directions. This arrangement counters the torque effect, so no tail rotor, or extra power to drive it, is needed. For the technically minded, the rudder pedals controlled differential collective pitch between the two sets of rotor blades.

With the Kamov's re-assembled, industry and press representatives were invited to a demonstration. A container, filled to a weight of around five tons was lifted by longline. I operated the radio on this flight, the Russians' English being limited. Our demo received a full page of complimentary press coverage. We could now offer clients the greatest lifting capacity available in PNG, at a very competitive price.

With the importation paperwork completed, I showed the Russians the way to Hagen and manned the radio. At least one of the crew spoke sufficient English to understand my basic instructions. I could also point at instruments, for example the compass, and write or show a number of fingers to indicate a requirement or change. I was allowed to fly the aircraft and found the stability augmentation and autopilot excellent. Plus stand alone doppler navigation, requiring no ground based navigation aids. With a short tail and no tailrotor, yaw sensitivity was evident at power changes – meaning it fishtailed slightly. But lacking a long tail, the Kamov was little affected by crosswinds on landing or takeoff.

Chevron wanted the Kamovs to begin work immediately so we quickly found ourselves based at Poroma, just south of Mendi. Accommodation, storage sheds and a hanger had been built to support helirigs proving oil reserves on their large lease. The area involved stretched for over one hundred kilometres from the southeast of Poroma to the southwest. A road over the highlands connected the port of Lae to our base, enabling thousands of tonnes of supplies to be trucked in.

Weather permitting, our camp was the scene of frenetic daily helicopter activity. Two Boeing Vertols, our two KA-32's and one Puma were based there, plus various smaller machines. Over three dozen helicopters in total worked to support Chevron's drilling and exploration project. One Hughes 500 was used solely as a dedicated postal delivery machine, servicing around twenty different camps and outstations.

We fitted into this maelstrom of activity with our two, quickly nicknamed, 'camels.' It was a fitting choice, both being ugly, and very good at their specialised roles. Specific procedures were followed to eliminate the risk of collisions with so many aircraft constantly using the same routes through narrow mountain gaps, most with cloud just above them. It was not uncommon to see a load mysteriously appear, apparently suspended from a cloud.

I knew the area and challenges but needed to instill a commercially oriented mindset into our newfound friends from Vladivostok. They told me a common saying back home was 'We pretend to work, and they (the State) pretend to pay us.'

That attitude was brought home to me at the end of a day's briefing session when the interpreter said, 'Tomorrow we are not flying.'

'Why, are both aircraft unserviceable?'

'No, it's Aviation Day in Russia tomorrow and we never fly then.'

'Like hell,' I said. 'You are not in Russia now and if you don't fly you can all go home and I'll get a new batch of pilots.'

That got their attention and they began to realise that future work in the western world was based on performing to the client's satisfaction.

Unfortunately seniority, not proficiency at longline flying determined some of the appointments to what was considered a plum overseas posting. They reminded me of my Indonesian students. In Russia, jobs for the boys meant a loadmaster peered through a half metre size hole in the fuselage floor above the load and told the pilot what to do. Now, the pilot had to lean out of his door and do it all himself. I struggled and eventually managed to kick the navigator/radio operator off the aircraft as well. The redundant crew didn't want to go back to freezing in Siberia. Naturally, Chevron wanted minimal bodies in an already overcrowded camp.

The necessity for one of us to fly as radio operator, plus a lack of basic English among their pilots provided many interesting moments. It was a huge cultural shock for the remaining crew plus being accountable and having to work hard seemed a new experience for some. It just amounted to more grey hairs for me.

I found this period at Poroma most depressing. The single mess had no common room in which to socialise, play cards or games during the evening or long daytime hours waiting for weather to clear. We each shared a minute twin bed space featuring an upper and lower bunk. Also, we were outsiders in the opposition's territory. Our deficiencies were music to their ears. The only superior card we held was the ability to lift heavier loads than they could.

My struggles to keep our client happy meant I even tried to teach some pilots basic longline skills. I was far from expert myself but knew the basic principles. It was bizarre, trying to teach non-English speakers, in a strange aircraft, a complex task without even having dual controls to demonstrate. In a letter to my mother during this stressful period, I wrote that retiring to grow mushrooms seemed a wonderful idea.

In the middle of this new activity, we flew Placer's first shipment of around seven hundred kilograms of gold from Porgera to Cairns on the 25th of August 1990. Just after this milestone, one of our aircraft went missing.

Bruce, a quiet bush pilot, enjoyed working with a small team in isolated camps. He was flying geologists searching for exotic minerals in a rugged, unpopulated high altitude area of the Western Highlands, close to the border with Irian Jaya, when we received a call saying he had crashed. All survived with only minor injuries, but needed to be rescued. Despite the difficult terrain and heavy vegetation, we achieved this without further drama.

Investigation revealed that the accident was caused by the governor failing and slowing the engine to idle.

Bruce described how, after falling through thick jungle, the aircraft came to rest upside-down with the engine still running. The outer parts of the five rotor blades had been torn off but the steel rotor head and blade stumps remained and began to dig a hole in the jungle floor, just above the upside down occupants heads.

Bruce, hanging from his seat belt and shoulder harness, tried to stop the noise and action by closing the throttle fully but it had disconnected in the crash so the tunneling continued. Then he tried to pull out the red knob activating the fuel shut off valve but it wouldn't budge. He said he and his passengers couldn't leave the stricken ship for fear of falling into the thrashing maelstrom. It would have been an interesting situation, hanging upside down while watching metal, earth and branches being beaten to death half a metre below your head.

Bruce's adrenaline must have kicked in when he gave the fuel shut off another mighty heave and it moved, stopping the engine and preventing the rotor head from possibly digging their grave. After evacuating and checking for injuries and fire, Bruce faced another problem, that of notifying the authorities of their plight.

The radio antenna was smashed, so in desperation Bruce found and attached a piece of wire instead. Amazingly, they managed to make contact with the outside world. It seemed a near miracle considering the state of the aircraft. This was vital to their survival, as Bruce had earlier committed the cardinal sin of deliberately failing to advise the authorities of their operating location, as required by law and good sense. Without that information it's unlikely they would ever have been found and surviving a trek to the nearest habitation was doubtful.

For example, I know of one instance where horrified onlookers saw a Cessna fall into the trees within sight of the airstrip. The wreck had not been found ten years later! In secondary jungle you could stand looking up, or search from above, and see no trace of an aircraft in the multitudinous layers of solid green.

Further checking found that Bruce had not reported being airborne for days, or indeed even left any details of their proposed survey areas back at base camp. Notwithstanding his very fortunate life-saving radio call, Bruce's earlier omissions were unforgivable. He was instantly terminated, his PNG licence cancelled, and was lucky not to have been prosecuted for breaking aviation law. An error of judgment can be forgiven but not daily, blatant flouting of elementary airmanship and regulations.

In contrast, James, while on a similar survey, lost his helicopter and was unable to report the problem. He chose to accompany his geologist passengers clambering down a narrow rugged stream. These rocky, jungle-lined waterways were often the only possible landing sites. When the water level began to rise rapidly, James scrambled back toward his machine and watched in horror as it met him tumbling down in a mangled state, amid a torrent of water. Isolated heavy rainfall can occur 'around the corner', while the sun is shining elsewhere and one is oblivious of this until the flood arrives.

That group was fortunate, having noted a nearby village, to which they managed to walk. We soon found them as their base camp knew the day's work schedule. James was not fired for losing his half-million dollar helicopter as he had learned a valuable lesson. Many years before, in Fiji, I almost suffered a similar occurrence and after that always stayed with my machine unless it was safe to leave.

Just three weeks after the KA 32s arrived, the world's largest helicopter, the MIL Mi26 flew in to Hagen. It initially travelled to Brisbane by cargo ship and after reattachment of the rotor blades on the dock; the Mil ferried to PNG. It was the first helicopter to fly from Cairns to Port Moresby direct, a distance of over eight hundred kilometres.

In Hagen, I again operated the radio for demonstration flights after a large dump truck was driven into the hold. I sat in the cockpit aisle, between the navigator and flight engineer, on a folding garden chair positioned behind the interpreter who occupied the jump seat between the captain and copilot. A loadmaster in the hold made us a crew of seven.

Captain Gennadi proved to be a great guy and an old school type of worker who helped move freight in and out of the twelve metre long cargo bay and also let me fly the big beast. It handled like any well mannered chopper except obviously had a lot of inertia so I had to think many miles ahead. Gennadi was also the last Mil 26 skipper still living who had dumped loads of sand onto the smoking Chernobyl reactor after its meltdown.

Gennadi did forget to secure his cockpit sliding window properly and it fell onto the grass beside the runway when we took off on our first flight. As the Mil has a pressurised cockpit, the window was strong enough to be undamaged by the fall.

We were not allowed to fly passengers but eighty-five of them could be carried if seating was fitted. I read that the military carried almost double that number of soldiers in extremis. This indicates the size of the machine. It needed a forty metre clear space from front to rear to turn the rotors. The maximum 56,000 kilogram gross weight was lifted by 22,000 Horse Power (16,400 kW), produced by two, three shaft, turbine engines.

Chevron utilised the Mil at a cost in excess of ten thousand dollars per flight hour plus fuel, consumed at the rate of three and a half thousand litres an hour. It immensely speeded up construction of their private airport on the shore of Lake Kutubu. That strip, on completion, would be the gateway to their oilfields and allow large fixed wing aircraft to fly in production equipment and supplies.

Due to the size and weight of the Mil, I had to obtain special clearances for it to land at provincial government airports. At our main loading point, Mendi, we were required to tow the Mil to a taxiway before starting engines to avoid possibly blowing away any nearby light aircraft in the parking area.

We flew the big beast to Poroma where a large new helipad had been bulldozed, a safe distance from the others. Chevron were a little dismayed at having to provide beds and meals for the crew accompanying the Mil, - seven maintenance men, two pilots, one flight engineer, a navigator, translator and finally myself working the radios.

Next morning a large group of spectators watched the monster preparing to depart. We were to collect our loads from Mendi airport, being able to lift more using a short running takeoff, not possible at Poroma. On the first attempt to start the five hundred HP (373 KW) starting engine, it shut down automatically. The second resulted in its fire extinguisher firing. The crew were greatly embarrassed on finding the engine's air intake plug had not been removed. With that out, all engines fired up normally and we soon landed at Mendi.

The big chopper always drew a crowd and hundreds of spectators quickly arrived, posing a danger to operations. Security staff were required to control them. Thereafter, whenever we flew, another chopper first brought in guards to secure the loading area.

When about to start engines on our first trip into Moro I noticed a Chevron employee still on board.

'Sorry Eric,' I said. 'We are not allowed to carry passengers. You need to use one of your other choppers.'

'Phil, if the Mil goes down I might as well go with it. My back's against the wall and I ain't got no future if this machine does not deliver.'

'Just this time then.'

I felt sorry for Eric as he went out on a limb to persuade an American company to use Russian machinery instead of bringing in larger equipment from the USA. The industry would not trust him again if we did not perform. On the other hand, he would be a hero if we delivered as promised.

We did. Gennadi and us crewmembers loaded large earthmoving

365

trucks, dozers, graders and other goods in at Mendi and out at the other end. It happened so quickly Chevron had trouble keeping us supplied with freight. Previously, all larger equipment had to be dismantled into numerous flyable pieces before being re-assembled in primitive conditions, taking months and much effort and expense.

I suffered worrying occasions when the Russian pilots flew into clouds before I could prevent it. It was second nature for them but we were not supposed to do so, relying on seeing other aircraft and being seen. We had no GPS or ground based navigation aids but the Russian machines all had doppler navigation systems fitted. They knew they were not descending into one of the many surrounding mountain ranges. It was unnerving; I didn't know what was going on apart from seeing our height indication decreasing prior to breaking out below clouds.

At the time, in many ways, the Russian machines were much better equipped than western civil helicopters. Stand alone navigation systems, as well as cockpit and flight data recorders were fitted as standard equipment. The state paid for these and didn't have to make a profit or account to shareholders. People often forget that the Russians were first to place a satellite into orbit.

As I got to know our eastern lads better they told me a story about military crews in Russia who they regarded as wimps because they wore parachutes. It seems that on one flight a red light came on in the cockpit, signaling impending doom, so all the crew jumped out. Some twenty minutes later a chopper turned up unannounced at an airport and came to a hover a metre above the runway.

The controller shouted at the unannounced arrival to go and park but the chopper didn't move or respond to radio calls. Eventual inspection revealed that the machine was uncrewed and waiting for further instructions. A pilot was found who climbed aboard, disconnect the autopilot and parked the chopper before it ran out of fuel. The machine's autopilot had been programmed to take it home so that's where it went, the indicated major fault not materialising. A somewhat sheepish crew eventually turned up by road to claim their aircraft.

In December 1990, I escaped from nurse-maiding the Russians and attended a memorable Christmas party in Australia with Andy and Heather, my old friends from Kota Kinabalu. The function was held at Fort Dennison, in the middle of Sydney Harbour. Ferry transport, sumptuous food and wine plus a jazz band were all provided for invited guests by an oil well service company.

After leaving that luxurious treat, I literally came to earth with a thud while playing touch football under a Morton Bay Fig tree. Slipping on ball bearing like fig seeds, I heard a loud crack from my right shoulder as I fell on it. The ligaments had been torn off the bone. A chemist provided me with aspirin for the pain and a sling for my arm. It took weeks before I regained reasonable strength in that arm, which still reaches out three centimetres further than my left one. Another effect is to make hitting a hard topspin shot in tennis more difficult.

Next day I flew to Adelaide, my leave would not be ruined by that injury. Before collecting a hire car, I removed my sling. I doubt I'd have been allowed to drive away otherwise. Driving a manual transmission single handedly just requires a bit more anticipation and concentration.

After church attendance's and Christmas celebrations with my mother and relatives I spent several relaxing days with Pamela, my first true love, at her home. She was now divorced, living alone and had retained her shapely figure. Our bond resurfaced but she was still a practicing Catholic so I didn't consider her a future partner.

Returning to Brisbane in January 1991, I bought a two bedroom, second floor unit in Toowong, Brisbane. I felt the need for a base in Australia, in a city serviced by regular flights to PNG. Gavin could also use it during his visits and he was considering attending university in Australia.

Meanwhile, a large contract to help build a powerline from BP's gas-fields at Nogoli to the gold mine at Porgera needed my attention. This logistical nightmare would require hundreds of towers for a line spanning sixty kilometres. It was to be built through jungle and rugged terrain rising to over three thousand metres. Few helicopters could lift and precisely place the towers at that altitude, but our Kamov's could. I prepared our winning tender document on that capability. It was a tricky task to precisely lower the single leg T-shaped tower onto its mount, then hold it vertically in position until guy wires were attached to keep the pole upright. I had employed a delightfully modest American specialist pilot for this project.

Ken knew how to safely pull lead wires over tower arms with a helicopter, to enable stringing of the conductor wires. He also scheduled our half dozen helicopters assigned to the task; virtually controlling the whole construction project as every phase relied on them. Dozens of clearing, pit blasting and concrete laying crews had to flown in and out of tower and line cutting sites daily.

At a crucial point the Russians, perhaps feeling usurped, decided that Ken could not occupy the left (command) seat on the Kamov. It was a

367

power play. With sites cleared and concrete set, construction of the line depended on Ken being able to place the towers. He could only do this from the command cockpit seat. Millions of dollars and many reputations were at stake.

For several nights, I was on the phone to heads of aviation and government departments in Moscow and Vladivostok, virtually until daylight. The Russians probably felt we wished to show them the West had better training and pilots than they did. That of course, was not the point – their crews had not built Western powerlines or spoke sufficient English!

This problem, which had probably festered out of sight, threatened our company and the future viability of Russian helicopters in Asia. Ken held a Russian Licence to command the Kamov after being tested in the USSR, so legality was not the issue.

Eventually our threats and good sense won out. The major project was completed ahead of time and, we were told, under budget. One Bell Long Ranger helicopter crashed into the jungle during the thousands of hours flown on that job. Only minor injuries occurred to the occupants who were found and flown out within hours. Considering the pressure our pilots faced to drop off and collect so many field crews daily, at extreme altitudes and weather, we were thankful nothing worse occurred. The pilot of the accident aircraft admitted that he became disoriented after flying into cloud when caught in a narrow steep-sided, high altitude valley late in the day. He was not fired, remaining a loyal employee. Helicopter pilots called the accident valley end Karl's Gap.

Late in 1990, my old friend and ex-boss, Pat Lloyd flew in from Singapore. He ran his own business in that bustling city and had made a deal to promote our company in Asia. We worked together for almost a week compiling a tender to supply several Kamov's and a Bell 212 model for a helirig job in Myanmar (Burma).

We were awarded the contract early in 1991. Soon after, I found myself in Yangon (Rangoon) visiting aviation authorities to obtain operating permits. Myanmar shared a border with Bangladesh and thanks to the isolation imposed by years of military rule, Myanmar was also a very poor country. A civil war was being fought in several provinces, attempting to overthrow the ruling junta and return the country to democracy. We stayed well clear of the internal struggles, however, virtually all communications out of the country were monitored. Even the oil company's satellite voice traffic to head office in the USA had to pass through military scrutiny in Yangon and could be cut at any time. It seemed the ruling generals were paranoid about security and censorship.

The capital city (like its neighbour Dacca) had only one hotel considered fit for use by Westerners, the Inja Lake. Built by Russians many years prior, it was so old that bathrooms featured rusty external plumbing and taps. Sometimes water didn't flow from pipes for several minutes, then arrived a muddy brown colour. The lift had a totally illogical mind of its own, it was a shock to arrive at the selected floor without a half dozen unnecessary, erratic journeys. It seemed the country's foreign exchange was used to buy military hardware, so only local, mostly tasteless food was available.

One evening after finishing our meal in the hotel restaurant I discussed business with two colleagues when we became aware that only one other person remained in our large, spartan eatery. She was an attractive, slim, fair-skinned woman of indeterminate age, seated at a table some distance away. The large corona cigar she lit captured our attention.

'She looks a bit of alright,' I remarked while wondering about her nationality and why she was eating by herself.

Speculation about the woman followed. Eventually my two companions bet I was not game to chat up the aristocratic looking lady composedly smoking her cigar between sips of after dinner coffee. It was a challenge I was only too happy to take on, besides, I had nothing else to do that evening. After introducing myself, I was soon seated at Danielle's table. I learned she was a divorced French lady, based in Bangkok who frequently travelled to Myanmar on business. An apparently successful businesswoman, she could read and write four different languages fluently and spoke several others.

We moved to the bar next door where Danielle provided me with many insights into the local people, culture and the country in general. Having lived in Yangon and now being a frequent visitor, it seemed most of the hotel staff knew her and respectfully addressed her by name. After several drinks we retired to our rooms. I asked her to have dinner with me in town the following evening but she politely declined. Next day, I happened to meet her in the hotel and she said she could join me for dinner.

During our meal at a restaurant in the city, our friendship deepened and the conversation became more intimate. After returning to our hotel, I invited Danielle to my room for a nightcap and she accepted.

The following night, after dinner, we became lovers. Danielle previously mentioned that she had two children, now attending university, but her perfectly proportioned body was like that of a thirty year old virgin. She knew how to use every part to excite and please a man.

They say French men are the best lovers, but I would rate their ladies very highly. The only difficulty was hiding the liaison from hotel staff who seemed to be found in public areas at all hours. We carefully checked hotel corridors before leaving each other's rooms as Danielle dared not compromise her reputation. Her business and personal connections depended on it.

I had won my bet and gained a wonderful partner. I even began to fall in love. It was a new element to consider in my life. Logistics were a problem but I would be travelling to Asia regularly. Danielle made up for some of the trouble and stress our Russian crew caused in Myanmar; we usually managed to synchronize our visits. I remember an idyllic long weekend with her at an isolated hotel on the beach in Southern Thailand, alternating between the restaurant, beach and bed. I became very attached to her and respected her mind. Our bodies seemed to have a natural attraction, like two magnets in close proximity.

This interlude was followed by a few weeks at my unit in Brisbane, then it was back to Singapore to nursemaid two Russian Kamov helicopters to Yangon. An interesting exercise as only the interpreter, Igor, and I spoke English. Both aircraft traveled in company and were treated as one as only I could do the radio reports and obtain flight clearances.

Having worked with Igor before in the Mil 26, he knew the routine but this time we had two aircraft. After receiving clearances, I told Igor what to tell the Russians. The first crew then relayed this to the other, following aircraft on a discrete frequency. The procedure worked as none of the four countries we traversed complained.

After a re-fuelling stop in Pinang we overnighted at Phuket where the Thai airport ground controller's English was so bad he was impossible to understand. I gave up and directed the pilot to park at what I thought was an appropriate place on the apron. No vehicles or officials appeared so we shut the helicopters down. Sometimes you just have to use your initiative.

It took me two and a half hours of running around to complete our incoming and out going paperwork for the overnight stay. The four bars on my uniform epaulettes and white skin enabled me, several times, to walk into the terminal via the departure area and out to the airside using incoming customs and immigration lanes. I just walked through whichever route was the shortest, during the struggle to complete a long list of official requirements.

Exhausted, I made it to a hotel where Igor had already checked in the thirteen crew.

'How are we going to ensure they'll all be ready to leave here at six am tomorrow' I asked?

'Don't worry, I've told them it's straight back to Siberia if they don't show. Also, none of them have any local currency.'

'Hope it works as we can't afford to leave late or we won't make Yangon.'

We did get away on time and after fighting shocking, notorious Bay of Bengal weather, made it to Yangon. The massive dome of that city's major temple, covered in shining tons of gold could be seen for kilometres and was an unmistakable landmark. Several days later I shepherded my charges, again in pounding monsoon rain, to their destination beyond Mandalay in Northern Myanmar. The site was bounded by the Chinese, Thai and Indian borders, all within a few hundred kilometres. There, other Australian radio operators took over from me.

Prior to the Myanmar operation commencing, I felt it time to relinquish the twenty four hour demanding role of chief pilot. Five and a half years of living mostly in PNG, had been enough strain. I was happy to hand over the reins to Trevor McGowan, a Kiwi, in mid 1991. He had been persuaded to move to Hagen with his lovely wife Joan. There were numerous other consulting jobs I was tasked with, beside sitting in for Trevor's leave breaks. I was easing my way out of PNG and in 1992 it was a great relief to pack up my belongings for shipment to Australia. It would be a homecoming of sorts, after spending more than twenty-one years based overseas.

Before that happened, the Russians in Myanmar caused problems requiring my presence. Two groups worked tours there, each having two aircraft on site. One lot was from Krasnodar, the other Murmansk. They didn't co-operate – not even lending each other spare parts. I was responsible to the oil company for their performance, but had no authority over them except to ship individuals out. That action would mean insufficient working crew on site as replacements took weeks to arrive. I could only point out their lack of performance might lose them their jobs and coveted hard currency allowance.

The other problem was the same as I had experienced in PNG – they were not properly trained for longline work and almost caused a disaster. Night after night I tossed and turned, becoming so stressed I hardly slept for weeks. For the first time ever I resorted to sleeping pills to maintain my health and sanity. We eventually eased out of trouble by importing Ken, the ace pilot who had bossed the power-line job. He trained the Russian pilots.

Personal problems arose at the remote campsite, several hundred kilometres north of Mandalay. The base was hacked out of the jungle on a bank of the Irrawaddy River. Heavy supplies arrived by boat when the river was high. Personnel and urgent freight arrived several times a week in a Twin Otter that could use the short purpose built airstrip. It took all day for the aircraft to complete the round trip.

Alcohol was banned, but the Russian's had imported drums of de-icing fluid for their aircraft. It was 100% pure alcohol, which they mixed with orange or other juice. I had previously been obliged to drink this concoction at a party in Hagen hosted by Russians, and found that it spun my head and rendered my legs useless after several generous shots. One pilot in PNG, from another company, lost his job after being unable to fly for several days because of a heavy night on that deadly drink.

It's likely that consumption of their de-icing brew resulted in fraternization with local women. One night the camp erupted when a soldier threatened the Russians with his machine gun. I believe a village woman was involved.

It seemed few days passed without new hassles arising. The years of staying alive in the air had tempered my attitude to stress but managing multi-million dollar contracts was another matter. The Russians managed to put my mental anxiety into the red, above the do not exceed area, many times. Delay in obtaining visas and lack of connecting flights meant a week or more passed before I arrived to try and resolve problems with our Eastern Block crews. Even after fifteen years my stomach tightened at the memory of that contract. It sure left a mark on me. In contrast, the one Bell 212 flown by my pilots caused virtually no trouble.

On completion of that drilling program, I heard the oil company say the one unsuccessful hole drilled in Myanmar cost them over twice as much as any previous well sunk on land.

The only benefit arising from these problems was that I continued meeting Danielle in Bangkok or Yangon. She also visited me in Hagen for several weeks and we managed to spend a few days relaxing at a hotel in Madang. A close bond was developing but sometimes I wondered if our relationship was destined to last. A near perfect woman in every way, except her citizenship meant one of us would eventually have to choose a foreign culture in which to be domiciled. Meanwhile, the journey was terrific, and worrying about a destination was postponed.

January 1992 began with a blaze. Nationals overran the defenses at CRA Exploration's camp at the Mt Kare gold deposit and set fire to our

Bell 204 helicopter based there, destroying it. While the invaders razed the camp, our pilot and engineer, fearing for their lives, escaped. They trudged all night for twenty-two kilometres through sticky mud, climbing the path to a three thousand metre gap before reaching safety at our base in Porgera. A harrowing experience for our lads. I believe a few looters were caught and punished. That gold deposit made some rich, ruined others and directly or otherwise caused many premature deaths. It seems to be the norm when riches are easily won.

February is normally the month when the biannual Asian Aerospace exposition is held in Singapore. Major companies set up large exhibits and the latest aircraft, civil and military fly in. In 1992, the overseas arm of our company was represented at this event and I helped man the booth. We were promoting our ability to perform a range of helicopter operations in Asia.

I felt privileged to mingle with world leaders in our gravity defying industry. One evening, Pat Lloyd hosted a tour. Perhaps thirty people boarded a chartered vessel for a harbour cruise. It featured four different mouth watering dinner courses being served to us on different islands in the harbour. Another unique experience and a chance to socialise with VIPs from different countries. I met Dick Smith for the second time, the first being at Seletar airport when he flew in on his round the world chopper trip.

March, 1992 was notable in that finally my stored possessions from PNG, Singapore, England and Adelaide (where wedding presents had been with my brother for twenty-two years) were all reunited with me in Brisbane.

In June that year, I was a company representative at Chevron's 'first oil' party at Moro. After their years of big spending on exploration in PNG, the black liquid provided revenue. For the first and perhaps only time, it was legal to drink alcohol at that small company town. However, booze intake was strictly limited by the two tickets given to each guest. No champagne for the masses. Another milestone and a first for the country.

Also, during that period, Gavin took a year off before beginning university. He flew out and stayed in my unit in Brisbane between fruit picking ventures in northern Queensland. With me now working tours, I was able to spend more time with him. He visited his grandmother in Adelaide and bussed back via the coast road, stopping off at his birthplace in Sale.

Friends convinced me to invest in Sydney as the Brisbane property market seemed stagnant. I was spending more time there so it made sense to have my own accommodation. While driving down via the inland highway in July, my car and I were shocked to find ourselves in a snowstorm soon after leaving sub-tropical Queensland.

Weathering that unexpected event, I found I could afford a small unit close to the harbour in Sydney's eastern suburbs, at Elizabeth Bay. It proved to be a good base for outings to sample exotic foods, attend the theatre, opera and other events I had missed for so many years. Gavin was impressed when we only took five minutes to drive to town and then walk to the Opera House in another five minutes. He enjoyed his first opera, Hansel and Gretel.

I felt my years of privation were rewarded when I savoured a succulent meal with wine while watching the sun go down over Sydney and the harbour. Followed by a few steps to enjoy a world class operatic performance. Especially as I had been a fan of Joan Sutherland for decades, having collected all her recordings – in those days on open reel tapes for high fidelity. Over the next few years I was privileged to attend almost every new opera during my time off. Not being involved in the 'rat race' or daily commuting I could fully enjoy what the city had to offer. I had gone full circle to my early days in Sydney, except that now I was seeking a permanent partner. My occupation and lifestyle still made that difficult.

Another downside was the stressful time I spent as the relieving chief pilot in Hagen and ongoing problems with our Eastern Block crews. In September 1992, we ferried a Bell twin-engined helicopter to Cambodia where it began work with the UN. Gareth Evans, Australia's foreign minister had worked hard there to organize the first election in local people's memory. Logistic support was required to ensure a fair ballot. Pol Pot's rebel faction had supposedly been subdued but we heard UN aircraft had been shot at. Soon, two more company aircraft were flown to Pnom Penh and I visited to check the operation and pilots.

CHAPTER 17

*Never let an aircraft take you somewhere your brain didn't
get to five minutes earlier.* ~ *The Aviators Guide Book*

Obtaining a visa to enter Cambodia took several days and during this time I caught up with paperwork in our Singapore office. On arrival in Pnom Penh, the primitive nature of the airport terminal illustrated how poor this country was in comparison to most of its neighbours. In contrast, the UN contingent seemed to have money to burn. Hundreds of their new, white, air-conditioned, four-wheel drive vehicles roamed the streets and highly paid expatriates lived in comparative luxury. I heard that half of all the UN people in the country were allocated a vehicle.

Our Company rented two houses adjacent to the city centre. One to accommodate the resident manager, visitors, an office and stores. The other housed our pilots and engineers.

The city, lining the banks of the wide, brown, sluggish Mekong River basked in tropical heat and crawled with salespeople selling everything imaginable. Electricity was expensive and distributed via a spider's web of wires reaching out from several poles in the street. Individual house meters didn't exist; it seemed only one was allocated to every city neighborhood. Generally they were located in a small concrete bunker, attended by the resident male bill collector.

It was he who decided how much each household should pay. I suppose his standard of living depended on the difference between collections and the amount he paid to an electricity provider further up the totem pole. Being rich foreigners, our electricity bill was determined by the company's willingness to pay. The cost of our power doubled every month. If the bill was not paid promptly in cash, disconnection or worse was threatened. Having our frozen food spoiling, or no air-conditioning, was unthinkable.

On reaching almost US $1000 for a month's supply, our manager Greg - a burly, forceful fellow - refused to pay the outrageous charge. He was well aware of the danger involved, having been told a local in our street had been murdered after a similar refusal. The electricity man was not one to be trifled with! A compromise was reached; the bill collector probably didn't want to kill this particular goose.

I was soon introduced to the social scene, which involved a bar. A private one, accessible only to expats, was tucked into a UN contractor's warehouse. We drank next to hundreds of new portable generators waiting to be spread through the countryside to power computers for the forthcoming elections.

At this bar, I met a polyglot, diverse bunch of men, most having been associated with UN projects all over the world.

'So, where are you going to settle when you give up this roving life?' I asked Fred, a trim dapper fortyish Brit.

'I'm not sure yet old boy but it must be somewhere warm, I can't handle the English winters any more.'

Over cold beers, Swedes, Canadians, Americans and German nationals joined the discussion. We decided that in addition to a warm climate, political stability, democracy and an English speaking similar culture was needed for retirement. The only two areas in the world that met those criteria were northern Australia and Florida. Few felt they could handle the American scene so were aiming for an Aussie passport.

Over the years I had been involved in many such discussions while sitting in jungle camps or breasting a bar somewhere in the world where professional expatriates meet. It's hard to give up a well paid, interesting, travelling life and settle down to routine, often mundane, suburban existence. To justify moving to a new life, the country and location was carefully chosen. It's also the reason why many well qualified and travelled foreign nationals with the means to do so settled in Australia.

Gossip during the next few days confirmed rebels were still active in parts of the country. In these areas it was wise to fly either very low and fast or at a height beyond rifle range. I heard of a French pilot who was injured by a bullet entering through the floor of his Puma helicopter, severing his penis before exiting through the roof. After this episode, steel plates were fitted under the crew seats in our machines. We were also told that the rebels were offering a bounty of ten thousand American dollars to anyone managing to down a helicopter. In Cambodia, this would have been equivalent to becoming an instant multi-millionaire.

Some Russian pilots flying above the clouds at ten thousand feet reported seeing anti-aircraft shells exploding some distance away. Fortunately the guns' radar aiming system was inaccurate and no machines were damaged. All the UN helicopters were painted white, with the circular blue UN logo providing a convenient bulls-eye for marksmen.

Every morning, seconded military personnel gave pilots a briefing on the latest reported hot spots and perceived danger levels in various parts of the country. Pol Pot's rebels were still causing problems and deaths. This talk was a sobering way to start the day but fortunately our crew or aircraft didn't sustain any damage during their months in Cambodia.

The environment in which I flight checked our pilots was treacherous. The airport held a tangled mess of helicopters from Russia, France and America. All parked among dilapidated and partly collapsed hangers, some still containing outdated cannibalised Russian jet fighters, howitzer guns and other rusting inoperative military hardware.

Many of the polyglot pilot contingent only had a nodding acquaintance with English so the Cambodian air traffic controllers' mangled language and accents compounded the communication difficulties. It became an interesting, yet serious game guessing who would take off from where and when. Various large airline jets came and went, at least they predictably used the runway.

Having flown clear of the airport to a 'safe' rural area in the south, an unseen danger lurked below ground - land mines. Normally I chose unpopulated areas to practise emergency landings and suchlike but in this country the only places we dared touch down were on paths bearing peoples' footprints.

One day another pilot and I flew a charter to an up-country airport. Enroute, I was astounded at the continuously pockmarked countryside. Countless bomb craters still scarred the terrain decades after the Vietnam War ended. These stagnant ponds were ideal breeding places for malarial mosquitoes.

After dropping our passengers, I began to conduct flight checks on the other pilot. We flew the customary left-hand circuits at this quiet rural airport. Then a radio call advised us that rebels had shot at aircraft from a nearby mountain range overlooking our flight path. After landing and checking for bullet holes we continued, flying on the other side of the runway. I certainly didn't envy the crew on this posting.

That evening I walked around the block to our crew house to brief pilots on possible unusual failures such as caused by projectiles. My knowledge was theoretical but I had heard many Vietnam veterans' war stories. I strolled home after several hours and had barely arrived when the phone rang.

A breathless voice asked if I was OK. They told me a gunfight started just after I left. Bullets had dislodged plaster from the balcony ceiling where we had been sitting.

I thanked my angel for getting me home safely again.

We didn't discover the reason for this shooting in the quiet suburban street. I guess it was none of our business.

Soon after that event, my work in Cambodia was completed and I flew back to Australia.

Early in 1993, I sold my unit in Brisbane as the real estate action seemed to be in Sydney. Having just gathered all my possessions under one roof, they went into storage yet again as my unit in Sydney was far too small for them. I sometimes wondered if my aboriginal walkabouts would end.

After several months careful shopping in Elizabeth Bay, my offer for a two bedroom apartment close to my existing unit was accepted and I became the owner of a substantial mortgage. Now I could move out of my 'cubby house' and rent it out. In my new harbour view premises friends could stay overnight without having to sleep on the carpet.

Among the first people I entertained for a long lunch were, by chance, the trio involved when I crashed on Ayers Rock – Smithy, the model Beverly, and Boris the photographer. Smithy happened to be visiting Sydney and I managed to track down the others whom I had not seen for many years.

I knew that Smithy had sold his enterprise and retired. Beverly now ran her own editing setup in Sydney while Boris bemoaned an acrimonious divorce and the loss of his business. What had I done with my life?

I had lost my faith in western religions and replaced it with a wider ranging undogmatic spirituality. Adult walkabouts, combined with aviation had certainly led to a nomadic, eventful life. My quest for a permanent compatible partner continued. I wished to settle back into rural living with a lady I could commit to. My heart was waiting to be claimed, after a candidate passed the obstacle course in my head.

In between stints as relieving chief pilot, I was commissioned to begin producing the documentation required to place the Mil Mi26, the world's largest helicopter, on the PNG aircraft register. It was a mammoth undertaking. Just one small aspect of the task was having to write the correct procedures to deal with a total of over two hundred red, amber, yellow and white; warning, caution and condition lights in the cockpit and aux panels.

Since early 1991, I had translated thousands of pages of Russian 'English' manuals and collated them into official flight manuals. First for the Kamov

Ka 32, and then for the Mil 171. The latter legally carrying twenty-six passengers in comfort. The first project took years to obtain official registration of that aircraft type in the Western system of certification in PNG. It required many trips to Russia for validation of their standards and systems by our chief, and government certifying engineers. Thankfully I managed to avoid that journey as the cold and food did not appeal to me.

It did however require me to spend many evenings with our Eastern crews in Mt Hagen, eating Russian dumplings and sampling their vodka in the barn-like company premises they occupied. In the early days, genuine caviar was served. For many of them, I became the go-between, addressing their concerns with management. The company even employed a teacher to school them in English and the western air law necessary to pass PNG pilot and engineering licence exams.

These projects involved liaising with specialists in Brisbane and Sydney. On one of these trips to Brisbane I met Dinah. She was born in England and attended boarding school in the UK before leaving a nursing career to drive overland to Australia with one Aussie and five Kiwis. I had planned to do the trip in the opposite direction but my career moves killed that prospect. Another co-incidence was that Dinah had worked for Connellan Airways in Alice Springs before marrying a local there. Then, with her husband, she raised two girls on an outback cattle station in the Territory. These details emerged over many months during my visits to Dinah's house in Northern N.S.W.

As our bond grew stronger I felt I'd met the person with whom I wished to share the rest of my life. Our personalities seemed to dovetail in the best ways. I was ready to pack up and move in with her after meetings over several months, but that was not allowed. First I had to prove myself. As an early innocent test, she served me catfish for lunch, caught by her in a nearby creek. I didn't much like it, but ate without complaint, not wishing to appear fussy.

Danielle and I were still corresponding but I felt our relationship posed too many geographical and cultural difficulties for my liking. I didn't speak her native tongue even though I'd learnt bits of half-a-dozen new languages since childhood. And I didn't know how or if I'd be accepted into her community in the south of France where she had property. I'd had enough of being an 'outsider' in society or foreign countries. Regretfully, I wrote her a Dear Jane letter and we have had no contact since. I thought it for the best, though I knew she would be hurt.

In September, 1993, I visited England for Gavin's 21st birthday celebration.

Unlike my uneventful coming of age, he had a small private party with some of his childhood friends. Thankfully, I was able to stay with Gavin and Mary at her husband's farmhouse. We enjoyed an easy relationship and Gavin's new father treated him as his own son, even spoiling him in some respects.

New Years Eve found me back in Sydney where the evening was spent at the Opera House with my ex Hagen friends, Jo and Nigel. Back then, it was the only night people were allowed to bring their own containers full of booze to the evening's entertainment. For us, our night began by drinking bubbly while sitting outside and watching the sun go down. Then we carried our drinks inside for a light classical music concert. The interval was timed to enable viewing of the early fireworks show through the large glass walls facing the harbour. Further musical entertainment followed and on conclusion pre-paid guests moved to another room to gorge on king prawns and other gourmet delights. Then the midnight spectacular began and filled a clear sky with colour. A prime location from which to see the world renowned fireworks display ushering in a New Year.

When the noise and light show stopped this unforgettable evening ended with us dancing to a live band, adjacent to the famed '*Blue Poles*' painting by Jackson Pollock. Peoples' eskys travelled everywhere. I felt extremely privileged to be able to afford the luxurious feast for eyes, ears and palate. It certainly helped make up for my many broke, miserable, nowhere days, during my first years in PNG.

The only let down was having to walk home dripping sweat as taxis were unavailable on that hot night. The early morning slog was spiced up by numerous 'ladies', wearing only miniscule knickers, parading up and down the Kings Cross end of William street.

Early in 1994, I was sent to New Zealand to write an Operations Manual as we planned to establish a logging venture with a Kamov. This meant learning a new system and meeting new regulators. An interesting exercise. I lived, studied and composed at my friend and co-worker, Dick Anderson's house in Nelson. His wife catered for me admirably.

After a month's intensive writing, I completed the task, then hired a car and toured the South Island for a week. In Christchurch, I stayed with our Mt Hagen ex-company accountant Richard and his wife Sue, who showed me the sights. One of the pilots I had employed, Rusty, who worked in PNG for some years, landed me on the top of the Franz Joseph glacier. Accompanying Japanese tourists paid for the flight. After completing this tour, I returned to Sydney.

The Bougainville crisis was occurring when I next filled in as chief pilot. We had several aircraft based at Buka providing logistic support to the military when a Kamov was requested to join them. I vetoed that as being too politically provocative and dangerous to the Russian relationship.

In August 1994, I happened to fly the regular bank run to the Porgera gold mine site. Flying into Porgera's steep-sided bowl from the east gap, I noticed the mid morning light in the valley was crisp and clear with the dark green rainforest trees embracing the sunlight. To the north, nature was in its normal cycle of constant growth and renewal. To the west the steep hillside was scarred and torn by massive yellow machines gouging the earth like hungry dogs after a bone. I noticed black and white smoke beyond the gold refining mill, offices and accommodation blocks clustered in the town area.

After landing at the large multiple helipad site, I discovered the smoke plume came from the remains of the explosives manufacturing plant. Three men had just been vaporised in a shattering explosion. Space was at a premium in the steep valley but it seemed a serious oversight that the explosives manufacturing facility had been left in its original position as the town grew. Incredibly, multiple housing blocks, mess halls and office buildings were situated within a few hundred metres of the potentially dangerous plant and stored dynamite. Even our helipad site had moved several times and was now well clear of the central town area.

I was told of the extensive damage to numerous buildings clustered in the blast zone; one large mess hall blown off its piles, hundreds of windows shattered and other facilities destroyed. Flying glass injured tens of people inside buildings, the final death toll being more than a dozen.

We stood and waited on our elevated helipad, wondering if the remaining tons of explosives stored in two dirty brown shipping containers were going to burn or explode.

The mine management had asked us to drop water on the fire but it was not a safe option. Our multi million-dollar helicopter could have been destroyed and the pilot killed if another explosion brought the chopper down. Besides, none of the mine rescue team waiting on the helipad were game to inspect the carnage and all personnel in buildings within hundreds of metres had been evacuated.

The suspense hung over us like a guillotine.

By chance, I was looking directly at the fire when the second explosion occurred. My memory cells will forever be imprinted by the pure white ten metre perfect sphere that hung in the air for a millisecond like a large

Christmas decoration above the site. Immediately afterward black hell erupted and the shock wave hit us - it almost knocked me over. Debris began to fall from the clear blue sky. Men ran for cover. I crouched onto the ground and looked up, ready to dodge any shrapnel coming down. Terry, one of our pilots, threw himself under his helicopter. We were about a kilometre from the blast and roughly two hundred metres above it and found only a few small pieces of twisted metal had fallen onto the helipad. Fortunately, none of our four parked helicopters was damaged.

'God, if anyone was still alive down there, they're history now!' someone said.

When the smoke cleared, nothing remained of the factory site, like it had never existed. Even the containers and a large diesel storage tank had disappeared. A large, black topped, mushroom cloud boiled into the atmosphere. It was eerily silent for a moment until a frenzied wailing began. A dozen trained guard dogs, kennelled about thirty metres away from the plant had amazingly survived both explosions. Unfortunately, they were now uncontrollable and had to be destroyed. The owner of the security firm was most upset, his dogs were imported from Australia at great expense and could not be easily replaced.

The hospital was filled with suffering people. The mine area employing over a thousand workers was virtually shut down. Vital facilities had been damaged and most employees were sent home. With the injured still being stabilised, I flew to Mt Hagen with a load of stunned personnel. Our other aircraft transported the casualties later.

The horse had bolted but questions were now asked - what was all this high explosive material doing on the fringe of office and mess buildings?

This disaster cost the mine operator millions as gold production ceased for weeks as the mine was closed, pending investigation. Eventually, the official finding was that a worn five-dollar bearing in a mincing machine probably caused the first explosion. A commercial version of those found in home kitchens. The mincer was fed with bulk explosive material to produce a uniform 'sausage' which fitted into holes drilled into rock or soil. The worn bearing was thought to have produced hot metal or a spark, which resulted in the devastation and loss of life.

Just before this disaster, a VIP and his family visited our company in Mt Hagen. He was a knight of the realm and controlled a major Asian airline and shipping interests. Our Chairman invited him to inspect operations in PNG with a view to investing in the company. The status of this gentleman was such that he was not allowed to fly in the same helicopter as his wife and family. I flew him, his family following in another machine. Their tour occurred only a week before the blast. While visiting Porgera, we flew above the explosives plant - a usual route when viewing the mine site and associated development. My angel was obviously still on guard.

I sometimes wondered about having avoided numerous disasters. Was it fate, or as some say, you reap what you sow. I tend to the latter, notwithstanding having cast wild oats in the past. But I was very careful with the odds that had claimed many of my colleagues.

The transport of Porgera's gold from the mine site involved a helicopter trip from the mine to Mount Hagen, then it was flown to Australia in our Beechcraft King Air turboprop. These random flights were never shown on our bookings white-board. On the helicopter flight, in addition to normal radio reports, coded messages were frequently transmitted so each flight could be monitored during the fifty-minute journey. Only one passenger flew on these trips, a burly male in plain clothes who carried a duffel bag that may have contained a change of clothes but I suspect also hid some interesting hardware.

Occasionally I flew the gold shipment to Hagen which didn't terminate at our normal parking area. Instead we landed next to the company King Air, which had been taxied to the end of the active runway during our approach. In under a minute the cargo was transferred and the aircraft took off, usually bound for Cairns or Townsville. Any knowledgeable onlookers only became aware of millions of dollars worth of gold departing at the last moment. Even the local police were not informed, it was just too risky.

During August 1994, Dinah visited me in Hagen for two weeks while I was busy producing paperwork for the Mil 26. Her visit coincided with the local Cultural Show which featured many different tribal groups performing in traditional costumes. It attracts visitors from worldwide, photographing bare breasts and the striking multicoloured Bird of Paradise personal decorations. Dinah was not intimidated by the locals and persuaded Elsie, the chief pilot's wife, to accompany her to the event. I happened to fly PNG's Governor into the showgrounds to open the biannual extravaganza, which attracted entrepreneurs of every kind. Unfortunately, after the fire brigade's demonstration, a stand caught fire. The onsite tender was empty so firemen were unable to douse the flames. The wooden structure was destroyed but other patrons prevented the fire spreading.

I was able to show Dinah views of PNG from the ground and air. We also spent a weekend at the relaxing, sleepy, coconut tree-lined coastal town of Madang before she returned to Australia. Her visit gave me further hope for our future.

Late in the year we were contracted to support construction of the Skyrail project from the outskirts of Cairns to Kuranda in Northern Queensland. The passenger gondolas were to travel on cables strung between tall towers over environmentally sensitive rainforest.

Cairns seemed to attract many unemployed people, especially younger ones. Some of these decided construction for the tourist trade was taking precedence over the environment and Skyrail seemed a high profile example to protest against. The protesters staged events for the media, symbolically attacking, and swarming around the fenced Skyrail bottom station. Television crews were notified beforehand, to ensure good media coverage. Some protesters admitted privately that it was just a good giggle and a chance to get on television. They really didn't know or care much about the project.

We were told the longer term, hard core jobless had set up camp in the jungle at the end of a narrow dirt road. One day I attempted to visit their village but was prevented from entering the national park area they inhabited by a smelly bearded youth. He told me I was not allowed to drive any further. Pleading ignorance as a lost visitor, I left. To have been exposed as a Skyrail spy was the last thing I needed.

One objector spent weeks living high up a tree and gave radio interviews by walky-talky from his nest. He was lured down to conduct a television interview whereupon police appeared, carting him off to be charged.

I was told the protesters caused more damage to sensitive rainforest than any of the Skyrail works. The company had all of its construction materials flown in by longline into miniscule clearings. The so called enviro-friendly 'ferals' stomped all over the jungle, leaving behind cigarette butts and other litter. They often filmed our operations to record any possible damage caused to trees during placement of loads into clearings, or our rotor downwash breaking branches.

For this, and future work, Hevilift set up an Australian operation with me being nominated as chief pilot. I had to pass a theory test in Cairns to fill the required statutory position. The position did not thrill me, not having flown as the single pilot in command in Australia for twenty years. I had become accustomed to flying in a system where the rules and pilots decisions were not heavily influenced by the possibility of a lawsuit. That prospect seemed to stifle a lot of productivity and initiative in Australia. Although keeping my licence current, there were many changes, which I only knew in theory. Of course my pilots working on the job knew all the local requirements.

Countering the effects of protests and doing pilot check flights meant I spent weeks in Cairns before our work concluded. Hardly a hardship post and once Dinah even accompanied me. When completed, Skyrail was to provide visitors with a close view of rainforest without setting foot in it, ensuring the jungle remained in pristine condition. Years later, I was greatly impressed with the information package and undisturbed treetop views after travelling on Skyrail.

The skills our pilots developed in the use of precision longline operations came to the fore when Sydney's outlying suburbs suffered devastating bushfires. Kerry, our Australian manager, had won a contract for the company to provide a Bell 212 fire-fighting helicopter.

When the fires hit, our pilots saved many homes by pulling water out of nearby backyard swimming pools surrounded by obstructions, their special buckets being far below them. Other helicopters flew for miles to collect water in clear areas, enabling hovering near the surface. Our crews could also place their water bucket close to flames or embers to avoid most of the dumped liquid being blown away or evaporating before reaching the target. This ability was especially useful in suburban areas and 'mopping up' operations such as extinguishing burning stumps among tall remaining black tree trunks.

Australian operators were upset by our crews showing them how to fight fires. Naturally, the locals soon adapted and many specialised aircraft, such as Elvis, have since appeared, along with new equipment and techniques.

When Gavin next flew to Australia, he met Dinah. Having decided we could live happily together, I was now sharing her double bed. It was time Gavin became aware of this intimacy and it didn't appear to trouble him. Soon we all drove to Sydney to meet with his mother and her husband who were visiting Australia.

By 1995, having known me for a year, Dinah accepted my commitment to her. I had fully confessed my past loves and affairs. She was ready for another man in her life, but wary in her choice, having divorced her ex-husband in 1991. I must have proved worthy and was allowed to move into her house in the country. A perfect semi-isolated location, just like my childhood. Nevertheless, only a forty minute drive to Coolangatta airport and two hours to Brisbane International, which made commuting to PNG relatively painless.

Yet again, the packers arrived at my unit in Sydney. It was my fourth move in four years. The furniture stayed as I was letting out the premises fully furnished to company clients organised by my agent.

Prior to departing, I modernised the kitchen. During this work, the water supply pipe sprung a leak, having rusted through. It could only be fixed by access from outside the vertical wall of the building, seven floors up. It happened that the very same side of the building was being painted for the first time in many years, so was covered in scaffolding. I just stepped out of the kitchen window and helped a plumber replace the piping, the task being done in no time. I thanked my angel for making such a potentially difficult and expensive job easy.

After settling in with Dinah, I returned to PNG and worked on Mil 26 certification, pilot checking and even flying the line. In mid year, Dinah and I visited England for Gavin's university graduation ceremony. Hiring a car ensured we were not reliant on others or expensive public transport. Our transport had only ten miles on the clock when collected, but no air-conditioner. It was a hot summer and being north London based at Dinah's friend's house, we sometimes found ourselves stuck in traffic jams. Especially on the notorious M25, London's North Circular bypass which was being improved. Being slowly cooked while a bus's high exhaust blew fumes directly into our car was awful. Winding up the car windows just made us sweat more.

Gavin's graduation day was also hot, guests being forced to sit for an hour in formal attire, in sweltering chartered busses on the way to the function. The ceremony, held in a vast hall, was impressive. Afterwards, sandwiches and booze were available while parents and graduates socialised amid much photographic posing.

It was also a graduation day for myself – Gavin would at last be moving into the workforce, no longer needing financial support. He had worked at a large celery farm near Cambridge during university holidays and was now to become a full time junior manager.

With the ceremony over, Dinah and I drove all over southern England meeting each other's friends and my ex brothers and sisters-in-law. Fortunately she is a good navigator so we were rarely lost. A greatly beneficial, mutual bonding process which I felt important. We met people who were otherwise just names in our past lives. I got on well with Dinah's well spoken kin, having long been schooled on proper procedures in English society. Besides, pub lunches are usually very convivial and some of our hosts even knew how to cook a backyard barbecue.

On my return to the Southern Hemisphere and PNG, an Israeli tourist disappeared while climbing Mt Wilhelm, the country's highest mountain. I joined the effort to find him and flew locals to search areas where he may have lost the trail. It's so easy to become disoriented when walking in cloud-covered mountains. The weather was kind which enabled me to spend several hours flying over the upper trails, above a camp at ten thousand feet. The search was repeated the following day and during that flight I made my highest ever landing and take-off, at just over fourteen thousand feet indicated on my altimetre. This height equated to a sixteen thousand foot density altitude if compared to air in a temperate climate.

The Israeli Government was very touchy about their citizens disappearing. Within days, three 'mountaineers' arrived from Tel Aviv to investigate and continue the search. Weeks later, the missing tourist's body was found – he had fallen into a ravine and would not have survived the drop. At least no foul play was suspected.

Soon after, my visits to PNG began to taper off. The company managers changed and my work on the Mil 26 project was cancelled. A specialist check and training pilot, Dave, was employed so that duty was largely removed from my area of responsibility. I continued to fill the chief pilot's slot when Ralph and Elsie took leave. They kindly let me baby-sit their company house which was luxury – otherwise it meant sharing a room in a noisy, crowded, rabbit warren-like compound. Many years previously I had employed Ralph as a line pilot and we developed a close friendly relationship.

I was happy to be withdrawing from the country and beginning to find working for other people rather tiresome. Also, I felt the country seemed to be heading downhill. Having to field the numerous customer and pilot queries after being away for months was stressful. The onerous tax regime was another disincentive. It just didn't seem worth it anymore. My age didn't help either. I couldn't even fly the odd trip for some of our regular clients, being over their company age limit for command pilots.

Numerous projects at home kept me fully occupied. Our water supply, from a creek at the bottom of a paddock, caused problems and a promised drought might see it run dry. I taught myself dowsing, or water divining and booked a driller to put in a borehole.

He confirmed my prediction and found good water twenty metres below the surface, just seventeen metres from our house. After plumbing that supply to our system, the rainwater tank needed replacement. This work plus sorting and equipping my new, large workshop utilised many old skills. My peaceful domesticity was a wonderful change from years of rush and drama. Sleeping in the same bed every night was pure luxury. I didn't want to go anywhere anymore either.

In 1996, my mother, chaperoned by a granddaughter, visited from Adelaide. I decided to behave normally, mother being on our turf. For example, grace was not said before or after meals, although we kept silent when she bowed her head to thank the Lord for her meal. I'm sure by now she was accustomed, if perhaps not personally accepting, of myself and others who chose to live together without the church's blessing.

She mentioned it was a pity her husband was not alive to see his offspring now.

'He would have been so proud. We never imagined our sons would have such successful, interesting and varied lives.'

No doubt she also prayed that our souls would not forever be cast into outer darkness. Did she rationalise that our good works counterbalanced the obvious lack of religious manifestation? I never did tell her of my present philosophical outlook. My much earlier period of rabid agnosticism was kept well away from mother. Likewise my further mellowing, embracing humanitarianism and general agreement with that best-selling author, Ann Rand's pragmatic philosophy.

For me, my church wedding in England had been in line with an attitude which seemed prevalent among ordinary people there – that the religious Institution is respected but mainly there to deal with birth, marriage and death. I had enjoyed the ceremony for the joy it gave to those around me but felt the occasion was mainly for the benefit of the bride.

The church also seemed to provide comfort to old ladies and people in distress. I didn't fit the latter category so drifted along, a happy agnostic but one with a belief in a universal form of intelligence in the cosmos who provided my Angel.

Much later, seeking to overcome a difficult health issue without drugs, I tried various healing modalities and began to meditate. During this educational process, I reconnected with the universe and probably my aboriginal totem, the Flying Termite. He was the Namatjira clans totem, which I'm told I can claim due to my parents' kinship with the famous artist and his family. I had quite forgotten him until my brother Peter reminded me of that spiritual association with my early desert backyard. The reopened link has helped take me back to childhood, before my mind was programmed by Western dogma and beliefs. My soul or spirit is now liberated and free, though hopefully grounded as well. Dinah helped with her blunt, no nonsense approach to life. Coupled with a complete disregard for many modern fashions, gadgets or what other people thought of her. She was just true to herself and had an amazing rapport with flora, fauna and the universe.

My mother and niece returned to Adelaide after a week's stay. The next visitor's, at years end, were Gavin and his university classmate Martin. They stayed for several weeks before leaving to find work in Sydney. Gavin planned to settle here, having decided better opportunities existed in Australia. His mother was unhappy about him departing to the colonies, but Gavin said he'd had enough of the cold, drab English weather. Besides, his workmates said he was crazy staying, they just wished for an Australian passport enabling escape from the windy Cambridgeshire fens and bogs. I helped the boys by providing my small apartment in Sydney for their use for several months, after which some rent applied.

They found it difficult to find full time work. Call centre and other unappealing short term jobs were necessary to meet their Youth Hostel rent after leaving my 'expensive' luxury accomodation. It was over a year before Gavin found a proper job in the finance department of a major bank.

My consulting work in PNG slowed so Dinah and I took a holiday. We joined a seven day 'Barrier Reef Discovery' voyage operating out of Cairns. Our hundred and twenty berth vessel was uncrowded with only half the possible number of paying guests on board. The weather was kind and we snorkeled, drank wine, and enjoyed a hedonistic time together. I was so happy to be with Dinah we didn't socialise or speak much to other people. It was another greatly appreciated, and I felt earned, reward for past deprivation.

The luxury cruise was soon forgotten when a phone call gave me just eight hours notice to join a flight to Hagen. The elections were on in P.N.G. and another pilot was required yesterday. Shocking weather greeted me – so bad that another pilot and I found ourselves struck overnight at a Highlands town called Wapenamanda. It was the first and only time I didn't make it home. Even 'old timers' were known to have been caught out so my angel served me well. On this occasion we found beds in a local politician's fly-screened house, avoiding having to sleep in our machines, unlike many other unfortunates. It was a lucky break. The weather improved and after five long days aviating I flew back to Australia, having been away for just a week.

In July 1997 I returned to occupy the chief pilot's chair for six weeks. I began to notice that us older pilots were being phased out. It didn't bother me much anymore as the company had changed greatly since being sold. The feeling of belonging to a cohesive team seemed to be fading. I could also sense that most pilots no longer felt they worked for me personally, now it was just another job so the kids were fed and the mortgage paid. The loss of teamwork was not just my opinion; other senior long-term employees felt the same. Dick and I had tried but could not change the new owner's management style that treated vital, treasured employees poorly. We had been cogs in helping the company grow enormously but all those achievements were behind us now. It did make my easing out of the industry quite painless. Besides, I still had plenty to do on the home property back in Australia.

The company's policies, my age and the insurance industry were conspiring to limit my flying options. My consultant's daily fee was another disincentive to further employment. I was reaching the end of the line but it was satisfying to think that during my thirty-five years in the helicopter industry I had helped it grow, take on new horizons and perhaps be more accepted by society. At least when saving lives or property, especially if it's possible without much noisy flying over people's backyards. I was also proud that during my years as the chief, very few lives had been lost in company aircraft flown by 'my' pilots in our challenging and often dangerous industry.

Christmas soon arrived, as did Gavin from Sydney to join us for a family gathering. He also accompanied Dinah's daughter Gail to the hot spots in town before returning to Sydney early in the new year.

Late in January 1998, I flew to Mt Hagen for what would prove to be the last time. My final flight in command was to check another pilot. It was symbolic, considering the hundreds I had trained and tested for competency during my career. The flight occurred a few days before my sixty first birthday and may, in retrospect, have been a fitting final aviation gift. It was time to fade out before people thought me an old fogey that should be put out to pasture. Had my time, effort and the enormous contribution in lives and taxpayers money up north been worth it? History may yield an answer.

It was also time for my logbooks to collect dust as defying gravity had lost its appeal. I felt my lifetime supply of adrenaline was almost depleted and some should be saved. Besides, I'm sure my angel's wings needed a rest. Most of our working life is spent 'selling' our physical effort and mental capacity to someone, for varying compensation. Some even, like my parents, laboured long and hard for a heavenly reward. I'd been fortunate that like my father, I'd been too young for one major war and too old for others.

I had not made a fortune or changed the world, enough people were busy doing that. My personal experiences were priceless. I felt very rich in that respect. I'd helped develop the Mount Tom Price mine site when it consisted of six tents and a small tin shed before the Hamersley Ranges in Western Australia became Japan's iron ore mine. I'd seen the sun rise on Mount Everest and enough accidents and scorpses for my lifetime. For almost a year I'd been the pilot helping shape the world's second largest copper mine – and flown the world's largest chopper. I'd shown that regardless of background, seemingly fanciful dreams can be achieved by those who try hard enough. Who could have guessed a country boy could do so much? Had all my good fortune made me a better person? I hope so.

My father was a pioneer and should have recorded his story for posterity. I have done so and hope readers have found some enjoyment in sharing my life journey, which has gone full circle. The Flying Termite, after growing wings, flew around the world touching down to refuel, work and play, before returning to his home country. His wings had been singed; he'd survived a few storms, sampled sweet nectar and finally found his queen.

It was time for me to leave the chase for minerals and oil in undeveloped countries. I'd explored many extremes (except hard drugs) and like Sir Isaac Newton now stood on a new beach while another unexplored ocean lay before me.

This bush boy was going back to bare feet and foraging in the countryside. I had been blessed and protected by my angel while being paid to see the world from a bird's view.

Now I'd just look up and enjoy the bird song.

THE END

GLOSSARY

A quid	colloquial for one pound = $2
Brumby	wild horse
Bung eye	infected with fly eggs, puffy, swollen eyelid partly or completely covering the eye
Bum, bummed	ask a favour, borrow, perhaps permanently
Bush	Australian natural growth of plants and trees, woodland
Bushfire	wildfire, uncontrolled burning on land
Collective lever	used to increase and decrease pitch (lift) on all main rotor blades. On helicopters fitted with efficient governors it also regulates engine power in flight, without use of the throttle.
Creek	small stream, with or without water
Cyclic (stick)	used to change the rotor blade pitch (lift) differentially ie to roll the chopper left or right or pitch the nose up and down
Dingo	native Australian wild dog
Dob, dobbed in	report an event to others, usually about a persons failure or misdeed
Jesus Nut	large nut securing helicopter main rotor blades to the mast
Jesus Button	releases all anchors on one side of a drillship to prevent it sinking if a gas blow-out occurs
Loo	lavatory, bathroom, toilet, outhouse
NT	Northern Territory of Australia
OZ	colloquial for Australia, Australian
PRIMUS (stove)	brand name for, originally, a portable kerosene powered flame cooking device operated similar to the Tilly lamp. Now burns bottled gas and lamp versions are available.

Rudder pedals	used to maintain a heading or turn an aircraft's nose left or right
Scrub	Australian, as for bush, without tall trees
Spinifex	spiky, stiff circular grass clumps that can grow over a metre (porcupine grass) high and two wide. Walkers avoid the 'hard' variety
Station	ranch or property, as in cattle or sheep station. Train stop
Swag	bedroll, usually with a waterproof outer sheet or tarpaulin
Telegram	urgent short message sent by telegraph from a post office and delivered to a postal address
Telex	early form of short fax like communication typed into a special machine that relays the message to another distant teleprinter
TILLY lamp	kerosene powered lamp providing bright light from an incandescent mantle. Required regular pumping to blow pressurized, atomised, heated fuel through a fine jet into the mantle
Top End (of OZ)	Northern Australia, area well above the Tropic of Capricorn
Tucker (box)	food (placed in a box for transportation)
Utility, ute	a small, smart, pickup truck with sides fixed to the tray, or, a sedan type of vehicle with a small rear tray and tailgate
Verandah	an open, roofed section attached to a dwelling, usually along a complete house wall. May be affixed to many or all outer walls
Expat	a person living in other than his or her native country

ORDER FORM

To obtain more copies of this book or DVDs containing photographs, specifications and exclusive limitations of the Mil Mi 26, please post this completed form to:

Zytal Press, c/o Stokers Siding PO, NSW, 2484

or email: pjlatz2@tadaust.org.au for a quote on large orders, online payment details, or bookshop terms of trade.

Name: _____

Address: _____

_____ Postcode: _____

Phone: (_____)_____

Your email: _____

BOOK   **DVD**
Flying with My Angel   Mil Mi 26 Limits, Ops. and Photos

2008 Costs
Book and DVD $25 each, plus Postage and Handling $9.60
Order BOOK and DVD together and pay only $40 + $9.60 (save $10)

Please send me _____ copies of _____

Please send me _____ copies of _____

TOTAL $ _____

Please enclose your cheque or money order, payable to P. Latz, unless paying online.
(Please allow up to 10 working days for delivery)